THE SPIRITUALIST PRIME MINISTER

Cover Images:

Volume 1: Prime Minister Mackenzie King in his Laurier House study, circa 1945. Library and Archives Canada C-075053.

Volume 2: The last Mackenzie King photo at Kingsmere, July 18, 1950, four days before his death. Library and Archives Canada PA-129854.

THE SPIRITUALIST PRIME MINISTER

VOL I
Mackenzie King and the New Revelation

Anton Wagner, PhD

White Crow Books in association
with the Survival Research Institute of Canada

The Spiritualist Prime Minister: Vol. 1, Mackenzie King and the New Revelation

Copyright © 2024 by Anton Wagner. All rights reserved.
Published by White Crow Books, an imprint of White Crow Productions Ltd., Guildford, Surrey, in association with the Survival Research Institute of Canada, Victoria, British Columbia.

The right of Anton Wagner to be identified as the author of this work has been asserted by him in accordance with the Copyright, Design and Patents Act 1988.

No part of this book may be reproduced, copied or used in any form or manner whatsoever without written permission, except in the case of brief quotations in reviews and critical articles.

A CIP catalogue record for this book is available from the British Library. For information, contact White Crow Books by e-mail: info@whitecrowbooks.com.

Cover and interior design:
Michał Kozłowski

Paperback: ISBN: 978-1-78677-264-0
eBook: ISBN: 978-1-78677-265-7
Revised: June 2024

Non Fiction / Body, Mind & Spirit / Parapsychology / Afterlife and Reincarnation

www.whitecrowbooks.com
www. survivalresearch.ca

THE SPIRITUALIST PRIME MINISTER, VOLUME 1:
THE NEW REVELATION

Foreword by Walter Meyer zu Erpen vii

Introduction: The New Revelation 13

1. The Magic Portrait of Isabel King 53

2. Mackenzie King's Family and Spiritualism in Canada 65

3. The First Medium: Mackenzie and Isabel King, "I Am Alive" . . .87

4. Joan Patteson, Mackenzie King's Spiritual Partner 109

5. Conversations Over the Little Table 123

6. Mackenzie King, Magnetic and Electric Sex Currents,
   and The Lost Leader 153

7. Mackenzie King and the Historians 183

8. *Fantasio*, an Interview in Ectoplasm,
   and the Duchess of Hamilton 199

9. The Spiritualist Cover Up by the King Executors 223

10. "Everybody Knew About It" – Circles of Spiritualists 241

11. King's Magical Thinking and the
    Canadian Origins of His Spiritualism 255

12. Dr. T. Glen Hamilton: Photographing
    Ectoplasm in Winnipeg 293

13. Mackenzie King, Ellen Elliott, and The Christ Presence 313

Acknowledgements 349

Chronology: Mackenzie King's Life and His Mediums 351

Bibliography 367

List of Illustrations and Photo Credits 383

About the Author 387

THE SPIRITUALIST PRIME MINISTER, VOLUME 2: MACKENZIE KING AND HIS MEDIUMS

Volume 2 contains:

14. Rachel Bleaney, Kingston Fortune-Teller, and the 1925, 1926, and 1930 Federal Elections

15. Etta Wriedt, American Direct-Voice Medium

16. Helen Lambert, Eileen Garrett, and Marie Carrington: Mackenzie King and New York Mediums and Psychic Investigators

17. Mackenzie King, London Mediums, Richard Wagner, and Adolf Hitler

18. Mackenzie King and Two Psychics During World War II

19. Mackenzie King and the Birth of the Atom Bomb

20. Canadian Psychic Friends and an Alternate Universe

Concluding Summary: Mackenzie King's Spiritual Great Chain of Being

Acknowledgements

Appendix A: Was Mackenzie King Guided from Beyond? Excerpts from the London Séances, 1945-1947

Appendix B: Contents: The Spiritualist Prime Minister, Volume 1: The New Revelation

Bibliography

List of Illustrations and Photo Credits

About the Author

FOREWORD

The Spiritualist Prime Minister (TSPM) by historian Dr. Anton Wagner presents former Canadian Prime Minister William Lyon Mackenzie King's quest for spirit communication within the historical and cultural context of British, Canadian, and American Spiritualism. Anton's introduction, "The New Revelation," highlights leading prophets of Modern Spiritualism including Sir Arthur Conan Doyle and Sir Oliver Lodge. The biography is the most thorough analysis of King's spiritualism ever published. *TSPM* provides an unprecedented first-hand account of one individual's encounters with some of the types of psychological phenomena now reported as exceptional human experiences.

The Modern Spiritualist Movement began in 1848 when inexplicable rapping sounds were heard within the walls of the Fox family's home in Hydesville, New York. The Canadian-born Maggie and Kate Fox were discovered to be the source of the phenomena, now considered a psychokinetic (PK) or poltergeist outbreak. Through the raps, the girls communicated with the alleged spirit of a pedlar who died in the house. Soon after the sisters began public demonstrations, mediums were facilitating spirit communication across North America, and American mediums introduced the practice of spirit communication in darkened séance rooms to England. Gradually, Spiritualism evolved as a new religion around the strange psychic manifestations attributed to surviving spirits, including rocking and floating tables, musical instruments played by unseen hands, and materialized forms. Investigative societies for study of spiritualistic phenomena attracted the attention of educated men and women.

Individuals convinced of authentic psychic phenomena were divided. Many attributed them to unseen spirits; a minority claimed they resulted from some little understood capacity of the human psyche. In 1882, a group of Cambridge scholars founded the Society for Psychical Research (SPR) to investigate the phenomena, independent of religion. Before he met leading Spiritualists, King had extensively read William James, the American psychologist and religious studies pioneer. A founding member of the American Society for Psychical Research (ASPR) in 1884, James served as SPR President (1894-1895) and lectured about immortality in 1898 during King's studies at Harvard. King also had a cordial relationship with British physicist Sir Oliver Lodge, who was SPR President (1901-1903) and President of the British Association for the Advancement of Science (1913). He met Lodge during the 1926 Imperial Conference and purchased ten of his books about survival. His friend Lizzy Lind-af-Hageby, President of the London Spiritualist Alliance (1935-1943), proclaimed Spiritualism as the meeting place of science and religion.

The elite circle in which King moved included world leaders and royalty, and an international network of individuals willing to discuss the evidence for post-mortem survival and spirit communication through mediumship. Those contacts facilitated introductions and significant readings with well-known mediums, often initially incognito: Etta Wriedt from Detroit; Eileen Garrett in New York; and Gladys Osborne Leonard, Helen Hughes, and Geraldine Cummins in England. King made detailed notes. Even Winston Churchill asked to read the transcript of King's 1947 séance with Cummins.

This major historical revision relies upon King's own words from his correspondence and his 30,000 pages of diary entries. The two volumes reveal several themes. *TSPM* may be read as a psychological study of a lonely man whose diaries record a decades-long struggle with a lack of female companionship, illustrated by the "electric sex currents" that tormented him. With the Princess Cantacuzene, granddaughter of American President Ulysses S. Grant, King attempted to discover whether those were part of an empowering divine fire. Another recurrent theme is King's conviction that he was an agent of God, working out His will "on Earth as it is in Heaven." The biography references many of the milestones and obstacles of King's significant role in Canadian political history, including candid comments about colleagues and adversaries.

The biography's focus is the record of King's meetings with Spiritualists and psychic investigators. He held an unwavering conviction that the surviving spirits of his mother and family supported him. Prominent deceased individuals who communicated regularly included Prime Minister Sir Wilfrid Laurier and his own grandfather William Lyon Mackenzie, leader of the failed 1837 Upper

Canada Rebellion. In 1934, Frederic W.H. Myers, an SPR founder and author of the pioneering *Human Personality and Its Survival of Bodily Death* (1903), became one of King's spirit guides. King's belief that he was a chosen instrument of God provided him with immense spiritual capital that helped him become the most powerful individual in the Canadian political field. *TSPM* delineates King's inner mind and explores how his spiritualist beliefs influenced his political decision-making. He believed that once humanity became convinced that human personality and a higher moral order continued in the world beyond, that human conduct would change and there would be peace on earth. In the concluding chapter, "Mackenzie King's Spiritual Great Chain of Being," Anton brings together the diverse aspects of King's spiritualism and occult practices that were integral parts of his spiritual journey.

King's spiritualism became newspaper headlines in 1950, when journalists exposed the deceased politician as a Spiritualist. Although King attended the Presbyterian Church, he accepted the main tenets of Spiritualism. The overlay of Spiritualist belief upon Christian faith comforted him, as did his various occult observances. Despite attempts by his executors to obliterate Spiritualism and the occult from his papers, enough evidence survived to allow Dr. Wagner to create a chronology of King's more than 130 known interactions with mediums, psychics, fortune-tellers, palmists, astrologers, graphologists, phrenologists, and psychic investigators.

His executors and fixers in the Liberal Party tried to control the political damage, denying that King discussed political matters with mediums or that they influenced his decisions. King's belief in his own psychic powers, and that he was part of a divine plan to save humanity from another world war, had led him to Berlin in 1937 where he misjudged Hitler and his intentions. Ultimately, King became party to Canada's integral role in the development of the atom bomb. Transcripts of King's séances with mediums in London in 1945 and 1946 (volume two) show that he was convinced of communication with the late President Franklin D. Roosevelt about whether the secret of the atom bomb should be shared with Russia.

Dr. Wagner's research demonstrates that King was Canada's most prominent psychic explorer from 1919 when he became Leader of the Liberal Party Opposition in Parliament until his 1948 resignation as Prime Minister. He sought the advice of Kingston, Ontario, fortune-teller Rachel Bleaney in the federal elections of 1925, 1926, and 1930. He met with leading psychic investigators such as Sir Oliver Lodge in London, Dr. T.G. Hamilton in Winnipeg, and Hereward Carrington in New York. In 1933, Dominion Archivist Sir Arthur Doughty introduced King to table rapping as a means of communicating with the spirit world.

In his diaries, King revealed his delight upon first contacting the spirit of his mother. He recorded his disappointment in fortune-tellers when their predictions about the future proved wrong and analyzed the reasons for their failures. We see also that King was alert to the possibility of manipulation, including by individuals attempting to garner favour through him on account of their claimed psychic gifts. During the 1930s, he turned increasingly to acting as his own medium in conversations over the "little table" with his séance partner Joan Patteson.

From the 1930s, the emerging field of parapsychology began investigation of psi phenomena in laboratory settings. With the shift of psychic research away from mediumship, individuals interested in survival of the human personality after death regrouped in new organizations. The Survival Research Institute of Canada (SRIC), founded in 1991, follows in that tradition. One of our dream projects was to undertake a comprehensive study of King's spiritualism. With the untimely passing of SRIC co-founder and archivist Debra Elaine Barr (1954-2008), our intended project to read King's Spiritualism papers, opened by Library and Archives Canada in 2001, fell by the wayside. In 2021, when Dr. Wagner contacted us, we discovered that he had independently undertaken this very project. His research goes well beyond what we could have hoped to accomplish.

In our conversations, Anton shared his desire to complete his revision and contextualization of King's story as a means of giving back to Canada. He expressed gratitude for having found shelter here in 1969, avoiding military service in Vietnam. Intended as a gift of cultural capital to Canadians, *TSPM* results from a decade of painstaking research and writing.

Working with Anton Wagner these past 30 months has been a great privilege; he is an exceptionally thorough scholar and researcher. Together we recovered the biographies of several mediums, notably direct-voice trumpet medium Etta Wriedt. Among the astrologers King consulted, Cecilia Stevenson proved to be the mother of noted

Canadian-born reincarnation researcher Ian Stevenson. The *TSPM* volumes are richly illustrated with photographs, historical documents, and astrological charts, many not previously published. Online family history data and digital newspapers facilitated the genealogical approach that allowed us to locate descendants of three of King's psychics who shared stories and portraits. The website of the International Association for the Preservation of Spiritualist and Occult Periodicals (IAPSOP) proved invaluable in demonstrating the flow of information about Spiritualism and psychic investigations from one country to another.

The Spiritualist Prime Minister provides an important new look at Canada's longest serving Prime Minister and a significant record of early twentieth-century Spiritualism. The biography demonstrates the extensive interest Canadians had in communication with deceased loved ones, especially following the World Wars. Gallup and Angus Reid surveys conducted since 1960 have shown that at least 60 percent of Canadians believe in some form of afterlife, with the possibility and nature of continued existence influenced by religious belief. The February 2024 Angus Reid survey suggests that only 13 percent of Canadians rule out entirely the possibility of an afterlife.

As an archivist and historian, I am grateful that Anton persevered in his determination to provide us with a better understanding of King's spiritualism and how it enabled him to retain the position of Prime Minister for 22 years. Without the faith William Lyon Mackenzie King had in his ancestors in spirit, it is doubtful he would have continued to run in election after election. The Survival Research Institute of Canada is pleased to have been able to support Anton Wagner's research and scholarship.

—*Walter Meyer zu Erpen, BA, MAS, Co-founder*
Survival Research Institute of Canada

INTRODUCTION

The New Revelation

On October 25, 1917, despite the threat from the strategic bombing campaign by Germany against England during the First World War, an audience packed the Salon of the Royal Society of British Artists in London to hear Sir Arthur Conan Doyle deliver an address to the London Spiritualist Alliance entitled "The New Revelation." The meeting occurred under dimmed lights and the police urged that the gathering terminate as soon as possible because of the danger of German bombing, so there was no discussion afterwards. Conan Doyle had published the essential points of his address in the Alliance's *Light: A Journal of Psychical, Occult, and Mystical Research* in November 1916. At that time, the Battle of Verdun and the Somme offensive had already wounded or killed 1.7 million Allied and German soldiers in ten months of horrific carnage.

World famous as the writer of the Sherlock Holmes short stories and novels, Conan Doyle described himself in "A New Revelation: Spiritualism and Religion," as a subscriber and contributor to *Light* for the past thirty years and as one of the oldest members of the Society for Psychical Research, founded in 1882. He affirmed that "In spite of occasional fraud and wild imaginings, there remains a solid core in this whole spiritual movement which is infinitely nearer to positive proof than any other religious development with which I am acquainted."

He found this positive proof in the psychic investigations by scientists and writers such as the chemist and physicist Sir William Crookes (discoverer of the element thallium), the naturalist Alfred Russel Wallace (co-discoverer with Charles Darwin of the theory of natural selection), the physicist and parapsychologist Sir William

Fletcher Barrett, the French astronomer Camille Flammarion, the physicist Sir Oliver Lodge, the newspaper editor and reformer William Thomas Stead, and Vice-Admiral Usborne Moore, the investigator of mediums and author of *Glimpses of the Next State* and of *The Voices*. Conan Doyle proposed, "We should now be at the close of the stage of investigation and beginning the period of religious construction." He was convinced that the psychic phenomena that had already been recorded by these, and other investigators, were "taking shape as the foundations of a definite system of religious thought, in some ways confirmatory of ancient systems, in some ways entirely new."

For Conan Doyle, the psychic phenomena confirmed the existence of "higher beings whom we may call angels and of an ever-ascending hierarchy above us, culminating in heights which are beyond our sight or apprehension, with which we may associate the idea of all-power or of God." The new Spiritualism proclaimed the continuing development of human beings on earth and after death and that there was no impassable chasm between the two worlds. The human body, personality and mind continued to develop in the spiritual body. "It is in the possibility of communion that the main feature of this new teaching lies," Conan Doyle suggested. The means of communication with discarnate entities included "Clairvoyance, clairaudience, the direct voice, automatic writing, spirit control – these are the various methods, all depending upon that inexplicable thing called mediumship, a thing so sacred, and sometimes so abused."

Sir Arthur repeated the tenets of his spiritualist philosophy in his public address to the London Spiritualist Alliance in 1917 and in the publication of *The New Revelation* in book form in March 1918. He saw only two alternatives in accepting or rejecting the vast amount of psychic phenomena that had been recorded in the United Kingdom and in America. "The one supposition is that there has been an outbreak of lunacy extending over two generations of mankind and two great continents – a lunacy which assails men or women who are otherwise eminently sane. The alternative supposition is that in recent years there has come to us from divine sources a new revelation which constitutes by far the greatest religious event since the death of Christ…a revelation which alters the whole aspect of death and the fate of man." Conan Doyle could not perceive an intermediate position between these two alternatives. "Theories of fraud or of delusion will not meet the evidence. It is absolute lunacy or it is a revolution in

Figure 01: Sir Arthur Conan Doyle's portrait in his 1923 Our American Adventure.

religious thought, a revolution which gives us as by-products an utter fearlessness of death, and an immense consolation when those who are dear to us pass behind the veil."

Referring to the slaughter of the World War, Conan Doyle concluded, "Men talk of a great religious revival after the war. Perhaps it is in this direction that it will be." Sir Oliver Lodge, who had presided at Doyle's address to the London Spiritualist Alliance, agreed. "It was a time of spiritual outpouring. All the great times in history had been marked by great sacrifices, and there must be a great outcome of all the sacrifices of the present time." In the expanded publication of *The New Revelation* in 1918, Conan Doyle cited in its preface the message received by the celebrated American trance medium, Leonora Piper, uttered in 1899: "Before the clear revelation of spirit communication there will be a terrible war in different parts of the world. The entire world must be purified and cleansed before mortal can see, through his spiritual vision, his friends on this side and it will take just this line of action to bring about a state of perfection."[1]

While Conan Doyle was addressing the London Spiritualist Alliance in October 1917, William Lyon Mackenzie King was at the bedside of his failing seventy-four-year-old mother Isabel, who was hovering near death in Ottawa. Conservative Prime Minister Robert Borden had called for the formation of a Union Government to prolong the life of Parliament during World War I and to enforce conscription. He announced elections for December 17. As described in Chapter 3, King supported former Liberal Prime Minister Sir Wilfrid Laurier who opposed conscription without a national referendum. He ran for Parliament in the riding of North York, Ontario, the region that had been represented by Isabel's father, William Lyon Mackenzie, in the Legislative Assembly of Upper Canada from 1829 to 1836. By force of will, Isabel managed to hold on until December 17, also King's forty-third birthday, but died the next day after hearing of King's defeat in the election and before her son managed to return home from campaigning. Years later he recalled that he travelled from Toronto on the train to Ottawa "to find that she had passed away, and her body been taken away when

---

1 Doyle, "A New Revelation: Spiritualism and Religion," *Light* 36:1869 (November 4, 1916), 357, 358. Doyle, *The New Revelation*, 53, 97, vii-viii. "The Reality of the Unseen: Address by Sir Oliver Lodge," *Light* 37:1921 (November 3, 1917), 347.

I arrived. That was the way of the cross if there ever was such; it all seemed defeat & sorrow."[2]

Mackenzie King had not yet embraced Spiritualism and therefore was not comforted by the "immense consolation" Conan Doyle held out for believers. Yet he had already been in direct contact with British Spiritualism and articulated a spiritualist worldview at an evening at Miss Gertrude Toynbee's in London during his year-long Harvard travelling scholarship in 1899. He was asked to respond to a presentation on materialism and modern science by Herbert Burrows, the prominent socialist activist and theosophist. Burrows criticized the materialist conception of the origin of mind in matter found in German psychology. He suggested that it could be proven to scientists that human consciousness could exist independently of the body "by experiments in clairvoyance, and 'spirits' where it was evident that the 'consciousness' was in [a] place other than the body at a particular time & distinct & might be free & was not annihilated on death."

King concurred with Burrows' spiritualist conception two decades before the death of his mother convinced him of the continuation of personality after death and caused him to engage in occult experiments in the 1920s, 1930s and 1940s. He expressed his belief that "everything acts according to law & nothing to chance, but the laws of the spiritual world are different in kind from those of the natural, though the latter may be part but not all of the former." Two weeks shy of his twenty-fifth birthday, he also stated his conviction, "I believe we have yet to discover to what a great extent the so-called spiritual laws, e.g. faith & result of, are acting in our lives regarding daily material experiences."[3]

As with so many others who had lost family members and loved ones, the death of King's mother led him to believe in Spiritualism. Two months after Isabel's passing, he recorded a dramatic dream vision in his diary. "Last night I dreamt that I saw dear mother's face in death; it was not worn by disease as I last saw it, but beautiful, radiantly beautiful though dead. I said to her – as though talking to her spirit apart – you promised mother – which she did – to tell me from the other world if you were still alive & near me & when I said this

---

2 Diary, September 21, 1944.
3 Diary, November 29, 1899.

her lips opened and she said 'I am alive' but it seemed as though it was forbidden her to say more."[4]

In his 1917 address, Arthur Conan Doyle affirmed that the system of spiritualist communication, "from the lowest physical phenomenon of a table-rap up to the most inspired utterance of a prophet, was one complete whole, each link attached to the next one, and that when the humbler end of that chain was placed in the hand of humanity, it was in order that they might, by diligence and reason, feel their way up it until they reached the revelation which waited in the end." Less than two years later, Mackenzie King began using the means of communion with his dead mother, father and sister Conan Doyle had highlighted in *The New Revelation* and often used mediums in Canada familiar with Spiritualism in the United Kingdom. He first contacted the English-born clairvoyant and clairaudient fortune-teller Rachel Bleaney in Kingston when he was re-elected to Parliament in 1919, in the 1921 election that made him Prime Minister, in the 1925 and 1926 elections, and in 1930 when the Liberals were defeated by R.B. Bennett's Conservatives.

As discussed in Chapter 14, Rachel Bleaney's mediumistic guidance was crucial in helping King navigate the Byng Affair, the 1926 constitutional crisis when Governor General Lord Byng refused King's advice to dissolve Parliament and hold new elections but then granted a dissolution to Conservative Leader Arthur Meighen since neither the Liberals nor the Conservatives could muster a stable majority in Parliament. The previous year, King recorded in his diary, "I cannot do other than regard all Mrs. Bleaney has told me as revelation."[5] He made the issue of a British Governor General refusing to accept the advice of his Canadian Prime Minister the central constitutional issue of the 1926 election and won a stable majority for the Liberals.

King began commissioning horoscopes from the English astrologer M.E. Young and from the Scottish-born Mayor William Duncan Livingstone Hardie of Lethbridge, Alberta, in 1924. He had his first meeting with that other great prophet of "The New Revelation," Sir Oliver Lodge, at Lord Grey's mansion in London during the 1926 Imperial Conference. Lodge, in addition to his sterling reputation as a

---

4 Diary, February 15, 1918.

5 Conan Doyle, "The New Revelation," *Light* 37:1923 (November 17, 1917), 366. Diary, October 31, 1925.

Figure 02: J.W.L. Forster's 1902 portrait of Mackenzie King.

scientist, had published in November 1916 his widely read description of the spirit world, *Raymond, or, Life and Death*, as communicated by his son to the trance medium Gladys Osborne Leonard via automatic writing. Raymond had been killed by shrapnel near Ypres, Belgium, on September 14, 1915. King held his first séance with Leonard in 1937 and remained in regular correspondence with her until December 1949. W.T. Stead, a year before his death in the sinking of the *Titanic*, selected the direct-voice trumpet medium Etta Wriedt from Detroit

Figure 03: Mackenzie King in his Laurier House study in Ottawa in 1932.

as a resident medium at his Julia's Circle in Wimbledon, Southwest London, in 1911. Arthur Conan Doyle, at the beginning of his 1922 American lecture tour, called Wriedt the "strongest medium in the world."[6] Chapter 15 cites Mackenzie King's vivid descriptions of his more than sixty séances with Etta Wriedt between 1932 and 1938, found in his legendary diaries.

Chapters 4 and 5 analyze how King began delving yet more deeply into Spiritualism and the occult after the English-born Dominion Archivist, Arthur Doughty, introduced him to table rapping in 1933. With his spiritual partner and life companion, the married Joan Patteson, he continued almost daily séance "conversations" over the "little table" until the end of September 1949. King's last extant handwritten transcription of a Laurier House séance is dated May 1950, just two months before his death. He met the Duchess of Hamilton and Louise (Lizzy) Lind-af-Hageby, the President of the London Spiritualist Alliance, after addressing the League of Nations Assembly in Geneva in 1936. Both subsequently introduced him

---

6 "Suicide Not an End of Ills, Says Doyle," *New York Times*, April 11, 1922, 11.

to half a dozen mediums in London with whom King held séances until October 1948.

In twentieth-century Canada, there were three individuals who engaged in extensive psychic investigations, which was the stage Doyle suggested preceded the stage of religious construction: T. Glendenning Hamilton and his wife Lillian Hamilton in Winnipeg, and William Lyon Mackenzie King in Ottawa. Hamilton's *Intention and Survival: Psychical Research Studies and the Bearing of Intentional Actions by Trance Personalities on the Problem of Human Survival*, edited by his son James after his father's death in 1935, was published by Macmillan in Toronto in 1942. Psychic Press in London published Margaret Hamilton's *Is Survival a Fact?* in 1969. It documented her mother's continued psychic investigations until 1944. After Lillian's death in 1956, Margaret also edited a second edition of *Intention and Survival* published by Regency Press in London in 1977. Mackenzie King was Canada's most famous spiritualist but the record of his personal psychic research and occult activities, so vividly recorded in his voluminous diaries and correspondence, has until now not received detailed analysis.

The Hamiltons and Mackenzie King had crucial connections with Spiritualism in the United Kingdom. King could meet and socialize with fellow spiritualists in London and arrange sittings with the mediums they recommended during his frequent trips to the Empire as a politician. The Hamiltons were inspired by the early British spiritualist and psychical research pioneers and had two thirds of their research published in *Light* and in the *Quarterly Transactions of the British College of Psychic Science* (subsequently cited as *Quarterly Transactions*). *The Spiritualist Prime Minister* examines why King could not openly declare himself as a spiritualist and be part of the kind of vibrant social and religious movement he had witnessed in London.

Mackenzie King was Canada's longest serving Prime Minister – from December 29, 1921, to June 28, 1926, September 25, 1926, to July 28, 1930, and October 23, 1935, to November 15, 1948. He was also one of the longest serving elected leaders in the Western world. As outlined in Chapter 7, historians ranked King as Canada's greatest Prime Minister in 1997 and 2011. Yet echoing Conan Doyle's reference to lunacy, several historians also debated King's sanity because of his spiritualist and occult pursuits. On the 100th anniversary of his birth, in December 1974, James

Eayrs, the prominent *Toronto Star* syndicated journalist, questioned assurances that the PM had not been influenced in his politics by his spiritual convictions. "Were Canadians throughout most of the 1920s, and from 1935 to 1948, governed by occult forces, or by King's perceptions of them?" Eayrs asked. "Here was no mere life of fantasy, it was the life of the dedicated Spiritualist, replete with mediums, trumpets, tambourines, flowers, ectoplasm – and cheesecloth." Referring to Etta Wriedt and other King mediums, Eayrs queried provocatively, "was Canada really run by these elderly lady necromancers?"[7]

Another historian, Reginald Whitaker, "staggered shell-shocked and blinking from the Public Archives" after his "descent into delirium" from reading King's 7.5 million words long diaries of 30,000 pages, described by Robert Keyserlingk as "this massive self-reflective labyrinth." Whitaker wrote that it was an image of a "whirling sea of insanity drawing one on to uncharted dreams and unseen disasters, that kept forming and reforming itself in my mind while venturing into the private diaries of William Lyon Mackenzie King." These were not like other matter-of-fact diaries Whitaker had studied. "I read on and then realize that I am losing my moorings. The man is quite crazy. The contradictions become noticeable, then significant, then insurmountable. The inner world of the public man begins in incongruity and ends in hallucination. The stream runs faster and wilder, the light darkens, and the shore is lost from sight."[8]

Derived from the Latin *occultus*, occult means knowledge of the secret, hidden and clandestine, and practices using supernatural forces to manipulate natural laws for personal benefit. Alex Owen, in *The Place of Enchantment: British Occultism and the Culture of the Modern*, writes that the term "encompasses such a broad spectrum of beliefs, ideas and practices that it defies precise definition. It is often applied without qualification to activities as diverse as divination (astrology, palmistry, tarot reading, crystal gazing, and so on), sorcery and black

---

7 James Eayrs, "Will Mackenzie King Attend His 100th Anniversary?" *Toronto Star*, December 14, 1974, B6. See also "Professor Jeers at Premier's Spiritualism," *Psychic News*, January 4, 1975, 2. Helen Duncan, one of the last psychics imprisoned in 1944 under the British Witchcraft Act of 1735, was accused of swallowing and regurgitating cheesecloth, claiming it was ectoplasm. See also "Editorial: Cheese-cloth Ectoplasm!" *Occult Review* 54:6 (December-January 1932).

8 Whitaker, 7, 6. Keyserlingk, 28.

magic (the manipulation of natural forces, often for self-interested purposes), and various kinds of necromancy or spiritualist-related practices. This diversity is underpinned, however," Owen continues, "by an implicit acceptance of the idea that reality as we are taught to understand it accounts only for a fraction of the ultimate reality which lies just beyond our immediate senses." Henrik Bogdan and Gordan Djurdjevic summarize in *Occultism in a Global Perspective* that "Broadly speaking, what distinguishes occultism as a branch of human activity is an orientation towards hidden aspects of reality, those that are held to be commonly inaccessible to ordinary senses."[9]

Mackenzie King expressed the same idea about what was real when he re-read William James' *Human Immortality* in 1902 and recalled the night James gave the lecture while King was studying at Harvard in 1898. "I have long in my real belief held to the conviction that the reality is the immortal life about us, that all our existence here is a sort of stage play. That 'the furniture of earth & chair of Heaven' may be but such that when we throw off the tenement of clay, our real life develops freed from the trammels of the ills & temptations that flesh is heir to and the limitations of finite barriers," he wrote in his diary. "I liked greatly James' interpretation of the truth, that every man has a soul within him bursting for immortal life."[10]

For King, Spiritualism was a belief bordering on faith and occultism practices to test and implement that belief, as an attempt to "see God." After nine séances with the direct-voice medium Etta Wriedt in February 1932, he wrote in his diary, "what has been truly remarkable is that what I have felt and accepted 'by faith,' is all being verified." He assimilated a trust in fortune-telling from his mother Isabel, who had her first encounter with a fortune-teller as a seven-year-old in Kingston, Ontario, in 1850 and had fortune-tellers predict her children's futures until the 1890s. King recorded the palmist Mrs. Lauretta Menden telling his fortune in Toronto in 1896, when he was twenty-two years old. He also recalled being taken as a child to see a phrenologist – presumably by his mother in the mid-1880s to determine his best future profession – and was told that "I ought to be an architect."[11]

---

9   Alex Owen, 19. Cited in Tatiana Kontou and Sarah Willburn, 6. Henrik Bogdan and Gordan Djurdjevic, 1.

10   Diary, February 2, 1902.

11   Diary, February 28, 1932, and May 15, 1948.

In 1894, King let himself be mesmerized by the English-born phrenologist and mesmerist Professor William P. Seymour (1842-1919) in Toronto. As Egil Asprem noted of Franz Anton Mesmer's notion of animal magnetism, "The different theories and practices associated with Mesmerism came to exert an enormous influence on nineteenth-century esoteric currents, notably occultism and spiritualism." Asprem summarized Mesmer's animal magnetism as "a pseudo-mechanistic theory of subtle fluids, interpenetrating the cosmos and living beings, accounting for various physical and psychical ailments as well as special mental rapports between human beings."

The twenty-year-old Mackenzie King consulted Seymour in January 1894 while attending the University of Toronto. He went to see "Prof. Seymour who is a phrenologist mesmerist. He mesmerized me & spent about an hour with him." King did not describe what proceeded while he was hypnotized or whether Seymour also performed a phrenological examination of his skull. The Professor probably referred to the sexual temptations faced by all young men. Like his phrenologist predecessors Lorenzo Niles Fowler and Johann Gaspar Spurzheim, Seymour contended that the human brain consisted of a plurality of organs and faculties. In *Seymour's Key to Phrenology and Mathematical Scale for Reading Character*, he had referred to "the triumph of the intellectual faculties and moral sentiments over the animal propensities."

The organ of Amativeness was said to be located in the cerebellum at the back base of the head. It was believed to greatly increase in size and become active at the age of puberty. In the *Key to Phrenology*, he wrote that when this organ was large and "if ungoverned by reason and the moral sentiments, it leads to abuse; either to self pollution or licentious conduct with the opposite sex." King had begun recording his occasional encounters with prostitutes in his diary in September 1893 and always felt guilt-ridden by his much more frequent masturbatory practices. He must have thought Seymour's phrenological observation applied to him for he added in his diary after his consultation, "I cannot but daily see how weak I am. I trust & pray that God will give me more strength to withstand all temptations."[12]

King maintained a belief in magnetic and electric currents and that there was a correspondence between the shape of the skull, brain

---

12 Asprem, 713. Diary, January 3, 1894. Seymour, *Seymour's Key to Phrenology and Mathematical Scale for Reading Character*, 3. Seymour, *Key to Phrenology*, 20, 65, 67, 68.

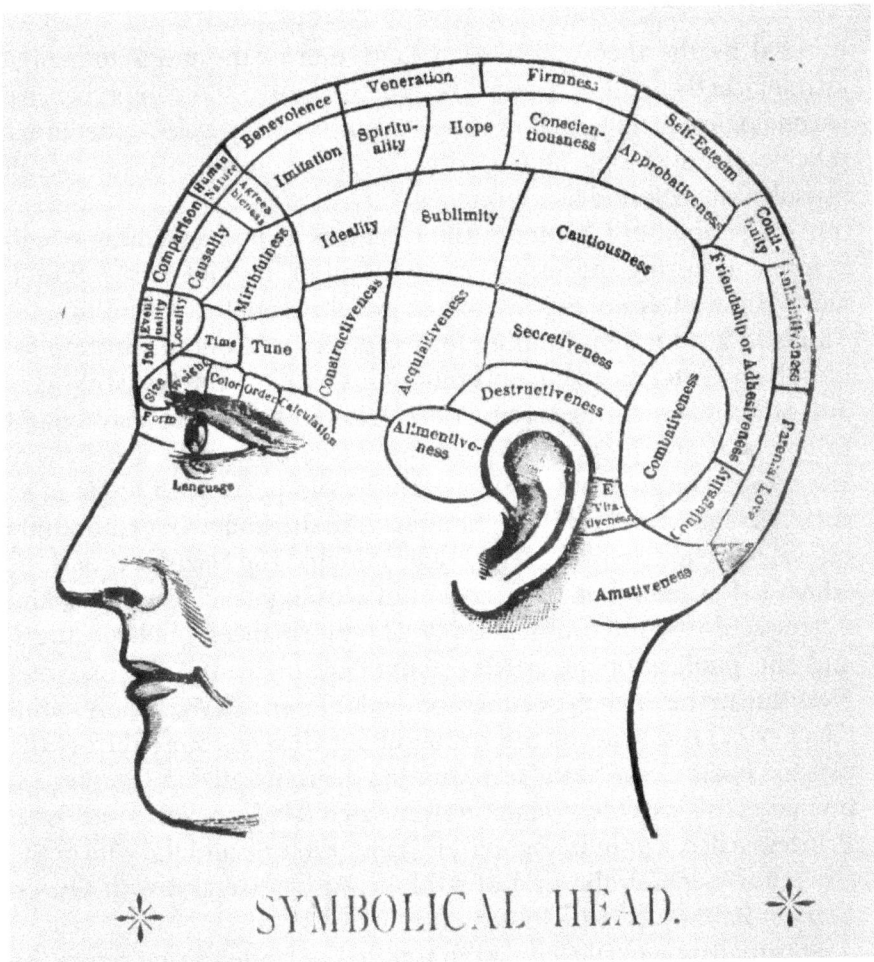

Figure 04: A phrenological chart from William Seymour's Key to Phrenology *(1890).*

functioning, the disposition of the mind, and the formation of character for decades. In 1900, he had his head read by the phrenologist O'Dell at the London Phrenological Institute in England. When he was Prime Minister and in 1923 invited Governor General Lord Byng to Laurier House, his residence in Ottawa, "We talked of phrenology which Lord Byng has specially studied. His Excellency said he had been studying the heads of all my ministers."

Mackenzie King's obsession with magnetic and electric sex currents and his fear that he was being controlled by outside forces is examined in Chapter 6. The monthly *Modern Astrology* in London which prepared M.E. Young's astrological charts for King in 1925 had been founded in 1890 by the theosophist Alan Leo, "one of the most influential astrological theorists of the early twentieth century."[13] A comprehensive chronological listing of all of King's contacts with psychics, mediums, psychic investigators, and spiritualists that documents his occult pursuits can be found in Chronology.

As described in Chapter 8, the Germans also accessed the occult before and during the Second World War. In the mid-1930s, Rudolf Hess, Hitler's Deputy *Führer,* and an occultist, applied for millions of Marks in government funding for his projected Central Institute for Occultism. After receiving a propitious horoscope from his astrologers and other psychic messages in 1941, Hess embarked on a solo flight to Scotland and parachuted from his Me-110 onto the Duchess of Hamilton's family estate in an attempt to win peace with England so that Germany would be free to attack Russia. Following Churchill's refusal to negotiate with Hess, Hitler initiated the Nazis' *Aktion Hess* which led to the arrest of hundreds of astrologers, clairvoyants, and other occultists, and prohibited public performances, public lectures, and the publication of articles about Spiritualism. King had met Hess during his own peace mission with Hitler in 1937 (analyzed in Chapter 17) and believed the visions about Hess he received from the psychic Jessie Coumbs in New York. As demonstrated in Chapter 18, he shared this psychic revelation from "an old lady in New York" with Princess Alice, a granddaughter of Queen Victoria and the wife of the Governor General, the Earl of Athlone, in Ottawa and with Queen Mary at Balmoral Castle in July and August 1941.

Spiritualism had started taking root in the United Kingdom in the early 1850s when mediums from America began travelling to England after Margaret and Kate Fox had launched Modern Spiritualism via their mysterious "Rochester Rappings" in 1848. According to Barry Wiley, "Table tilting and domestic circles became popular throughout Great Britain, with the wealthy, fashionable classes well represented. It was this penetration of the intellectual and moneyed classes that further distinguished European Spiritualism from the American movement, which was rooted in rural and working families and the newly developing middle class." But Spiritualism in the United Kingdom was not confined to the middle and upper classes. As Janet Oppenheim documents in *The Other World: Spiritualism and*

---

13 Diary, March 11, 1923. Campion, 598.

Psychical Research in England, 1850-1914, the social reformer Robert Owen endorsed Spiritualism in the 1850s and promoted it in the working-class labour movement. The British National Association of Spiritualists was founded in 1873, *Light* in 1881, the Society for Psychical Research in 1882, the London Spiritualist Alliance in 1884, the British Spiritualists' Lyceum Union in 1890, and the non-Christian Spiritualists National Federation in 1891. It subsequently incorporated as the Spiritualists' National Union.

By 1887, *Two Worlds* "listed more than one hundred available spiritualist 'Services for Sunday' in Temperance Halls, Co-operative Halls, Mechanics' Institutes, and other assorted meeting rooms of urban Britain." Over a dozen publications and over two hundred provincial and London-based spiritual organizations were founded before World War I. Oppenheim roughly estimates the number of spiritualists at the time between ten and one hundred thousand. R.H. Yates, the secretary of the Parliamentary Committee of the Spiritualists' National Union, affirmed in December 1918 that over the years "In our Lyceums, hundreds of thousands of children have been reared in the tenets of Spiritualism. They know very little about the fall of man, or about the miraculous conception and the doctrine of a vicarious Atonement, but they do know something about evolution, about the rise of man and eternal progression and about the laws that govern their being; and their lives are shaped and guided by the fundamental principle of personal responsibility."[14]

By 1920 David Gow, the editor of *Light*, identified the Spiritualists' National Union, operating mainly in the Midlands and Northern counties of England, as the largest body of spiritualists in Great Britain. It worked with some 370 societies throughout the country and had a membership of approximately 30,000. Writing on "Spiritualism: Its Position and Its Prospects" in the review *Quest*, he described the Lyceum Union as representing two hundred forty lyceums with a membership of some 24,000 young people and gave the membership of the London Spiritualist Alliance as 1,500. The Society for Psychical Research had a membership of 759 in 1933. In 1935, the British College of Psychic Science, publisher of the important *Quarterly Transactions BCPS*, reported a membership of 584. The following year, the Spiritualists' National Union announced at its convention in London

---

14 Wiley, 118. Oppenheim, 40, 42, 103, 52, 99, 44, 50. R.H. Yates, "The Witchcraft and Vagrancy Act," *Light* 38:1979 (December 14, 1918), 398.

Figure 05: Barbara McKenzie's portrait in Psychic Science, January 1926.

that there were probably about 600 services held each Sunday. Lind-af-Hageby, addressing the Marylebone Spiritualist Association in 1935 on the topic of "The Rapid Growth of Spiritualism," referred to these "hundreds of churches and societies" and stated, "I am sure our movement has millions of adherents in this country."[15]

For many non-Christian spiritualists, the Bible was not infallible holy writ, and Christ an extraordinary medium rather than the son of God. One of the most prominent was James Arthur Findlay, founder of the Glasgow Society for Psychical Research in 1920 and one of the founders of *Psychic News* in 1932. He published a widely read investigation of psychic phenomena titled *On the Edge of the Etheric*, in 1931, and *The Rock of Truth, or, Spiritualism, the Coming World Religion*, describing the persecution of mediums by Christians, in 1933. After three months of persistent criticism of *The Rock of Truth*, Findlay lectured on "Why Spiritualism Must Become the Only World-Religion" at the Grotrian Hall in London. He stated that there was no historical basis for the Christian religion and that Christianity was not the teaching of Jesus. "There was no more similarity between the Christianity of to-day and the teaching of Jesus than between chalk and cheese." Findlay was certain that "The truths for which Spiritualism stands will be accepted in time by all races, by all peoples, and that creeds, dogmas, rites and ceremonies which surround this basic truth in all religions will be dropped." "Some day all such labels as Christian, Moslem, Hindu and Buddhist will disappear and there

---

15 Gow, "Spiritualism: Its Position and Its Prospects," 256, 257. "Report of the Executive Council," *Quarterly Transactions BCPS*, 14:3 (October 1935), 228. "Dangers of Popularity," *Light* 56:2888 (May 14, 1936), 318. Lind-af-Hageby, "The Rapid Growth of Spiritualism," 402.

will be no need for the label Spiritualism, as all will merge into one great religion of humanity. Spiritualism is not *a* religion, it is religion."

In May 1934, in addition to serving as chairman of *Psychic News* and the International Institute for Psychic Research, Findlay accepted the presidency of the London Spiritualist Alliance and chairmanship of the Board of *Light*. Six months later, however, he presented such a strongly anti-Christian lecture to members of the LSA that its Council inserted a notice in the December 6, 1934, *Light* dissociating the Alliance and its publication from his views. Findlay promptly resigned from both organizations.[16] As shown in Chapter 15, this conflict between Christian and non-Christian beliefs on the part of mediums and spiritualists created a major crisis for Mackenzie King when he participated in séances with Etta Wriedt in the mid-1930s.

The main debate within the Christian spiritualist movement was about its relationship with other faiths and the form and nature of the spiritualist creed itself. Barbara McKenzie from the British College of Psychic Science published "Can Spiritualism Replace Christianity?" in *Light* a few months before Findlay's sudden resignation. She suggested, "If Spiritualism needs the best that Christianity can offer, Christianity certainly needs the contribution of Spiritualism, for the facts by which the latter stands form not only 'the preamble' of Christianity but its completion. Dogmatic theology, alien to modern minds, has side-tracked the Churches from the Universal Message attributed to the historic Jesus, in which he affirmed his belief in the spiritual nature and survival of man." McKenzie pointed to the Spiritualists' National Union and its goal of promoting the religion and religious philosophy of Spiritualism. "The bulk of Spiritualists in Britain are gathered out of the various denominations. They need a spiritual home and are justified in their formation of Societies and Churches, for it is their privilege to conserve this new knowledge for the people with freedom of thought, a task no Church is prepared to undertake." Geraldine Cummins – with whom Mackenzie King had sittings in 1947 and 1948 – affirmed, "The faith of the early Christians was founded on that great psychic phenomenon, the Resurrection of Jesus. If Christ had not risen from the dead on

---

16 "Mr. J. Arthur Findlay Replies: Why Spiritualism Must Become the Only World-Religion," 764. "Notes by the Way," *Quarterly Transactions BCPS* 13:4 (January 1935), 316. "Mr. J. Arthur Findlay," *Light* 54:2816 (December 27, 1934), 804.

Figure 06: Louise (Lizzy) Lind-af-Hageby's portrait in Light, November 1913.

that Easter morning, if Paul had not in mediumistic trance seen the Vision on the road to Damascus, I do not believe that there would have been a Christian faith."[17]

A completely contrary conception of Spiritualism was advocated by Hannen Swaffer, the popular journalist, drama critic and one of the co-founders of *Psychic News*. He succeeded Arthur Conan Doyle as the honorary president of the Spiritualists' National Union and was described by *Light* in "Hannen Swaffer on Future of Spiritualism" in 1933 as an "untiring propagandist for Spiritualism." "I draw a line between Spiritualism as an organised movement and as a systemless truth. As a movement, Spiritualism will never become a great force. As a truth it will permeate and conquer the world," he stated in his interview. "The spirit world, in my experience, desires no churches, organisations, speakers, researchers or newspapers. What it desires is Mediums. To get more Mediums we have to encourage the home circle. To them solely is due the fact that in the last ten years Spiritualism has made more progress than in all its history."

Swaffer had worked for the Fleet Street publishing magnate Lord Northcliffe, owner of the *Daily Mail* and *Daily Mirror*. After his death in 1922, Swaffer established contact with Northcliffe via the trance medium Gladys Osborne Leonard and published an account of the séances in *Northcliffe's Return* in 1925. He was therefore convinced of the crucial primary role of mediums in the spiritualist movement. "The job of Spiritualism is to comfort the mourners and transform the world. Nothing can do it more effectively than the home circles

---

17 Barbara McKenzie, "Can Spiritualism Replace Christianity," 496. Cummins, "Survival and Immortality: A Modern Revelation," 276.

and I insist on their decisive importance even as regards science and Psychical Research."

As outlined in Chapter 16, Swaffer's call for a great increase in the number of amateur mediums via home circles was completely contrary to J. Hewat and Barbara McKenzie's aim in establishing the British College of Psychic Science in 1920 for the careful training of professional mediums. Frederick Bligh Bond, editor of the College's *Psychic Science*, cautioned in 1926, "Public speakers on spiritualist platforms are apt to recommend the cultivation of mediumship by development in home circles. There is danger in this unless the process is guided by some knowledge of the pitfalls incidental to such efforts. The development of mediumship needs expert advice and careful watching. We cannot wholly exonerate our leaders or ourselves from an occasional lapse from discretion by too free an advocacy of this home culture of such gifts as trance mediumship and clairvoyance."

Lizzy Lind-af-Hageby, who succeeded James Arthur Findlay as the President of the London Spiritualist Alliance, agreed with Bond. "Some people are inclined to think that a Medium is an empty vessel – a person without much brains, much balance, much knowledge. They are inclined to think you have got to be empty within in order to be able to commune with and transmit knowledge from others. This I utterly deny." The Duchess of Hamilton also believed "in the need for perfecting and developing the brain of the Medium, so that he or she may be better attuned to co-operate with other intelligences, as a crystal cup will reflect the colours and transmute the light that it receives. The question is one of 'cooperation' as against 'control.' The more developed a Medium is, the more his or her mediumship will pass into co-operation and be less and less a matter of control."[18]

The London Spiritualist Alliance promoted itself as the oldest representative spiritualist organization in the British Empire and perceived its membership – as it stated in 1917 – as "forming a kind of middle class between the almost purely academic activities of the Society for Psychical Research and the propagandist energies of the numerous Spiritualistic societies carried on in the Metropolis and at many other centres in the United Kingdom." By the time Mackenzie King contacted the organization in 1936, Lind-af-Hageby had largely

---

18 "Hannen Swaffer on Future of Spiritualism," 677. Frederick Bligh Bond, "Editorial Notes," *Quarterly Transactions BCPS* 5:1 (April 1926), 4. Lind-af-Hageby, "Place of Spiritualism in Modern Thought," 82.

defined what in her view Spiritualism and the LSA represented. She had stated her thesis in an address delivered at Caxton Hall, Westminster, in January 1935 entitled "The Place of Spiritualism in Modern Thought." "First, Spiritualism, in the sense of the recognition of the spiritual, the unseen, the intangible, the divine, has existed from the dawn of human thought. To-day it contains the mass feeling, the mass thought reflected in all of religion, literature and art that transcends materialism. Secondly, Spiritualism in its knowledge of human survival and its personal avowal of the reality of spirit communication, is no modern event. It is manifest in the utterances and writings of thinkers of all ages and of very many races."

Lind-af-Hageby contended that the spiritualist movement had already achieved a partial victory for the acceptance of the basic principles of Spiritualism, "the victory taking the form not only of a measurable growth of adherents, but of a penetrative influence, an infiltration into practically all departments of human thought." Unlike Findlay, she perceived no need for throwing over Christianity. "You cannot be a Christian without accepting the Spiritualistic basis, for the whole of the Christian religion is founded upon these very things, and there is no denying it. Voices, visions, 'miraculous' powers, the story of the Christian faith as it runs through the Church, as it is accepted to-day in the Roman Catholic Church, is the story of Mediumship." Above all, she believed Spiritualism could encompass both science and religion. "I believe that Spiritualism, in its scientific aspects, has played and will play an enormous part, breaking down intolerance, opening new vistas, giving men of intellect new visions," she stated in her address. "I believe that it is the meeting place of Science and Religion – that Religion will become more and more scientific, and Science will become more and more religious."[19]

In an apparent reference to Max Weber's *The Sociology of Religion*, Lind-af-Hageby acknowledged the persistent opposition from science and other faiths to Spiritualism. "In Religion you have always had and always have the Priest and the Prophet. The Priest is addicted to dogma, to formalism, to stating the creed. The Prophet, on the other hand, is the man who sees, who desires additions to knowledge, who

---

19 "The London Spiritualist Alliance (Ltd.): Its Past and Its Future," *Light* 37:1881 (January 27, 1917), 28. Lind-af-Hageby, "Place of Spiritualism in Modern Thought," 81, 83.

is capable of vision, who is mobile in his mind, in his whole mental, intuitive, and spiritual outlook."[20]

The French sociologist Pierre Bourdieu (1930-2002) also drew on Weber's study to quantify the struggle for power between conservative, established agents and institutions and new subversive cultural agents in specific social fields such as religion. Such contending power relationships could be monitored, he believed, not only by the measurement of the accumulation of financial capital as Weber had established but also of symbolic capital, including social, spiritual, cultural, and political. Bourdieu's insights and concepts help explain the relative success of the spiritualist movement in the United Kingdom and the failure of such a collective movement to develop in Canada.

He expanded Weber's model of religious change presented in *The Sociology of Religion* – in which "priests" with conservation strategies and charismatic "prophets" with subversion strategies compete among the "laity" for consumers of their respective symbolic goods – to encompass all phases of cultural and social life.[21] "Those who, in a determinate state of power relations, more or less completely monopolize the specific capital, the basis of the specific power or authority characteristic of a field," Bourdieu wrote, "are inclined to conservation strategies – those which, in the fields of production of cultural goods, tend to defend *orthodoxy* – whereas those least endowed with capital (who are often also the newcomers) are inclined towards subversion strategies, the strategy of *heresy*."[22] The crux of the struggle for religious power between "priests" and "prophets," Bourdieu believed, centered around the question of who had "the *monopoly of the legitimate exercise of the power to modify, in a deep and lasting fashion, the practice and world-view of lay people*."[23]

In his analysis of *The Sociology of Religion*, Bourdieu noted that Weber defined "prophets" – for example, individuals such as Arthur Conan Doyle, Oliver Lodge, Lind-af-Hageby and other prominent leaders of the spiritualist movement – as "the bearers of metaphysical

---

20   Lind-af-Hageby, "Place of Spiritualism in Modern Thought," 81-82.

21   Swartz, 73-74, 80. Lash, 195.

22   Bourdieu, "Some Properties of Fields," 73.

23   Bourdieu, "Legitimation and Structured Interests in Weber's Sociology of Religion," 126. Italics in original.

or religious-ethical revelation." He posited that "The prophet's charismatic action basically achieves its effects by way of the prophetic word" and defined their charisma as "*the symbolic power that confers on them the ability to believe in their own symbolic power…it supports the faith of the prophet in his own mission.*"[24]

Lilian Whiting gave an example of the impact of the prophetic word and of the prophet's charisma in a description of Oliver Lodge's presentation in Boston during his 1920 North American tour. "The deeply religious feeling of Sir Oliver Lodge is impressed upon every audience privileged to listen to his inspiring lectures. He is one of the most sympathetic of speakers, establishing a *rapport*, at once, between himself and the immense throngs that crowd Symphony Hall to hear him," Whiting wrote to *Light*. "His clear, sympathetic voice and charm of manner captivate all…Sir Oliver Lodge comes to the States divinely commissioned." Whiting cited part of Lodge's address demonstrating the prophet's faith in his own mission. "Do not think of the departed as far away. I assure you they are not. Only the veil of sense separates us, and there are those who have their moments of clairvoyance. The departed may be all about us now, especially if attached by links of affection. There may be myriads here now," Lodge told his Symphony Hall audience. "They tell us we are the dreamers, the ghosts, while they are the reality. They see the world from one aspect, we from another. Sometimes I think there is but one world."[25]

We can also sense the power of the prophetic word in a description of "Propaganda Meetings" held by Hannen Swaffer and Maurice Barbanell in 1931. "I have heard many great orators in my time; I have been carried away into new realms of realisation by the magic of the spoken word; but I have never before experienced the thrill of losing myself in the speaker's simple sincerity as I did on Wednesday last listening to Mr. Hannen Swaffer address an audience of over 3,000 people in the Free Trade Hall, Manchester, on 'Spiritualism, the Plain Truth,'" James Norbury reported to *Light*. Swaffer proclaimed to the assembly that "Spiritualism is the greatest truth in the world, behind it is a great Spirit Power that will stop all wars and all brutality among men." Introducing him a year after Conan Doyle's death, Maurice Barbanell told the

---

24 Ibid., 120, 127. Bourdieu, "Genesis and Structure of the Religious Field," 20. Italics in original.

25 Lilian Whiting, "Sir Oliver Lodge in Boston," *Light* 40:2043 (March 6, 1920), 75.

audience that "Mr. Hannen Swaffer is ably filling the place occupied by Sir Arthur Conan Doyle as Spiritualism's leading propagandist."[26]

When he expanded Max Weber's model of religious change to encompass all phases of cultural and social life, Bourdieu suggested that neither orthodox "priests" nor subversive "prophets" could succeed without building a community of followers. "The prophet's power rests upon the force of the group he can mobilize." Even the charismatic "prophet" could not succeed in the competition with "priests" without first building a community of followers. "Prophecy cannot completely fulfill the claim that it necessarily implies, of being able to modify the lives and world-views of the laity in a deep and lasting fashion," he observed, "unless it succeeds in founding a 'community.' This is in turn able to perpetuate itself in an institution capable of carrying on a lasting and continuous activity of winning acceptance for and inculcating the doctrine." He concluded, "The prophet's power rests upon the force of the group he can mobilize."[27]

Spiritualists in the United Kingdom succeeded in building a community, attracting a significant number of followers, and institutionalizing their creed in churches and in local, regional, and national organizations. They also had respected prophets with considerable social and cultural capital, a multitude of mediums creating new adherents, and means of communication via publications, large and small public meetings, and countless home circles. In emergencies and for special occasions, they were also able to raise financial capital from their members to commemorate or defend Spiritualism. Doyle sent his annual donation of £10 to *Light* in 1918 with the brief note, "you are in a position, I consider, not to beg for but to demand a sufficiency, in the spirit in which St. Paul demanded the needful money for himself and his propaganda from the early Churches. You represent the most living religious cause now existing upon earth, the only conclusive answer against materialism, and to let your work languish for want of funds is unthinkable."[28]

Yet the very success of the spiritualist movement generated attacks from established faiths, scientific disciplines, the press, and the legal system defending the established order. Conan Doyle observed in his

---

26 J. Norbury, "Propaganda Meetings," *Light* 51:2657 (December 11, 1931), 598.

27 Bourdieu, "Legitimation and Structured Interests in Weber's Sociology of Religion," 129, 127, 129.

28 "The Maintenance of 'Light,'" *Light* 38:1933 (January 26, 1918), 29.

"The New Revelation" address that there were always two main lines of attack made by opponents against spiritualists. "The one was that their facts were not true…The other was that they were upon forbidden ground." *Psychic Science* cited a Bishop of a northern diocese regarding spiritual healing as reported in the *Sunday Express* in 1925: "The healing of diseases is the physician's task. It cannot be the duty of the Church to return to beliefs and methods of a primitive and superstitious past, but rather to follow the evident leading of the spirit of truth, to support the labour of scientific men…The healing ministry of Christ…was to be traced not in sporadic prodigies of faith-healing but in the majestic and unfaltering movement of medical science." The quarterly's editor, Frederick Bligh Bond, editorialized that "An ecclesiastical hierarchy, jealous of its privileges, will always repudiate the spontaneous exercise of prophetic and other allied gifts by those outside clerical orders."

When the Bishop of London attacked Spiritualism in a diocesan leaflet and forbade any church or church building to be used for spiritualistic séances in 1935, Lind-af-Hageby responded with her own broadside in *Light*. "The Church has encouraged communion with the Saints, prayers to them, answers from them, visions of them… if it be right to seek inspiration from a recognised Saint, it cannot be wrong to seek the same from one as yet not recognised…Millions of people have become Spiritualists because the evidence of Survival and communication have convinced them of the facts."[29]

Mackenzie King's views on Spiritualism were identical with those that Mercy Phillimore, the Secretary of the London Spiritualist Alliance, presented to the Archbishop of Canterbury's Committee on Spiritualism in March 1937. "Spiritualism means the Demonstrated Survival of Human Personality after Bodily Death. It includes the knowledge of the interaction of matter and spirit. Further, it implies a comprehension of the intelligent progressive spiritual principle which underlies the whole of creation, of mankind and nature in this present life, and of the continuous individual progressive spiritual life in the Hereafter," Phillimore stated to the Committee. "The endeavour to prove continuity of life of Human Personality after bodily death is

---

29   Conan Doyle, "The New Revelation," *Light* 37:1923 (November 17, 1917), 365. Frederick Bligh Bond, "Editorial Notes," *Quarterly Transactions BCPS* 4:1 (April 1925), 4-5, and 3:3 (October 1924), 164. Lind-af-Hageby, "Questions for the Bishop of London," 434.

a science...The scientific findings of this examination have implications which involve philosophy and religion. Therefore, Spiritualism may rightly be claimed fundamentally as a combination of Science, Philosophy and Religion."

Seven out of ten eminent Committee members were sympathetic to Phillimore's presentation. The controversial section of their 1939 *Report* stated, "When every possible explanation of these [spirit] communications has been given, and all doubtful evidence set aside, it is generally agreed that there remains some element as yet unexplained. We think that it is probable that the hypothesis that they proceed in some cases from discarnate spirits is a true one." But the Archbishop of Canterbury, Cosmo Gordon Lang, suppressed the public release of the Committee's *Report*. Its majority findings were only leaked to *Psychic News* in 1947.[30]

The government also sought to limit the growth and influence of the spiritualist movement. In 1935 and 1936, the British Broadcasting Corporation refused requests from the Spiritualists' National Union that it broadcast a Spiritualist Sunday Service. The *Sunday Referee* justified this appeal to the B.B.C. for radio coverage in 1936 by asserting that Spiritualism in the United Kingdom "has at least one million adherents. Every week hundreds more are being converted. At more than 2,000 Spiritualist churches throughout the country the average attendance at Sunday evening service totals a quarter of a million." The B.B.C. Religious Advisory Committee justified its exclusion of spiritualist services by stating, "Before a request for an evening service is granted, the Committee shall have satisfied itself that the teaching of the applying body is such as can be said to be in the main stream of Christian tradition. Inasmuch as discrimination of some kind is absolutely necessary, this would seem an obvious condition to lay down in a country with many centuries of Christianity behind it and still largely Christian in sentiment and belief."[31]

---

30 Mercy Phillimore, "The Terms of Reference of Committee," p. 2. Copy in King Spiritualism Papers. Phillimore comments on the decision by the Archbishop of Canterbury's Committee on Spiritualism not to publish its report in *Light* 60:3104 (July 11, 1940). Georgina Byrne, "Spiritualism: Some Elements as Yet Unexplained," *Church Times*, January 31, 2020. "Archbishop's Report," *Psychic News*, no. 805 (November 8, 1947).

31 "The B.B.C Again," *Light* 55:2846 (July 25, 1935), 466. "B.B.C. and Spiritualism," *Light* 56:2887 (May 7, 1936), 299. "The B.B.C. and Spiritualism," *Light* 56:2895 (July 2, 1936), 424, 426.

Figure 07: Mercy Phillimore at the London Spiritualist Alliance in 1926.

In the House of Commons, Ernest Marklew, the only openly professing spiritualist Member of Parliament, declared in 1936 that he was proud to state he had been a spiritualist for the last forty years. "I owe everything I have, everything I am and all the hopes that I entertain so far as the future is concerned to Spiritualism." Speaking in the discussion on the Government proposals for the future of the B.B.C., he claimed that there were hundreds of thousands of spiritualists in the country and that "We have no more right – less, if any – to repress a man in the effort to give expression to his religious convictions than we have the right to repress him when he desires to give expression to his political convictions." Marklew also endorsed the opposition by spiritualists to the Medicines and Surgical Appliances (Advertisement) Bill in Parliament which would have subjected spiritualists who practiced healing and diagnosis to fines and imprisonment. The Bill, as Markle stated, "was not designed to protect the public, but to establish a vested interest for orthodox healers – doctors and surgeons." He had cured his own ill son by calling "on the help of the spirit-world, and himself acted as the intermediary by the 'laying on of hands'" after his doctor said his son's case was hopeless. A public meeting organized by the Spiritualist Joint Council on Healing at the Friends' House in London estimated it would cost between £500 and £750 [£29,000 and £44,000 in 2023] to oppose the Bill.[32]

The government exerted its greatest threat against spiritualists and Spiritualism in the United Kingdom via the Witchcraft and Vagrancy Acts of 1735 and 1824, which were also used to suppress psychics and mediums and the taking of money for predictions of the future. In 1876, the mediums Henry Slade and Francis Monck were arrested and charged under the Vagrancy Act. It made punishable as a rogue and vagabond every person "using any subtle craft, means, or devices by Palmistry or otherwise to deceive and impose on any of His Majesty's subjects." The High Court of Justice found that the accused "attempted to deceive and impose upon certain persons by falsely pretending to have the supernatural faculty of obtaining from invisible agents and spirits of the dead answers, messages and manifestations of power, namely, noises, raps, and the winding up of a musical box." Slade and Monk were sentenced to three months of hard labour.[33]

Four decades later in 1917, Olive Bush – described by Lind-af-Hageby as a genuine psychic – and Madam Claire were sentenced to three months imprisonment and fined £35, respectively, and the astrologer Alan Leo fined £5 and £25 in court costs. Lind-af-Hageby

---

32 "'The People Called Spiritualists:' Plea in the House of Commons for Their Rights," *Light* 56:2897 (July 16, 1936), 454. "Spiritual Healing: Protest Against Proposed Restrictions," *Light* 56:2881 (March 26, 1936), 200. See also "The Threat to Spiritual Healing," *Light* 56:2882 (April 2, 1936).

33 "Rogues and Vagabonds," *Psypioneer* 2:9 (September 2006), 203. For Spiritualism and criminal prosecutions in the United States, see Dyson.

addressed a large mass meeting at the South Place Institute demanding the amendment of the Witchcraft and Vagrancy Acts in May 1917 and explained the greatly increased activities of mediums resulting from the First World War. "The sacrifice of so many young lives in the fulness of health and strength and vigour naturally brought home to thousands of hearts the questions, Where had they gone? Where were they? Was the tie of love finally severed? If there was another world, was the veil between the two impenetrable? Thus it was that the war had given a great impetus not only in this country but in all other countries to psychical research and Spiritualism. Many thousands were looking to Spiritualism, to its literature, to its meetings, to its exponents, who would not have come but for personal bereavements." She called for the licensing of mediums so that they could earn a modest livelihood like other professions and be connected to churches, societies, and scientific institutes. "There is no science which can compare in importance with the science of the soul, of the higher powers of the mind, which brings the Unknown within the realm of the visible and tangible."[34]

At the conclusion of the First World War in November 1918, R.H. Yates and the Spiritualists' National Union launched a drive seeking 600,000 signatures for a petition to Parliament to amend the Witchcraft and Vagrancy Acts. Yet a decade later, Mercy Phillimore, the LSA secretary, was herself charged by the police with "aiding, abetting, procuring and counselling" in arranging séances in the Alliance's facilities for one of its mediums, Mrs. Clare Cantlon. In June 1928, the medium was accused of having "professed to tell fortunes" while in trance under the control of the Indian spirit White Chief. A meeting of representative spiritualists presided over by Arthur Conan Doyle, the President of the LSA, at its headquarters at 16 Queensberry Place, South Kensington, determined to use the case as an opportunity to obtain Parliamentary reform of the Witchcraft and Vagrancy Acts. The meeting established a Spiritualists' Defence Fund with the Doyle family and Hewat and Barbara McKenzie among the first donors. *Light* published contributors' names and amounts donated followed by the statement, "All Spiritualists must value the psychic faculty as the bed-rock of our Movement, and will thus realise the need of safeguarding its legitimate use." By the end of September, £688 out of £879 in legal fees had been covered by

---

34 "To Amend the Witchcraft and Vagrancy Acts," *Light* 37:1897 (May 19, 1917), 157.

donations to the Defence Fund, with some contributions received from outside the United Kingdom[35]

When the case came to trial as Rex v. Cantlon and Phillimore at Westminster Police Court, Mrs. Lilian Wyles, an inspector of women police at Scotland Yard, testified that she had paid 17s. 6d. to Phillimore for a séance with Cantlon. The counsel for the LSA, Sir Patrick Hastings, KC, presented the Alliance as an institution which had nothing to do with fortune-telling but was occupied with the investigation of evidence of human survival after death. He indicated that the LSA had severed its association with Cantlon – who had pleaded guilty as charged – and maintained that "the conviction against Miss Phillimore would sound the death-knell of this and every other association of people whose endeavour to arrive at the truth or falsity of these [spiritualist] ideas and doctrines." Arthur Conan Doyle testified that he had been the Alliance President for about three years, that it was not-for-profit and existed "purely for furthering investigation and the study of the science in which the association believed," and that it tested and watched the careers of its mediums.

Sir Oliver Lodge caused a sensation in the filled court when he left the bedside of Lady Lodge, who was ill, to give evidence on behalf of the LSA. He testified that he was not a member of the Alliance but had been a member of the Society for Psychical Research since its founding in 1882 and had served as its President in 1901-1903. He stated that there were perfectly genuine psychics and that mediums were required for his psychical research since "I have no power myself." Mercy Phillimore, who had pleaded not guilty, testified that she had never accepted sitters who asked to have their fortune told. Cantlon had had about fifty-nine sittings during the current year out of a possible one hundred and six and no one had ever reported that the medium had told their fortune. The LSA deducted 2s. 6d. from each fee received by a medium to cover overhead expenses and made no profit out of its activities.

In his judgement the magistrate, Mr. Oulton, declared that he had an open mind about Spiritualism but that he thought both accused guilty as charged under the existing laws. "The history of Spiritualism is tarnished by fraud and chicanery. On the other hand, there have been, and are, great men and women whose honour is unquestioned,

---

35 "L.S.A. and Action of the Police," *Light* 48:2479 (July 14, 1928), 336.
"Defence Fund," *Light* 48:2490 (September 29, 1928), 468.

striving to show that from the undiscovered country the traveller does return," he stated in court. "But the earnest searcher after truth must be amenable to the law and must not break it. If he deems the law out of date and thinks it frustrates his efforts, his remedy is to alter and modernise the law." Oulton dealt with the case as leniently as he could. He dismissed the summonses in both cases under the Probation of Offenders Act but charged £20 in court costs to Phillimore and £10 to Cantlon. *Light* editorialized that the magistrate's decision really amounted to finding Phillimore and Cantlon guilty and that "This might mean very serious results if the offence were repeated. The legal weapon has been brandished even if it has not been used with full effect."[36]

In his "The New Revelation" address, Doyle had asked if Christ returned to London in 1917 "could we be certain that some Pontius Pilate in a police-court would not be sorely puzzled as to whether he should not be indicted under the Blasphemy Act as unsettling the old religion or under the Vagrancy Act as a prophet and a medium?" After Doyle's death in July 1930 and after the Home Secretary received a deputation, Oliver Lodge helped to draft an amendment to the Witchcraft Act which he and the Spiritualists' National Union hoped could pass the House of Commons. Frederick Bligh Bond editorialized in the *Journal of the American Society for Psychical Research* (subsequently cited as *JASPR*) in 1931 that "The Home Secretary, Mr. J. B. Clynes, is stated to have declared himself in favor of it" and that the immediate effect of the passing of the bill would be "the elevation of mediumship to a status of public respect as a recognized calling or vocation…Doors will open in the clerical and academic world which have hitherto been jealously guarded."

The Home Secretary was still making similar promises for an enquiry into the use of the Vagrancy Act two years later. In 1935, the Spiritualists' National Union presented a manifesto, questionnaire and a draft of the Bill previously presented to Parliament to all candidates in the November General Election. The following year, *Light* cited the *Sunday Referee* "that when Parliament reassembles, 'Britain's million Spiritualists' will press for the hearing of a Bill designed

---

36 "The 'Fortune Telling' Case," *Light* 48:2480 (July 21, 1928), 340. "The Police Court Prosecution" and "The Police Court Case," *Light* 48:2842 (August 4, 1928), 362, 363, 364, 366.

to prevent the prosecutions of Mediums under the Witchcraft Act of 1735 and the Vagrancy Act of 1824." But the Witchcraft Act was not repealed until 1951, with the support of Labour Party MP and spiritualist Thomas Brooks, when it was replaced by the Fraudulent Mediums Act. Yet this new Act, given Royal Assent on June 22, 1951, still provided for fines and imprisonment ranging from £50 to £500 and four months to two years for "any person who – (*a*) with intent to deceive purports to act as a spiritualistic medium or to exercise any powers of telepathy, clairvoyance or other similar powers, or (*b*) in purporting to act as a spiritualistic medium or to exercise such powers as aforesaid, uses any fraudulent device." This Act was not repealed until 2008.[37]

Fraudulent mediums and psychics had already started the greatest *internal* conflict within the spiritualist movement only a few years after the Fox Sisters seemed to prove the existence of a spiritual world that made its presence known through mysterious knockings. In the United States, fake spirit photography began appearing from the mid-1850s on and during the American Civil War. In a sensational trial in 1869, the New York lawyer and reformer Elbridge Thomas Gerry unsuccessfully prosecuted the photographer William H. Mumler for soliciting money by pretended "spirit" photography. Mumler was found not guilty because Gerry could not prove how Mumler combined faint images of the deceased with his living subjects. The photographer subsequently widely circulated an image of Mary Todd Lincoln with her dead husband. *Light* and the *Quarterly Transactions BCPS* strongly endorsed spirit photography as they did virtually all phenomena that seemed to prove the existence of a spiritual world. Mackenzie King, like W.T Stead and the College's J. Hewat McKenzie, also "believed that spirit photography would in the future supply the principal body of evidence to prove the continuity of life beyond death."[38]

---

37 Conan Doyle, "The New Revelation," *Light* 37:1923 (November 17, 1917), 366. Frederick Bligh Bond, "The Statutory Protection of Mediums in England," *JASPR* 25:1 (January 1931), 1, 2. Ernest W. Oaten, "The Vagrancy Act – An Enquiry Promised," *Light* 53:2742 (July 28, 1933), 471. Frank T. Harris, "Spiritualists and the General Election," *Light* 55:2860 (October 31, 1935), 695. "The Fraudulent Mediums Bill," *Journal of the Society for Psychical Research* (subsequently cited as *JSPR*) 36:662 (January-February 1951), 370.

38 J. Hewat McKenzie, 102. On Mumler, see Manseau, Gerry, and Chéroux. By coincidence, Mackenzie King tutored Gerry's sons Robert and Peter at Harvard in 1898-1899 while studying for his PhD.

One of the most respected psychical researchers who uncovered fraud was the physicist Eleanor Mildred (Balfour) Sidgwick, the Principal of Cambridge University's Newnham College. Her husband, the philosopher and economist Henry Sidgwick, was one of the founders and the first President of the Society for Psychical Research in 1882. She was the sister of Arthur Balfour, President of the SPR in 1893 and Prime Minister in 1902-1905. Her brother, Gerald Balfour, served as Chief Secretary for Ireland in 1895-1900 and as SPR President in 1906-1907. Elected as the SPR President for 1908-1909, Eleanor Sidgwick was re-elected President – with Oliver Lodge – for the 50th anniversary of the SPR in 1932. Her paper "On Spirit Photographs," published in the *Proceedings of the Society for Psychical Research* (subsequently cited as *PSPR*) in 1891, critiqued Alfred Russel Wallace's endorsement of spirit photography as tangible proof of the existence of spirits and debunked the fraudulent photography of William Mumler, the British photographer Frederick Hudson, and the French photographer Édouard Isidore Buguet. In 1918, she praised Oliver Lodge's *Raymond, or, Life and Death* but regretted that his book would lead many readers to consult professional mediums in order to communicate with their lost loved ones and thus "encourage a very undesirable trade." Sidgwick stated of professional mediums that "many of them – perhaps most, are more or less fraudulent. Even when there is some real power it acts fitfully, and the temptation to supplement genuine with manufactured evidence must often be great when the medium's living depends on satisfying sitters."[39]

Two other psychic investigators and SPR members, Harry Price and Eric J. Dingwall, published a facsimile edition of *Revelations of a Spirit Medium; or Spiritualistic Mysteries Exposed*, first published anonymously by "A Medium" in St. Paul, Minnesota, in 1891. In the preface to their 1922 edition, published in London and New York, they echoed Sidgwick's warning about professional mediums. "If genuine physical phenomena exist (and we believe such phenomena to be excessively rare), it is scarcely conceivable that such manifestations could take place at the will of any medium on whom a sitter happens to call," Price and Dingwall stated. "Public mediums therefore are to be especially guarded against, and any apparently successful results obtained with them should be scrutinised with the greatest care. The

---

39 Sidgwick, "Review: *Raymond, or, Life and Death*," 409, 408.

Figure 08: William H. Mumler's 1872 photograph of Bronson Murray with the spirit of Ella Bonner.

present great increase of interest in psychic phenomena will probably result in the production of spurious physical phenomena by the less honest mediums, and it is with this thought that we have decided to reprint the *Revelations of a Spirit Medium*."[40]

Sidgwick's criticism of dubious psychic phenomena contributed to the well-known spiritualist and medium William Stainton Moses' resignation from the Society for Psychical Research. Arthur Conan Doyle engaged in a public debate about Spiritualism and fraud with Joseph McCabe, representing the Rationalist Press Association, in Queen's Hall in 1920. McCabe went on to describe an account of his debate with Doyle, entitled *Is Spiritualism Based on Fraud?*, later the same year. In his opening statement, *Light* reported, McCabe bluntly declared that Spiritualism "was born in fraud, cradled in fraud, nurtured in fraud, and it was based to-day to an alarming extent all over the world in fraudulent performances." While totally disagreeing with McCabe's presentation, Doyle did concede that "there were some mediums with the real power who, when that power failed – and it was an intermittent force – were immoral enough to fill up the gap by fraud."[41]

Yet in his 1926 *The History of Spiritualism*, Doyle sharply criticized the Society for Psychical Research – particularly Eleanor Sidgwick as "one of the worst offenders" – for accusing mediums of fraud and denying the reality of physical psychic manifestations. "The central machinery of the society has come into the hands of a circle of men," Doyle charged, "whose one care seems to be not to prove truth but to disprove what seems preternatural." Four years later, Theodore Besterman, the SPR's librarian, investigating officer and editor of its *Journal*, wrote a review of Gwendolyn Kelley Hack's *Modern Psychic Mysteries, Millesimo Castle, Italy*, with a preface and articles by the prolific Italian parapsychologist and spiritualist Ernesto Bozzano. Five months before his death and already ailing, Doyle found Besterman's review so antagonistic and offensive that, after thirty-six years, he resigned his SPR membership. He asked others to resign as well as a "public protest against the essentially unscientific and biased work of a Society which has for a whole generation produced no constructive work of any kind, but has confined its energies to the misrepresentation

---

40 Harry Price and Eric J. Dingwall, *Revelations of a Spirit Medium* (London: Kegan Paul, Trench, Trubner, and New York: Dutton, 1922), preface, vii-viii.
41 "The Conan Doyle-McCabe Debate," *Light* 40:2045 (March 20, 1920), 91.

and hindrance of those who have really worked at the most important problem ever presented to mankind." In a public circular, he urged SPR members to resign and to become members of the "progressive" British College of Psychic Science. The circular called the SPR "an anti-spiritualist organization" and charged that "the influence of the Society is entirely for evil."[42]

Sir Arthur also resigned as President of the London Spiritualist Alliance because it withdrew from a July 1, 1930, deputation of leading spiritualist organizations and individuals that lobbied J.R. Clynes, the Home Secretary, to revise the Witchcraft and Vagrancy Acts. The strain of organizing this lobbying effort hastened Conan Doyle's death. A month after his passing, R.H. Saunders, the frequent contributor to *Light* and author of *Healing Through Spirit Agency*, lauded "The Chief Apostle of Spiritualism" in the *International Psychic Gazette*. "When we remember that it was at the apogee of a popularity second only to Charles Dickens he risked all, and, throwing to the wind all personal considerations, devoted himself to the public advocacy of an unpopular subject many authors were content to espouse *sub rosa*, we may glimpse some measure of his courage. He lifted the subject of Spiritualism to a pinnacle it would never have attained without his eloquent advocacy. We have able men and women in the Movement, but none can adequately wear his mantle, for he was the Chief Apostle of Spiritualism, without a peer."[43]

This is the context for Mackenzie King's direct contacts with British Spiritualism in the 1930s and 1940s. Arthur Conan Doyle, Oliver Lodge, and many other advocates for Spiritualism toured Canada, spoke to large audiences and held private meetings with Canadian spiritualists and psychic investigators. The effects of their visits on Spiritualism in Canada is referred to in the chapters that follow.

Mackenzie King had also encountered deception and fraud in so-called spiritualist presentations. In 1906, while Deputy Minister of Labour in Wilfrid Laurier's Government, he paid one dollar to attend

---

42 Conan Doyle, *The History of Spiritualism*, 86. "Sir Arthur Conan Doyle's Resignation" and "Sir Arthur Conan Doyle's Circular," *JSPR* 26:463 (March 1930), 45, 47, 48. For an extensive critique of Besterman and the SPR in support of Conan Doyle, see Bradley. See also A.C. Cummings, "Spiritualists 'War' Over Mediaeval Castle," *Winnipeg Tribune*, May 10, 1930, 13.

43 By One of the Delegates [sic], "Sir Arthur's Last Work for the Cause – Introduces Deputation on the Witchcraft and Vagrancy Acts," *International Psychic Gazette* 18:203 (August 1930), 173. Saunders, 172.

the Russell Theatre in Ottawa where the Fays were presenting psychic readings and other spiritualist phenomena. Anna Eva Fay's son, John T. Fay, caused a woman to float in the air. In a complete copy of his mother's routines, his wife, Eva (Norman) Fay, made musical instruments jump around on stage. Most of the performance consisted of tests of Eva's clairvoyance and mindreading. King recorded in his diary, "Mrs. Fay's reading & answering of questions was quite mystifying; our questions were not answered & none for persons I know." He believed "it is done by the writing on pads & by accomplices in the audience & through the city. Still it is quite remarkable. Culbert & I went up on the stage as a committee from the audience to tie her hands, examine tables etc. in a few preliminary tricks. The people in the house called out our names to go up. It seemed to me all the tricks we witnessed could be easily explained by means of mechanical devices."

The *Ottawa Citizen* acknowledged the entertainment value of Eva Fay's performance with reservations. "Regarded strictly from the standpoint of entertainment no exception could be taken to them. Those who went got the worth of their money." Yet Fay could not answer the test question of the *Citizen* reporter made in advance in a public challenge: "When was I last in Toronto?" He subsequently noted in his article, "So clever was the exhibition of ostensible mind reading that it unduly impressed the superstitiously inclined to the extent that they were prepared to accept the answers of such a marvellously endowed woman as prophetic and towards the close of the engagement it took on the characteristics of a high class fortune telling performance. The effect of such an influence on superstitious minds cannot be beneficial." Two decades later, while struggling to remain in office as Prime Minister in 1925, King was still leery of public demonstrations of Spiritualism by medium performers. "My nature & reason revolt against 'spiritualism' & all the ilk – but not against the things of the spirit – the belief in spiritual guidance – through intuitions. It is the spiritual manifestations I feel charry [sic] about."[44]

Yet, as with hundreds of thousands who had sittings with mediums in the United Kingdom, on the continent and in North America,

---

44 Diary, March 3, 1906, and Cash Account for March in the diary for December 31, 1906. "The Test That Failed," *Ottawa Citizen*, March 5, 1906, 6. On the Fays, see also "Mrs. Fay Challenged," "A Discontented Deity," "The Test That Failed," and "Mrs. Fay Failed," *Ottawa Citizen*, March 3, 1906, 11, 8, and 6, and March 5, 1906, 2, and Wiley, 267-290. Diary, October 31, 1925.

Figure 09: Etta Wriedt at Mackenzie King's Kingsmere estate, August 28, 1934.

Mackenzie King became totally convinced of the genuineness of many mediums after he and Joan Patteson held séances with the American direct-voice medium Etta Wriedt in 1932. Through Wriedt, King and Patteson conversed with their loved departed mothers and other family members in the world "beyond the veil." The discarnate spirits spoke of experiences, persons and events Etta Wriedt could not possibly have known about. "There can be <u>no doubt whatever</u> that the persons I have been talking with were the loved ones & others I have known and who have passed away," he recorded in his diary. "It <u>was the spirits of the departed</u>. There is no other way on earth of accounting for what we have all experienced this week ... I <u>know</u> whereof I speak, that nothing but the presence [of] those who have departed this life, but not this world, or vice versa could account for the week's experiences."[45]

Mackenzie King's certain belief in the continuity of life after death and in the existence of a spiritual world that interacted with and guided him in the material world presents dangers when found in a politician, especially a head of state. Several of Lillian Hamilton's mediums described encountering Christ in their séances. So did Ellen Elliott, the head of Macmillan's – King's publisher in Toronto – whose wrenching cathartic description of séance contact with a Christ Presence is cited in Chapter 13. Herself a clairvoyant medium, Elliott participated in a séance with the Prime Minister and the Toronto medium Alma Brash on August 5, 1942, at the height of World War II. Christ appeared and placed a crown of thorns on King's head and told him he would suffer and be persecuted as He himself was persecuted. The Christ Presence and Elliott's spiritual director, the "White Brother," informed the Prime Minister that "this war is now to be God's war. It is to be taken out of the hands of man, and now He is to direct [King's] steps in the direction He commands."[46]

Readers will be able to judge for themselves whether King believed the spirit of President Franklin Roosevelt three years later when the PM asked for his advice regarding the revelations of a Soviet atomic espionage ring in Canada, Great Britain and the U.S. made by the Russian cypher clerk Igor Gouzenko, who defected in Ottawa in September 1945. The transcripts of four October 1945 séances with mediums in London in which King asked whether the Russians should be given the secret of the atom bomb, as well as transcripts of three additional séances in 1946 and 1947 – one of which King passed on to Winston Churchill – can be found in Appendix A of Volume 2.

---

45 Diary, June 26 and 27, 1932. All underlined text in original.
46 "Record of a Sitting with A.B. (psychic), Mr. X, and E.E.," August 5, 1942.

The chapters that follow describe how Spiritualism was a central part of the Prime Minister's worldview and how his executors sought to suppress knowledge about his spiritual activities. As he recorded in his diaries, King's spiritual mission was to achieve a state of grace in which – citing the Bible – he could "see God" and be one of His instruments to bring about "a new heaven and a new earth." The diaries – like the medium in a séance – are the means by which we can bring back their author from the valley of the shadow of death. They contain code words like King's sexual "restlessness" that must be deciphered and document the innumerable special "associations" he projected onto physical objects and human beings.

The two volumes of this biography reference thousands of entries from King's diaries and correspondence because determining his mental states and spiritual views is best accomplished through a direct encounter with his thoughts and words over a period of decades. In August 1949, less than a year before his death at the age of seventy-five, King invited Joan Patteson to join him in a spirit "conversation" over the "little table." One of the discarnate entities that communicated with them was one of the Prime Minister's spirit guides, Frederic W.H. Myers, author of *Human Personality and Its Survival of Bodily Death*. King recorded, "I believe there is much truth in what Meyers [sic] has said by way of interpretation. It will be seen it parallels my own. It is clear to me that there is a great danger of my life purpose & story being misunderstood unless told & explained by myself."[47]

Was Mackenzie King mad as some have argued, or did he use his spiritualism and occult practices to enhance his emotional well-being and assist – as we see in the chapter on the Kingston clairvoyant Rachel Bleaney – in making difficult political decisions? The chapters document the Canadian and British origins of his spiritualism, how King has been misjudged by historians, and how his executors sought to suppress knowledge of his spiritualist beliefs to protect his reputation and that of the Liberal Party. Chapter 6 examines King's fears that he was being influenced by outside psychic forces attempting to control his libido and that his failure to control his sex drive resulted in his becoming a "Lost Leader." The study of Dr. T. Glen Hamilton's and Lillian Hamilton's psychic investigations in Winnipeg discusses the fact that the Hamiltons were Christians, not spiritualists, and how

---

47 Diary, August 22, 1949.

the lack of strong prophetic spiritualist voices in Canada impeded the development of a vibrant public spiritualist community as had emerged in the United Kingdom.

After the focus in Volume 1 on the social context of Spiritualism, Volume 2 concentrates on King's personal interactions with several of the world's most respected mediums – Etta Wriedt from Detroit, Gladys Osborne Leonard in London, and Eileen Garrett in New York – as well as with other psychics in the United Kingdom, Canada, and the U.S. Chapters analyze the influence of Spiritualism on King's appeasement of Adolf Hitler prior to and after his peace mission to the German dictator in 1937, his views on race, his contacts with psychics during World War II, and his intimate involvement in the creation of the nuclear weapons still menacing our civilization today.

The concluding chapters of Volume 2 describe how Mackenzie King's magical thinking created an alternate universe for the PM. His beliefs and behaviour compare with neuroses described in the American Psychiatric Association's *Diagnostic and Statistical Manual of Mental Disorders*. The revision of the fifth edition of the *DSM*, released in February 2022, features a controversial new disorder named prolonged grief disorder.[48] King's relationship with his mother and the grief at her passing was the springboard for his decades-long pursuit of spirit communication with deceased family members.

The chapter which follows presents an initial glance at Mackenzie King and his unbreakable bond with Isabel King that compelled him to explore various occult means of maintaining contact with her. The entire biography can be seen as a meditation on the iconic image of King communing with his mother. Violet Markham, his close friend and benefactor, referred to Isabel's portrait and its altar as "that mausoleum of horrors."[49] For King, the painting was one of the primary means of communicating with the spirit world.

---

48   See Ellen Barry, "How Long Should It Take to Grieve? Psychiatry Has Come Up with an Answer," *New York Times*, March 18, 2022.

49   Levine, *King*, 33.

CHAPTER 1
The Magic Portrait of Isabel King

Figure 10: Prime Minister Mackenzie King in his Laurier House study, circa 1945.

"Father knew what was wrong. It was the Prime Minister. The Right Honourable William Lyon Mackenzie King was undoubtedly an odd man, but subsequent study has led me to the conclusion that he was a political genius of an extraordinary order. To Father, however, he was the embodiment of several hateful qualities ... Mr. King's conjuror-like ability to do something distracting with his right hand while preparing the denouement of his trick unobtrusively with his left hand had not the dash and flair my father thought he saw in British statesmanship; but the astonishing disparity between Mr. King's public and his personal character was what really made my father boil.

'He talks about reason and necessity on the platform, while all the time he is living by superstition and the worst kind of voodoo,' he would roar. 'Do you realize that man never calls an election without getting a fortune-teller in Kingston to name a lucky day? Do you realize that he goes in for automatic writing? And decides important things – nationally important things – by opening his Bible and stabbing at a verse with a paper knife, while his eyes are shut? And that he sits with the portrait of his mother and communes – *communes* for God's sake! – with her spirit and gets her advice? Am I being taxed almost out of business because of something that has been said by Mackenzie King's mother's ghost? And this is the man who postures as a national leader!'"
—David Staunton in Robertson Davies' novel *The Manticore*, 1972.

* * *

On July 21, 1939, five weeks before he invoked the War Measures Act and subsequently asked Parliament to declare war on Germany on September 10, Prime Minister Mackenzie King granted the *Toronto Star*'s Gregory Clark a rare interview in Laurier House, his home in Ottawa. He had met with Adolf Hitler in Berlin in June 1937 and wrote at the end of that "miraculous year" in his diary, "clearly the purpose of God is related to my securing the good will of Germany & the British Empire, working with Hitler towards this end, and saving France thereby & much else." The following March he recorded his conviction that the spirits of King's and Hitler's mothers were guiding them on the path to peace and in 1939 that he and the German *Führer* "were 'communicating' with each other through the world of thought."[50]

---

50 Diary, December 25, 1937, March 27, 1938, and July 21, 1939, p. 13.

After Clark's interview, King had invited the German Consul General to Ottawa, Erich Windels, who had delivered a letter from King to Hitler offering himself as a conciliator between Germany and Britain and France to prevent Europe plunging into war. On what he called "a day of Destiny," Windels brought a response from Hitler inviting the Prime Minister to head a twelve-member Canadian delegation on a three-week peace mission as Hitler's personal guests. King "said at once I was greatly pleased & deeply moved, that it confirmed the confidence I had in the *Führer*, and in his belief, I believed, he had in me." He described the day as "one of the most significant in my whole life" and Hitler's proposal as "a sincere gesture based on mutual faith in each other on the part of Hitler & myself." Above all, he "felt that 'forces unseen' – loved ones in the beyond – were working out these plans, that there were no accidents or chances in this but all part of a plan in which God was using man to affect His Will in answer to prayer, the Mediums being those in the beyond who were working for peace on earth."[51]

The Prime Minister met with Clark and Windels in his library in Laurier House in front of a large portrait of his mother, Isabel King. Painted by John Wycliffe Lowes Forster in 1905 when King had not yet been elected to Parliament and was still only the Deputy Minister of Labour, the portrait depicts Isabel seated on a chair before a fireplace, her hand pointing to an open book resting on her lap. Only King and his mother knew that the volume was John Morley's biography of the British Liberal politician he idolized, *The Life of William Ewart Gladstone*, at the chapter entitled "The Prime Minister." An early manifestation of King's magical thinking and belief in his God-given destiny, the commissioned painting, which King wrote "has been a great comfort to me. It has been constantly before me," was one of the means the Prime Minister used – as Robertson Davies described it – of *communing* with his dead mother.[52]

Clark informed him that Howard Ferguson, the former Conservative Premier of Ontario whom King considered a bitter opponent, had been studying him for years to discover the secret and purpose of his political work. Ferguson concluded that King was striving to rehabilitate the memory and implement the political ideals of Isabel King's

---

51 Diary, July 21, 1939, pp. 9-12.
52 Diary, September 10, 1939, p. 3.

father, William Lyon Mackenzie (1795-1861), the leader of the failed 1837 Upper Canada Rebellion. The Prime Minister was "amazed, and equally pleased," that Ferguson had come to this conclusion on his own, he noted in his diary. "It bears out the theory which I hold very strongly, and which I mentioned to Clark, namely, that there is an intuitive or psychic sense which the people have which is much greater than most realize, and" – corroborating Robertson Davies' reference to the Kingston fortune-teller Rachel Bleaney – "which comes to be a determining factor in settling questions of elections, etc."

When King read to Clark from Charles Lindsey's introduction to his 1862 *The Life and Times of William Lyon Mackenzie*, which related to his grandfather "desiring above all else to bequeath to his children the title of 'unpurchasable patriot,'" the reporter asked whether his photographer "could take a picture of me with this book in my hand, at that page, standing beside Mother's picture." He was deeply moved and "experienced one of the greatest joys, one of the greatest rewards of my life" when he read Clark's article, entitled "Unpurchasable Patriot," accompanied by a photo of King and his terrier Pat, published in the *Toronto Star Weekly* of August 5, 1939. But ten days later he wrote the *Star* "asking them not to publish photo taken in my library at Laurier House beside Mother's painting. It is too sacred – the photo reveals details of bookset of the bible etc.; scoffers would ridicule the whole thing & say I was seeking to capitalize on the most sacred things of life."[53]

The Prime Minister was secretive about his direct communications with his dead mother. His family friend, the British MP Malcolm MacDonald, son of former Prime Minister Ramsay MacDonald and former Secretary of State for Dominion Affairs, was a regular visitor to Laurier House as Britain's High Commissioner in Canada from 1941 to 1946. MacDonald recalled discussing every topic under the sun with King except his occult practices. "It is true that whenever we talked in his upstairs study in Laurier House a painted portrait of his dead mother stood on an easel alongside us, almost as if she were alive and joining in our deliberations. He sometimes expressed his deep love for her during our conversations, but he never told me what her counsels to him were."

But to many other politicians, King had no such reservations. When Willis Keith Baldwin, MP for Stanstead, Quebec, came to Laurier House in 1928 to inform him that he wanted to resign his seat

---

53 Diary, July 21, 1939, pp. 2, 3, and August 4 and 15, 1939.

in the House of Commons, King "asked him not to, spoke of keeping Parliament & country & Empire united as Mother had told me to keep the family united." Baldwin, looking at Isabel King's bust the Prime Minister had commissioned from the Italian sculptor Giuseppe Guastalla, said, "then I will stay. I could not add to your burdens. I [King] pointing to the bust said, 'There is the Prime Minister, not here.' He understood & neither of us could speak."

King commented on his mother's portrait after MP William Horace Taylor, Liberal Whip of Ontario, read him a unanimous resolution passed by the Liberal Caucus in 1938 expressing its complete confidence in his leadership. "Just behind me was the painting of my mother," he noted. "I turned to look and smile at it as Taylor was reading the Resolution, knowing full well that my mother was conscious of all that was transpiring." Visitors to the PM's library realized the importance of admiring Isabel King's portrait. When he showed the painting to Winston Churchill in December 1941, "he spoke of how very beautiful her face was, kept repeating: a lovely face; a lovely face."[54]

And when the German-Swiss writer Emil Ludwig wrote the PM in 1943 requesting an interview for what became his *Mackenzie King: A Portrait Sketch*, he asked, "Perhaps I can sit quietly under the magic portrait of your mother as a symbol for my study." Governor General Lord Tweedsmuir (the Scottish writer John Buchan) had first introduced Ludwig to King at a Canadian Club luncheon in December 1935. Tweedsmuir suggested to King that the internationally known biographer of leading world figures such as Goethe, Napoleon, Bismarck, Stalin, and Jesus "had some interesting views concerning Mussolini; that I would like to have a talk with him. This was arranged after lunch."

When Ludwig was again in Ottawa eight years later, MP Brooke Claxton, then King's Parliamentary Assistant, suggested that he write a biography of the Prime Minister. King showed Ludwig around Kingsmere, his country home in the Laurentian hills on the shore of a small lake, told him his family history and life in politics, and inquired how he wrote his biographies. "I asked him if he did not think there were forces about us which continued to carry the existence of the soul of the person who had gone; if he did not think that in the world, there continued to be the spiritual substance of whatever there had been of reality in the life of a person, and that there were forces beyond that had

---

54 MacDonald, 52. Diary, December 12, 1928, December 19, 1938, and December 30, 1941.

their relation to lives that had passed away, and which continue to influence and inform our own." Recording Ludwig's visit in his diary King wrote, "I have seldom felt more elevated in my thoughts & feelings – as if I had been with a soul who saw into and understood mine. I loved his appreciation of art, of portraiture, as the key to all his writings, human character as the real study – the <u>flaw</u> of life – the river of life."

A year later, the Prime Minister read the page proofs of *Mackenzie King: A Portrait Sketch* two weeks before its publication and changed Ludwig's opening sentence, "A quiet, distinguished library, lined with books, is dominated by the portrait of a woman. It also dominates the man who in this room prepares his task of governing a great nation." King's revision read, "A quiet, distinguished library, lined with books, is made radiant by the portrait of a woman. It also inspires the man who in this room prepares his task of governing a great nation."[55]

It is precisely King's use of paintings, sculpture and other materials, his Bible, and the occult practices which he used to communicate with his deceased mother, grandfather and others in the Great Beyond – and indeed with God Himself – that is investigated in *The Spiritualist Prime Minister*. Such an examination of the ritual objects King used and his beliefs about the spiritual and occult provide a completely new assessment of Canada's longest serving Prime Minister. King was fully aware of the "associations" of the symbolic items lying on the small altar in front of his mother's portrait when he had his photo taken in 1939, including a little casket containing her wedding ring and a lock of her hair, an original photograph of Mackenzie that had been in his possession, and a small Iona cross similar to the one standing over the King family grave in Mount Pleasant Cemetery in Toronto. "The whole story of my life can pretty much be told by these bits of material, symbolical of the spiritual realities which they in part disclose."

He also referred to what he perceived as these spiritual realities after Parliament declared war against Germany in 1939 and he received a tremendous ovation from his Liberal Party caucus for keeping the country unified. "The world in which we live," the Prime Minister suggested to his fellow MPs, "was the world of our thoughts, not what we saw with our eyes of the physical aspect of this universe."[56]

---

55 Diary, November 21, 1943, December 19, 1935, and August 25 and 26, 1943. Ludwig, 1. Diary, July 15, 1944.

56 Diary, July 21, 1939, p. 4, and September 12, 1939, p. 3.

He had knelt in prayer before Isabel King's portrait after voting in the December 1921 federal election that made him Prime Minister and thanked God for His protecting providence through the campaign. Even before votes were counted, King believed "I shall see fulfilled what dear Mother and I saw together in the page of Gladstone's life open on her lap in the painting of her – 'The Prime Minister' – but it is all as God wills."

Only hours before taking his first oath of office as Prime Minister, Minister for External Affairs and President of the Privy Council on December 29, 1921, King invited the prospective members of his Cabinet to the apartment he had shared with his mother in The Roxborough in Ottawa to discuss their portfolios. He recorded in his diary, "the Cabinet for the most part has been made in its entirety in this room in which dear Mother died, the Ministers sitting beneath her painting or facing it, the paintings of the other loved ones round about. Here when I told dear mother some day I would be Prime Minister of Canada, and where her great suffering taught me how to be brave and to endure … I felt today the nearness of those who have gone before more than any other moment or time in all these momentous transactions."

That evening he invited Andrew Haydon, his friend and national Liberal Party organizer who had helped lead the Liberals to victory, for dinner in his apartment. "I had left on my table Gladstone's *Life* by Morley beside Mother's picture by Forster at the open page 'the Prime Minister.' It was Mother's secret and mine when the painting was made that the book should be open before her eyes at that page. Today she sits and looks at it over my fireplace in the room in which she died and in which I have entered as Prime Minister of Canada." He added, "and yet there are those who discount faith! I knelt down and prayed when I came into my room & after looking at this picture…to bed at midnight feeling that a good piece of work had been accomplished & oh so glad that my mother had been spared to see this day."[57]

But Isabel King was not only embodied in and evoked by physical objects. She lived and was burned in Mackenzie King's heart and mind and appeared in his almost nightly dream visions. In 1937, he described one of her visitations as a "Vision of Guardian Angel" in

---

57 Diary, December 6 and 29, 1921, pp. 2, 5.

his life-long struggle to control his sex instinct. "I seemed to be in a restless mood and seeking relief from the pain of passion; some one seemed to want to soothe me. I was not anxious, however, that they should. Just then I saw dear Mother come into a part of the room. (…..) She looked very beautiful & very calm & her presence seemed to say to me 'Your soul needs a bath' – or she seemed to symbolize any soul & the bath, the symbol of washing away all that was impure. I felt grateful for her presence which was that of a guardian angel." In 1946, nearly three decades after Isabel King's passing, he recorded "a remarkable psychical experience" while shaving. "The lather, which I placed on tissue paper, made a perfect picture of my mother seated with a book in front of her, much as in the Forster painting, but with her feet much as they were where she is sitting beneath a tree at Kingsmere at the time of her last illness. It was a very remarkable bit of sculpture in its way."[58]

The PM retained such guiding visions in his personal life and in politics until the end of his life. A year before his death, he still recalled the inscription from Tennyson's *The Holy Grail* he had engraved on a gold bracelet for his spiritual partner, Joan Patteson, at the time of his first general election in 1921 after he assumed the leadership of the Liberal Party: "A strength was in us from this vision." He noted in his diary, "I must above all else watch to be true to the vision which I had as a young man and which has been my guide through life."

On New Year's Day 1950 – suffering from the heart condition that would kill him less than seven months later – King "thought of all the loved ones and slipped out of bed to kiss the portraits of my mother and father and sister and brother which were on the mantle. To quietly have a word of prayerful communion with them. I had missed not being in my library at the midnight hour where I have knelt each new year on my knees before my mother's portrait…I had allowed the nurse to come with me and showed her the lock of my mother's hair and wedding ring which is the first thing I looked at at the beginning of each new year."

Three months before his death, he wrote to one of his London mediums, Geraldine Cummins, "There certainly can be no truer explanation of the terrible condition through which the world has recently been passing and is still suffering from than the conflict of

---

58 Diary, December 6, 1937, and March 20, 1946.

materialism and the spiritual interpretation of life. Like you, but in a different way, I have sought to wage war on the former, and shall continue to do so to the end."[59]

So, who was the real Mackenzie King, what did he believe and how did his beliefs affect his actions for decades? Where did his dream visions come from, from his unconscious or his conscious desires and wish fulfillment? Which enduring visions guided him through life? What was the inner logic to his thinking and the psychological meaning of his superstitions? What made him engage in ritualistic behaviour like kissing the cold marble lips of his mother's bust before and after elections, kneeling in prayer before her portrait and contemplating the lock of her hair he held in the casket on the altar below her painting? Can we create a hologram of the man and what he thought and said? Has that authentic King been portrayed in our histories, in fiction, in newspapers and on radio, television and in film?

Heather Robertson defended her portrayal of King and his mother in her historical novel, *Willie: A Romance*, in an interview with Barbara Frum on the Canadian Broadcasting Corporation's *The Journal* in 1983. She had to make an imaginative leap about King's life from a fictional point of view, Robertson said, because "many of the King documents are still under lock and key and will remain secret until 2001. So a great deal of King material is simply not there."[60] Donald Brittain, in his 1988 National Film Board/CBC-TV co-production *The King Chronicle: Mackenzie King and the Great Beyond*, portrayed the Prime Minister as a blundering fool and mocked his spiritualism. He showed King and Joan Patteson just before the outbreak of World War II sitting with both of their hands flat on a heavy-looking wooden table. After a few faint knocks, Joan declared, "Hitler is dead, shot by a Pole." King replied, "so says grandfather."

Director Matthew Rankin, by contrast, stated at the 2019 Toronto Film Festival premiere of his political satire, *The Twentieth Century*, that he had been inspired to create the film about King at the beginning of his political career by reading his diaries. Yet he still saddled King with an invented orgasmic fetish for ladies' footwear that appears nowhere in his diaries and portrayed Isabel King as a

---

59 Diary, July 10, 1949, and December 31, 1949. King to Cummins, March 15, 1950.

60 "A debate on the Merits of Fictionalizing WLM King's Life," CBC-TV *The Journal*, December 30, 1983.

cackling Mad Hatter, hilariously enacted by an aged Louis Negin. The film would have been still more pungent, however, if audiences were more familiar with the actual Mackenzie King being satirized. If we do not know the real King and what he thought and did, he will remain a farcical figure in the popular imagination that fails to do justice to the complexity of the man and politician.

The Spiritualist Prime Minister finally establishes the genesis and nature of Mackenzie King's spiritual beliefs and occult practices that have made him a figure of derision in popular culture and diminished his stature as a statesman. The chapters that follow describe how the Prime Minister's Spiritualism became public knowledge and has been assessed by historians to date, how his spiritual beliefs first developed in Canada and were widely shared by others, and how his executors sought to suppress knowledge of his occult practices to save his political reputation and that of the Liberal Party. Subsequent chapters and the biography's Conclusion in Volume 2 support C.P. Stacey's contention that the war between King's spirit and flesh at times brought him to the brink of insanity. The chapters reveal how King himself became a medium and psychic to commune with his dead mother through his dream visions and Bible readings and with other members of his family and political leaders in séances over the "little table" at Laurier House. The chapters also describe the essential role his life-long friend Joan Patteson played in these spiritualist pursuits.

The eminent historian Jack Granatstein conceded that Mackenzie King had séance "conversations" with the deceased Prime Ministers Laurier and Gladstone "and people of that sort" but stated "whether and to what extent he believed it is another question."[61] *The Spiritualist Prime Minister* proves conclusively that the Prime Minister did indeed believe that his destiny was inscribed in the stars and in the palm of his hands, that his future could be foreseen by the fortune-teller Rachel Bleaney holding his handkerchief or neck tie, that discarnate spirits spoke to him through the end of Etta Wriedt's telescopic trumpets, and that he was on a mission from God and the spirit world when he met with Adolf Hitler in Berlin in 1937. The chapters trace King's contacts with mediums, psychics and psychic researchers in Lethbridge, Kingston, Detroit, Winnipeg, New York, London, Toronto, Kitchener, and Vancouver. A chronological listing of King's

---

61 Stacey, *A True and Faithful Account*. Jack Granatstein, CBC-TV *Saturday Report*, November 16, 1991.

contacts with mediums and psychics as well as of major events in his life can be found in Chronology.

Like Goethe's *Faust* which he cited in his first diary entry in 1893, Mackenzie King can be seen as a tragic figure who sacrificed his personal happiness to achieve earthly power and to comprehend the laws of the universe and the infinite knowledge of the Beyond. Along with many spiritualists, he believed the world stood on the verge of a new era of thought and discovery of psychic phenomena and investigated the latest psychic findings for a quarter of a century. As in *Faust*, Joan Patteson was his Marguerite whose love he sacrificed for the world of politics, his mother the angelic presence who interceded with God and rewarded his endless striving. *The Spiritualist Prime Minister* documents how King sought to accumulate spiritual capital to win elections in Canada, become a peacemaker on the world stage, and serve as God's agent on earth.

CHAPTER 2

Mackenzie King's Family and Spiritualism in Canada

Mackenzie King referred to the North American origins of his spiritualist beliefs when Lizzy Lind-af-Hageby asked him in Geneva in 1936 how he came to be interested in Spiritualism. He "gave her an outline," naming the Kingston fortune-teller Rachel Bleaney, Mary Fulford (widow of the multi-millionaire Liberal Senator George Taylor Fulford), in Brockville, Ontario, and the American direct-voice medium Etta Wriedt in Detroit, "with experiences, etc." Only after naming these psychic encounters, did he refer to Sir Oliver Lodge whom he first met during the Imperial Conference in London in 1926 and whose ten books on Spiritualism in his library he began reading in 1929.[62]

King was receptive to all these spiritualist influences because he had already absorbed the belief in a Christian afterlife as well as the occult from his mother during his childhood in Berlin, Ontario, where he was born on December 17, 1874. Charlotte Gray writes of Isabel Mackenzie's religious background, "For Scots Presbyterians like the Mackenzies, the Sabbath was not a day of rest and joyful hymn-singing. It was a day to reflect on their sins and misdemeanours and the slim hope that, despite their wicked thoughts and actions, after death they might find themselves among the elect in Heaven."[63]

King's Calvinist family background, instilled by his Presbyterian Church and family upbringing, conceived a world in which men and

---

62 Diary, October 7, 1936. Bedore, 198-199.
63 Gray, *Mrs. King*, 6. Dawson, 17.

women, since Adam's fall, were born in deepest sin. In the Calvinist doctrine of election, two out of ten were predestined to go to heaven and the other eight predestined to go to hell. Murray Nicolson, in his study of the King family, noted that his father, John King, like his father before him, "was a firm believer in Presbyterianism" and that at St. Andrew's Presbyterian Church in Berlin, in the 1870s and 1880s "he would conduct discussions or write letters about unconditional predestination or man's free agency."[64]

John King was deeply religious, a non-drinker, and active in the St. Andrew's Presbyterian Church in Berlin for twenty years as secretary of its board of management. According to Nicolson, "Another link which bound the family together and formed a major part of the socializing aspects of the King home was their profound belief in their religion and interest in their church...there were several religious paintings in the home and...the religious feasts were celebrated in a solemn way with the reading of selected literature." King and his siblings attended Sunday school, and with their parents, Sunday services in the morning and evening. His sisters Jenny and Bella taught Sunday school at St. Andrew's. This generational transmission of religious beliefs is also illustrated by King's recollection of reciting Psalm 40 from the Scottish Psalter to his mother as a child and receiving "a penny for learning paraphrases by heart." After reading the Sermon on the Mount to Isabel King in 1917, he "reminded mother how I had learned it off by heart for her as a boy."[65]

While both Isabel and John King socialized their children in conventional religious beliefs, his mother also nurtured Mackenzie King's emotional belief in magical thinking that exerted such a powerful influence in his later life. Nicolson notes that at Woodside, "When the children were young Isabel read and told fairy tales to them at bedtime." King recalled an even earlier residence in Berlin on Margaret Street where the family lived from 1878 to 1886 and hearing his mother "tell in bed, stories of the life of Christ and crying as a child when we came to the part of His Crucifixion."[66] After attending Sunday communion on

---

64 Klempa, 101. Nicolson, 22.

65 Nicolson, 20, 54, 38. Diary, April 24, 1938, and November 4, 1917. King cites one of the paraphrases he learned as a child in his diary for June 21, 1937: "He took me from a fearful pit, and from the miry clay, and on a rock, set my feet, establishing my way."

66 Nicolson, 36, 39.

his birthday in 1905 he recorded, "as always happens" he "was unable to sing through the paraphrase 'Twas on that night' without crying bitterly. Ever since a little child, the sacrifice and love of our Saviour as portrayed in that hymn has moved me deeply." He added, "The tragedy of the Cross is very real to me; the pain of it, is in the love that was misunderstood, and the injustice. One cannot think of the sadness of the heart of Christ who loved those who crucified him without grief. It is impossible to imagine anything more tragic."[67]

He also recalled the story told by his mother of going to see an old black fortune-teller with two or three other girls in Kingston when she was seven in 1850. "One of them had referred to the fortune teller as a nigger wench (she was a coloured person). When they went in, this fortune teller said to one of them: so you have come to see the nigger wench. Your tongue will tie a knot which your teeth cannot undo." She correctly predicted that when Isabel returned home, she would discover that her brother had narrowly escaped drowning while canoeing and also rightly predicted that the girl who had insulted the fortune teller would make a very unfortunate marriage.[68] This incident appears to have occurred while King's grandfather William Lyon Mackenzie, was amnestied in 1849 and returned with his family from exile in the U.S. and briefly stayed with his brother-in-law, George Baxter, on his farm near Kingston before settling in Toronto in May 1850.

Mackenzie, too, held superstitious beliefs. His son-in-law and biographer Charles Lindsey – referring to the death of Mackenzie's beloved twelve-year-old daughter Margaret in 1848 – wrote that "In his children he took the greatest pride; and the stern politician, who carried on so many relentless contests, wore the watch of his eldest daughter around his neck for twelve years after her death, in almost superstitious veneration of her who had passed away."[69] Mackenzie King's mother's superstitious folk belief in fortune-tellers persisted for decades and was an activity also engaged in during social occasions with friends at Woodside. His sister Bella wrote him in 1893 that their mother wanted "to get the fortune teller to tell our fortunes. I don't know whether it is right or wrong."[70] The town of Berlin had in fact

---

67 Diary, December 17, 1905.
68 Diary, December 17, 1905, and March 22, 1946.
69 Lindsey, *William Lyon Mackenzie*, 504. Kilbourn, 265.
70 Nicolson, 32.

passed a by-law in 1873 prohibiting (along with vagrants, mendicants, prostitutes, and gamblers) "every person pretending or professing to tell or using any subtle craft, means or device, by palmistry or otherwise to deceive or impose upon any person."[71]

Spiritualism at the turn of the century was most often practiced in private, limiting possible contact with other spiritualists in more public manifestations. Lady Matilda Ridout Edgar, wife of the Speaker of the House of Commons, James David Edgar, appointed to the Privy Council by Prime Minister Sir Wilfrid Laurier and knighted in 1898, turned to Spiritualism when her husband died the following year. She became president of the National Council of Women in 1906 and was re-elected in 1909. Mackenzie King mentions Lady Edgar in his diaries as one of the guests at a large dinner party given by Governor General Earl Grey at Government House five days after his election to Parliament in 1908 but she makes no further subsequent appearances in his writings.[72]

Some Berliners engaged in spiritualist activities within a small circle of associates. King would be nearly sixty before he discovered through the painter and fellow psychic explorer Homer Watson that his "old schoolmaster" David Forsyth and his French and German teacher, Adolph Mueller, at the Berlin High School, from which he graduated in 1891, were spiritualists. Watson "told me of Dave Forsyth coming in when Otto was at a table with some boys & heard the table give the Morse Code, telegraph. He then listened to what was said & remarked that there was intelligence behind it; from that time on he followed it with scientific interest & he & Watson took trips together to Lily Dale [the large spiritualist community in southwestern New York] & elsewhere, Arizona etc."[73] Watson, Mueller and Forsyth were in their 20s when they made their month-long trip by canoe and train to Lily Dale in 1879. Forsyth and Watson delved deeper into Spiritualism three decades later following the death of their wives when they sought to communicate with their deceased loved ones. King's "old schoolmaster" became president of the Kitchener-based Ontario Society for Psychic Research. Watson participated in séances at his home in Doon and with the Kitchener-Waterloo Psychic Society.[74]

---

71 English and McLaughlin, 49, 216, fn. 58.
72 Diary, October 31, 1908.
73 Diary, December 11, 1934, June 18, 1933, and April 14, 1934.
74 Noonan, 202, 72, 210. For an account of their trip to Lily Dale, see Noonan's

Spiritualism, the belief that one could communicate with the dead in the afterlife, flourished in North America in the second half of the nineteenth century. For tens of thousands who had lost their children and other loved ones to disease or the hundreds of thousands who had lost relatives in the American Civil War, and later in World War I, the belief that their family members, husbands, wives, and friends were still present in another dimension provided great consolation, comfort, and hope. As Peter Manseau noted, "In the aftermath of the Civil War, during which more than three-quarters of a million were killed, the nation exploded with interest in the possibility of making contact with the spirit world." The grief-stricken Mary Todd Lincoln and President Abraham Lincoln attended spiritualist séances in the White House in which they attempted to communicate with their son Willie who had died there of typhoid at the age of eleven in 1862.

Mackenzie King retained copies of the February 10, 1942, *Psychic Observer*, published in Lily Dale, New York, with its front-page articles "That Abraham Lincoln Was a Spiritualist Is an Established Fact" and "Emancipation Proclamation Induced by Knowledge Received Thru Spiritualism." The *Psychic Observer*'s Ronald Thomas, in "Washington Was Psychic," similarly assured its readers that "One of the greatest proofs of psychic phenomena is to be found in the fact that scarcely a single great man in history has not had supernormal powers of prevision or been guided by intelligent entities from another world."

Jane Pierce, the wife of President Franklin Pierce, invited the Fox sisters to Washington to demonstrate their famous raps and table-tippings following the death of her youngest son Benjamin in a train accident in 1853. Harry Houdini exposed Spiritualism and mediums as fraudulent before a U.S. House of Representatives committee investigating whether Congress should outlaw fortune-telling in Washington during Calvin Coolidge's presidency in 1926. In "Hints of Seances at White House," the *New York Times* reported, "statements were made that spiritualistic seances were held at the White House for the benefit of the President and his family, and testimony was given that four prominent members of the Senate – Senators Watson of Indiana, Capper of Kansas, Dill of Washington

---

chapter "SPIRIT: Earthbound." Roxanna Watson died in January 1918. For Watson and his paintings, see Foss.

and Fletcher of Florida – frequently consulted mediums for counsel and advice."[75]

The strong appeal of Spiritualism and other metaphysical beliefs to assuage human emotions and explain the purpose of human existence also manifested itself in Canada. As Ramsay Cook observed in his chapter on Spiritualism in *The Regenerators*, "By the 1850s in Canada, as in the United States and Great Britain, spiritualist activities had begun to arouse public interest. Spiritualist lecturers, like itinerant preachers on virtually every other subject from secularism to temperance, crossed the intellectually undefended frontier with increasing regularity during the late nineteenth century."

In 1848 – just two years before Isabel King's encounter with a fortune-teller in Kingston – the Canadian-born Fox sisters of Hydesville, New York, the eleven-year-old Kate and the fourteen-year-old Margaret, "introduced to a credulous world spirit-rappings, an apparent method of communicating with the dead through a series of cryptic knocks and bumps." By 1850, it was estimated that "there were a hundred mediums in New York City, and fifty or sixty 'private circles' in Philadelphia." According to S.E.D. Shortt, in the United States "By the mid-1850s an avalanche of publications on spiritualism greeted a burgeoning audience, with conservative estimates placing the number of formal believers at over a million in a population of twenty-five million." Stan McMullin noted in *Anatomy of a Seance: A History of Spirit Communication in Central Canada* that "In Ontario in the last half of the nineteenth century, spirit communication continued to interest those caught up in the theological issues raised by science and its manifestation, materialism." The first Swedenborgian church was established in Mackenzie King's hometown, Berlin, Ontario, in 1854. One of the three houses the King family lived in before moving into their fourth home, Woodside, was located on King Street, near the Swedenborg Church.[76]

The *True Witness* noted the arrival of spiritualist séances in Canada in its June 11, 1852, issue while the *Moniteur canadien* discussed

---

75 Brandon, 28, 36. "Hints of Seances at White House: Witness at Capital Asserts a Spiritualist Said Coolidge Family Attended Them. Story Officially Denied. Row Between Houdini and Mediums Breaks Up Hearing on Bill to Regulate Clairvoyants," *New York Times*, May 19, 1926.

76 Cook, *The Regenerators*, 66. Brandon, 42. Shortt, 339, 340. McMullin, xvi, 14. Peter Sims to King, December 1, 1924.

Figure 11: Thomas M. Easterly's 1852 daguerreotype of Kate and Margaret Fox, Spirit Mediums from Rochester, New York.

the phenomenon of table-turning in Montreal on December 22, 1853. "Aujourd'hui la tablo-tournomanie n'est plus un jeu, c'est une passion, c'est une fureur, c'est un délire!" George Edward Clerk, the editor of the *True Witness*, similarly deplored on December 23, 1853, that "Spiritual Rappings ... have, we regret to say, made their appearance in a very striking manner in this good city of Montreal: and, if the public journals may be relied on, have found partisans, and believers, amongst men, pretending to a smattering of education, and – oh disgrace! – calling themselves Catholics."[77]

The writer Susanna Moodie (1803-1885) met Kate Fox in Belleville, Ontario, in 1855. She described her as "a very lovely intellectual looking girl, with the most beautiful eyes I ever saw in a human head...I cannot believe that she, with her pure spiritual face is capable of deceiving." Susanna and her husband John Dunbar Moodie became

---

77 Sylvain, 223, 233. For additional newspaper reports and condemnations of Spiritualism by religious authorities, see Massicotte, *Talking Nonsense*, 11-15, 179, 181, and her bibliography.

interested in Spiritualism following the drowning of their five-year old son in the Bay of Quinte in 1844. Susanna Moodie also described séances with the Scottish medium Mary Williamson in Belleville. She saw a large heavy English dining table "rise in air repeatedly, without contact, have seen the leaf of the said table, rise in air repeatedly, without contact, have seen the leaf of the said table, fly up, and strike the snuffers out of my husband's hand, and put out the candles, have heard drums play, martial tunes where no instrument of the kind was to be found for miles, have been touched by unseen hands, and witnessed many curious phenomenon."

Moodie nevertheless maintained a sceptical attitude towards the spiritual origins of the phenomena she witnessed. But by 1858 she came to the same conclusion – as did Mackenzie King decades later – about the psychic messages she was receiving from Mary Williamson. They were "a mystery, strange, solemn and beautiful, and which I now believe, contains nothing more nor less than a new revelation from God to man. Not doing away with the old dispensation, but confirming it in every particular." Dunbar Moodie designed a "Spiritoscope," similar to the Ouija board with which Susanna Moodie was able to receive messages without the use of an outside medium. She recorded that her sister, the writer Catharine Parr Traill, used the Spiritoscope and was "a powerful Medium for these communications, and gets them in foreign languages." However, she also noted that Traill's spirits "often abuse, and call her very ugly names."[78]

By 1868, the twentieth anniversary of what became known as the Fox sisters' Rochester Rappings, "there were eleven million believers in America alone." But in 1888, in the packed New York Academy of Music, Margaret and Kate confessed that the knocks and rappings heard during the Fox sisters' séances had been produced through the cracking of finger, knee, toe and ankle joints.[79] Susanna Moodie had already written regarding Kate Fox in 1856, "I can make the same raps, with my great toes, ankles, wrist joints and elbows." Her servant "tried it also, and she exceeds me in the loudness of these noises. Which so perfectly resembles those produced by the Medium, that it has greatly surprised me." Yet Moodie, a reliable skeptical witness, also reported phenomena that still appear inexplicable today. In one of her letters

---

78 Ballstadt, 91, 93. McMullin, 22, 27, 23, 24.

79 Brandon, 37, 229.

to her English publisher, Richard Bentley, she reported that when she received Kate Fox in her home in Belleville in 1855, Kate "told me to lay my hands upon the table and ask the spirit to rap under it. This I did."

> The table vibrated under my hand as if it was endowed with life. We then went to the door. Miss Fox told me to open the door and stand so that I could see both sides at once. The raps were on the opposite side to my hand. The door shut and vibrated. Miss F. had one hand laid by mine on the door. I am certain that the sounds were not made by hands or feet. We then went into the garden. She made me stand on the earth. The raps were under my feet, distinct and loud. I then stood on a shallow rock under the window. The raps sounded hollow on the stone pavement under me…The strange vibrations of the knocks was to me the most unaccountable. It seemed as if a mysterious life was infused into the object from which the knocks proceeded.

In another demonstration of her powers, Fox asked the writer if she would like to hear her piano, "closed as it is, play a tune." Moodie reported, "I heard the strings of that piano accompany Mr. Moodie upon the flute, Miss Fox and I, standing by the piano, with a hand of each resting upon it. Now it is certain, that she could not have got within the case of the piano." Susanna Moodie wrote her publisher about those, and other phenomena, produced by Kate Fox that although she was "still as great a sceptic as to the spiritual nature of the thing, the intelligence conveyed is unaccountable."[80]

It suffices to point out that – like Mackenzie King – many other leading public figures turned to Spiritualism after the death of loved ones. The feminist, political activist, and Whitmanite Flora MacDonald Denison – the mother of playwright Merrill Denison – became active in the Canadian Association for Psychical Research after her dead sister materialized before her in a very bright light in the mid-1880s. She described her psychic experience in her biography *Mary Melville, The Psychic* and in "The Vision of Mary" included in Rev. B.F. Austin's *What Converted Me to Spiritualism: One Hundred Testimonies*, published in Toronto in 1900 and 1901.[81]

---

80 Ballstadt, 93, 91-92. On Moodie's experiences with Spiritualism, see Massicotte, *Talking Nonsense*.
81 Cook, 78-84. McMullin, 35-62.

Denison, after reading Dr. Albert Durrant Watson, felt that "a message in *The Twentieth Plane* was so significant of Whitman, that I longed for an evening where Whitman might converse freely with me about the work I am doing to propagate his Democratic Ideals." She communicated with him and his biographer Dr. Richard Maurice Bucke and others for one and a half hours via the Ouija board operated by a trance medium. The séance was arranged by Dr. Watson, President of the Association for Psychical Research of Canada, in his home in February 1919.[82] McClelland and Stewart had published Watson's *The Twentieth Plane: A Psychic Revelation*, his record of conversations with the spirits of great men of the past such as Lincoln, Emerson and Whitman, in 1918 and two years later published his *Birth Through Death: The Ethics of the Twentieth Plane*.

Psychic occurrences, such as Flora MacDonald Denison's vision of her dead sister when she was about twenty years old, often had profound life-long effects on those who experienced them. The same year that Denison published the accounts of her psychic experience, Canada's leading psychiatrist, Dr. Richard Maurice Bucke, dedicated his monumental *Cosmic Consciousness: A Study in the Evolution of the Human Mind* to his thirty-one-year-old son Maurice whom he had lost in a fatal accident the year before. "I will say that through the experiences which underlie this volume I have been taught," Bucke wrote his son, "that in spite of death and the grave, although you are beyond the range of our sight and hearing, notwithstanding that the universe of sense testifies to your absence, you are not dead and not really absent, but alive and well and not far from me this moment … Only a little while now and we shall be again together and with us those other noble and well-beloved souls gone before. I am sure I shall meet you and them; that you and I shall talk of a thousand things and of that unforgettable day and of all that followed it; and that we shall clearly see that all were parts of an infinite plan which was wholly wise and good."[83]

---

82 See "A Seance: Walt Whitman Communicates from Beyond the Grave," in Greenland and Colombo, 205-207. It cites the communication from Whitman as well as from Dr. Richard Maurice Bucke as quoted in Denison's article "The Twentieth Plane," *The Sunset of Bon Echo* 1:5, 1919. Cook, 249-250; McMullin, 365. On Denison's experiences with Spiritualism, see Massicotte, *Talking Nonsense*.

83 December 8, 1900, dedication from the first edition of Bucke's *Cosmic Consciousness*.

Mackenzie King was introduced to Bucke's *Cosmic Consciousness* in December 1937 by the physician C.A. Waterman. Like King a graduate from Harvard, Dr. Waterman had a prominent practice in brain surgery, neurology, and psychology in Boston. His patients had included King's favourite professor at Harvard, the economist Frank William Taussig, as well as William James. The Prime Minister dined at Dr. and Mrs. Waterman's beautiful summer home on 200 El Bravo Way while vacationing in Palm Beach, Florida. Waterman discussed telepathy. "The Doctor told me of interesting experiments which, he thought, had proved conclusively the fact of telepathy." King in turn described communicating with departed family members via the "little table" and the direct-voice medium Etta Wriedt and gave the physician "an account of some of the interesting experiences I had had on occasions, and which I had noted in psychic records. He clearly goes beyond the view that the sub-conscious mind contains what is disclosed, and that this rather comes from the appreciation of the universal."

Waterman suggested King read *Cosmic Consciousness*. "Said it had to be read slowly but believed the author had come to a real truth which was that there were individuals in all generations who were more highly developed spiritually than others, and who came to share a knowledge of the future as well as the present and the past. Also a knowledge of realities; spoke of Christ as the outstanding example." The PM told Waterman he would like some time to confer with him. The Dr. replied that if King would come and see him in Boston, "'I could do many things with that mind of yours,' meaning he could help me, and I could show him how to supplement some of his interests." King came away feeling that "he was the type of man I had been wanting to meet for years past, and that my researches on psychical lines were to go much further as a consequence of meeting him." Seeing an airplane directly above Waterman's house the following day was "so significant I felt it meant the right direction – That in Cosmic Consciousness he had recommended me to read, I have the right book."[84]

On Christmas day, King discussed cosmic consciousness with Joan Patteson and read Bucke's chapter on Jesus before and after church. "I liked it all except his treating him as a man; the emphasis should have been on the revealed God." A psychic session on "the little table" produced the usual "remarkable results" of his departed loved ones

---

84   Diary, December 11 and 12, 1937.

Figure 12: Dr. Richard Maurice Bucke's frontispiece portrait in Cosmic Consciousness *(1901).*

"all joined together for Christmas greetings" and a significant record re the <u>Second Coming</u>. The Prime Minister believed "it will be with the growth of 'Cosmic Consciousness' & the spread of spiritualist teachings & evidence there." Were Christ to return to the earth even now, He would not only be heard all over the world via radio but, "as television improves, it will be possible for any one to be seen all over the world. This is true of the material, mechanical world; how much easier & swifter of all is the spiritual – That we have even here & now – the ear & the eye of the spirit."

King believed he was receiving such spiritual communications while writing his ten-page typed Christmas day diary entry. While looking at his mother's portrait, he heard church chimes playing "Jesus Loves Me" and read a Christmas telegram, "We both thank you for your kind message of good wishes." He observed, "Is not this very significant – The first 8 words were as if direct from father & mother ... I am as sure as I am writing this that this is a direct 'communication' this Christmas season (Christmas chimes as I wrote) ... It is in this way that God reveals Himself – that cosmic consciousness is understood & known."

He had received letters and telegrams from several heads of state including President Roosevelt who asked him to make another visit. The sun came out and briefly illuminated another letter and envelope stamped Bethlehem before again disappearing behind the clouds. "It was the most direct thing I have ever seen – I was about to write everything points to something, telling me I have been chosen (I feel I cannot apply to myself the word anoint) for some special work ... all these things at this time in this way are making clear God's purpose – 'Cosmic Consciousness' – the sea – the air, etc. – all making the purpose clear ... I feel I am now on the threshold of the higher plane that leads to the fuller inheritance & that my real work may even yet now begin."[85]

The Prime Minister also thought it very significant when in March 1938 he received in the mail at the same time the first volume of the magazine *Public Relations* and the first volume of the *Journal of Parapsychology*, edited by William McDougall and Joseph Banks Rhine at Duke University. The association of these two publications was "significant," particularly in combination with John Gunther's two-volume *Inside Europe*, which King had begun reading in December and found an "extremely helpful review of the events in Germany since the Great War and up to the present." He recorded in his diary that he believed "the whole business bears out what Taylor [James Samuel Taylor, former CCF MP for Nanaimo, then sitting as an Independent] curiously

---

85 Diary, December 25, 1937.

enough said to me he believed were the new forces which were being felt throughout the world, namely, an understanding between minds in different parts of the world without any exchange of correspondence. Certainly that has been the case between Roosevelt and myself. I believe it to be equally the case between Hitler and myself on what he, at heart, has mostly in mind. It relates itself also in a way to sharing in 'Cosmic Consciousness.' All, of course, had to do with public relations and psychical phenomena in relation thereto."[86]

King easily incorporated Richard Maurice Bucke's concepts within his own spiritual beliefs, even in his life-long struggle to control his sex drive. Only two days after his illumination on Christmas day 1937, he awoke from a dream vision and "found my passions were tormenting me. I made the sign of the cross & sought to subdue them, saying I did not want to have any physical sensations. That they were the self conscious self which leads into error and helps to destroy or conceal the cosmic consciousness." In April 1938, he again "prayed earnestly to have peace of mind & rest of body restored. I have lost something of late, my spirit, its contact with God's holy spirit. I can see that sensual thoughts (uncontrolled) have worked havoc – brought on through fatigue & seemingly overpowering one's will. I pray for the return of holiness, and cosmic consciousness."[87]

Two weeks previously, he had read Bucke's chapter on Walt Whitman and "was impressed with his thought of making the ordinary man the real hero. William James has the same thought. I think that is what the world needs today, getting rid of its false notions of the truly great which is the simple and the natural and the humble." He "was struck with resemblances between Whitman, in some particulars, and Hitler. Love for the simple people, the natural things of the world, etc." In 1939, after going to bed, he read his "Song of the Open Road" from his *Leaves of Grass* and simply described it as a "poem by Walt Whitman – cosmic consciousness."[88]

As Mackenzie King's encounter with Richard Maurice Bucke illustrates, he assimilated both his mother's supernatural folk beliefs and the increasing literature seeking to establish Spiritualism on a scientific basis. While attending the University of Toronto in 1894, the

---

86 Diary, December 13, 1937, and March 29, 1938.
87 Diary, December 27, 1937, and April 13, 1938.
88 Diary, March 27, 1938, and July 2, 1939.

twenty-year-old went "to see Prof. Seymour who is a phrenologist mesmerist. He mesmerized me & spent about an hour with him." Two years later, he paid $1 to the palmist Mrs. Lauretta Menden at 309 Ontario Street in Toronto, "who told my fortune in a remarkable manner" and "told me some strange truths." Among the dozen accurate observations recorded in his diary was that he "was fond of intellectual girls & did not care particularly for dances." In January 1899, Mrs. Menden was arrested and convicted of having "unlawfully undertaken to tell fortunes and of unlawfully pretending to exercise or use a certain kind of witchcraft, sorcery, enchantment or conjuration contrary to the Canadian Criminal Code."[89] The Canadian Code, enacted in 1892, incorporated the prohibition against the practice of witchcraft from the British Witchcraft and Vagrancy Acts.

King also recalled having been taken to see a phrenologist as a child – who told him that he ought to be an architect – and was again astonished when he had his head read for a shilling by the phrenologist O'Dell at the London Phrenological Institute in England in 1900. He had initially gone to see O'Dell "as a sort of joke to take advantage of the rate offered to persons of limited means." But afterwards he concluded, "All that he said as to faults, as to acceptance of beliefs, facts, opposition, desire to lead & impress men etc. I think is true." Among the detailed observations of O'Dell's reading was "my reason controlled my lower nature" and "I was domestic in my tendencies & would like home life but that most women would not interest me. I needed a woman whom I believed to be better than myself."[90]

Paul Craven noted an example of magical thinking at the very beginning of King's diary in 1893 during his third year at the University of Toronto. Craven referred to King's "first contact with the supernatural: for seven nights in a row he opened his Bible to 'Chapters in which I found some verse which spoke of my going into the ministry.'"[91] On one of these he recorded, "Last night again I read

---

89 Diary, January 3, 1894, and May 2, 1896. "'WITCHCRAFT' As Set Forth in Toronto, Can.," *Progressive Thinker*, 19:478 (January 21, 1899), 5, and "Fortune Tellers' Fate," *Windsor Star*, February 2, 1899, 5.

90 Diary, May 15, 1948, and January 11, 1900. King's reference is probably to Stackpool E. O'Dell or Geelossapuss E. O'Dell, the authors of *Phrenology: Essays and Studies*, published by the London Phrenological Institution in 1899.

91 Craven, 60. See references in King's diary, November 10, 11, 12, 13, and 14, 1893.

a similar verse directing me to go into the ministry. This has been the most wonderful revelation I have ever known."[92] On March 8, 1894, he opened his Bible "after praying that God would show me how matters would turn out." The following day, King "found again encouragement from my bible last night reading verses in which I know God was speaking directly to me."

F.A. McGregor wrote in his biography that opening a book at random had become an enduring "practice of his." On the morning of the balloting at the 1919 Liberal Leadership Convention that would elect him Leader of the Liberal Party, "His first impulse on waking was to reach for his book of devotional readings, *Daily Strength for Daily Needs*, to see what 'message' it might have for him on this momentous day, what augury for good or ill it might reveal, what word that could be interpreted as divine guidance." The future Prime Minister "was always resentful of any scoffing of 'unbelievers' so blind as not to see, as he did, that the divine will could be revealed through such common-place acts as the opening of a book." Recording these "messages" in his diary he admonished sceptics, "Look ye who doubt, and say whether or not ye believe there is a God who rules the world."[93]

There are several references in King's diaries where he recalls incidents during his childhood of magical thinking, the belief that wishing or praying for something can bring about desired effects, and countless indications that such beliefs extended to his adult life. In January 1917, eleven months before his mother's death, he refused to accept the prognosis of doctors that his mother was dying. "I was thinking today of the time as a child I prayed to save a kite from escaping & the string was caught in the clover. I prayed for a dog 'Gyp' that was lost and found him in a street in Waterloo. I prayed for [his brother] Max's recovery from typhoid after the doctors gave him up in 1893 & he recovered. I prayed again in regard to his tuberculosis after the Drs. including Dr. [Thomas] Gibson said there was no hope. Now after the doctors have said the same regarding mother, I see her recover now. God grant she may keep my faith strong despite my fatigue & help me to continue to pray."[94]

---

92 Diary, November 13, 1893.
93 McGregor, 342.
94 Diary, January 29, 1917.

When King in 1939 described praying and using faith healing to cure his ailing terrier Pat he again noted, "That belief started as a child in the finding of my little dog 'Gyp' when I could not have been more than 10 or 12 years old." In his *Canada's King: An Essay in Political Psychology*, Paul Roazen commented, "King's tendency towards magical thinking was obviously marked even if it rarely seemed to surface politically." George Serban, in *The Tyranny of Magical Thinking: The Child's World of Belief and Adult Neurosis*, related magical thinking to primitive man's belief in animism, the thinking of children, neurotics and believers in religion, and to dissociative psychological states. He also noted, "the specific patterns of adult thinking are rooted in childhood thinking."[95]

The extent of King's magical thinking appears paradoxical because he was Canada's best-educated Prime Minister. His university degrees included an honours BA, LLB, and MA from the University of Toronto in 1895, 1896, and 1897, and a MA and PhD from Harvard in 1898 and 1909. But as S.E.D. Shortt points out, "Akin to phrenology, spiritualism is often viewed as little more than a quaint illustration of habitual Victorian gullibility in matters of faith and science. In fact, however, it was a topic which exercised leading Anglo-American scientific and medical minds in the two decades after 1865."

King read Maurice Maeterlinck's essays "The Pre-Destined" and "The Awakening of the Soul" in his *The Treasure of the Humble* while in London in 1899 during his year-long Harvard travelling scholarship. He "enjoyed the latter the most; there is a strange mysticism about the book which rather appeals to me, and I think the author is right in regarding the existence of a spiritual here & now, as evidenced by intuitions in silence, instinctive dread and trust etc. etc.... That the spiritual life will be more & more understood seems to me probable & that an understanding of it will lead to nobler action & life is inevitable, but centuries, not decades, are essential in the reckoning." Reading Henry Drummond's *Ideal Life* the following year confirmed his belief in a moral universe, "that nothing exists which is not governed by law, that nothing is ruled by chance, that for everything there is cause and effect, and that nothing exists without its influence for all time." His belief that God resolved the scientific and philosophic conflict between the spiritual and material is suggested by his comment

---

95 Diary, March 10, 1939. Roazen, 133. Serban, 141.

in 1930, "Einstein's theory of Space being everything seems to me sound. Space & Ether = God, that was the equation."[96]

King made one of his clearest statements on the relationship he perceived between Spiritualism and psychic phenomena after reading Anita Mühl's *Automatic Writing* [Dresden: T. Steinkoff, 1930] in December 1934. Mühl viewed automatic writing and astral projection as natural phenomena that had nothing to do with Spiritualism. King commented that "The 'scientific mind' so-called will accept nothing but natural phenomena, is determined to have nothing 'supernatural' or spiritual about the phenomena it examines. To my mind we should view the real universe or rather Reality as Spiritual, all material things as 'manifestations.' Then it becomes easy to see where in the present, we are in the future and in the past, where in the past, we are in the whole…I do believe the spiritual interpretation of all things as contrasted with the materialistic alone gives us a rational and true explanation of psychic phenomena." Three months later he reaffirmed his conviction in his diary that automatic writing was "in part inspired. These pages are inspired and I can now write."[97]

King's rejection of the scientific mind and materialism in favour of a spiritual conception of the universe allowed him to magically believe in virtually anything he wished, despite his PhD from Harvard. His idol, Sir Wilfrid Laurier, had been in love with Émilie Barthe, the wife of his law partner, Joseph Lavergne, in Arthabaskaville, Quebec, after his own marriage to Zoé Lafontaine in 1868. He had no children with Lady Laurier. Barthe's son Armand Lavergne, however, had a striking resemblance to Laurier, giving rise to rumours that he was his father. When Armand died and was buried in Arthabaska in 1935, King noted in his diary that "All this revives in public & private gossip, the story of Lavergne being an illegitimate son of Sir Wilfrid." King disbelieved this, calling the rumours "another Tory method of detracting and libelling." "What well may be the case," he ventured implausibly, "is the pre-natal influence of the admiration Lavergne's mother had for Sir Wilfrid who was her husband's law partner, and without doubt, thoughts of Sir Wilfrid in her mind daily, and watching his actions, conversing with him, while the

---

96 Shortt, 339. Diary, December 12, 1899, April 12, 1900, and June 18, 1930.
97 Diary, December 15, 1934.

child was being born, may readily have occasioned reproduction of certain features – even mannerisms etc."[98]

Mackenzie King never wavered in his belief in the functioning laws of the spiritual world. At times he referred to them under the Greek concept of nemesis, "the working out of the eternal laws of truth and justice," and wrote of "the nemesis that seemed to follow yielding to temptation as revealed in writings, plays, the scriptures, etc." He saw the same concept at work as karma, "the Hindu doctrine of our paying ourselves for all the evil we have done and receiving our reward to the extent that we, ourselves, have given 'help to others.' With it is accompanied the thought that we work out, in this station, our own fate while here on earth and before passing into a higher realm of existence. It is a doctrine thus expressed in which I believe absolutely."[99]

Appointed Deputy Minister of Labour at the age of twenty-six in September 1900, King could believe in the supernatural because so many other persons of stature in his social circle did so to varying degrees. He recorded that after a skating party at Government House in 1904, the wife of his friend and family physician, Dr. Thomas Gibson, "read hands" and told Lady Violet that she would marry very young at eighteen and have eleven children, "to which she said 'monstrous, I will not have more than three.'"[100] After he was elected MP for North Waterloo, Ontario, in 1908 and was sworn in as Minister of Labour in Sir Wilfrid Laurier's Government the following year, King discovered that even his political idol and mentor believed in psychic phenomena. At a dinner given by U.S. Consul General Foster at the Rideau Club to discuss U.S.-Canada tariffs, Laurier "told speaking of mind-reading of a man Lacroix, a customs official, an old fellow who liked to surround himself with clouds of smoke & then say that he had communication with spirits etc., claimed to talk with St. Paul, & others."

Laurier related in the presence of three members of his Cabinet and three deputy ministers that in Athabasca "When we were young fellows, had just graduated in law [in 1864], had nothing to do, there were 4 of us, two young lawyers, two students; we were joking with

---

98 Diary, March 9, 1935. See also Réal Bélanger, "BARTHE, ÉMILIE (Lavergne)," in *Dictionary of Canadian Biography*, vol. 15, University of Toronto/Université Laval, 2003. http://www.biographi.ca/en/bio/barthe_emilie_15E.html

99 Diary, November 2, 1935, December 4, 1938, and October 1, 1943.

100 Diary, February 27, 1904.

him in a room. He said Laurier, you will go into politics, you will be successful, you will go on & told me that I would rise to a high place (Later questioned by Mr. Foster if he said Premier he said, be leader of my party, that is the way he put it) & many things everyone of which have happened." He also accurately predicted the highly varied fortunes of the three other individuals, "just as Lacroix said."

Mackenzie King recorded of his conversation with Laurier, "This led me to speak of psychical forces" and asked the Prime Minister whether he believed man was immortal. "I told him I thought the resurrection of a physical body was 'nonsense' & he repeated the words, 'yes nonsense.'" But Laurier recalled the death of his father and, "speaking thoughtfully & earnestly," declared "I do not like it, I must confess I do not like the thought, but I cannot but feel that when life ends, it is all over, that that is the end." Laurier also referred to "a great friend with whom I used to talk of these things. He was a Scotchman & a thinker. He told me I had a brother; we were much together, when we were apart, I thought his thoughts. He thought mine, we compared notes. When he died, I could get nothing, I felt it was all over. And yet if death ends all, we are cheated. That is what I feel, we are cheated."

The thirty-five-year-old King offered Laurier two lines of arguments to refute that all ends with the grave. The first was "All science teaches us that nothing can be destroyed; there may be change, but not destruction, least of all can life be destroyed. He thought it was true, life in some form might continue but not conscious personality." King countered that conscious personality "was the only real thing about man; it was not what we saw, or what composed the physical man, that all changed in 7 years, but there was the personality which we loved."

> The other point was that Nature made nothing in vain, that everything had its end, its purpose, that this was the teaching of life. I believed it was true even to the last desire in the breast, the longing for immortality, was an evidence that it had its satisfying somewhere. That Christ's teaching was Life & death, more life, fuller life, no destruction that we brought on ourselves, & quoted Matthew Arnold's 'They mount but hardly to eternal life.' That where a man won here, conquered himself, conquered circumstances & surroundings, he had won immortality, had freed his soul.[101]

---

101 Diary, March 3, 1910.

King posited that because of Laurier's doubts about the continuity of life after death, he may not have been able to appear to him in his dream visions until February 1928 when the PM recorded, "It is the first time I have been consciousness [sic] of a nearness of Laurier. I have had a feeling as if his disbelief had made his soul foreign to mine." While at Laurier House three days after the death of former British Prime Minister Herbert Henry Asquith (and the day after the anniversary of Laurier's death in 1919), he "had a feeling as of the nearness of Sir Wilfrid's spirit, guiding me to higher resolves."

> It became very strong, as I dressed in the room where 9 years ago he died, so strong did it become that I felt like praying reverently to God to help me to keep that presence about me & to Sir Wilfrid to be near. I went and knelt at the sofa near where his bed was and prayed very earnestly. I experienced a feeling as of being endowed with a spirit ... I got up and had very strongly the feeling of one who is clothed in the armour of the spirit, if such is possible. As I walked to my car out of the front door, I felt like Sir Wilfrid, had a feeling as of a noble man, felt as I have seen him look – almost in fact as if I were him, as if his spirit were a part of me. I sat erect in my car as he sat, and all evening till midnight that feeling was with me.

Laurier, Asquith, Gladstone, and other great Liberal leaders "had been carrying on the work of Christ, the liberating of the spirit, the breaking the bond, the freeing the oppressed etc. & Christ was carrying out the mission of God in the world. It is the inspiration of the Spirit."[102]

But if human personality continued "somewhere" as Mackenzie King believed, how could one communicate with another "soul," either living or in another realm? When he discussed psychic forces and thought transfer with Princess Patricia, a granddaughter of Queen Victoria, at a Government House dinner in 1914, "she thought the psychic sense might be developed by concentration. She herself had been able to bring a flower before her mind by thinking of it, but could not retain it. She thought it ought to be possible to control this psychic power, that it was annoying not to be able to ... by reaching out in faith one could bring certain things to one. She

---

102 Diary, February 19 and 18, 1928.

thought the invisible reality greater than the things seen, was sure there was a psychic wave at the present time influencing thought." At the end of the year, John D. Rockefeller Jr. asked him to work as a labour consultant for the Rockefeller Foundation. King told Rockefeller that it was "not a mere chance we have been thrown together and that out of this association there is going to come some great service to mankind … Clearly there is a spiritual or psychic power that has attracted and that attracts and holds; what two men of earnest purpose can accomplish with such an opportunity who can say!"[103]

In August 1918, eight months after his mother's death, King read William James' *Is Life Worth Living?* After touching things that belonged to Isabel King, her old shawl, and the dressing gown she gave him, he recorded in his diary, "How unhappy I should be without the belief I have in the continued existence of those I love. I have been thinking that dear mother's long illness & patient suffering may have been in the nature of vicarious atonement for the errors of my life, and that its meaning will yet be apparent to me."[104]

Earlier in the year, King believed he had discovered how to communicate with Isabel King in the Beyond and that he had become his own first psychic medium.

---

103 Diary, January 7, 1914, and December 4, 1914.
104 Diary, August 3, 1918.

CHAPTER 3

The First Medium: Mackenzie and Isabel King – "I Am Alive"

Mackenzie King would not have delved into Spiritualism with such unwavering determination without the impetus of his mother, Isabel Grace Mackenzie. His older sister Bella had died in 1915 and his father, John King, became nearly blind and died in Toronto at the end of August 1916. When Isabel's health began to fail four months later, King asked her to live with him in his Roxborough apartment overlooking the Rideau Canal in Ottawa and engaged three doctors and a day and night nurse to look after her. She became unconscious on January 25, 1917, and the doctors told King that she could not recover. As he cared for his frail mother, their love and bonding deepened still further. The forty-two-year-old King noted in his diary that Isabel "keeps repeating it was a kind of Providence that brought her here. To me it is as Dr. Gibson said, like being a boy over again."

He had already recorded in 1898 that he loved his mother more than anyone in this world. Now at times near death and thinking of her husband and children, Isabel spoke "often of her love for me, has said while she loved all the others deeply, there was something between each of us 'deeper' than all the rest." In April 1917 King wrote, "I was privileged to have her arms around my neck again today, and to kiss her dear lips many times. I said to her there was no love like a son for a mother. There was none like a mother for her boy. She said she loved me more than she could say. That I was so good, etc."[105]

---

105 Diary, January 25, 1935, January 11, 1917, September 28, 1898, January 24, 1917, and April 21, 1917.

As Isabel hovered near death, at times comatose or speaking incoherently, King sat beside her bed facing his painting of Christ, *The Crown of Thorns*, and resorted to prayer and faith healing. He prayed, "saying I believed God would give her consciousness & impart His power through me. I had little more than expressed this belief when she opened her eyes many times at me, and put her arms around me. I rested & prayed in her arms for a long while. When I went to bed to lie down at 5, I felt I had learned what love is. The purest, strongest, truest love in the world. I felt a great holiness about me." He began to believe "more & more in Christian Science" and assured Dr. Gibson, who was certain of Isabel's imminent death, "there were two things stronger than all else – love and prayer & that he would see what they could do in mother's case." He was convinced that "now for my faith in God & His power & the power of prayer, I believe dear mother will come through this yet, but it will be the power of God not of man." He soon believed that a miracle had been worked in his apartment. "I cannot but know that dear mother's life was saved here by the grace of God. The picture of 'The Crown of Thorns' over her bed at the time was very real to me through that terrible crisis."[106]

For the next ten months, King recorded his mother's steady physical and mental decline and her medical treatment on an almost daily basis. Isabel could not move her legs and as her organs began to fail her face, hands, feet, and body became so swollen with fluid that it became difficult to move her. Very weak and in great pain, she asked King to let her die two days before her 74th birthday on February 6. "She came back to asking me if we could agree to end it now, to let it end now. She asked how long we were going to 'keep up this play' – how long 'this caper [was] going to last.' When she spoke of wanting to go, I broke down; this made her draw me to her and she said she would get better."

Their family friend and physician, Dr. Thomas Gibson, had found that Isabel had intestinal growths and told King that all signs indicated she was dying and that there was no hope. Upon discovering that the doctor, against King's wishes, had again given his mother morphine as a sedative, he dismissed Gibson and put Dr. McCarthy in charge of her care. King had commissioned the Italian sculptor Giuseppe Guastalla to create a large marble bust of Isabel just before her illness.

---

106 Diary, January 26, 27, and 25, 1917, and March 13, 1917.

When he showed her the artist's sketch at the end of February, she "seemed pleased about her bust, yet asked me what I wanted it for, and said 'You want me to live till you are prime minister' – this in a whisper so no one could hear it."[107]

McCarthy believed King's mother was starving from the liquid infant food prescribed by Dr. Gibson and changed her diet. But over the next seven months he diagnosed Isabel as having cerebral arterial sclerosis, mucous colitis, hemorrhaging of the bowels, a growth in her rectum and an increased mass in her lower bowel. He prescribed injections of morphine and strychnine and suppositories of morphine and belladonna. Isabel rallied somewhat at the end of June and King was able to move her, confined in her wheelchair, to his summer cottage at Kingsmere Lake. They returned to the Roxborough after nearly three months in September when his mother was again in great pain and had difficulty breathing. In his diary King recorded, "as I write she is calling out with pain, little plaintiff [sic] moans. It breaks my heart to hear her, like the bleating of some little lamb. I feel this cannot last long."

To alleviate Isabel's swelling, McCarthy performed an operation called aspirating or "tapping" at the beginning of October. King's description of the procedure was apparently so appalling that his private secretary, Fred McGregor, did not transcribe this section of his handwritten diary but indicated "[details omitted]." He did report Dr. McCarthy's statement that Isabel "was as brave as a lion, that not only did she not utter a cry, or say a word, but actually helped to press the needle into her body & then crushed & worked her sides to get the water out." The next day, King recorded that she had "got rid of an immense amount of fluid, and as a consequence rests better. I would much rather see her pale & thin than swollen out of proportions as she has been."[108]

The year 1917 was King's *annus horribilis*. The stress of caring for his mother and witnessing her suffering left him distraught and depressed. He was on salary with the Rockefeller Foundation but found it very difficult to concentrate on writing the chapters for his study *Industry and Humanity*. In September, he began to feel more certain that he was "on bedrock in founding the book on an order which is part of the underlying order of the world & evidence of God

---

107   Diary, February 4, 10, and 25, 1917.
108   Diary, September 28, 1917, and October 4 and 5, 1917.

in the universe and His purpose." Conservative Prime Minister Robert Borden urged the formation of a Union Government to prolong the life of Parliament during World War I and to enforce conscription – which Wilfrid Laurier and King opposed without a referendum. But ten other Liberal leaders abandoned Laurier and joined Borden's Cabinet and a Union Government that announced elections for December 17, 1917.

King was unsure whether he himself could win in the riding of North York because of his opposition to conscription and contemplated not running for office. Yet he also realized that because of his loyalty to Laurier, "it is even possible, this coming political contest might give me despite defeat such a place in the ranks of Liberalism as to become a leader in the new parliament when Sir Wilfrid drops out." Because of the support he would receive from Quebec MPs, "there is a real chance for the future leadership of the Liberal party ... Most of the possible leaders have now destroyed themselves."[109]

Isabel had already "referred to me as 'a future Prime Minister' while I was still in infancy" and encouraged King to contest the riding of North York, the region that had been represented by her father in the Legislative Assembly of Upper Canada from 1829 to 1836. She laughed with a hearty satisfaction when he told her that the MP Charles Murphy had said he had made a speech like William Lyon Mackenzie, "though the laugh betrayed how weak she was. She is the link between his past and my future. How I pray she may be spared to see me the member of North York that the link may bind these political careers." He campaigned in Newmarket in mid-September despite the "greater sacrifice of absence from mother...All the day I felt the keenest anxiety concerning her & when I heard a phone ring feared it was word that the end had come."[110]

As the election neared, King found little time to write his daily diary. He made only seven entries before the election for November and then December 1 and 2. On November 29, he spoke to Rev. Thomas Eakin "about the use of St. Andrew's Church & rang up Miles, the undertaker, about Toronto arrangements" for his mother's funeral in case of her passing. "It was sad and dreary business; could anything be more heart-rending at such a time! I can just pray for strength &

---

109   Diary, September 7, 1917, and October 12 and 13, 1917.
110   Diary, August 25, 1940, July 22, 1917, and September 15, 1917.

Figure 13: Giuseppe Guastalla's 1922 marble bust of Isabel King.

pray that God may spare dear mother, that I may see her alive again." The next day, his sister Jennie sent him a telegram, "Mother wants you. Condition serious."

When he returned to Ottawa and reached the Roxborough, Isabel "was changed. She looked a mere shadow of herself of ten days ago, her face drawn & thin & full of pain." She told him, "this is the morning of the day I am to die." As King rested on a sofa from the exertions of campaigning, "the elections hardly gave me a thought…Everything seemed trivial & I gladly accepted the will of God." On December 1, he arranged with undertakers in Ottawa in case of his mother's death while away campaigning. "Could circumstances more tragic be imagined, in the thick of a campaign."

He last saw his mother alive on December 9, 1917, when he again left Ottawa to campaign. In 1929, King would refer to leaving his mother at a dinner party at Laurier House for British Prime Minister Ramsay MacDonald at which Sir Robert and Lady Borden and Sir William Mulock were also guests. "I told Sir Robert Borden & others about mother's death at the time of my defeat in 1917 & of Mother telling me that Sir Wilfrid was an old man & needed my help, that he had been good to me when I was a young man, to go & help him, though she was dying, not to mind her."[111]

By the force of her will and care by Jennie, Isabel managed to hold on until election day December 17, also King's forty-third birthday. He phoned the next morning from Newmarket and told Jennie he had been defeated, losing by 1,078 votes. When he later asked Miss Petrie, the devoted nurse who had looked after Isabel in her illness, whether word of his defeat in North York had hastened her end, "she said Jennie had told me that after she told Mother the result, Mother 'never lifted her head again.' Miss Petrie said when she came in the afternoon, Mother just looked at her, one look, said nothing. She became unconscious towards five and died about midnight, laying her head on Miss Petrie's shoulder … She said she never knew anything like our love, that even my look brought mother strength, that she lived for me." On the twelfth anniversary of Isabel's death he still recalled, "It was just about midnight so Jennie told me, difficult to say whether the 18th or the 19th. It was the day after my birthday (a day on which she sent her

---

111 Diary, November 29 and 30, 1917, December 1, 1917, December 9, 1930, and October 19, 1929.

last message to me) and the day of my defeat in North York, her father's old battleground."[112]

King wrote Violet Markham, one of his closest friends, financial backer and fellow reform Liberal in London, two weeks after Isabel's death. "I write you as I do because to you, better than to any other person in this world have I been able to express what there is of spiritual reality in my nature." "It was her marvellous will, her simple and steadfast faith, and her unfathomable love for me which kept her alive so long," he informed Markham. "She literally fought off death day by day through the whole year…I can see now so plainly my dear mother's eyes after she had given me her last kiss and waved to me with her hand the final farewell from the pillow on which she lay."

King wrote he lost in North York by only about 500 votes and attributed his loss to the addition of over thirteen hundred pro-conscription women voters with relatives in the armed forces who were added to the voters list under the War Times Election Act passed by the Borden Union Government. When he phoned the election results to his sister Jennie in Ottawa and gave her the message of his defeat for Isabel, "'Poor soul!' were her words when she heard it. Then she said, 'Tell Willie I am glad that he is speaking in his grandfather's name.' That was her last message to me… her one last thought was her feeling of joy and satisfaction that I was continuing in Canada the battle on behalf of the rights of the people to which her father had sacrificed his all." Significantly, he added about one of the major guiding narratives in his life, "This, as you know, has been the silent inspiration of my life. It has been the base line on which all my decisions have ultimately been made."

King compared Isabel's funeral service at the large St. Andrew's Presbyterian Church in Toronto to a state funeral in its solemn dignity and impressive beauty. His friend, Rev. Thomas Eakin, presided. The organist played Isabel's favorite hymn, "Lead, Kindly Light." She lay in state in a great edifice in the city where her father was the first mayor and in the county that he had represented for many years in Parliament where he had struggled for responsible government. King felt that his mother's life "spoke of God's wonderful ways and the eternal justice which underlies His love for the children of men. There was nothing suggestive of death anywhere. Everything spoke of the

---

112 Diary, February 5, 1920, and December 18, 1929.

triumph of the spirit over all human limitations and of the might and majesty of spiritual power."

Isabel's painful death did not separate him from God. On the contrary, as he wrote Markham, "How can I but believe in God when vision after vision born of my heart's desire has been fulfilled in the wonderful and mighty manner? Long and secretly have I cherished this hope of the reality of God's justice. He tried my faith but as respects my mother it never wavered and He gave me the answer to my prayer." When he returned to Ottawa from his mother's burial at the Mount Pleasant Cemetery in Toronto, he opened his little inspirational book *Daily Strength for Daily Needs*, by Mary Wilder Tileston, and found and marked the verse, "Within Thy circling arms we live, O God! In Thy Infinity: Our souls in quiet shall abide, Beset with love on every side."[113]

Mackenzie King often used his diary as a confessional – sometimes unwittingly – particularly when his memory was triggered by an object, action, or locale with strong associated meanings. Reading *Daily Strength* in 1943, he "found great comfort in little passage by [Adeline Dutton Train] Whitney, 'The Nature that could fall into such mistake exactly needs, and in the goodness of the dear God is given, the living of it out.'" This then elicited his admission, "The great mistake I made, the saddest of my life was not returning to Ottawa the night of my defeat in North York on Dec. 17, 1917, escaping that night in Newmarket & being instead on the train, on the way to Ottawa and with dear mother on the 18th to have had the last day on earth with her."[114]

What was this "escape" in Newmarket the night of his greatest defeat? In *A Very Double Life*, C.P. Stacey reported that Isabel King almost died on Easter Monday, April 9, after King had become "restless" and left her to look for a prostitute, following "a path of pleasure when one of duty was so plainly mine." Isabel's life was saved thanks to Nurse Petrie and her doctor but "her lips were almost lifeless when I kissed them, and she was too weak to put her arms around me." He thankfully recorded in his diary afterwards, "God has mercifully spared me an affliction the most terrible I could ever know and one I have secretly dreaded for many years – that when Mother might be

---

113 King to Mrs. James Carruthers [Violet Markham], January 2, 1918. Diary, September 21, 1944.

114 Diary, December 19, 1943.

in a critical condition I might be away from her, and possibly selfishly indulging myself, when I should be at her side."[115]

Was King's "escape" that he had gone drinking after the great strain and disappointment at his election defeat and – aroused by alcohol – possibly even consorted with a prostitute afterwards? His diary gives us a partial answer. In 1936, he received a letter from Mrs. Nottingham of Newmarket saying she was at the Chateau Laurier and recorded, "Strange that it was at their house in Newmarket I was at the time of my defeat in North York & the night before dear mother's death. Had I left Newmarket that night I might have reached Ottawa before dear mother died."

Three months later, the Prime Minister was with Jennie and her family in Newmarket. "She spoke of dear mother having become unconscious after 7 o'clock (or 9), having wakened up after going to sleep at 3. She said I have had 'a wonderful dream. I dreamt mother was here beside me'...She told me that Mother died at 12 p.m. between the 18th & the 19th of December; it was this side – so the date has been the 18th." King had also invited the two sons of his brother Max, Arthur and Lyon, to join him before departing for London and Geneva where he would meet the Duchess of Hamilton, Lind-af-Hageby and mediums who put him in touch with his mother, Max and many, many others.

Lyon brought up the question of drinking, since he was the only one in his circle of young doctors who did not drink. King spoke out strongly against the folly and danger of alcohol. He reflected, "To have Lyon speak of the subject was strange – I could not but feel that I would have been a greater man if I had stuck to my principles in this regard. I would have had a better summer this year if I had not touched wine or spirits. The pain in my heart at Newmarket was that I could have ever thought of taking anything after the defeat & not kept the banner flying above defeat; there would have been none then – all this perhaps is the way the loved ones are taking to make me strong on my great mission overseas." He concluded,

> It seemed to me strange I should be in Newmarket as we talked of this. How poignant was the pain in my heart as I thought of how I was defeated on the night of the 17th & instead of leaving for Ottawa that night had remained over & not gone up till the 18th. Had I left that night I should have been with her at the end and had her words & farewell, and that wonderful memory.

---

115 Stacey, *A Very Double Life*, 153-154. Diary, April 9, 1917.

> To think that I was not there, when I might have been, is the greatest sorrow of my life – the fact that my lamp was not burning brightly; but had been dimmed – at the last watch. Perhaps it was to save me that error at the close of my own life. I believe it was. (.....)[116]

The Prime Minister believed that Adeline Whitney's verse in *Daily Strength* pointed to an absolution for his most terrible affliction and greatest sorrow. "The dear God has given me the chance of 'living it out' that mistake – my nature needed it. The rest of the passage is true – that in the living of it out we find that the finger of God has been at work among our lives, and that the emerging is into His blessed order, 'that He is forever making up for us our own undoings – that He evermore restoreth our souls.'" King also read the verses for December 18 in Constance M. Whishaw's *Being and Doing: A Selection of Helpful Thoughts from Various Authors Arranged for Daily Reading*. They asked, "has there been growth? (Hands exactly at 12). If so we are licensed to claim forgiveness. That I feel – there has been growth. Tonight contrasted with that of those years, leaves no doubt – my soul has been largely restored."[117]

But such quiet faith and religious certainty were not sufficient to satisfy Mackenzie King's emotional and psychological needs immediately after his mother's death as Spiritualism could. Two years after her death, he attended the funeral of Mrs. Larmonth and thought of his mother as he saw Larmonth lying in her coffin with her pure white hair. "Both fought a good fight to the close. Mother's suffering was greater & fight harder & to a finer finish; to the last second she fought for life. There was nothing left of her little frame when her spirit was taken away. The bible at best gives us little assurances as to life hereafter."[118]

Like his mother's passing in Ottawa, King had also not been present at the deaths of his sister Bella and his father in Toronto and of his brother Max in Denver, Colorado, and developed a belief in the continuity of their personalities after death. Recalling the first anniversary of his father's last visit to Kingsmere shortly before he died,

---

116 Diary, June 19, 1936, and September 5, 1936. When King campaigned in the Newmarket area again on August 18, 1920, he recorded that he "motored back to Jackson's Point where I spent the night with the Nottingham's at their summer cottage."

117 Diary, December 19, 1943.

118 Diary, November 27, 1919.

he paraphrased Matthew Arnold's *Rugby Chapel*, which the poet had written in homage to his father, Thomas Arnold. "'Somewhere afar I believe he lives & practices that strength, zealous, beneficent, firm,' a lovely father & a good man." On the anniversary of John King's death ten days later he recorded, "It seems impossible that a whole year has gone by since I was wakened at early morning by a voice telling me that he was dying."[119]

To honour the memory of his late sister on her birthday anniversary, King had contacted the publisher J.B. Lippincott in Philadelphia regarding the publication of his brother's manuscript, *The Battle with Tuberculosis and How to Win It*. When ten weeks later Max sent a telegram on his mother's birthday announcing that Lippincott had accepted the book for publication and offered a ten per cent sales royalty, King rejoiced. "Dear little Bell – her birthday gift to mother. – Yes somewhere near by she watches and helps to plan & arrange." On the second anniversary of her passing, King read one of Frances Ridley Havergal's poems, "God's Message," "a poem on peace to one who seeks God. It was like a word from little Bell herself and as I was thinking this & wondering if she could hear me & know of me, my eye fell on the following words underlined in another poem 'To me thy voice is sweet prevailing in thy feeblest prayer.' It came so suddenly, unexpectedly & pointedly that I exclaimed, 'Oh Bella, that is too wonderful.' I cannot believe this is all coincidence. I believe Bell is nearby, watching over my life." On the eighteenth anniversary of her death he noted, "Since then I have talked with her and know that she is not far away even as I write; also I am sure her sweet influence continues to guide and direct me and to help me on my way."[120]

Four weeks after he won the December 1921 federal election and became Prime Minister, King travelled to Denver to see his dying brother. Dr. Macdougall (Max) King had been diagnosed with advanced tuberculosis in 1913 and was convalescing in Colorado where he would die bedridden from a crippling progressive muscular atrophy, at the age of 43, in 1922. Before they parted for the last time, "I told him we would ever be together; shortly

---

119 Diary, August 20 and 30, 1917. King had already cited the poem in the frontispiece of his 1906 memoir to his late friend Bert Harper, *The Secret of Heroism*.
120 Diary, February 6, 1917, April 4, 1917, and April 4, 1933.

Figure 14: Mackenzie and Isabel King at Kingsmere, circa 1915.

before our last talk he said to me, 'You will be with me and I will be with you always.' I was glad of this. I told him I would count on his help from the Great Beyond." Upon his return to Ottawa, he engaged Miss Petrie to help care for his brother until his passing two months later.

What impressed him most as Max was buried next to his mother, father, and sister Bella in the family grave in Toronto was the moment just as the benediction was being pronounced. "The sun came out from under a cloud & shone with a wonderful brilliance upon the grave & the flowers. I could not but look into it & smile. It was as though dear Mac was giving us all evidence of his power beyond the grave & of the realm of light in which his spirit dwells. I shall never believe this was mere accident or chance happening of nature."

On the seventh anniversary of his death, he recalled his brother as "a lovely noble man ... a great power" and again cited Matthew Arnold's *Rugby Chapel*. "I believe he is today in 'the sounding labour house vast of being.' I am sure his noble soul lives on, guarding those he loves & helping us all." On the twelfth anniversary of Max's death he recorded, "How marvellous to have talked with him tonight and to have been thanked by him for the message & for the kindness shewn

[Max's son] Lyon in Toronto. Nothing quite so wonderful as this can be found elsewhere than in the experience itself."[121]

Mackenzie King's deep love for his mother led him to transform his memory of her into an even greater tangible spiritual entity than his sister, father, and brother. Six weeks after her death he recorded, "How do I miss her dear tender loving presence – my consolation lies in the thought that she has entered upon life eternal, and that she is ever near by, though unseen." On the anniversary of Isabel's last visit to Kingsmere he wrote, "I am grateful to God for the summer we had together and the memories it has left. Somewhere her spirit dwells, not far from me here. Did I not cherish that belief I should be unhappy beyond words." And two years after he last saw his mother alive, he recalled "the deep, deep blue of her eyes – the blue of eternity, her very soul. That she lives & is near me, I believe. I resolve again to make my life pure & good & great because of her. She is the inspiration & strength of my life, more like Christ than anyone on earth. God make me true to her memory ... Oh that I may be like her."[122]

Passages in King's daily reading of the family Bible and other devotional books often triggered memories of his mother's passing and of her promise to communicate with him after her death. On Christmas day 1930, he "spent most of the morning seeking to commune with dear Mother's spirit and the spirits of the loved ones in the Great Beyond. How could Mother guide me, how send the word I long to have – The Bible is the medium of which we spoke." Earlier in the year, he had read the verses from Isaiah 25:8 "He will swallow up death in victory and the Lord God will wipe away tears from off all faces." "Immediately I recalled my last talk with dear mother, when believing her to be dying I leaned above her and asked her to send me a message from the other world sometime to let me know she was near me, and I cried a little & she raised her hand & with her handkerchief wiped away the tear from my eyes & said to me 'I'll be like God Himself and shall wipe away every tear.'"

In 1948, he read the daily message from Corinthians 13 in his *Devotional Diary*, "the greatest thing in the world that now abideth are Faith, Hope and Love. These three, and the greatest of these is Love." He then recalled, "These were the last words I read aloud to

---

121 Diary, January 8, 1922, March 23, 1922, March 18, 1929, and March 18, 1934.
122 Diary, February 1, 1918, June 27, 1918, and December 9, 1919.

my mother at her bedside when she was dying. I asked her then to let me know from the Beyond that she was still alive and was helping to guard and guide my life."[123]

Almost anything could lead him to reference Isabel speaking to him such as when singing the verse from Mary Lee Demarest's poem about death, heaven, and immortality, "'My ain countree – a wee birdie to its nest.' I always associate birds with messages from mother ever since when partially unconscious she spoke to me of being as a bird." In a moment of mental confusion in October 1917, Isabel stated that her name had been Bird. "That before she had been a bird. Later when I asked her why she was pressing her side, she said she was trying to hold down a pair of wings she had added." On Christmas morning in 1931, he listened to the church bells and hymns from the All Saints' Church across from Laurier House and understood the meaning of a dream he had that morning before waking. "I am convinced this is all dear mother remembering our talk together before her death and her promise to come to me from the Great Beyond & let me know of her existence – This is her guidance."[124]

In 1938, he paid $25 [$501 in 2023 dollars] for Mrs. J.A. Stevenson's horoscope and was not surprised when she told him that his mother's influence (the Moon) came through so strongly and that she had seen nothing like it before. "The truth is mother and I talked of spiritual things when we were together, and of seeking to communicate after she had gone. It was the God-like I always saw in her, and in her beautiful life so pure and holy and Christ-like I felt all the time that her power would be very great. The only enduring & great power is that of the holy spirit and mother was filled with that and has it now as also father & Max & Bell – they are strong guardian angels. I believe too what mother & father tell me of what was revealed & is being revealed to them." And he thought a crimson light reflected from his red Prime Minister box in his study before the 1945 federal election was a visible sign from Isabel. "I have not the least doubt in the world that it all relates to my mother watching over me at this critical time in my life where so much depends on the forthcoming campaign and so much relates to the last of one's days. I missed being with her at the end of her life which has been

---

123 Diary, December 25, 1930, February 6, 1930, and July 28, 1948, p. 6.
124 Diary, July 30, 1928, October 13, 1917, and December 25, 1931.

the greatest of the sorrows I have had to bear. I want to be with her above all else at the close of my own life."[125]

J.W. Pickersgill, in his four-volume *The Mackenzie King Record*, largely omitted references to Spiritualism in King's diaries from 1939 to 1948 and trivialized his life-long religious and spiritual aspirations. In the introduction to the first volume, he stated that the Prime Minister "was sincerely religious and an almost militant Presbyterian; his beliefs, however, were highly personal and he was convinced that a host of unseen witnesses hovered about him and guided his conduct in emergencies."[126]

How could Mackenzie King communicate with these invisible spiritual entities? From examining his mother's correspondence written when King was already thirty, Murray Nicolson observed, "Isabel's superstitious nature allowed her to worry about what she considered inexplicable dreams. This was particularly disturbing to her when the dreams involved her children and as she got older her apprehensions about them increased. As a result she kept John King awake at night, fretting until she wrote or phoned the children to see that all was well."[127]

Mackenzie King often had similar dreams expressing separation anxiety. In 1944, he had a vision symbolic of old age and endurance just before waking yet could not recall its details. But "it carried an experience which has been frequent in dreams, namely, of feeling that my mother was alive, some distance away, and was anxious to see me." He could not quite get the complete meaning of another vision of running alongside a departing train and holding on very precariously but noted, "the train so often means the danger of separation from those one loves, through one's own acts." In another dream vision in 1933, he saw his mother going away by herself, leaving the family home bereft of everything, without furnishings or food. "It made me terribly distressed to see the condition and I felt no matter what came I could and would not let dear mother go away in her frail condition and alone. The pain that came into my heart as I saw the situation was very great. It was as if a spring of pain bubbled up within my heart – a pain that distressed me terribly. I cried out with it and wakened as I cried."

---

125 Diary, April 22, 1938, and January 24, 1945, p. 3.
126 Pickersgill, *The Mackenzie King Record. Volume 1*, 4.
127 Nicolson, 32.

King interpreted a great many of his dreams as warnings against what he perceived as sinning or moral transgressions. After seeing this vision, he instantly "asked God to forgive me for what I had done that was evil or wrong in His sight or offended against His holy law ... I think this was a vision – a vision telling me that I was not doing what was right – was being separated from my guide – wherever mother seems to be getting away from me, or I begin to lose her on a journey, there I believe is a sign that I am following a wrong course, and separating myself from her, with pain perhaps to her as well as to me." In another dream vision the same year in which he "had been in some other far away place" distant from his mother, "I could feel a physical pain in my heart; it was so great, there seemed to be a straight golden pathway as it were between me & her."[128]

Though he began recording dreams twenty years before his mother's death, Mackenzie King learned from Isabel how to distinguish between dreams and visions. In 1932 he entered in his diary, "This morning before beginning work I wrote out the dream (or rather vision as dear mother said) of the morning at the time of waking." Visions had to convey a clear important message. He dismissed one dream two years later because "I have not seen any significance thus far to make the dream a vision." While awaiting the provincial election returns in Ontario and Saskatchewan in which the Liberals swept the incumbent Conservatives from power in June 1934, he had been puzzled by another confusing dream in which he found himself stripped of all his garments near the edge of the sea. Only after a convoluted accounting of all the pieces of clothing he put on that morning, which corresponded in some fashion to what he had seen in his dream, "came the amazing 'evidence' of the dream being a vision, the full confirmation ... I was being shown the 'clean sweep' that was there all the time (Nature – God's garment)."[129]

The majority of King's dreams involved members of his family. He reported after a good night's sleep, "Toward waking, heard my sister Bella's voice quite distinctly but could not make out what she was referring to. It was quite a loud call and I saw her distinctly." In another dream vision, he "dreamt of different individuals who passed away – one night, of Lapointe [Ernest Lapointe, his former Minister

---

128 Diary, February 5, 1944, June 30, 1935, April 29, 1933, and August 25, 1933.
129 Diary, April 16, 1932, January 22, 1934, and June 20, 1934, p. 6.

of Justice and Quebec Lieutenant] and last night, of my brother Max. It would seem almost like a portrait gallery of friends who were in the Beyond. I seemed to sense in Max's presence an understanding and guardianship in connection with my life." He also dreamt of singing with his mother. "The tunes that were clearest and most beautiful of all were 'He came sweet influence to impart' – very very beautiful. I heard her voice very clearly and there seemed to be a holy light, revealing almost her face and presence."[130]

He physically felt Isabel in a very clear "Vision of Mother's presence." Before waking, "I felt my mother's arms as it were materialize and fold themselves around my head as it lay on the pillow. I said to myself at the time, that is what is happening, Mother is here and is making her presence known in that way." He perceived Isabel's presence to be "a message of comfort I believe to bring me more of rest and peace against the constant contending of flesh and spirit." In another dream vision, he brought his secretary Lucy Zavitske forward so that Isabel might kiss her. "Instead mother kissed my face, over & over again, until I told her she must not forget Miss Zavitske. It was a very real experience – I saw her face most distinctly, with her lovely hair and felt the kisses on my own face."[131]

King's father also helped him in his life-long struggle to control his strong sexual drive. In a "Vision of father's presence – guidance and prophecy," he described that "I found myself very restless during the night & with a tension hard to control. Nature's demands are very strong at times. After wrestling with the need for rest & peace, I fell asleep and have [sic] a very clear vision of dear father coming to me and placing his forehead against mine … His face was so clear I could see distinctly the hairs of his beard. It was most comforting coming after the other experience which at 60 I had hoped to be free from. I thought of his words to me in one of the 'conversations' with Mrs. Wriedt that he understood all that side."[132]

As Isabel hovered near death in 1917, she dreamt of and at times spoke to her deceased mother, father, and husband and became confused between her dreams and reality. King noted that his mother "told me this morning when [she] woke she had been dreaming she

---

130 Diary, August 7, 1943, January 5, 1946, and December 19, 1943.
131 Diary, May 1, 1938, and Daily Diary, Book H, January 5, 1947.
132 Diary, December 28, 1934.

had the lace for the artist who was to do her bust, that Jennie had sent it to her & that father was sitting beside her on the bed as she was sorting it. He had been there beside her. She gave a little cry but was very calm." This liminal stage probably led to her promise – prompted by Mackenzie King – that she would communicate with him from the Great Beyond. Two months after Isabel's death, King recorded perhaps his most dramatic dream vision.

> Last night I dreamt that I saw dear mother's face in death; it was not worn by disease as I last saw it, but beautiful, radiantly beautiful though dead. I said to her – as though talking to her spirit apart – you promised mother – which she did – to tell me from the other world if you were still alive & near me & when I said this her lips opened and she said 'I am alive' but it seemed as though it was forbidden her to say more. I felt she had told me all she could – All day the dream has been with me.[133]

Roy MacLaren sarcastically referred to King's mother as "by far his most frequent and reassuring extraterrestrial interlocutor," not fully understanding the origins and effects of his spiritualist beliefs. In a dream vision of her in 1933, he indeed "did not see her – but felt the reality of her presence as of a living fire. She seemed in the building nearby to which we were to go, but it was as if the radiance of her being made itself shine through all material things."[134]

Subsequent chapters will follow how Isabel King became an increasingly powerful construct in her son's spiritual universe. What clearly emerges from King's diary is that he perceived his mother as a divine figure even before her death and becoming Prime Minister in December 1921. He noted during her illness ten months before she died, "As I looked at the profile of her face, it was more like the pictures of the beautiful faces of Christ than anything I had ever seen. I was so struck by it that I pointed it out to the nurse." Isabel became a central agent in what King perceived to be his own spiritual mission on earth as determined by God Himself. After completing *Industry and Humanity* the following year, he felt "the possibilities of my book, the eternal greatness of the things of the mind & of the spirit ... I feel that to reveal Christ's mission to the world is the one great thing to

---

133 Diary, September 2, 1917, and February 15, 1918.
134 MacLaren, 8. Diary, September 11, 1933.

Figure 15: King's shrine to his mother in his library at Laurier House.

seek to do. I feel more my real self, more at one with God & my own soul & near to those dearest to me who have gone before … Spirit is the only reality."

In February 1919, he viewed Sir Wilfrid Laurier's "too wasted, too worn" remains lying in state in the Commons' Chamber and spoke with many MPs who encouraged him to seek the Liberal Party leadership. He had opened his Bible "believing I should receive a word of guidance" and was struck by the remarkable sentence in the Acts of the Apostles, "For if this counsel or this work be of men, it will come to naught; but if it be of God, ye cannot overthrow it." King commented that he believed these splendid words "sum up all I feel and believe at the present time. They express my attitude toward the possible leadership of the Liberal party. If it be of men, it will come to naught. If of God it cannot be overthrown. That makes it God's work, if it comes. God's work to be done in the world."

Four months after winning the 1919 Liberal Party leadership election, another Biblical passage "too seemed so appropriate, and almost in part as if a message from dear Mother herself, and through her from God Himself." On the twentieth anniversary of having been chosen Party Leader, King still recalled, "Others may not have known. I knew or thought I knew 'God whispers some of us in the ear' that I would be chosen leader, that forces were working to that end in the beyond."[135]

Even before her death, he had come to identify the birth of his mother – a "seven months' delicate infant, born in exile amid conditions of penury" – with both the Virgin Mary and the birth of Jesus in what he referred to as the miracle of Bethlehem. Isabel was born on Chambers Street in New York while William Lyon Mackenzie served as an actuary at the Mechanics' Institute. "He in exile, the family so poor as not to be able to afford a physician other than a midwife who could only make her mark, not write her name." Her parents debated "whether they had food or whether her life was worth saving, as they had so little in the way of food wherewith to supply the needs of the children." King recorded that three weeks before Isabel's 74th birthday in 1917, his mother thought she was dying but recovered. "Then speaking of herself as a little child – the 13th in the family, so frail that it hardly seemed to her mother advisable for her to live – here I am at 74 holding the hand of the future prime minister of Canada."

When he checked Norman McLeod Rogers' biography *Mackenzie King*, published by George Morang before the 1935 federal election, he "worked into the paged proofs a reference to mother being born in exile – it is there that the secret of my life lies." After he defeated the Conservatives' R.B. Bennett and was swept back into office as Prime Minister with a great majority in that election, he read the Christian hymn *The Magnificat* on Christmas day in which Mary praises the greatness of The Lord. "He has put down the mighty from their thrones and has exalted the lowly." For King, "It clearly meant dear Mother was speaking to me through its words – the Miracle of Bethlehem being repeated – a mother & her son – dedicated to the service of God … It seemed to me everything was intended to signify 'the Holy Spirit' with power from on High."[136]

---

135 Diary, February 26, 1917, July 14, 1918, February 18, 1919, p. 4, December 18, 1919, and August 7, 1939.

136 Diary, February 6, 1917, May 25, 1944, January 17, 1917, and February 22, 1935. Rogers, 18. Diary, December 25, 1936.

This was Mackenzie King's magical thinking about Isabel Mackenzie as an intermediary with God already in his first term as Prime Minister from 1922 to 1925. Travelling in his private railroad car to address "a magnificent gathering" of 600 at the Montreal Women's Liberal Club held at the Windsor Hotel in 1923, "the thought came to me in a very real way that she was in a way as near to God as to me even in life & I gave expression to this idea. Indeed she was a revelation of God. I am sure she is guarding me and that her spirit is very near me." At the Women's Liberal Club, he had felt "a real power in speaking at the close and exercised it with might. I received a great ovation at the close."

That Christmas, he sent out four hundred cards of J.W.L. Forster's 1905 painting of Isabel, *Light at Eventide*, and felt "a happiness from the distribution of dear Mother's picture which is now lending its radiance & sweet influence to many homes in England, U.S. & Canada." He was convinced the distribution of his mother's portrait was "a great influence to have abroad in the world. I shall make it felt not only throughout Canada but throughout the Empire. It is she who rules & God through her. Every passage in the scriptures of meekness, humility etc. has been proven true in her case."[137]

The Prime Minister believed it was direction from Isabel and not mere coincidence that he read Isaiah 9:6 on Christmas Day morning, "that it should have been of the Mother and her son, that 'the government shall be upon his shoulder.' It is strange that I should have been impressed feeling as I do how much this is coming to be my lot in the affairs of our country. This mystical relation between mother & son & between both and God was the great illuminating perception of my soul this day." Hearing the bells from All Saints chime out *Oh Come All Ye Faithful*, he "felt like a soldier of Christ's army – that I could follow with pride & confidence and right & be one of that great procession that has marched through the centuries from the days of Bethlehem and the cross to today – for once I felt the thrill of a crusader, of a Knight of the Holy Grail. I was deeply moved." On New Year's Day, he viewed the symbolic objects on the "altar" in front of J.W.L. Forster's painting of Isabel King and remembered "all I love most dearly before God. Dear mother's hair & wedding ring like the Holy Grail in the casket lined with red."[138]

---

137 Diary, February 19, 1923, and December 23 and 25, 1923.
138 Diary, December 25, 1923, and January 1, 1924.

He could *commune* with Isabel through Forster's image even in his tea leaves. In 1935, "in the tea cup at noon I saw as plain as day & McLeod [his butler] saw in a way that impressed him very much dear mother as she sat in Forster's painting – shewing me she was here & near." When he received a posthumous portrait of Isabel from the English painter Frank O. Salisbury in 1944, it engendered "the thought of my own relationship to my grand-father, my mother being a guiding spirit helping me to serve my country so as to make clear the real mission of my grand-father. The coming of her portrait at that moment was like her spirit making itself manifest in a picture."[139]

---

139 Diary, January 25, 1935, and September 21, 1944.

CHAPTER 4

Joan Patteson, Mackenzie King's Spiritual Partner

C.P. Stacey was the first historian to describe the major role Joan Patteson played in Mackenzie King's life. After delving into his diaries, he concluded, "Obviously, one could write a whole book about King and the Pattesons ... Perhaps, if justice were done, the Liberal party of Canada should raise, in some secluded corner at Kingsmere, an appropriately modest memorial to Mary Joan Patteson, one of the founders of its fortunes."[140]

King first referred to Godfroy and Joan Patteson, who also had an apartment in the Roxborough, when he held a dinner party at the Hull Golf Club on October 2, 1918, to celebrate the completion of his study for the Rockefeller Foundation, *Industry and Humanity*. When they met, Joan was 49 and King 44. Godfroy Barkworth Patteson was the son of Thomas Charles Patteson and Marie Louise Jones. Born in England in 1836, T.C. Patteson studied at Eton and Oxford and emigrated to Canada in 1858. After working for a prominent law firm in Toronto and for the Ontario government, Patteson was asked by Prime Minister John A. Macdonald to become the founding manager and editor-in-chief of the Conservative party organ, the Toronto *Mail*, in 1872. After resigning from the paper at the end of 1877, he received a government appointment as the postmaster of Toronto.[141]

Godfroy Patteson was born in Port Hope, Ontario, on October 27, 1867, and died in Ottawa on April 7, 1954, at the age of eighty-six. He

---

140 Stacey, *A Very Double Life*, 125, 138.

141 Levine, *Scrum Wars*, 15-18.

attended school in Cheltenham, England, Trinity College in Port Hope, and the Royal Military College in Kingston. Godfroy began his forty-five-year banking career in 1887 with Molson's Bank in Toronto and subsequently in London, Ontario, and in Ottawa. After Molson's Bank merged with the Bank of Montreal in 1925, he became associate manager of the main branch of the Bank of Montreal in Ottawa, retiring in 1932.

Mary Joan MacWhirter (alternate spelling McWhirter and Macwhirter), daughter of James Alexander McWhirter and Jessie Allison Kennedy, was born in Woodstock, Ontario, on November 27, 1869, and died in Toronto on April 23, 1960, at the age of ninety. Godfroy had married Joan in the First Presbyterian Church in London, Ontario, on November 21, 1895. His religious denomination was Episcopalian and Joan's Presbyterian. Their son John Coleridge ("Jack") Patteson was born in London, Ontario, on December 5, 1896. He became the General Agent for the Canadian Pacific Railway Steamship Passenger Department and subsequently General Manager for the CPR for the United Kingdom and Europe, with headquarters in London, and at times facilitated King's transatlantic travel in the 1930s. He died in France in January 1954. Joan Patteson's great-grandson, John McCallum, was a Member of Parliament from 2000 to 2017. He served as Minister of National Defence, Minister of Veteran Affairs, Minister of National Revenue, Minister of Immigration, Refugees and Citizenship, and as the Canadian ambassador to China in the Liberal Governments of Jean Chrétien, Paul Martin, and Justin Trudeau.[142]

When King met the Pattesons, Godfroy was manager of the Molson's Bank in Ottawa. Like Marjorie Herridge who had been estranged from Reverend W.T. Herridge, Joan Patteson was also in an unhappy marriage. When she told her mother in one of Etta Wriedt's direct-voice séances in 1932 that she was happy, her mother replied, "Well it's better than it was 15 years ago. This is true. Fifteen years ago my domestic affairs were terrible & they are at least peaceful today though not very uplifting – I am glad she knows what I have gone through."

In addition to their son Jack, the Pattesons had a daughter Rose Allison, born in 1906, who died on Easter Sunday the same year,

---

142 "Obituaries: G.B. Patteson," *Montreal Gazette*, April 10, 1954, 17. "Former Leading City Banker Godfroy Patteson Dies," *Ottawa Journal*, April 8, 1954, 28. "Mrs. Patteson: Widow Dies, Was Friend Of Mr. King," *Ottawa Citizen*, April 28, 1960, 2. "Mrs. G.B. Patteson Dies in Ottawa in 91st Year," *Ottawa Journal*, April 28, 1960, 5.

stimulating her mother's – but not Godfroy's – interest in Spiritualism. After King and Patteson began using the "little table" in 1932 to communicate with spirits in the Beyond, Rose communed with them using the name Nancy. Again, like Marjorie Herridge, Joan shared King's love for literature and the arts. He wrote in his diary in September 1920 that she had "a nimble mind, a fine appreciation of literature, keen intelligence and wit; a most delightful intellectual companion, she could rise to the greatest heights, but in Godfrey [sic] she has not her equal intellectually. His tastes are on a different level. Her nature needs the spiritual, and that side is far from developed in him."

Citing the original handwritten diaries – these references to Patteson were expunged from the online diaries – Stacey recorded that King and Joan felt a strong sexual attraction within two years of meeting. "It seems so hard to overcome oneself, and this morning it was nearly desperation ... These storms of passion – for that is what they are, are madness and wrong. They 'rock the mind' and must cease. We both have strength enough to see that, and we will help each other to what is best for each, hard as the struggle may be – and it is hard in this lonely solitary life." As Allan Levine commented, "We will never know if he and Joan succumbed to temptation, since King sliced the next five days of entries from his diary." In another entry the following year again excised from the online diary, Joan "spoke of her fondness for me, and of having to give me up ... she feels that a great struggle has been come through successfully – she said she felt she had nursed me through a great illness for which she had been partly responsible – How true. She spoke of the anxiety she has suffered for months. Her sorrow & tears were a reaction now that the struggle was over – dear little soul – she would have been an ideal wife – if we only could have met years ago."[143]

Louise Reynolds, in *Mackenzie King: Friends and Lovers*, cites other references to the Prime Minister's relationship with Joan Patteson expunged (.....) from the Library and Archives Canada online diaries. When King saw *Parsifal* and its conflict between sexual passion and the quest for the Holy Grail at the Metropolitan Opera on March 25,

---

143 Joan Patteson, "Mrs. Wriedt's Visit – Feb. 24, 25, 26, 1932." Stacey, *A Very Double Life*, 121, 122-123. Cited by Levine, *King*, 120-121. The citations are excised from the September 6 and 7, 1920 and May 21, 1921, online diary. In his diary for May 10, 1935, King noted that Joan "has all the artistic qualities, would have made a good musician, writer, artist, decorator, teacher of art or poetry – a very lovely nature."

1921, he "wished so much Joan had been with me. It was <u>our</u> play. The Holy Grail. I was amazed to see how unconsciously we had hit upon the central theme in life." King "wondered if I could be as Amfortas, stricken with a wound that will not heal." When he and Joan subsequently studied the libretto in Ottawa, "we came to one passage which suggested a train of thought that immediately changed our whole evening ... It was very sudden, very unexpected ... Joan was quite frank & honest about its effect upon her and by speaking the truth openly we were able to face the question before us. This problem is increasingly difficult to solve but we are determined to solve it."[144]

The extent of King's feelings for Patteson is indicated by a 1921 will which he showed her three months before his death while sorting old documents and records for what he hoped would become his memoirs. "I had willed to her all my property at Kingsmere for her lifetime but with the understanding that it would be, after her death, used as a sort of community property for girls in civil service, shops, etc. where they might have a chance for rest and recreation."[145]

H. Blair Neatby, the second "official" biographer appointed by the King executors, had asserted that it was "a tribute to Mrs. Patteson's discretion and transparent dignity that any unfounded rumours about the nature of her friendship with the Prime Minister appeared ridiculous to all who knew her." Allan Levine, in *Scrum Wars: The Prime Minister and the Media*, similarly reported that no one in the Ottawa press gallery "speculated (in public in any event) about King's relationship with the married Joan Patteson." He called Heather Robertson's assertion in *More Than a Rose: Prime Ministers, Wives and Other Women* that King had an affair with Joan "pure speculation, based on a reading between the lines of his diary." Yet in his subsequent King biography, Levine also affirmed that "From 1920 onward, Joan Patteson shared Mackenzie King's life as much as it was possible for a married woman to do so."[146]

But a careful reading of even only the online diary minutely traces the intimacy of their three- decade-long relationship. After the death of Marjorie Herridge, the PM purchased her large house at Kingsmere

---

144 Reynolds, 174.

145 Diary, April 29, 1950.

146 Levine, *King*, 120. Neatby, *William Lyon Mackenzie King: The Lonely Heights*, 199. Levine, *Scrum Wars*, 134. Levine, *King*, 120.

in 1924, renamed it Moorside, and provided the home for Joan and Godfroy Patteson. C.P. Stacey commented, "Thus the woman who had succeeded to the place Marjorie had once held in King's heart succeeded also to Marjorie's summer home." In 1929, he moved the Pattesons to still another cottage at Kingsmere, "Shady Hill." In his diary he explained, "I must keep my little cottage by the lake a sanctuary... There will not be the too close identification of my life with theirs. I will be able to get back to the old days where there can be companionship without absorption, and where I can be apart and alone, with God, with Nature & the loved ones who still 'lead me on' ... This is better in every way and I am immensely relieved in feeling. It avoids the intimacy in the relationship which is certain to occasion comment."[147]

The Prime Minister was very much aware that his liaison with Patteson could seriously damage him politically. Reading the Conservative Party's *The Canadian*, prepared for the 1930 election, "the cartoon shows what is to be expected, a vile campaign of slander, insinuation, lying & whatnot. It will be very nasty." He concluded: "I can see they will try to make something yet of my friendship for Joan. I shall have to be circumspect in that particular." In a dream three years after his electoral defeat in which he again saw himself as PM, he was determined "not to give political traitors or enemies or anyone a chance to question Joan's relations & mine by travelling together." Patteson had also been receiving this counsel from her deceased daughter in the Beyond so that King "could not but think of what Joan told me of Nancy warning her about not going to New York – this was much the same true guidance – the dream was with me throughout the day as I am writing it up tonight – so that it is a vision."[148]

There are several references in King's diaries to his masking this personal relationship with Joan. In April 1934, he had purchased George Goodwin Kilburne's oil painting "The Trysting Place" at auction in Ottawa for $65 [$1,393 in 2023 dollars] along with other canvases. He described the painting as "a beautiful soft & tender picture" and intended it as a gift for Patteson. When he showed her the paintings, however, he "did not make a presentation, as I saw she was doubtful about the trysting place one, as being too much like 'her & me.'" There are indeed at least four references in his diaries to "our trysting place," "our little trysting

---

147 Stacey, *A Very Double Life*, 126, 127. Diary, May 26, 1929.
148 Diary, April 2, 1930, and November 5, 1933.

place on the moor" and "our little trysting place of a year ago" on the Kingsmere estate. He had made a cryptic reference two years previously to his conflict between his religious ideals, political ambitions, and his strong sex instinct, writing of "the struggle I had had all my days – my political days – where the Holy Grail was seen burning at the end of the journey, in 1921, having kept the tryst, having overcome. Surely all this is parable & at the end of it all I shall yet see the holy Grail."[149]

Unlike Rev. W.T. Herridge who had slammed the door in King's face when he returned late at night with his wife Marjorie in 1902, Godfroy Patteson does not appear to have resented the PM's constant presence with Joan, perhaps because of his prestige. In Paris at Molyneux's in 1934, King bought a black velvet gown for her birthday that she tried on immediately in front of him and her husband upon his return to Laurier House. "She had quite a time fitting it on," King recorded. "Godfroy had to give her a hand & I had to explain it had an 'inside' as well as an 'out'. It fitted her perfectly & she was delighted with it."

Two weeks later, he had a dream vision of Venus, "an amazingly distinct vision of a perfect statue. It was an exact reproduction of one of the statues – not the de Milo but of one with both arms preserved and brought before the body. When I looked at it closely it was living, and was Joan – a figure of perfection in the human form, exquisitely beautiful ... I should not be surprised if it related to her appearance tonight in the black velvet dress I brought her from Paris, and which is perfect in its fit. She looks beautiful in it. Her figure so refined ... she told me that really nothing was worn beneath the dress because of the style in these things and its close fitting character; the dress being dark did enshroud or rather surround a perfect Venus." Writing up this vision in his diary King added, "everything appeared to me to be as devoid of the sensual as anything in the world could be and to be rather an exhibition of innocence and perfection."[150]

He had a more Freudian phallic dream, "Vision of clearing away encumbrances," in Naples the previous month after being "restless" and having yielded to the "magnetic" sexual current discussed in Chapter 6. The dream vision hints King may have subconsciously desired to castrate himself to resolve his ever-present conflict between his robust sexual

---

149 Diary, April 7, 9, and 10, 1934, July 10, 1939, September 3, 1939, October 3, 1939, April 14, 1941, and November 6, 1932.

150 Diary, November 23, 1934, and December 7, 1934.

Figure 16: George Goodwin Kilburne's 1896 "The Trysting Place."

instinct and equally strong spiritual aspirations that was obstructing his public duties. "Before waking I had a vivid dream of standing at the foot of a small hill, down which there ran a small road," he recorded.

> I had an axe in my hand and was about to cut off the last branch – it was really a limb of a tree in the nature of some large palm or pine (of the kind one sees here) which was out of place by itself, the other pieces all having been cut off. A bare stump was shewing except for this piece of green – rather luxurious remaining. Joan seemed to be standing near me & to be approving what I was doing. She looked very happy & very beautiful.
>
> This remaining branch seemed to be falling or leaning over the road in a way which obstructed a cart loaded with wood & being drawn by a single horse making its way down the road, the driver, a poor man, seemed to be throwing off some of the split pieces of wood to (so it seemed to me) make the load low enough to be able to pass under the limb which was obstructing him … all was clear – the end of the road, the foot of the hill, the last of the tree, myself with the axe doing the cutting & Joan standing by heartily approving & looking very beautiful.

King added, "What it means I do not know." Returning from the trip to Europe during which he had come to acknowledge his unquenchable sexual nature he wondered, "Is it the last lap of the journey homewards, have I cut off all the branches save the one remaining & which obstructs something – Is it some fault or weakness that remains … perhaps it is this branch that is to be hewn away & Joan will help me to it."[151]

He had another dream vision in which Joan appeared a few days before Parliament opened in January 1935. He saw himself in some small community in England such as Stratford-on-Avon where amateurs were rehearsing a new play. Before entering the theatre, he gave his ticket to an actress dressed in a black costume that concealed her identity. The lady in black put an arm around his back as if they had long known each other. King found her "most companionable and comforting – She gave me a sense of strength and power and vitality" and so offered to take up a small part in the play. "This would shew great sympathy with the whole theatrical movement as apparently at that moment I was again Prime Minister."

The scene being rehearsed featured a throne that occupied the centre of the stage. "Joan came into the picture as the lady in black drew nearer to me as we were watching the performance. Joan too drew nearer and seemed a little concerned. I thought of my loyalty to Joan, and while the attraction of the other was very great I felt I should cause Joan no pain nor give her cause for pain, so I withdrew towards her from the other, though there was great power in the other and seeming frailty at the moment or time in Joan. Her look of distress was sufficient to appeal to me."

King believed "the whole vision has to do with the political stage as it is being set for the ensuing battle – something being sent me to give me confidence in my right to assume sovereignty in control of parliament, not to permit dictatorship – to claim power as of right, where it relates to the people and is on their behalf. Who the lady in black was I do not know, unless it might be someone who has sought to claim sovereignty over me – over the mind & the affections. All these things are a part of the reality of the next sphere of existence – the reality of the things of the mind & the spirit – the material things are but appearances, are in reality all symbols or shadow shapes – the true and the false, the real and the seeming."[152]

---

151 Diary, November 12, 1934.
152 Diary, January 13, 1935.

Three months before the 1935 federal election, King had a dream "Vision of race successfully won" after having "looked long at dear mother's picture and prayed that some vision might be given me which would help to restore my faith and courage in the task ahead." He saw himself running in a long track race for which Stanley Baldwin, the Prime Minister of Great Britain, was the presiding judge. To his amazement, he came in first in the race. Later in the vision, the sixty-year-old King saw a gentleman of distinction, "a scholarly retired & rather austere type kissing a very beautiful lady at a window. She had her head as it were at the open window and he was kissing her because of her sheer loveliness and beauty. It seemed perfectly right that he should so enjoy the loveliness in human form. When she smiled, a laughing smile, he made one rush to her lips, something that seemed to me quite irresistible and natural, and right."

King awoke at this point. When he later wrote up this dream vision in his diary in his upstairs study in Kingsmere, he heard Joan in the garden beneath "looking very beautiful. I spoke to her through the window. In reading the little book today [Mary Wilder Tileston's *Daily Strength for Daily Needs*], I reread yesterday's messengers which speak of loving each other & not emphasizing faults etc. Last night, being fatigued, I was inclined to do this, and to feel exhausted & the vision lost. I believe the last part of the vision meant to be loving, to be kind with Joan, and to enjoy her beauty and loveliness of spirit – that it was not wrong so to do, but 'a present help in time of need.'"[153]

Joan Patteson, too, had dream visions about the nature of their relationship. Two weeks before the outbreak of World War II, she "told me of a vision she had had this morning and which was as follows. She had dreamt that we were married & were at Laurier House trying to decide which rooms should be occupied for different purposes. She seems to feel that the marriage was one of minds and souls, that it had no thought of human love, of any carnal nature, but a holy divine love – all was quiet and perfect peace."[154]

The PM's intimate friendship with Patteson complicated his decades-long debate with himself whether he should marry. He was never satisfied with his staff at Laurier House and needed someone

---

153 Diary, July 10, 1935.
154 Diary, August 14, 1939.

to organize the many dinners and other entertainments he held there for dignitaries, politicians, and other acquaintances. He wanted a wife who would not only foster the nobility of his character but also share his many personal and political obligations as Prime Minister. In 1926 he wrote, "It all comes down to this living alone business, of which I have spoken a good deal to Joan of late. She has come to see that it is better for me to marry if I can find the right one and she has bravely said she will do her part. She thinks I should marry someone young enough to have children. I would like a son and daughter if they were to be strong and noble characters."

Two years later he commented, "It is the great handicap in not being married, where life & ambitions could be shared with the wife, who would be keen to watch & further one's purest & highest interests." In 1929, he considered inviting his late brother's wife May and her two boys for a brief visit to Ottawa. "There is a chance of being able to see them for a day or two this summer & I shall do what I can to this end. The placing of a memorial over Max's grave will be an occasion when we all might be together. How I wish I were married to have someone help me in all this which is my obvious duty."[155]

King's defeat in the 1930 election and becoming Leader of the Opposition only increased his dissatisfaction with his bachelor status. When he heard that Joan's lost watch had been found in church, he was "so glad, for the loss would have seemed a bad omen, just as the recovery in church is a good one. I imagine the fastening was not complete, which is true of the relationship I have." Discussing the question of servants and running Laurier House after dinner with Patteson, King "got all out of sorts, really complained & grumbled at length & was most unkind towards Joan herself, when she has been doing what she can to help me. It is part of the reaction or complex which sets in so often when we are together. The unnaturalness of my solitary life at this stage. There is a real problem ahead. How I am going to manage alone both the house & my very responsible duties in politics?"[156]

Despite all her bravery, Patteson was jealous of King's other marriage prospects. After tea with Jessie Dunlap of Toronto in 1931 he noted, "it was amusing to see how keen Joan was on questioning her age, whether

---

155 Diary, January 23, 1926, June 17, 1928, July 15, 1929, and February 2, 1931.
156 Diary, November 30, 1930, and November 1, 1930. See also Diary, May 8, 1931.

I liked her etc. etc. It is quite apparent some are of the view it would be a good match." Alice Massey and Senator Cairine Wilson again invited King to dinner with Mrs. Dunlap, the widow of David Dunlap, co-founder of the Hollinger Gold Mine, in 1935. "These two wealthy women are evidently seeking to 'throw us together' for the good of the party," King noted. "How little they know what I really care for. I would rather have Joan's friendship with her pure sensitive and tender heart and faith and love than all that the world could bring."

In a dream vision the previous year in which he wondered whether it had revealed "the one intended for me," he esteemed Patteson higher than his English friend and financial supporter Violet Markham who "seemed to be moved by deep feeling – anxious to have me express a deep feeling for her." He acknowledged Markham's great soul, progressive politics and wealth and recalled that before he entered Parliament in 1908 "speaking to mother of her, and dear mother being so gentle in her words 'just to be sure.' I do not remember ever speaking to mother of any other of whom I had thoughts of the possibility of marriage." But of Patteson he recalled "the beauty of soul, just simple beauty – such as Joan possesses ... With Joan it is just the beauty of pure and loving soul wholly disinterested."[157]

Mackenzie King's return as Prime Minister in the 1935 election greatly increased his political workload and social obligations. In 1937, he "felt very tired all day – weary, weary, weary; I cannot throw off a sort of endless fatigue. I am lonely, see the mistake I have made in life in not marrying & continuing to live alone. I feel the years coming over me." After an argument with Patteson the following year, he "could not help saying aloud to myself – a selfish woman – It is at these moments I see the great mistake I have made in not marrying long ago & having a real companion to share my life. However, I have gone on as I have & shall have to continue rather than hurt her feelings; but for that I would certainly even yet get a wife & live the home life that would be most precious to me of all."[158]

King's and Patteson's liminal relationship would continue for another thirteen years, with Joan often embarrassed at social functions. The Prime Minister had already complained in 1935 that she

---

157 Diary, February 2, 1931, February 22, 1935, and October 1, 1934. King attended the opening of the Dunlap Observatory in May 1935.

158 Diary, November 7, 1937, and April 10, 1938.

lacked confidence when entertaining VIPs because of her undetermined social position. At a dinner at Laurier House for the Japanese minister and other diplomats, King very much needed "some one to help me get through a night like the kind; Joan is most helpful, but is so self-effacing that I have to make the moves myself." Patteson explained she did not like socializing because she found she was "very impressionable & weak in some ways, that if she got into social round, she would find it difficult to keep up her spiritualism etc. I pointed out that the very fact that she was psychic made this an inevitable danger; the impressions bad as well as good quickly register themselves."

When the Governor General, the Earl of Athlone, and his wife Princess Alice paid an official visit to Kingsmere in 1941, Joan pleaded illness and could not come to arrange flowers. Exasperated, King recorded, "I might have assumed as much – it is terrible how almost invariably she gets these 'inferiority' attacks. It seems to me they are that, where royalty or Government House is concerned ... It may have been her way of not wishing 'to receive' with me."[159]

Mackenzie King did acknowledge the tremendous support he was receiving from Patteson. In addition to her companionship and assistance at social functions, she gave him ideas for his speeches and brought relevant books and articles to his attention. C.P. Stacey recorded that Patteson had already assisted King in the 1921 election that made him Prime Minister. Four days before polling day, he bought her a gold bracelet for $125 [$1,917 in 2023 dollars] and inscribed it with a reference to Tennyson's *The Holy Grail*: "'A strength was in us from the vision,' *The Campaign of 1921*." Three months before the 1930 federal election, he spoke with his Minister of Finance, Charles Dunning, and "suggested he see if china from England could not be given additional preference. (This was a suggestion from Joan)." Three days later, "Council agreed to china (porcelain, ironstone etc.) coming in free from Great Britain; this was Joan's suggestion to me. With free tea, it will make a fine 'talking point' for elections." When Dunning brought down his budget in the House on May 1, "the free list British Preference, the countervailing duties, the free tea, free china sets etc. brought forth prodigious applause."

After his electoral defeat, King presented Patteson with a framed photo of himself "with the inscription 'to dear Joan with heartfelt gratitude for

---

159   Diary, December 28, 1935, March 13, 1935, and July 21, 1941, p. 4.

the help you have been to me during the years I have sought to serve my country as Prime Minister, Rex' – the date 1921-1930 engraved at top. Godfrey [sic] was there as it was opened & said it was a time when the tears could not be kept back. They were I think both greatly pleased. I told Joan it was my last stroke of the pen as P.M."[160]

In 1933, he heard of the death of Sir Henry Thornton whom he had appointed President of the Canadian National Railways in 1922 and drafted an appreciation which he read over to Joan. "She made a suggestion or two & later wrote out something which she read over the phone. I added another paragraph or two with ideas of hers & mine combined." When he was too tired in 1935 to work on a speech for delivery the next day and found it difficult even to think out the outline of his presentation, "Joan helped me very much by a suggestion or two over the telephone which she wrote out for me later in the day. I often think she is a sort of medium through which comes to me or is sent ideas which I seem too dense to acquire."

On election day in October 1935, he said to himself "'a new heaven and a new earth – God's will be done on earth as it is in heaven.' That was the prayer I prayed most earnestly this morning – also that I might be an instrument to do <u>His holy will</u>. These words are my desire beyond all else." In preparing a victory statement for the press "giving Bennett a broadside he deserved; I waited five years to do that," Joan was "most helpful in her critical attitude towards thoughts & expression." After the scope of his great electoral victory became clear, King "spoke to Joan of our victory – and of our consecration anew to God's service – at last the holy grail has been found. After many fights it has been won. We have seen the vision face to face." In 1941, he showed her page proofs for his collection of speeches, *Canada at Britain's Side*, and noted, "She was immensely pleased. She certainly has helped in the making of that book." When he read the Speech from the Throne to Patteson in January 1944, "she remarked that it needed some additional statement which would deal with human lives, their sacrifices, suffering, etc., instead of mere statistics and records which is what I myself had so keenly felt. I spent some time, after she left, in revising the speech."[161]

---

160 Stacey, *A Very Double Life*, 123. Diary, April 6 and 10, 1930, May 1, 1930, and August 9, 1930.

161 Diary, March 14, 1933, March 19, 1935, and October 14, 1935, pp. 1, 3, 5. Diary, August 15, 1941, and January 15, 1944.

Figure 17: King with Etta Wriedt, Joan Patteson, Pat I, and Derry at Kingsmere, August 28, 1934.

Joan Patteson's greatest contribution to King's life and career was serving as his supportive partner who participated in and affirmed his spiritualist pursuits. Joan, too, had vivid dreams which she asked the PM to interpret. After seeing his mother in a dream in 1929, "she asked me tonight if I thought she were going to die, as Mrs. Bleaney [Rachel Bleaney, the Kingston clairvoyant] had spoken of seeing her mother before the door open & she thought it could be for no one but for her." The following year King shared a dream he had on his birthday and "we had an earnest talk together of its significance & the significance of our lives in relation to res aeternalitis." In 1933 he wrote, "Whatever Joan picks up in this way of books, papers, etc. is apt to be significant; she is being used as a messenger, is a psychic person – one who quickly gets impressions." He also added, "Joan's visions usually concern us both and I have never known one not to have significance. Just now the note of prophecy seems to be the one we are getting."[162] Joan Patteson's participation in King's "conversations" over the "little table" is discussed in the next chapter.

---

162 Diary, January 15, 1929, January 4, 1930, October 8, 1933, and September 2, 1934.

CHAPTER 5

Conversations Over the Little Table

Mackenzie King's and Joan Patteson's lives were transformed when the Dominion Archivist, Arthur Doughty, introduced him to table rapping in November 1933. King had invited Doughty and his wife, Kathleen Rathburn (Browne) Doughty, as well as Madame Marika Pouliot, the wife of the Liberal MP for Témiscouata, Quebec, Jean-François Pouliot, for dinner at Laurier House. "We had an amazing evening," King recorded. "The first time I have seen table wrapping [sic] & having messages come through to me from father, mother, Max & Bella. There can be no shadow of doubt as to their genuineness. The messages to Tiny Doughty [Mrs. Doughty] were also amazing. I pray the warning given her may be heeded. It apparently is needed. Doughty is a dear soul and I am very fond of him." He added, "see the journal page 323 for the account" but the editor of the online diary, F.A. McGregor, annotated that this important description again was "not transcribed."[163]

T. Glen Hamilton and Lillian Hamilton had been similarly amazed when they first encountered table rapping a few months before Conan Doyle arrived in Winnipeg in 1923. The table rap message they received in their living room, letter by letter, "Go on with your work. More ahead. W.T. Stead," stimulated them to test mediumship and investigate psychic forces. Lillian Hamilton recalled that "Never before had I seen my husband so impressed. All had been simple, four people alone in the room while the fire light played over our hands, and yet out...there was a mind communicating who belonged to an invisible state."[164]

---

163   Diary, November 13, 1933.
164   Keshavjee, 49.

When Joan and Godfroy Patteson returned from a trip five days after Arthur Doughty initiated King in table rapping, King showed them the "little table" just before the arrival of the Rev. Dr. Thomas Eakin, principal of Knox College at the University of Toronto. "Joan and I had started to see if we could get results from placing our hands on the small table. It had spelt out the word 'Godfroy' & was under way with other words when we had to stop for Eakin. He joined us & the first word he spelled when he came in was 'Eak' – later we got quite a number of messages. See account of same [not transcribed]. It was our first experience at 'table wrapping' [sic] and was amazingly successful. I was delighted to find Joan and I had the power."[165]

No account has yet been located in which King described precisely how he and Patteson worked the "little table." In his diary he never refers – perhaps out of discretion – to a Ouija board though he did note in March 1934 that before going to church, he and Joan "began our 'conversations' over the Board & continued them after I returned, a most remarkable evening – see other book." He had written up five pages in his diary on his 59th birthday reporting that the "table" again "spelt out" very brief, repeated, responses from his family such as "love" and "happy birthday." When the initials of his mother, I.G.M.K., were spelled out, "I asked the question was I a 7 or an 8 month's child. Table spelt – <u>Seven</u>." Since the Toronto Art Gallery wanted to borrow King's paintings of William Lyon Mackenzie and his wife for an exhibition during Toronto's centennial year, he asked his deceased grandfather: "When & where were the paintings of grandmother and yourself made? The answer came spelled out <u>In Canada, in 1848</u>. (In getting the date the table spelled the numerals stopping after each one; we checked etc. by asking questions as before the Rebellion (answer No), after the Rebellion (Yes). After return to Canada (answer Yes). To the question, Do you know by whom? – The answer was <u>No</u>."

Through his communication on the "little table," King was able to compile a genealogy of his family that "takes me back 7 generations ... the answers were coming faster than I could work out the connection in my mind & write them down." He concluded that this conversation with twenty deceased family members in the spirit world "has been a truly amazing evidence not only of survival, knowledge, interest nec-

---

165 Diary, November 18, 1933.

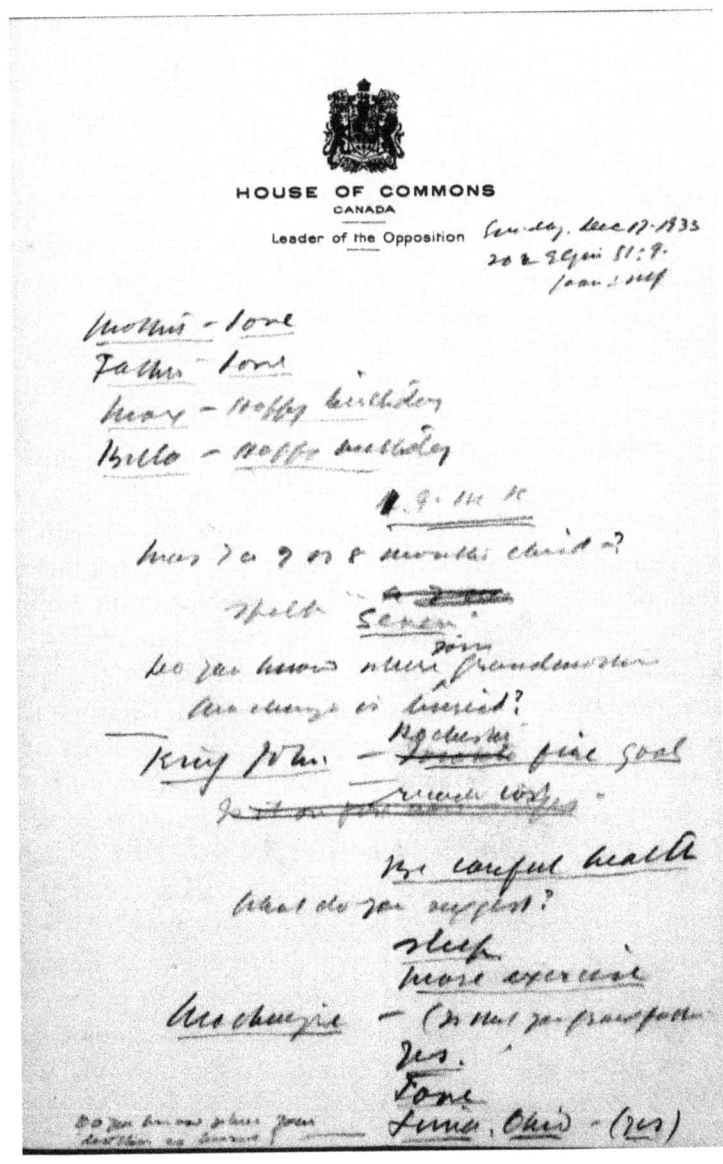

Figure 18: Record of King's and Joan Patteson's table rapping on his birthday, 202 Elgin St., Ottawa, December 17, 1933.

essary etc. etc. but of tenderness & love as well. How infinitely more interesting than anything else one can think of for a birthday party!" Joan Patteson, who believed she was related to the Scottish landscape painter John MacWhirter, communicated with "MacWhirter Father" and "MacWhirter Mother" as well as her deceased daughter. For her birthday the following year, King presented her with a framed copy of MacWhirter's painting, "flowers in spring in the Tyrol."[166]

In Susanna Moodie's description of spirit rapping with Kate Fox in 1855, discussed in Chapter 2, three responsive raps on the table to a question meant yes. C.P. Stacey reported, citing a note by King on a memorandum of a sitting at Joan's home at 202 Elgin Street on March 25, 1934, "Two raps meant Yes … and one presumably No. Where detail was required the table 'spelled out' the answer in code; the method usually accepted seems to have been that one rap meant A, two meant B, and so on through the alphabet. No doubt Rex and Joan used this system, though I have not found specific confirmation of it. Obviously it was a slow and cumbersome procedure." The awkwardness of this method may be reflected in King's diary entry of January 14, 1934: "At 5:30 spent an hour before dinner with Joan at the little table – too short a time for much, but enough to know that the loved ones are all near-by and close in touch. On little Nancy's say I decided to go to Church, when I was hesitating about it."

After initially struggling correctly to identify single words at their first table rapping session on November 18, 1933, King managed to capture brief statements over the weeks that followed. Since his transcriptions of spirit communications soon extended up to a page in length, Stacey commented, "It is rather hard to imagine this sort of thing being laboriously spelled out letter by letter." He speculated, "Is it possible that King had turned himself into a medium and believed himself to be receiving, in his head, messages which he repeated aloud for the benefit of Joan Patteson and then wrote down?" Stacey admitted, "How the rapping was produced I do not pretend to explain; doubtless there was some form of 'unconscious pressure.'" But he concluded, "the matter of technique is not of primary importance. What matters is that Mackenzie King was convinced that he was receiving communications from the Beyond, and that he made a full record of those communications on paper."[167]

---

166   Diary, March 18, 1934, and December 17, 1933. Stacey, *A Very Double Life*, 119. Diary, November 27, 1934. Patteson had given King MacWhirter's *Sketches from Nature* for his birthday in 1930. See Diary, December 21, 1930, January 23, 1935, and July 5, 1935.

167   Ballstadt, 91. Stacey, *A Very Double Life*, 172, 173, 174. Diary, January 14, 1934. In his biography, Allan Levine thought that as late as June 9, 1935, after the memorial service for Governor General Lord Byng at the Capitol Theatre

Stacey's hypothesis that King became his own medium and heard answers to questions in his own head is supported by Percy James Philip's recollection of private conversations about Spiritualism with the Prime Minister while crossing the Atlantic for the Paris Peace Conference on the S.S. *Georgic* in July 1946. King recorded, "Had Philip of the N.Y. Times in to dinner" on the train to Halifax to board the *Georgic*, that he also had dinner with the reporter on ship, and that he had "a short walk around the deck with Philip of N.Y. Times." While crossing the Atlantic, he dictated to Edouard Handy from notes two sittings with Florence Jane Sharplin and one with Helen Hughes in London on October 26, 30, and 31, 1945 and subsequently checked Handy's transcriptions of the sittings. "If one believes in God and a life after death," he told Philip in one of their conversations, "it is inevitable that one must believe that the spirits of those who have gone take an interest in the people and places they loved during their lives on earth. It is the matter of communication that is difficult. For myself I have found that the method of solitary, direct, communion is best. After my father and mother died I felt terribly alone. But I also felt that they were near me. Almost accidentally I established contact by talking to them as if they were present and soon I began to get replies."[168]

The Prime Minister also communicated with his family in his dreams. After his last night in England in November 1945, he recorded, "I slept well last night. Just before waking, had a very beautiful experience and heard some voice whispering to me: 'My peace I give unto you, not as the world giveth give I unto you; let not your heart be troubled.' I am sure it was my mother's voice speaking to me on this last morning of this memorable visit to England." Before he became Leader of the Liberal Party in 1919, King's benefactor Peter Larkin and his wife Jean hoped that he would fall in love and marry their daughter, Aileen. Fourteen years later, Aileen wrote King that

---

in Ottawa, "the Pattesons and King summoned the spirit of Lord Byng at one of their mystical seances around his 'little table,' at which the dear and departed communicated through a series of knockings." He also refers to "King's plea for assistance at a table-rapping sitting at Kingsmere on July 26, 1936." Levine, *King*, 165, 259.

168 Diary, July 18, 21, 22, 24, and 25, 1946. Philip, "I Talked with Mackenzie King's Ghost," reprinted in Colombo, 177. Transcriptions of the Sharplin séances on October 26 and 31, 1945, and the Hughes sitting on October 30, 1945, are published in Appendix A of Volume 2.

she was selling all her possessions and was entering a convent. King was uncertain whether he should try to dissuade her from withdrawing from the world. He "knelt down & prayed for guidance as to what I might say or should say in replying…I spoke to Mr. Larkin – in my thoughts, and asked him to let me know what it was best to do. Before I had retired, I had come to the conclusion that my vision had meant to signify 'Consent.'"[169]

This form of mental communication is probably what Mackenzie King meant when he recorded in his diary that "higher & unseen intelligences flash thoughts to us, which we take up" and that he received similar messages from the Beyond "in 'words' over the Table." Reviewing his debates in Parliament in 1938 regarding a new Canadian flag, political corruption and the exclusion of Orientals, the Prime Minister noted that "while speaking I am sure I was being 'impressed' with thought – 'inspired' – something coming from spirit to spirit. It seems to me that out of 'the conversations' at the Table & direct voice, I have received clearly that the spirits – who have gone – continue to influence our thoughts, that in their work further we attract those we seek & get impressions to the degree of our receptivity."

King and several of his mediums such as Rachel Bleaney, Etta Wriedt, Gladys Osborne Leonard, and the psychic Ellen Elliott often used the word "impressions" for the spirit messages they believed they were receiving from the Beyond but distinguished these from thought transfers or messages from the subconscious. So, when King ate dinner at Joan Patteson's in 1934 and "had a few minutes at table afterwards" during which "Jacob Koehler, who died yesterday and whose body is to be buried tomorrow came & talked, spoke of being with grandfather," King added, "He was not the least in my thoughts."

He contrasted "impressions" sent from the spirit world with subconscious thoughts and "conversations" over the "little table" after another séance the following year. "It may be one's own wish was a controlling factor in what was received…It may be to get accurate results we must not summon but await those who came – we shall see," he recorded in his diary. "I can see where what was said had been impressing itself on my mind – it would seem that the recorded table conversation bears out the view that these impressions come apart altogether from the record – which might be regarded as in

---

169 Diary, November 3, 1945, and November 21, 1933. The 1945 citation is from John 14:27.

part automatic or mechanical in view of what precedes. The real 'impression' is the one experienced as we work and write. That is why, no doubt, we are told it is as well to use the table only occasionally – not to let what it says gain undue emphasis or proportion in one's mind." King concluded that when he acted upon the genuine "impressions" from the spirit world, "quite apart from the table…I was a medium in a larger way for the forces beyond."[170]

C.P. Stacey's hypothesis that King's "conversations" over the "little table" were a form of automatic writing is supported by a diary entry in March 1935 when his father and grandfather incorrectly informed him that Prime Minister Bennett was dying. "Some mundane influence has crept in with regard to what is said of Bennett," he noted. "Over the Radio at 11 came word that Perley [Sir George Perley, the Conservative MP and Minister without portfolio] had been talking with him and that he was much better. I had a sort of feeling when the word 'death' was mentioned that it was not grandfather speaking – or father save in part. Yet I took it all down as it came – it may even be correct."

The incident troubled him for several days and he returned to it in his diary. There was "something false coming in when I was talking with father & grandfather re Bennett being unconscious etc. & going to die – there was an evil spirit crept in there. When Joan and I talked of the casting out of devils into swine, I had been reading that chapter [Mark 5] that morning and felt certain that it related to the kind of evil spirits that creep into our flesh – possess our bodies at times – that something of the sort must have happened last Sunday night through fatigue … the voice that crept in 'savored' to be at the time, not of father not of grandfather – not of God – but of what some men might wish."

Despite his immense hatred of Bennett, King did not consider whether the wish for his death emanated from his own mind. Over the years, he had a number of spirit controls who brought other spirits with whom he wished to communicate. One of these controls was Phillip and King noted – making the connection between automatic writing and "little table conversations" – that "I will ask Phillip tonight re all this, for it has troubled me a lot in getting at the truth through the mediumship of automatic writing (or rather 'conversation of table.')" Commenting on his own writing up of spiritual experiences

---

170 Diary, April 18, 1934, June 20, 1934, p. 8, February 20, 1938, p. 2, January 21, 1934, and January 27, 1935.

in the pages of his diary, he also added, "This I believe to be automatic writing and true, some spirit is influencing this page, or my writing upon it." That the thought of Bennett's demise emanated from King's mind is suggested by the fact that it returned a week later at a "conversation" in Joan's home. "We each discerned in a moment where an outside evil influence came in re Bennett being paralysed – Fatigue I think is largely responsible." King had also noted the previous year that in reading the verses of his devotional "little books," "I have just been struck by how the style of repetition of the first part corresponds with much we get through automatic writing on the table."[171]

Stan McMullin, in *Anatomy of a Seance: A History of Spirit Communication in Central Canada,* noted that the Ouija board "usually has a polished surface upon which the alphabet has been printed. Two people rest their hands lightly on a tripod, which moves of its own accord over an alphabet printed on the board and stops with its apex pointing to letters to spell out messages." If King and Patteson indeed placed their hands on a Ouija tripod in this manner – rather than King being the automatic writing medium for spirit communications – the experience must also have been a sensuous one, once again confirming C.P. Stacey's conviction that the spirit messages received came not from the Beyond but "subconsciously out of King's own head."[172]

In January 1934, just before an important session in Parliament, King entered in his diary that "Before waking I had another very remarkable vision which I recorded immediately after breakfast and prayers."

> It would seem from the directions given me by father, as to the reading of Corinthians, the 'coming through' of the Hindoo priest Karo Mura when he did, the chapters read yesterday and today, that their 'intelligences' not only were working together, but were doing so in the light of what was going to happen some time hence – that the future, the past and present to them are one. I was deeply impressed by what I recorded. Even more amazing was the mere chance by which Joan stayed for dinner tonight and we took an hour together afterwards to talk 'over the table.' That I should ask if Meyers [sic, Frederic W.H. Myers] were present, as though he had suggested it to me, and then to obtain from him direct confirmation of his having sent the vision

---

171 Diary, March 17, 22, and 31, 1935, and November 21, 1934.
172 McMullin, 110. Stacey, *A Very Double Life,* 174.

at the instance of Karo Mura and that my interpretation etc. was correct. What he told me in addition was more wonderful still – a consecration to God's service in the service of Humanity – God's grace having saved me from my sins and His love chosen me to help to work out his will 'on earth as it is in Heaven.' – The supreme prayer of my life heard, and answered with the assurance of God's strength & vision being vouchsafed in time of need. There have been forecastings of this all along the way, but nothing so direct & immediate and now that it has come, I can hardly believe it. The time chosen is that which above all others I would have – just before the important speech on the address which opens the real work of the session.[173]

The following week, in Patteson's home, the two again communicated with "the beautiful spirit Koramura." A month later, however, after he had sent a wire responding to a letter from another romantic interest, the Princess Cantacuzene, King and Joan had a quite different encounter with Koramura. At a sitting in Laurier House, they were "expecting to speak with the loved ones. The experience was grievously disappointing (See other volume) but one of amazing enlightenment in some respects." The following day he added in his diary, "The experience of last night has been like a hideous nightmare; it was all so subtle, and of a character to cause one to feel that the 'conversations' had to [be?] admitted, but as phenomena were what the Roman Catholic Church says 'the work of the devil.' On the other hand, a clear head & the scientific method of approach enables one to see them in their true perspective & brings out in bolder relief than ever the conflicts of forces that seek to gain the soul, or are fighting for the souls of men. (All this I have written up fully in the other volume, the reference here is needed to giving the colouring to the day's events.)" H. Blair Neatby cited parts of the March 9 diary not transcribed for the online LAC diaries. One of the messages King and Patteson received "was in praise of love and King recorded that both he and Joan sensed they were being tempted by earthly passion. Joan wanted to end the session immediately but King persuaded her to go on 'for scientific reasons.' The messages then 'became very personal and direct, so much so that I would not write down what was said.'"[174]

---

173 Diary, January 27, 1934.
174 Diary, February 6, 1934, and March 9 and 10, 1934. Neatby, *William Lyon*

C.P. Stacey was also able to examine King's "other volume" before his executors burned his spiritualist binders in 1977. He wrote, "There had been a sitting on 9 March 1934 which strengthens my belief that the relationship between King and Mrs. Patteson was entirely platonic, even if King sometimes wished that it was something more. A 'Hindoo' priest of ancient times, 'Koramura,' spoke, and at the end of a long rigmarole said, 'Hail God who has ordained that you should love each other,' and more to the same effect. King recorded, 'Joan at once protested … She took her hands off the table and shook them away from her as if to protect herself … King wished to go on and for a time they did. But next morning he decided that Koramura was 'a pagan spirit that I do not want to have around.' No more was heard of him." Yet at another sitting at Laurier House the following month, "As soon as we began an evil spirit came in with 'glory Halleluiah' God wants etc. We stopped it at once & later got mother and her verification of the fact that it had been an evil spirit that came in at the start, that came in last week etc. It seems the mention of & thought of them serves to bring them. Unbelief is a cause – pure thoughts the strongest armour."[175]

In May 1934, King experienced "quite the most remarkable of all my psychical and religious experiences … Nothing comparable to what I have known and experienced today has ever come before." He awoke one morning "with a feeling that some voice near me was speaking of 'kindly thoughts and words' – these related to the natural experiences of life, those having to do with human relationships, including those of birth. It is difficult to describe but was as it were the presence of the Holy spirit in relation to human love and its expression in the birth of a child." In contrast with such pure love, sexual desire for mere physical gratification prevented spiritual growth. King thought of "our natures being like a mixture in a glass, which could settle and clear, and that we came nearer the spiritual realm as all material things settled. I was going to speak to Joan of it as evidence of how we got our best impressions, the soul rising into the region of clearer vision, nearer the source of all knowledge as it came out of the murk of doubt, disbelief & strife."

However, during a sitting after Joan's birthday anniversary dinner that November, they encountered yet another evil spirit "of untruth &

Mackenzie King, The Prism of Unity, 1932-1939, 74-75.

175 Stacey, *A Very Double Life*, 183. Diary, April 20, 1934.

carnal affection ... on mention of a name in London associated with a love affair there ... Joan & I were frightened we might encounter an experience such as we had once before and which neither of us wish ever to encounter again & most of all, not on an evening such as tonight's anniversary."[176]

Despite these occasional encounters with "evil spirits," King's "conversations" over the "little table" were so real for him that he not only believed in but also took guidance from them. As C.P. Stacey observed, "The year 1934 is perhaps the moment in King's life when he came closest to losing contact with reality." In June, he had admonished himself "not to be disobedient to the heavenly vision, to do as I am directed" and marvelled that a "little table" conversation with his dead father at Kingsmere "was almost like being in the room together – 'the reception' was exceedingly good, everything came through as clear as possible. It was a marvellous experience & made me feel father's presence as very real."

By the end of the year, he had come to believe as much in the reality of these "conversations" with spirits of the departed in the Beyond as he did in the reality of the Bible, his dream visions and reading the tea leaves in his tea cup. We are fortunate that F.A. McGregor included in what is now the existing online diary such numerous and detailed extracts from King's 1934 loose-leaf spiritual notebooks later burned by his executors. Considering the political and social context of the time, it is understandable what so infuriated Stacey.[177]

R.B. Bennett had been dealing with labour and social unrest resulting from the Depression since becoming Prime Minister in 1930. Unemployment exceeded thirty per cent in many regions of the country. Tens of thousands of young, unemployed men were sent to 237 remote work camps in British Columbia, Alberta and other provinces established in October 1932 by an order-in-council. It authorized a government expenditure of $668,000 [$14,200,000 in 2023 dollars] for their construction. By the time King closed the camps in 1936, one hundred seventy thousand unemployed had laboured in them.

The Communist Party infiltrated the camps and agitated for improved living and working conditions through the Relief Camp Workers' Union. In August 1931, Bennett had used Section 98 of the

---

176 Diary, May 20, 1934, and November 27, 1934.
177 Stacey, *A Very Double Life*, 176. Diary, June 11 and 10, 1934.

Criminal Code, which made it illegal to advocate force or violence to promote political change, to imprison Communist Party leaders Tim Buck, Sam Carr and six others for unlawful association and seditious conspiracy. When a delegation from the Communist-led Canadian Labour Defence League travelled to Ottawa in November 1933 to protest the imprisonment of the labour leaders in the Kingston penitentiary, Bennett had the delegation forcibly removed from his office.[178]

Reading the 1934 diaries explains what made C.P. Stacey so exasperated at what he considered King's superstitions. On April 5, King finished Geraldine Cummins' book, *The Road to Immortality*, purporting to be a description of the afterlife communicated by the late F.W.H. Myers. He recorded, "This book has thrown more light on my path, done more to convince me & to confirm my beliefs than anything I recall having read. I find in its every page, paragraph & here & there line something that confirms an experience or answers a call – and what is most remarkable – tells as of scientific truth much that I have worked out in my own thoughts & researches & had in my consciousness for some time – some years. It has made the whole of the Bible truer than ever, given life to its passages & strengthened my belief – and put me again on solid foundations where there had come to be uncertainty. It is epoch making with much still to be gathered from it. I am deeply grateful to Myers."[179]

The following day King took Joan and Godfroy Patteson to the opening sale of paintings at the James Wilson auction room on Sparks Street between Elgin and Metcalfe and – from 8:30 to midnight – spent $540 [$12,000 in 2023 dollars] on nine canvases, "exceedingly good bargains." They included four scenes of Venice, a Roman ruin, two of sheep at eventide, "one an interior of a Welsh home – a little family – the abode of the poor & a little landscape. Each made its special appeal to my soul – seemed to give me the inspiration I wanted – the beautiful bright blue of the Venetian skies, a city rising out of the sea – the sort of thing that John had in mind in Revelation. I am certain there is a spirit helping me & directing me in all this, bringing me to the realm of light."

He was so delighted with the paintings he had purchased "to keep my spirit soaring" and so elated by viewing their distant vistas that

---

178 Boyko, 314, 317, 319, 324-326.
179 Diary, April 5, 1934.

when he left the auction room he was completely disoriented. "For a few minutes I did not know where my home was. I thought of the Roxborough – I had to ask where I lived to Joan & Godfroy. I must have been on another plane – of light altogether ... I really did not know just where I was in the car & had to ask where my home was so I saw Lay driving on – It seemed to be the Roxborough & Laurier House a long way off. It was a sensation I have never experienced before – the lights of the city – with its darkness & long streets & open park space were for a moment like Paris or some European city."[180]

On April 8, he also recorded his belief that "a group beyond are working together to aid me, in being an instrument to work out better conditions re labour. How happy I would be if this all works out no one can say. I would rather have my life count for the people in that way than anything else in the world." Joan Patteson assured him, "the meaning of the vision I had keeps coming stronger than ever to me – that you are the one to guide the forces at work, that you cannot help the torrent coming on, but you can turn it into quiet ways. – I said that is the whole thing. I welcome the torrent of social unrest and change, but I want to direct it through the right channel – that being our parliamentary institutions, if it don't [sic] go through that channel it will overwhelm the people – This I believe with all my heart – I believe equally and this I told Joan that a group are working over yonder to use me – and equally her as means to work out this change – that Sir Wilfrid [Laurier], Sir John [Macdonald], Lord Oxford, Mr. Larkin, father, grandfather, Goldwin Smith & others and most of all perhaps [F.W.H.] Myers & some of his group William James, Balfour, President Eliot [of Harvard] & others: All seeking to work out what is best and intend to use me to that end. That in all things I am being guided 'from on high.'"[181]

When he had to speak in Parliament ten days later attacking Bennett's Marketing Act, "a terrible measure, most important debate," he "felt all day as I was preparing being 'impressed' with certain ideas & thoughts." Consulting the "little table" with Joan, "it was interesting how the conversation began at once on the really important theme."

> I spoke about tomorrow's debate – I notice they usually wait to be asked questions before saying much. I had spoken to

---

180 Diary, April 6, 1934.
181 Diary, April 8, 1934.

Lapointe about the Act being unconstitutional, but never saw it in the larger sense & meaning of the word as I began to the more [sic] I worked upon it. Sir Wilfrid's saying to refer to it as 'unconstitutional' helped me very much. Also his reference to Stubb's Charters [William Stubbs, *Select Charters and Other Illustrations of English Constitutional History*. Oxford: Clarendon, 1845], which I had thought of, not consulted & finally the reference to the British North America Act – Trade & Commerce – Gladstone's reference to Greene [John Greene, *A Lecture on Magna Charta*. Bury St. Edmunds: G. Thompson, 1850] & 'great traditions' was another sound note – the advice to <u>make plain my points</u> was most needed. I had been hesitating about speaking at length – Lincoln's advice – to let them see I knew what I was talking about was excellent – and also to stress <u>Limited Production</u> – that gave me the key to an underlying principle & a third division of the speech etc. The conversation was as follows: [not transcribed.]

King added about this advice from the spirit world, "I am inclined to believe re so-called mind-reading that these higher & unseen intelligences flash thoughts to us, which we take up, rather than it being 'our thoughts' which are being expressed over from them." Finishing up his hour-long presentation to Parliament the following morning, he "went to work on my speech for the afternoon with the full conviction that I was being helped by those who spoke to me last night and others as well. Indeed I modelled what I thought of saying largely on what was told or said to me … I kept in mind Mr. Gladstone's advice to speak long enough to make my points clear."

When he prepared for the discussion of the Marketing Act in committee the following month, King "got a very clear perspective of the Imperial situation as I worked and felt quite sure I was being 'helped.'" He also believed he saw Wilfrid Laurier communicating with him in the tea leaves of three cups of tea at his luncheon on April 18, 1934. The leaves of the third cup showed "there was as distinctly as could be, two people, a man and a woman, the latter following, who had just gotten out of the aeroplane & were going forward. It looked exactly like Sir Wilfrid and Lady Laurier. To me the whole was as clear as could be; Sir Wilfrid was coming to help me. I was being given that assurance."[182]

---

182 Diary, April 18 and 19, 1934, May 20, 1934, and April 18, 1934.

Figure 19: Joan Patteson at Kingsmere Lake, mid-1920s.

Joan Patteson at times tried to moderate King's obsession with the occult. At a "little table" sitting, his mother informed them that one of the Laurier House servants, Nancy, had become pregnant by another servant, MacLeod, and "gave directions of first importance." Though MacLeod would confess his responsibility the next day, "Joan became so alarmed that she did not want to talk further." During a walk earlier in the month, King had "talked of psychic research, getting a little roused (unnecessarily) in trying to clear away what seemed to me a determination on her part to close her mind to some things & not keep records etc. I am anxious that we get truth & wisdom."

When he informed her that the number five had appeared very distinctly to him "and also the number one seven and three one – all of which spoke of the immediate presence of those who were guiding me, Joan said she thought I was wrong in expecting so much, particularly regarding names and numbers which were always difficult, that she doubted if they over there had knowledge of time etc." Regarding such difficulties and errors in spirit transmissions, "Joan thinks proper names etc. & dates not possible – I believe both possible but most difficult." King was impressed by one of Patteson's remarks which he recorded, "'You know I am truthful,' she said, 'and also I must hold to the truth as I see it,' etc. That I wanted her to do. 'There has been great subtlety in what has been said to us, in advising us to hold fast to the truth,'" she continued. "'I confess when we went on to question of marriage & date of & of death I did not like it & felt it was going too far.' (…..)"[183]

King's belief in the veracity of his communications with spirits in the Beyond was severely tested in 1934 after he sought to use his "conversations" over the "little table" to foresee the future in the political arena. When he visited Homer Watson in Doon again in April 1934 while campaigning in a by-election in the riding of Oxford South, Ontario, he had full confidence in his own mediumistic abilities. The tea leaves in his teacup already predicted a Liberal victory on April 12. He had a feeling that "these <u>tea leaves were 'thought formations'</u> sent as a further evidence of the truth that is being revealed in these many ways 'nothing too small' to be ordered by the Father of all, nothing that cannot be known by faith. If we win Oxford by a good majority, it certainly sounds the doom of the present administration & will mean the elections this fall of a certainty." King was scheduled to speak for two hours the next day, his speech also to be broadcast over radio, to a large audience in Ingersoll on behalf of the Liberal candidate, Almon Secord Rennie, and spent the night with the Watsons. After dinner, the painter showed King some of his automatic writing between slates. "I showed Mr. & Miss [Phoebe] Watson the Hamilton psychic pictures, tried the table with Watson & got some splendid results … Miss Watson made the notes as I called out the words. (…..)" They reached Senator Lawrence Alexander Wilson – who had just died on March 3, 1934 – and asked him whether the Liberal candidate will win the by-election. "Yes – by how much – <u>1600</u>. (…..)"[184]

After returning to Ottawa, King transcribed another "conversation" with Laurier just before the by-election in Oxford South. "Question: Sir Wilfrid is it – Yes – Glad to be here tonight. Look out for a big

---

183 Diary, April 22 and 2, 1934, June 12 and 4, 1934, and July 5, 1934.
184 Diary, April 12 and 13, 1934.

majority tomorrow – Gag the Tories. Question: How big a majority do you think we will get? – 1800. What you saw in the tea cup is correct. Glad you believe in this medium of transmission. Tea cup will tell you much." When he had examined his tea leaves, King had only seen the number 16 but realized that "the 2 little dots were not leaves but decimals … they would make the 1600. I wrote it down at 1800, though feeling 1600 correct." Joan laughed when he told her about the tea cup but King explained, "it was from the higher realm, the one of light (or beyond) where there is knowledge of all – past, present & future – that the thought comes in answer to prayer which gives the expression in the leaves. This medium of transmission – it is one of the very many media. It may not be given to those who have not yet gone that far to know save what they are told … This source I have worked out myself, as I have the bible & little books – and now the table which I find I can use with others & may be able to operate alone."

Initial election returns ranged from 800 to 1,000 but finalized at "about 1500, or 1600 majority." King had become anxious "less on account of the election than for fear Sir Wilfrid's prophecy might not work out." In the final election results, Rennie did indeed defeat his Conservative opponent, Donald Sutherland, 6,692 votes to 5,199. King was given a great reception by Liberal MPs when he entered the House while R.B. Bennett "never even looked up or across at me but kept his head down in much the same way he does whenever I get up to speak."[185]

Homer Watson was amazed by the accuracy of Senator Wilson's election prediction in their "little table" conversation of April 13, 1934. "The prediction gave you a majority of 1600. I notice there is a discrepancy between the Conservative figures and the Liberal. When all is vetted I believe the figure given by the prediction will prove to be accurate. This is wonderful. It shows how our friends on the other side think of us and in consideration of more forces to work for our benefit. They can influence by the power of mind and thought the natures of us in these material realms." King had telegrammed the painter the day before, "Returns just received indicate splendid victory South Oxford. Please keep strictly private and confidential our conversation Friday evening." Watson assured King that "our friends

---

185 Diary, April 15 and 16, 1934.

Figure 20: Homer Watson surrounded by spirits, 1930.

over there know and influence us more than the people here have any idea of" and that he and his sister Phoebe "will keep to ourselves all that was received in the conversation on Friday night. I was impressed and delighted to see you had such psychic power."[186]

Mackenzie King's certainty about Wilfrid Laurier's prophetic powers was shattered by the provincial elections in Ontario and Saskatchewan in June 1934. Sir Wilfrid had prophesied to him in a "conversation" the day before the election that Ontario Premier

---

186 King to Watson, April 16, 1934. Watson to King, April 17, 1934.

Mitch Hepburn would lose his own seat and that his Liberal Party would go down to defeat. King believed the prophecy was true and that it "will confirm other prophecies." Instead, the Liberals swept both provinces. King was "really more anxious (at heart) to have the prophecy fulfilled, that my faith might not suffer a shock, than I was to see a great Liberal victory in both provinces. It could not be otherwise." He felt "an anguish of mind and heart, in discovering that this 'prophecy' had failed, that Sir Wilfrid had not had the knowledge evidently required and had seen only so much of the whole. I did not want to have any feeling of disloyalty to him, nor to doubt it was he who was speaking, as in fact I did not – I believe it was he but that he was unable to foretell, had based his knowledge on what he had gathered, but the knowledge was insufficient."

Despite his initial disillusionment, King "felt it was all for a purpose, that behind this disappointment in this feature, there was some great good which I would soon see, that God was helping me to get a clearer vision of His laws and purposes, that it was all to help me in an understanding of psychic phenomena and spiritual realities." He nevertheless dreaded "what the undermining effects of inevitable disbelief & doubt might come to mean." In order not to lose his faith in spirit communication, he rationalized that "the knowledge of those who spoke is inadequate – it means that <u>it is not for them or for us to know the future</u> – or <u>the time or occasion save as God Himself reveals them to us</u>. There are some who are taking on themselves the function of directing and advising who have not the right or the power so to do. Even if it meant I had to conclude that Sir Wilfrid who has done so much for me, and who has my interests so greatly at heart, and can have but one motive & desire, has still not passed into realms of light sufficiently clear to have the larger vision – out of partial darkness into the full light – I must so conclude … Also I felt that it was meant to teach me that 'Thou shalt have no other gods before me' – that <u>God alone could reveal the truths that related to the future</u>, with certainty of no failure."

King therefore determined that he should only trust communications from his own family in the Beyond because of their greater spirituality and since they had put all their faith in God's will. "I thought <u>our own family</u>, in the value its members attached to <u>spiritual things</u>, were nearer to God than others whose careers had been greater in the eyes of men, that in the sight of God they were the greatest in the kingdom of Heaven. I thought of <u>little Bell</u> & <u>dear mother</u> having <u>a spiritual power</u> much greater than that possessed even by Sir Wilfrid because of a greater spirituality, also of <u>dear father</u> with his unswerving loyalty to <u>truth & justice</u> & unwillingness to condescend to any dishonourable act, equally <u>Mackenzie and his hatred of corruption</u>."

We can trace King's thought process in explaining the failure of Laurier's prophetic powers thanks to F.A. McGregor who excerpted no less than thirteen pages from his June 20, 1934, entry in his spiritual notebooks for inclusion in the existing online diary. These show that King concluded that he had been shown the sin of blasphemy, "of <u>those who would appear as gods in the eyes of men</u> – or rather who would seek to take to themselves what belongs to God in the matter of foretelling events, seeking to direct, where conscience – that 'celestial and immortal voice' should be every man's guide – not any lesser powers."

He affirmed his belief that "Christ alone was the revelation of God – and that <u>only as we approach his spiritual nature can we be like him in power – of healing, of foretelling etc. etc.</u> I went to my chair & knelt & prayed to God to let me have no other Gods – to <u>follow Him only & the One who revealed His life</u> & nature to mankind. I prayed God to forgive Sir Wilfrid if in anything he had presumed to say too much and to help him to rise higher out of the earth influences … if these in any way impeded his upward and onward progress, to bless him – to forgive me, for having trusted any voices that I should not have trusted & to lead me too onward & upward."

In retrospect, King was struck by the fact that he had not received a dream vision prior to the Ontario and Saskatchewan provincial elections that would have revealed their outcomes. He had relied on the "conversations" over the "little table" and "in listening to other voices, I had not sought the vision – been satisfied with the lesser & not been concerned with the greater, had been content with what was nearer earth & not sought my intuition and knowledge from 'the highest heaven.'" He asked God to send him a vision "which would let me know my prayer had been heard & which would give me light & comfort & truth."

That night he dreamt he was near the edge of the sea with the ocean rolling in in a complete sweep beyond and believed this "Vision of 'complete sweep'" referred to the elections in Ontario and Saskatchewan and that God had answered his prayers. "I began to feel more strongly than ever the truth of what I have all along felt, that those alone who are spiritually great can know & reveal God & His knowledge, that the visions which I have been receiving were true – <u>they have never failed</u> – because being inspired by those who know and believe in God and Christ as the revelation on earth to man of God as He is in Heaven – the infinite being revealed to the finite, in terms that the finite can comprehend – that much that I have received in 'words' over the Table – has been true – but not all – true where it has come from the highest sources, less true as the truth became obscured by the human channels through which it had to pass – or the souls of men not yet lifted into the highest realms of light and truth." King's mother and Joan Patteson held special positions in this Great Chain of Being between himself and God. "I thought of mother as the sublime human revelation I had known in life itself of God-like character – and Joan as embodying the Spirit of Truth and many similar attributes."[187]

Mackenzie King was almost immediately shocked again by Laurier's false prophetic powers. He had fiercely attacked Prime Minister Bennett in January 1934 for reviving the practice – in abeyance since 1919 – of recommending Canadians to the British Crown for knighthoods. He believed it was the difference "between Tory & Liberal – the power in people not the Sovereign – in House of Commons not the throne," and that the names of those knighted would be announced on King George's birthday on June 3. "Then will come the names of those who have been carried away by false standards – poor weak vain creatures."

C.P. Stacey, who was able to consult King's later-burned spiritual notebooks, reported, "on 13 May his father's spirit gave him a long list, including Bill Herridge (who had become a close associate of Bennett and had married his sister, and who was now Canadian Minister in Washington), H.J. Cody, Vincent Massey, and Herbert Marler." What Stacey missed was that on May 13, 1934, King, in his regular diary, also indicated that an evil spirit was again intruding in his and Patteson's "little table" conversations by conveying thoughts of a sexual nature. After church, at a session in Joan's home, "Intervening was a conversation in which some third party came in, someone who was deceptive. I had at church feelings which have disturbed me in the past. It was singular how very strong were some of the feelings

---

187   Diary, June 19 and 20, 1934.

& impulses as we were recording conversations almost as if an evil influence were again at work seeking in a subtle way to mislead, both Joan & myself. While there was evidence of reality in the conversations, there was as it were, control of thoughts from which one would wish to be released & I felt this was perhaps the means to the end of release that was being sought. (…..)."[188]

On June 3, 1934, to his question "Can you tell us about the knighthoods?" "a lying spirit" King identified as "K.L.M." gave him and Patteson a list of ten names. But that evening news came that only Dr. Frederick Banting, one of the discoverers of insulin, and Dr. Charles Saunders, the inventor of Marquis wheat, had been knighted. He had a dream vision in which Joan had moved to another city but had not given him the number of her new house. He made a frantic search, "having some doubt as to Joan not letting me know," and entered doors that led to "'fake' astrologers – palmists – mind-readers etc. I said to myself, these people are not genuine (…..)."

This made King wonder about other spirit predictions, such as Bennett's impending marriage to Hazel Beatrice Colville. "I began to think there had been deception, that an evil spirit had crept in & something 'faked.'" His tea leaves suggested the announcement of the full honour list of titles would be made on Dominion Day. On June 24, he and Patteson had a "conversation" with Laurier, Clifford Sifton, his brother Max, and F.W.H. Myers, "quite the most significant & sacred evening we have had yet. I felt we were getting very near to Reality – to Truth & Justice & the source of Love & Power. The record is complete in the other book." Yet again, no additional knighthoods were announced on July 1, 1934, "making clear we were wrong in what we get via the means of communication used (the table wrapping [sic])."[189]

He consulted his other means of spiritual communication beginning with the inspirational "little books," Mary Wilder Tileston's *Daily Strength for Daily Needs* and Harry Emerson Fosdick's *The Meaning of Prayer*, which he read every morning along with his Bible. "The other little book spoke of purpose to conquer for God His unhappy world; that I felt to be my real purpose in this world so full of unhappiness and mistaken aims and purposes at the present time."

---

188 Diary, January 1, 1934, and June 3, 1934. Stacey, *A Very Double Life*, 178. Diary, May 13, 1934.

189 Diary, June 3 and 4, 1934. Boyko, 257-258. Diary, June 24 and 30, 1934.

He read the Acts of the Apostles and found it "full of messages, fuller than anything I have ever read before" and later added in the margin, "This was most significant. The true guidance to be found in the bible – not in table wrappings [sic]." King even thought of "the article on numerology – by the man in Montreal – given me by Quest Brown, in which Mother, Home & Heaven are related, and my life's purposes revealed through numerology."[190]

The Montreal numerologist W.J. Morran (telephone Harbour 3658) had written Quest Brown in 1931 that he had worked out King's "Number Symbology." "I find that the Honourable Gentleman chose to contact Earth life carrying twenty five vibrations. This indicates to me that before making choice of his Parents, he had definitely decided to, what Theosophists would call, 'work out a heavy load of Karma.'" According to Morran's Number Symbology, the name Mackenzie King "vibrated" to the number 11. "He is the Poet; the Aaronic Priest who ministers in the Inner Temple; the guardian of the Holy of Holies; he is the great transcendentalist; the mystic in the shrine of life: He keeps God alive in the minds of the world: He is the Man with a Vision…He is close enough to God, not to be mistaken about himself, and close enough to Man, not to be misunderstood: He is both the Messenger and the Message; the message is of God and about the Good."

Moran closed his letter to Quest Brown by adding, "Being a good Conservative, myself, I cannot pray that he may soon be restored to Power in Canada, but I must confess that I find it difficult to conceive of a better man to lead Canada, now, or hereafter, than the man whom Numerology reveals to me in 'Mackenzie King.'" In his diary, King recorded that Brown "felt what he had written squared so exactly with her reading of the palm that she was more convinced than ever of the accuracy of her prophecy. This remarkable document for such it is I am fyling [sic] away with other papers. It may mean nothing and it may mean everything. I am convinced it means something most significant. It is based on the theory of reincarnation which I have never accepted or believed in, but which may be true in ways we do not dream of."

King noted that Brown believed "'There is a fortune-teller in every womb,' meaning that spirits who have been progressing through the years chose their reincarnations & may come back to this world in that way to work out their destiny. I would be my grandfather reincarnated

---

190 Diary, July 1, 1934.

(supposedly). She believes or Morran states, I am at the point of nearing the highest realm, if I do not fail in renouncing weaknesses. All of this is very strange at a moment when these weaknesses are most in evidence to my own mind." King also recalled "what Mrs. Bleaney said to me of seeing the No. 3 as the mystical number for me. 3 seemed to be the number to be guided by…This Number symbology is quite remarkable…a really remarkable confirmation of an almost a scientific exactness in deciphering of findings."[191]

On July 1, 1934, King still believed that R.B. Bennett's honours list of the ten individuals nominated for knighthoods that had been revealed to him over the "little table" would be announced. "How much might become known or foretold would depend on how high those imparting knowledge had risen in spiritual power and how much those receiving had equally risen in spiritual power – to get the perfect relationship required for prophecy that would not be false depended on the spiritual height of the one revealing in God's name and the one receiving equally in God's name. The power is that of 'the Father.'" Reading Acts of the Apostles, he saw that "all this chapter is full of 'spiritualist' phenomena as Joan & I know & have seen it. Christ being taken into Heaven, the angels present, dematerialization and manifestation."

When the Monday morning papers brought no mention of knighthoods on July 2, he was convinced that this only meant a delay. As he had read in Acts, "God's holy spirit coming to all through Christ – so that sons & daughters shall prophesy, young men see visions, and old men dream dreams & on servants & handmaids – so they shall prophesy & see 'wonders in heaven above' & signs on the earth beneath – just as Joan and I are now being given to see – all necessary at the time to give Christianity its start – necessary to Joan and me to help me to begin aright with confidence & trust." Another "conversation" over the "little table" with Joan that evening assured him, "I was able to interpret aright, an assurance God has special work for Joan & myself, an assurance God will guide and protect & continue to love us both." In this test of faith, he was still certain "as to it being Sir Wilfrid who is speaking and as to his having this time accurate knowledge. I believe it is Sir Wilfrid speaking, also that his knowledge is 'exact.'"[192]

---

191 W.J. Morran to Quest Brown, April 12, 1931. Diary, February 18, 1931. I cannot account for the discrepancy in the dates of these two documents. King had sittings with Brown on February 16 and 18, 1931, and April 16, 1931.

192 Diary, July 1 and 2, 1934.

On July 5, there was still no announcement of titles. Joan Patteson informed King of a dream vision in which she thought Sir Wilfrid and F.W.H. Myers were very near. She "had prayed very earnestly about our being led aright, and I said to them, how was it that Rex said what he said about the government, the last words. I knew you were worried about them ... The voices said to me, 'It was an evil spirit – the fact that he was tired and eaten too much & not had enough sleep etc. let it come in and take possession of him.' She went on to say that she thought the mediums the best way to get information, as they were usually ignorant people – their minds a blank – that with our minds so strong & feelings etc. entering as we wrote, and especially saying we would call on so and so to tell us, Laurier & the like, we were not getting the right source; we were either using our own subconscious thoughts, or an evil spirit was creeping in."

King wrote about Joan's explanation, "I confess I felt she was right – that the vision alone is the true guide & there great care to be taken in interpretation – the bible the surest guide of all."

> Soon now we shall know whether the Bible is the only guide or <u>the</u> Guide. That God speaks to us through its pages as nowhere else, I know, and I believe its teachings and words mean more than all else beside, and that all else must be read and considered in the light of them. But I also believe that as we advance in spiritual knowledge and perceptions, everything speaks of and helps to reveal God, and that we discover to some have been given the gifts of tongues, or of prophecy or of healing etc., diverse gifts. All may fail – but God will never fail – for God is Love eternal – but all were meant to help to lead us to God, and His guidance is something given through Nature, through the minds of men, in books and expressed in voices, through men here below, and men being transformed into God's likeness in the Great Beyond, the extent of their knowledge and spiritual power being dependent wholly upon the nearness of their approach to him for <u>to the Father alone is given to know the time and the seasons</u>.

King was very anxious about whether the spirit predictions would prove to be correct and carefully reviewed the previous night's "conversation."

> The positive statements that Knighthoods had been conferred, that the morning papers would announce them etc. makes quite clear that it has been some evil spirit that has come in, that it is not Sir Wilfrid who has been communicating, nor indeed Mr. Myers, except possibly the latter part – that Myers has been sending the visions or helping in that I am sure – they have never failed but this is wrong, and with it goes by the board completely all that may be said of a definite character re events, times, seasons etc. and prophecy – save as may be evidenced in other ways …
>
> Either these men are yet men seeking to be Gods, or as I more truly believe, an evil spirit is usurping their place at times. It is answering something in one's own nature – a hidden desire or suspicion, they belong to the realm of earth – they are not of the higher regions, the highest heaven, where alone God is to be found. It comes back to the celestial and immortal voice of conscience – to the revelation that comes through the Scriptures, to much told truly by those we love & who love us, to mother & father, Bell & Max & especially grandfather, as continuing to shape my life. Sir Wilfrid also yes – but not to the degree of my own parents and grandparents, home etc. I come back to the highest spirituality being the real power, and to faith being better than the things we are told, faith in the unseen reality, God whose nature has been revealed through Christ, who said it is not for us to know the times or the seasons.

At nine in the evening on July 5, 1934, King and Patteson decided to have another "conversation" on the "little table," "just to get matters straightened out."

> At the beginning 'Laurier' was supposed to be speaking. Then Mr. Myers. I felt it was a lying spirit and asked for proof of its being Myers. Immediately the spirit disappeared. Mother then came, I feel sure it was mother, with the words to leave alone 'that person,' 'the father of lies,' – the subtle crafty devil. Then going on to speak of loving one's enemies, blessing those who despitefully use you etc. There was, too, the clear conflict between the spirit of hate, jealousy etc. that would destroy one's soul & the spirit that would save souls.
>
> Joan said it was an 'immense relief' to her mind that we had had this further talk – that she saw what was meant, that we draw to ourselves the spirit of evil, if our own thoughts or desires are evil, that we should not approach this work except

where we are sure our thoughts are high & pure & unselfish & those of love and kindness. In all this she was expressing what I have seen and written out before, but appear to have been falling away from in insisting that she should believe in what we were being told – taking our word from voices of departed 'men' rather than from God alone. The subtlety of what was said by 'that person' is quite remarkable – Note the approach via the belief in the bible – and then on to error.[193]

King would go on to analyze this major failure of his spiritual belief system for weeks. On July 15, he noted in his spiritual journal that he was still writing up the record for June 30 "in the other diary." He found it very fatiguing, "having allowed so long a time to elapse. I could see wherein I had been paying too much attention to detail, and perhaps drawing into the web of my thoughts and imagination too many 'coincidences.' One has to be careful not to overdo in that respect." He had concluded on July 6, "As to the table, I think it well to use it sparingly and as dear mother said to let God send who He will, not for us to call those we want. I believe that it brings both truth & error. I think the two are distinguishable – We have seen over & over again how an evil spirit has crept in where desires have been concerned & wishes – both are of the earth – earthy & earth bound spirits respond. God alone can send his messengers from on High. They are helping, all who love us, but by working for the Divine idea & its fulfilment in our lives."

After reading Chapter 6 of the Acts of the Apostles, he wrote, "Surely, surely here is Divine guidance – Not voices concerned with the things of earth, but celestial voices, messengers of God bringing assurances from Him & comfort & guidance." "Now comes consideration of what all this teaches –"

> 1. Great care must be exercised in discerning truth and error, good & evil to be sure it is the spirit of good not the spirit of evil that is influencing the mind.
>
> 2. The two are subtly intertwined as joy and sorrow – but prayer and faith can separate the two and give the true vision.
>
> 3. Spiritual phenomena must be spiritually discerned – the distinction between the spiritual and material continually kept in mind.

---

193 Diary, July 5, 1934.

4. We are not to be concerned with matters of position, events, etc., the time or seasons; it is the divine idea alone that is important.

5. It is advisable to give up looking for signs etc. in <u>everything</u>. In some things where they impress themselves beyond mistake, it is well to recognize they are Heaven meant and Heaven sent but our business is not to be looking for groundhogs but to be in search of the souls of men.

6. Hold fast to vision – as a method shown in the bible to be one used by God in making His will and pleasure known to individuals.

7. It is safe to follow anything revealed in the bible – as to methods of knowing God – visions – significance of miracles, happenings etc. But above all let us say 'Christ is the way, the truth & the life;' to follow Him is the surest guide of all.[194]

On July 12, 1934, King determined to apply the lessons he had learned spiritually to the political realm. "I must never again let myself be 'driven' by any one ... I was the best judge of 'the times and the seasons' to be speaking." He greatly resented and blamed his ill health on the constant pressure exerted by Vincent Massey, President of the National Liberal Federation, to undertake numerous speaking engagements, a speaking tour of Western Canada in 1933, and conferences and meetings in an effort better to organize the Liberal Party. "I can see wherein for the problems of government," he wrote, "I must now & hereafter as before be my own master and yield to no one – follow the guidance that cometh from on high – also not listen to voices, either in 'conversations' at the table or from without in the world, that are begotten of human <u>desire</u>, either my own, or the desires of others. Seek only to know the will of God and be guided by it in so far as it may be revealed to me."

Four days later, his late brother Max identified the origin of the recurring "evil spirits" in King's and Patteson's spirit communications as emanating from Mackenzie King's subconscious. He had himself written the introduction to Max's *Nerves and Personal Power: Some Principles of Psychology as Applied to Conduct and Health* (1922) and

---

[194] Diary, July 15 and 6, 1934.

described this table "conversation" as "an experience in separating truth from error – the evil spirit crept in, was recognized – its origin explained by Max, much in a way that helped to make clear the significance of the morning vision. The subconscious self the source of Evil – the realm of beauty the source of truth."[195]

Yet King was not ready to accept that all messages he was receiving from the Beyond emanated from his own subconscious mind. After reading Anita Mühl's *Automatic Writing* in December 1934 he commented, "I do not believe 'the subconscious,' our subconscious, accounts for everything in automatic writing. We would perhaps recognize nothing that did not come out of the subconscious – it would seem unreal. There would be no way of proving it did exist etc. In this way much may seem to be subconscious or unconscious. But what is the power that brings it into consciousness, causes it to appear in some form of manifestation, writing, speaking or something else, if it is not a mediumistic influence which links our finite existence and knowledge with a wider existence & knowledge which becomes the infinite as the soul rises towards God. All things work together for God & for God for those who love God – for faith – to complete belief in His power & existence as the All in All."[196]

In August 1934 rumours, which Mackenzie King attributed to "mostly Tory propaganda, a desire to weaken my hand & that of the party," circulated that he was very ill. He wrote, "I am coming to the conclusion that 'the table' and these mental conflicts re spiritualism have also been sapping my strength and that I have been undernourished, not eating enough solid foods. All of these are matters which from now on I shall seek to remedy." But like his resolve to control his sex instinct, abstain completely from consuming alcohol at social functions, and not overeat, King was unable to implement this resolution regarding these spirit "conversations." His 1949 diary still references sixteen sessions on "the little table" with Joan Patteson before his death in July 1950.

He had recorded a "triumphal note" already on New Year's Day, 1935. His tea cups showed "a bird resting on its nest – then a bird soaring through the sky" and he transcribed a prophetic "conversation" with

---

195 Diary, July 12 and 16, 1934, and January 1, 1935.
196 Diary, December 15, 1934.

another of his many spirit guides. "If I asked my heart's greatest desire it would be summed up in what Lorenzo di Medici said tonight will happen in the years to come. How I pray it may be so … may this be an epitome of the beginning and the end of this life's journey."

> Lorenzo di Medici – a happy new year to Mrs. Patteson & you.
> You will be Prime Minister this year.
> You will have a great name in History.
> You will be a peace maker.
> You will make many people happy.
> You will have a long life.
> You will teach many nations the way of peace.
> You will work hard to achieve that end.
> You try to sleep all you can.
> Good night.

"I had said earlier to Joan as she played 'Afton Water' & I looked at the works of art about & thought of Schubert's 'Serenade' – 'Home Sweet Home' etc. that I wished I might do one thing that would live. Could it be that this prayer will be answered as above? To further peace & good will on earth I should love above all else."[197]

Rather than cutting down on the "little table," two months later, "feeling that there was some communication I would receive," King "took the little table by myself to see what I might get." His father informed him: "Bennett is crazy; he will never be back. He will go to England. He will bring on the elections when he returns in May. He will go to pieces during the campaign. He will look to Rhodes [Edgar Nelson Rhodes, the Minister of Finance] to succeed him. You will win easily. Love from all here. Good night. Self: Will Bennett be back in Parliament – or do you know what he is going to do from now on? The answer: He will go to England soon. Will he come back to parliament?: No." After receiving this spirit communication King hoped, "can it mean that I am at last to be relieved of the punishment I have had of having to sit opposite that man for 7 years? … At last am I to be released from that thraldom – and all the misrepresentation and abuse of which he has been guilty – in that period of time?"[198]

---

197 Diary, September 1, 1934, and January 1, 1935.
198 Diary, March 9, 1935.

CHAPTER 6

Mackenzie King, Magnetic and Electric Sex Currents, and the Lost Leader

When King began drafting *Industry and Humanity* in January 1916 – a year before the death of his mother – he again began coping with an aggravated nervous condition and conflict with his sex instinct. "My thoughts have turned away from the ideals I have cherished and I have found myself in an encounter with my own nature such as I have never known before," he recorded in his diary. "It has been at times as though a fire would devour me and I have been unable to get rest by night or day."

In June, he resolved to seek medical assistance in Ottawa fearing, "there may be some injury to my spine, that the pressure on the nerves of it is the cause. I shall consult a physician if the rest and change does not eliminate the feelings I sometimes have, for it holds me back in my work and besides makes me most uncomfortable both alone and in the presence of others." Dr. R. Chevrier examined his spine on July 1, 1916, and found him in perfect physical health but "nervously overwrought." At the end of the month, Chevrier certified that King was "suffering from the incipient symptoms of a severe form of neurasthenia which have been brought on by overwork." Neurasthenia was a widely used medical term encompassing a range of meanings from tired nerves and excessive work and family pressures to Freud's emphasis on sexual factors such as insufficient sexual activity.[199]

---

199 Diary, June 22 and 27, 1916, and July 1, 1916. Roazen, 63, 64-65. Dr. Chevrier was Sir Wilfrid Laurier's physician and announced his death following a stroke in February 1919. See "Sir Wilfrid Laurier Dies at Ottawa," *Edmonton Journal*, February 17, 1919, 1.

King had been coping with tremendous work and family pressures. His favourite sister, Bella, had died in 1915, his only brother Max was suffering from tuberculosis, his mother was ailing and on August 30, 1916, he suffered another blow with the death of his father. King was close to suffering a mental breakdown and, at the suggestion of John D. Rockefeller Jr., was examined at the Johns Hopkins hospital and medical school in Baltimore by the Canadian-born and educated Dr. Lewellys Franklin Barker, president of the American Neurological Association. Barker referred King to Dr. Adolf Meyer, whom Paul Roazen – who analyzed King's medical records from 1916 – called "the most important single figure in the history of North American twentieth century psychiatry."

When Dr. Barker examined him at Johns Hopkins in October 1916, he again insisted that his spine be x-rayed to try to locate the cause of the very physical tingling sensations that were tormenting him. We know what these sensations were from Barker's examination of King and his records of this "very interesting case." "The principle [sic] subjective disturbance is that of being influenced electrically by others and of influencing others in this way." In his physical examination, Barker observed that King had "hallucinations of perineal sense … Has sensations; referred to the perineal region."[200] The perineum is the erogenous zone between the anus and the bulb of the penis in the scrotum, behind the tip of the coccyx, the final segment of the vertebrae column.

Dr. Barker and Dr. Meyer assured King that his tingling sensations were hallucinations and that his sexual feelings were normal. After King had an abscessed tooth and adenoids removed – suspected physiological causes of his "hallucinations" – Barker informed him that the x-ray of his spine showed that everything was in order. He spoke to him again "of my view of sex problems, said he thought I over exaggerated significance of perfectly natural phenomena, that there was danger in so doing by a healthy man; he advised reconciling in thought any conflict between the animal and spiritual nature. He had to do this himself, had been through the same conflict."

King was extremely grateful to Barker for his counsel and the free treatment he received thanks to the Rockefeller Institute for Medical Research. "I told him he had been like a little saviour to

---

200 Roazen, xlii, 73, 75, 77.

me, in helping me out of the torment of the sinner." When he was discharged from Johns Hopkins on November 11, 1916, his hospital diagnosis included "Psychoneurosis" and "Psychasthenia" which Paul Roazen explains were "a Freudian term implying the existence of a sexual conflict" and "phobias and obsessions." King himself had recorded in his diary at the end of October 1916, "I have been practically free from the dread I had since speaking with Dr. Barker of it, and almost free of the symptoms which produced it. How grateful I am I did not delay longer in speaking."[201]

King felt immensely relieved after his treatment at Johns Hopkins and published his 567-page *Industry and Humanity* in 1918. But the physical and psychological conditions that produced his symptoms had not been addressed nor eliminated by his treatment in Baltimore. In June 1918, he confessed that "carnal temptations have absorbed too much of my thought. I have not exerted the will to overcome I should have. I am not satisfied with myself as a man." In December 1920, he "had another day of terrific struggle" because of "thoughts wandering in other directions" and "found it next to impossible to work." The following day, King "suffered a terrible depression this afternoon from yesterday" and concluded, "There are mysterious phenomena of which we have not begun to gain a knowledge that control and sway our lives." A little more than a year after he became Prime Minister on December 29, 1921, he again experienced a "terrible depression which made me feel that death itself would be a happy release from everything." He could not sleep, "was restless and thoughts difficult to control" so that he "felt a violent impulse almost to go out and waste time in revelry of any kind."[202]

References to magnetic currents begin to appear in Mackenzie King's diary in 1928 when, as Prime Minister, he gave a dinner in honour of the British MP and Colonial Secretary, Leo Amery. He considered his toast to Amery and the Empire a failure, the result of problems that had been affecting him for some time. "I had hoped I might do well in speaking tonight but somehow all day I felt a great depression, as though I might cry. I found it hard to have a clear free mind when I got up to speak. It is the sex passions I think that when one is asleep, tear & wear one & a magnetic force that at times

---

201   Ibid., 98, 100, 77. Diary, October 29, 1916.
202   Diary, June 24, 1918, December 13 and 14, 1920, and February 3, 1923.

reacts, or allows itself to be drained by others. I cannot understand the mystery of it."

King had recorded in April, "I was so filled with a sort of internal fever as not to be able to care about anything or anyone & in a combative sort of mood. It is I believe a sort of passion fever, that it is hard to account for, the worm that never dies." The following year he noted he was "reading each night a little of a volume entitled 'Personal Magnetism' [Theron Q. Dumont. *Personal Magnetism: The Secrets of Mental Fascination* (1914)], a simple book but with much good teaching. I have been happy today & more my real self in overcoming self than for a long time past." He would read the book again in 1933, commenting that he found it "full of useful and helpful ideas, much that explains what is most puzzling about one's self."[203]

That September, King attended the week-long Liberal Summer Conference for young Liberals on international politics, economics, electoral reform, and the role of government in society organized by Vincent and Alice Massey at their four-hundred-acre Batterwood estate near Port Hope, Ontario. Conference presentations, which attracted Brooke Claxton and Paul Martin Sr., future progressive members of King's Cabinet, were held at Trinity College School. "With his soft bulk squeezed into a student desk several sizes too small, King squirmed uncomfortably as Massey forced him to listen to Canadian and British intellectuals, as well as prominent American 'New Dealers' Raymond Moley and Averell Harriman, extol the benefits of a regulated, planned economy."[204]

King opposed government intervention and was appalled by the economic and political measures President Roosevelt had introduced in the United States to alleviate the worst effects of the Depression. When he dreamt he saw two snakes come out of a marshy ground and later actually saw such snakes at the Massey's estate, he "wondered if it could mean that by any chance my hosts at Port Hope were not to be trusted." He had consumed sherry, white wine and port at dinner and so also interpreted the snakes as "the two temptations – wine & women – wine the lesser of the two & leading to the second." King danced with several of the young women attending the Conference and later felt sexually aroused. "My contact with two or three of the young persons possessing a certain attraction

---

203 Diary, June 23, 1928, April 23, 1928, October 9, 1929, and April 11, 1933.
204 Donaghy, 31.

should have been avoided – the magnetic touch is not something to be either sought or played with. It would have been wiser not to have danced."[205]

While attending the Conference, King read "a quite amazing chapter on the search for God by the soul being symbolized in sex relationship" in Lawrence John Ronaldshay's book, *The Heart of Aryavarta: A Study of the Psychology of Indian Unrest* [London: Constable, 1925]. He found its contents "about as dangerous a doctrine as is conceivable," and was prompted to reveal his own views on the "proper" function of sex. "I can well understand love being based on the search for the beautiful, and a supreme expression of human love in marriage, leading the way to the conception of a 'glory that excelleth beyond,'" he wrote. "But where the marriage consummation is made 'a means to an end' in a search for God instead of for its real purpose the perpetuation of the species, and the expression of the mutuality or oneness of love between individuals whose very souls seek only the highest in the other, religion of the kind becomes the very essence of heathenism and subtlety carried to an 'nth degree.'" He reproached himself that during and immediately after the Conference his own thoughts were "not controlled as they should have been."[206]

What was different about King's belief in electric and magnetic currents was his fear – already expressed during his near-nervous breakdown in 1916 – that he was being controlled by others. After Dr. Lewellys Franklin Barker examined him at the Johns Hopkins hospital and medical school in Baltimore and referred him to Dr. Adolf Meyer, he wrote Meyer that their patient "is in good physical condition but has peculiar ideas in regard to his own person and other people. Has the idea that other people are influencing him by electric currents." According to Paul Roazen's examination of his 1916 medical records, "King thought he could influence others electrically as well."

---

205 Diary, September 3 and 11, 1933. King commented on "duty dances" at social occasions, i.e., dances "with those who expect it" – particularly the wives of MPs and their friends – five years previously. "There is an attraction which meeting & dancing with women begets and it creates a conflict in the mind, between sense & soul, duty to work & fondness for pleasure; moderation is difficult in my position." Diary, February 17, 1928.

206 Diary, September 9, 7, and 10, 1933.

Figure 21: After Meet the Navy, *Ottawa, September 15, 1943.*
Contact with young persons, possessing a certain attraction, should be avoided.

When he attended *Parsifal* in New York with his friend Mary Ashley Hewitt in 1921, he awoke sexually aroused at six o'clock the next morning "with feelings akin to those experienced in Ottawa." Though distressed by his bodily sensations, he actually felt "a source of mental relief, as I was able to assure myself, they rose from within myself & were not directly attributable to power possessed by one which is not possessed by another. I knew Mrs. H. [Hewitt] would exert no occult influence – was able therefore to feel that what I have been experiencing is largely due to my own thought & subconscious life."[207]

His conviction about "currents" persisted throughout the 1930s and the Second World War, simultaneously with his laments about the fire burning in his veins. In 1930, he entered in his diary, "I must find out the cause of my feeling as I do. These passions that cause me to wake up in the morning as if on fire are a curse. I do my best to keep calm, to subdue them, to keep thought & mind pure." The following year he was so overworked and exhausted while attempting to write his speech on R.B. Bennett's budget that "I can do little, then my whole body seems afire, whether it is nerves or passion or what I don't know, but I seem to be almost consumed alive, and it leaves me in a very distressed condition. I cannot think as I ought or work out what I have in mind."

On the morning of March 5, 1932, just before meeting with Winston Churchill at Government House in Ottawa, King dreamt "that voices were speaking with me – there were very many and with great force – it was as if very strong electric forces were sweeping by." The magnetic currents struck him not only while dreaming at night but also in his daytime activities as a politician. He referred to one such physical reaction after speaking in the House of Commons for four hours and twenty minutes as Leader of the Opposition in January 1934. "On the way driving home in the car & after going to rest I felt that physical sensation of the sexual organ which I have experienced after great efforts in speaking before, but I felt it possible to control it. It must have to do with some magnetic power which develops as one speaks."[208]

One night during 1935, he could not fall asleep for some time, "a sort of magnetic current having been started which it seemed impossible to control. It left me a little 'on edge' throughout the morning & day, inclined to be more sharp & quick with others." Travelling by train from Calgary on his Western tour for the 1935 federal election, King slept fairly well "but was a bit wakeful and felt the magnetic urge but managed to control it." In 1937, he had a dream that he interpreted as being either about black magic or animal magnetism. He

---

207 Roazen, 77. Diary, March 26, 1921.
208 Diary, November 11, 1930, June 9, 1931, March 5, 1932, and January 30, 1934.

"thought of the former as I woke for the person I saw & who seemed to influence me was dressed in black & of the latter looking into little Derry's [Joan Patteson's terrier's] black eyes as he stood & gazed at me motionless for some time." He concluded, "I suppose this is the magnetic force which destroys the body unless controlled & which controlled becomes celestial fire, stimulating the creativeness of the mind & causing one's thoughts to be transmitted."[209]

Before waking after another dream a month later, he "was strangely affected by the sense of some attraction not possible to control. I find it quite impossible to comprehend the cause, origin or truth of what I experience at such times. Magnetic currents very strong and not to be suppressed." He had seen a dream vision of a dance in which he partnered Princess Patricia, "with whom I danced with the utmost freedom and joy on the part of each," and with Mrs. John Bassett, the wife of the publisher of the Montreal Gazette, "who was in light attire – spoke of her appearance." His eyes closed up and he experienced a feeling of blindness. When he awoke he concluded, "physical attraction of the kind experienced was dangerous to one's vision. It might be spiritual vision. It might be physical – or mental vision – all three in all probability."[210]

King could not control or eliminate his almost nightly visions. In 1938, he dreamt of being inside a building with a swimming pool where "there were a number of women bathing, one lying on the pavement near where I was resting. It seemed to me she tried to exert some sort of magnetic power – animal magnetism, or the like. I determined to be free of the influence and got up (.....)." Two months later he was greatly impressed and aroused by "a photo of a beautiful painting" sent him from "half way round the globe" by a friend whom he does not name. King speculated whether the cause of his sexual arousal was "telepathy, or whether (as is probably true) 'imagination' & 'more imagination' working on the nervous system – or some sensory perception, or extra-sensory perception – as it were the ethereal body, leaving the natural body, and encountering other like bodies, still natural, not yet wholly spiritual. That is something that may become clear in time & this doubtless is guidance. It was all very real."

---

209 Diary, September 11, 1935, October 1, 1935, and October 17, 1937.
210 Diary, November 13, 1937.

In 1942, a gift of Chinese vases and a photograph from Mrs. Soong, the wife of the former Minister of China to Washington, Dr. T.V. Soong, caused King again to speculate about "some force or directing influence, making itself felt & known – the power of attraction – a strange mystical sort of thing."[211] He recorded beginning "to feel a surge of unrest, which it was difficult to control," "found it hard ... to control my thoughts" and "feelings began to control me" before falling asleep as late as September 1949, less than ten months before his death at the age of 75 in 1950.[212]

King, of course, could also be sexually aroused without feeling electric currents. He had observed that before he spoke at the Prince Albert Exhibition in August 1933, "the performance in front of the grand stand of girl dancers, in costume of Indians, was quite beautiful to watch." That evening he experienced another restless night and wrote, "the performance of the dancers at the Exhibition was not without its effect on my emotions, in occasioning restlessness. All this is interesting as revealing one's nature and the forces that play upon it, what has to be guarded and guided day by day & hour by hour." In 1934, after he had felt "'the thorns in my flesh' buffeting me during the night," King thought "this morning's chapter on Corinthians seemed to point to it being the conflict arising from natural or spiritual impulses ... I want to be wholly freed from these conflicts of sense vs. soul."[213]

King had first heard about electric currents from his mother who told him in 1914 that William Lyon Mackenzie, "used to put glass non-conductors on the foot of his bed to help store his nervous energy." His preoccupation with magnetic forces intensified in the 1930s when he felt not only powerful physical sensations and magnetic currents but found these combined with dream visions of not only the living but also the dead. Before she died in 1917, Isabel King had promised her son "to come to me from the Great Beyond & let me know of her existence." In 1932, King felt the sexual electric current when he dreamt of his mother. When he took her in his arms, "she reached over & kissed me very sweetly. As she went to kiss me I

---

211 Diary, January 11, 1938, April 29, 1938, and September 3, 1942.

212 See Diary, January 18 and 30, 1949, February 1, 1949, June 6, 1949, July 14, 1949, August 26 and 27, 1949, and September 27, 1949.

213 Diary, August 2 and 3, 1933, and February 18, 1934.

felt as it were an electric current from her lips to mine ... I thought of her promise to come to me in dreams when she could & her saying in our conversation when she could get in touch with my magnetism she would. Clearly what I felt in the electric current was that."[214]

Heather Robertson, in *More Than a Rose: Prime Ministers, Wives and Other Women*, cites another of his "Vision of dear mother – celestial materialization" in 1935 in which he gave her "a pretty little gown I had secured for her while abroad." King "seemed to be in my underclothing as I came near her side" when he took her in his arms. "She put her lips to mine as I lifted her up & kissed me, in a manner that it seemed to me, breath seemed to come from her to me." Robertson speculated about the origin of this and other King dream visions. "What really happened between Mother and Willie? Was King, at sixty, having incestuous fantasies about a woman dead nearly twenty years? Or was he playing out, in the safety of a sleeplike trance, a sexual trauma that had actually occurred?" He had recorded another "very very vivid" dream in his diary in 1929 in which he seemed to be sleeping at home. "Suddenly dear mother came to my room & slipped quietly into my bed beside me as if not to alarm me."[215]

This suggests King could acknowledge a sexual feeling for his mother in his dreams. In his diaries, he also recognized breaking social and religious taboos with other women. Whether King had a strictly platonic relationship with the married Joan Patteson has been a subject of debate. That he considered her not only his closest friend and spiritual companion but also had sexual feelings for her is indicated by a 1933 diary entry. When he phoned her and "was delighted indeed to hear her voice – the electrical effect of it & our talk together was a phenomena I watched deliberately with interest. It was useless for me to try to control it, as it took possession of me as if I had a battery within which was being charged. There is something here I have yet to understand, a physical hour of magnetic attraction that defies space."

He again referred to the magnetic current between himself and Patteson – and King's medical condition identified by the Ottawa physician Dr. Chevrier just before he was examined by Barker and Meyer in Baltimore in 1916 – after King and Joan watched a film

---

214 Diary, December 11, 1914, December 25, 1931, and April 12 and 14, 1932.
215 Diary, January 5, 1935. Heather Robertson, *More Than a Rose*, 210, 211. Diary, March 24, 1929.

about Franz Schubert's life in 1934. "With the sympathetic attraction of Joan's nature & mine, there was the drawing out of a natural magnetic current – which in Nature has its natural outlet in marriage & which leads to marriage in Nature – but which when thwarted leaves the nerves drawn, as it were & produces reactions which occasion a sort of Neurasthenia."[216]

King also felt a strong sexual attraction for Princess Cantacuzene whom he had first met in Newport, Rhode Island, in 1899, when she was still Julia Grant, a granddaughter of President Ulysses S. Grant, before her marriage to a Russian prince, whom she divorced in October 1934. In 1932, he believed she was exerting a sexual influence on him and became "conscious as I have never been before of magnetic forces sweeping as it were through me – some attractive power which it was impossible to resist, and which seemed to gain an almost infinite strength." "I seemed to be certain that it was thoughts on the part of Princess Cantacuzene to whom I had written and who in all probability had received my letter ... This afternoon about three thirty I received a wire from Princess Cantacuzene as follows: 'Deeply grateful for your thought of me.' ... I am wondering if what I experienced last night was self-intoxication, as it were, my own thoughts, or influence of spirits round about, brought near my own thoughts, or nature's urge swept free as it were after being dammed. This I have to learn. I felt I was 'experimenting' and as such alone permitted my thoughts to have the sweep they had."[217]

When he received a letter from the Princess at the end of May, he once more became "very conscious of strong forces uniting my life with some vital force elsewhere."

> From what Princess Cantacuzene says I feel convinced that there is a play of forces which unites thoughts; how far it may be real or imaginary is something that correspondence or conversation alone can determine. I can see, however, that it is something which must be guarded, and that experimenting with one's will incurs dangers with it which cannot be too greatly guarded against. What I want to record here is the certain knowledge of the influence of forces which affect one's entire being and which are so real as to be unmistakable. Are there evil forces as well as

---

216 Diary, November 16, 1933, and December 28, 1934.
217 Diary, May 10, 1932.

good at work & do evil spirits find their way into control that is the question to be solved.

The following morning King recorded in his diary that he had had some sort of sexual experience. "There has been a reaction today which makes clear that whatever forces are at work, they are not the ones to encourage and must be controlled. This morning when I wakened I soon experienced all that I experienced before going to sleep last night, and it is clear to me that this is not mere self-hypnotism; it is some sensory centre that begins work on its own, as a result of an outside impulse or stimulus – but the reaction is a nervous one and one is left with a feeling of irritation, impatience, unrest, etc." He noted, "It may be it is just the passions let loose within one & stirred in a manner which affects one's being. Throughout the day I found it difficult to talk quietly or pleasantly & was inclined to be short & irritable. This is quite wrong and I know it."[218]

After speaking to Princess Cantacuzene in New York on the telephone from Laurier House in July, King once more confessed the next day, "I was not true to my best self last night." "Why I do not hold to the way that I know to be right, I cannot say. It is a lack of discipline of the will and a desire to follow the path of inclination through lack, I imagine, of not having a home of my own and partly a desire to experiment. Last night's conversation over the long distance left no doubt as to the experiment." This remark may mean that King masturbated either while speaking to Cantacuzene on the telephone or afterwards. He wanted to understand why he was feeling "fire through the veins" and to "comprehend my own nature & learn above all else to control & subdue every part that does not administer to what is highest and best in life." He feared that "I have aroused part of my nature which should be subdued by writing the letter I did to Princess Cantacuzene – that may be the fire that shuts us out of Paradise. It may, on the other hand, be part of a divine fire which controlled means, power and understanding."

In October, he wrote the Princess and "told her just what I felt to be right & know she will help to work out the problem that has so curiously grown out of our occult experiments." Yet two weeks later, King had other "strange occult experiences" related to her and wrote that he "must ascertain later whether they had foundation only in my own imagination or as I believe they were – part of an invisible reality

---

218 Diary, May 31, 1932, and June 1, 1932.

Figure 22: Princess Cantacuzene from the frontispiece of her Revolutionary Days *(1919).*

– related to forces that are at work in the world & a part of Nature's laws. In any event they were quite amazing."²¹⁹

---

219   Diary, July 28, 1932, May 7 and 8, 1932, and October 4 and 19, 1932. In 1943, King would record another sexual experience after speaking on the telephone

In November 1932, King received a letter from the Princess describing her visit to the medium Etta Wriedt in Detroit who connected her to her deceased father and aunt. He was convinced her attestation about the séance was "further confirmation of the survival of those who have gone in much the same or exactly the same personalities as they possessed while here." Cantacuzene reported that Isabel King had also appeared during the séance and had approved of their relationship. The night before receiving her letter, King had "felt another influence sweep over me and was perfectly sure it was that Julia Grant was seeking to communicate with me; the impression became overwhelming."

When he went to sleep, however, his mother appeared to him in "a most remarkable vision, the most important, I believe of all I have had." "She was making clear to me that carnal love was wrong, that it separated one from the divine and spiritual, and that what I had been experiencing was that." He prayed "I may not be disobedient unto the heavenly vision" and subsequently informed the Princess that there was no chance of them marrying. Yet he again recorded her electric and magnetic effect after reading the Princess' autobiography, *My Life Here and There*, in January 1933.[220]

King was probably also thinking of Princess Cantacuzene when two months later he dreamt in the morning seeing a young woman undressing in a building opposite. "These Freudian experiences are being noted for what they are worth; just why they should come I don't know except from the play of instincts repressed," he recorded. He felt the "irresistible impulse" again when he lay down to rest. "All forenoon it seems to me as if some outer force were playing against me. I am quite certain that [X] has probably been thinking of me in some way that has occasioned this feeling. I wish I could get some authoritative book to read which would explain this phenomena to me. I had no desire to do other than to forget everything of that kind and have my mind and thoughts turned in other ways. I know, too, this is injurious to my eyes & nervous system & yet it seems impossible to control."[221]

---

with Elize Tintet at the Ball Clinic in Ottawa who gave him electric and massage treatments. Evoking his previous experiences with electric and magnetic currents, he recorded a dream vision in which he came "under an influence I could not control & which would not let me rest." Diary, October 25, 1943.

220 Diary, November 7 and 6, 1932, and January 7 and 8, 1933.
221 Diary, March 29, 1933.

Regarding another sex dream, he described having "the distinct sensation of being both asleep and awake, of seeing something that was a dream & being conscious of my faculties working as when awake. It was the borderland region and an interesting experience as such. I suffer a good deal from the way the passions seem to rouse themselves in one's lower nature with the least extra bit of bedding. I suppose it is a part of the struggle on the borderland as well as the brute and the spirit, each seeking its right of control. The conflict is an exhausting one. With God's help the spirit will yet ride supreme in its own orbit."[222]

According to C.P Stacey's research in the King diaries, he and Julia Grant "had a 'sitting' in which her grandfather, General – and President – Ulysses S. Grant, spoke to them" in Washington in November 1935. The recently re-elected Prime Minister had travelled to the American capital to finalize a new Canada-U.S. trade agreement with President Roosevelt in the White House. Once again troubled by his sexual conflict, "a sort of destiny" had compelled him to secure Dion Fortune's *The Esoteric Philosophy of Love and Marriage* [London: Rider, 1929] from the cupboard containing his books on psychic phenomena. The volume had been loaned to him by Marie Sweet Carrington, Secretary of the American Psychical Institute in New York. King began reading the book on the train to Washington and "was immensely impressed with what seemed to me a true statement of the different planes through which we evolve," an evolution upwards from the instinctual to the seventh spiritual plane where "all are one and one is all." He nevertheless commented, "This book reduces everything too much to Sex, in terms of positive and negative forces – but in this also there may be much truth."[223]

Mackenzie King had achieved greater insights about his sexual instincts during his 1934 European tour through his contact with the Italian sculptor Giuseppe Guastalla. He had first discovered the artist while touring the Panama Pacific International Exposition in San Francisco with former Governor General Lord Aberdeen and Lady Aberdeen in November 1915 and purchased Guastalla's silver bronze head of a young woman entitled *Visions*. He commissioned Guastalla

---

222 Diary, September 16, 1932.

223 Stacey, *A Very Double Life*, 134, 238, fn. 41. Stacey cites a "Pencil memo of sitting" omitted from the online diary for November 16, 1935.

to sculpt a bust of his mother before her death and commissioned a bust of his father and modelled for his own bust in 1934. He was "restless" the night before visiting the artist's studio in Rome, "due to thoughts that were not free from desire – It seemed impossible to avoid the latter last night, they were overwhelming, a magnetic current due to proximity I imagine of someone equally so." A week later, after having several drinks of Scotch before going to sleep, "all the energy within me [seemed] suddenly directed towards desire for union with the other sex."

A door opened that let in "some other force, of possible evil, or may be that beauty itself creates passion and passion demands some satisfaction – but there it is – the feeling that the desire is being satisfied from somewhere – some magnetic force outside – created it may be by the imagination – rather I imagine by a similar force of an opposite sex elsewhere – a sex attraction – from where difficult to understand – unless it be minds uniting, with some overwhelming desire." He once again "seemed to be completely overwhelmed by magnetic attraction from some source, where I cannot say, but nothing has ever been stranger or less possible to resist. I could not but yield to it despite all I know & believe & have experienced. It was as if all the force within me were being driven towards someone who was completely answering the need. This I cannot explain. It is some phenomenon doubtless associated with failure to have married." He felt this "influence of another" particularly "when partially asleep than when awake & when the control of the will was not so strong."[224]

King believed this experience had been sent to him by his loved ones in the spirit world "to help me onward" and to enable him "to see from a greater height just what the forces are that are contending for supremacy in my nature, and how most effectively to combat them." He interpreted the vision to mean that through prayer mankind could rise "from the beast to man and man to God … a consciousness of evolution from a lower order of creation into a higher." The same night he had as well clearly seen in his tea cup "two horses (or animals) with their heads in opposite directions & bodies joined … I said to myself that means facing both ways – I saw also a hand pointing to the head of a woman, a perfect head, looking straight ahead," much like the sculpture *Visions* he had purchased from Guastalla.

---

224 Diary, November 5, 12, and 13, 1934, and April 23, 1934.

> The two together symbolize & are The Sphynx [sic] – the animal in man, which causes him to face both ways ... the animal nature perhaps – and the head of the woman – the divine. And so at the end of this journey I am brought to an understanding of the riddle of the Sphynx – finding it, myself ... I pray I may rise Sphynx-like out of the ashes of a dead self to the great purpose of my life – that the Sphynx in me may slay itself & only the God-like remain – the one true man looking straight ahead, being guided by the divine on earth and in Heaven. To God I pray that my prayer may be heard – and this journey and the old life and see me drawing nearer the Infinite alike in life & love.[225]

King kept two sphinx candelabra on his desk at Laurier House as a reminder of this insight and prayer, but these did not alter the frequent sexual content of his dreams. In his diary, he used "unrest," "restless," and "restlessness" as code words to indicate that he had been sexually aroused and rarely described in detail his dreams and dream visions that had stimulated him. One exception was on the night before his sixtieth birthday in December 1934, just a month after returning from Rome, when he described a "<u>Vision of The Way, through surrender of one's Thoughts. The overcoming of secret sins – the cross vs. the flesh. Assurance of ultimate triumph</u>." He felt this dream was "very real:" "I was lying in bed, and that some woman in white silk nightgown was lying there, and seeking to have me come close to her, urging me it was rest of this kind that I needed, that it would give me the sleep I required, and fit me the better for my duties. The way to rest in this regard was made very clear."

In another part of his vision, "a woman giving herself to someone beneath her also presented itself to my mind but I did not allow it to influence my thoughts." Walking on a long path between rows of plants and flowers, he was followed by a lady and a little girl. At the end of the path, "another lady was waiting, garbed in white silk and anxious to indulge in pleasures that were forbidden – the little girl seemed to be very tender in her touches and to be quite unconsciously, as though quite right seeking to influence my passions. The first woman was also clearly intimating her desire for love of an earthly sort." Partly awake, King was conscious "the dream might go in any

---

225 Diary, November 13, 1934.

direction and that if I lay still covered with the warmth of the [bed] clothes the intentions would be fulfilled. I said this is not for me, will not have it, this is not the way I want to go, and I made the sign of the cross in front of my breast and said if there were evil in what I was being told was natural, I wanted it to flee away."

Trying to interpret his vision while dressing, King noted of the "beautiful ladies" of his dream that "each one seen in the vision was a person truly beautiful in character and well known to me." He also realized, "it is the thought which is real; we may sin in thought quite as effectively as in the body, that my most difficult temptation is that subtle one where the thoughts possess one and one yields in the imagination to them. I believe the world is really spirit in essence – and that we do go to any part in thought – and are capable of any & all acts in thought." He believed that, paraphrasing Matthew 5:8, "vibrations bring us all each to his own place & we see God as we vibrate God's nature of purity etc. in our being. Then the pure in heart see God and are blessed on that account."

He felt blessed at the end of fifty-nine years "to have been permitted to glimpse reality – to touch on its fringes the outskirts of the spiritual world" and prayed for "nothing quite so much as a pure heart, and through that medium more and more of insight into God's will and ways and the strength and the power to do and to say that which is right and which serve to cause His will to be done, on earth, even as it is done in Heaven." The next day – on his sixtieth birthday – he admired a vase given to him by Joan Patteson, which she had inscribed with the weighty words, "increasingly significant with the years, 'And one hath seen the vision face to face.'"[226]

Mackenzie King almost never identified the women who aroused him sexually in his dreams by name – even those "well known to me" – and was also terribly embarrassed speaking with women about sexual relations. One exception was the wife of the Polish Consul General in Ottawa whom he met three days after his "Vision of The Way, through surrender of one's Thoughts." He recorded "a very pleasant talk with Madame Adamkiewicz who has much charm & poise" during a dinner at the Rideau Club in honour of Lady Perley and Sir George Perley, a Minister in R.B. Bennett's Government. That evening before going

---

226   Diary, December 16 and 17, 1934.

to sleep on the seventeenth anniversary of his mother's burial, King "felt the forces of physical attraction again at work, no doubt due to the associations of the evening. I tried to hold myself in check but find the subtlety of the forces at work great indeed."

After receiving a letter from Adamkiewicz a few days later thanking him for the conversation at the Rideau Club and an evening at Laurier House, King described receiving a "Vision of freedom of <u>Spirit</u> vs. Money Power." "I saw Madame Adamkiewicz before my eyes in the flowing garb as it were of some Greek goddess, like the Thraecian Victory, but bound with strappings around the waist, sufficient strappings to make it appear she was bound. She seemed the embodiment of woman with a spirit – the spirit of her was very real. She was not standing but in a lying posture; her face was not visible in features – but I knew it to be her."

In his "very real" vision, King had been studying banking issues (R.B. Bennett had established the privately-owned Bank of Canada in 1934) and saw a block of gold next to the bound and prostrate Adamkiewicz. "I said to myself this means, it is the spirit of woman that must be freed. It is <u>the freedom of the human spirit versus gold</u>. That is the great problem of today. I was being shown the two side by side, the woman bound, lying there with great beauty of form & nature – her spirit to be freed. To free the spirit it seemed that the weight of gold, money and its power would have to be removed."

Although he could not see Adamkiewicz's face, King "was conscious of her whole body and of a great soul being housed therein. I thought of her as 'altogether elemental.'" In this juxtaposition of spiritual and physical beauty, he believed the spirit, "(the head) will become increasingly revealed as 'the evil spirit' is driven away. I believe she will be helpful in revealing some great truths to me. I feel much attracted by her personality." He subsequently identified Adamkiewicz with Giuseppe Guastalla's bust of ideal womanhood, *Visions*. "She reminds me much of the conception of woman which Guastalla had in his other great work of art at the World's Fair – the natural physical being – absolutely true and truthful."[227]

In January at dinner at Senator Cairine Wilson's (King had appointed her as the first female Senator in 1930), the conversation turned to the question of our human natures. Madame Adamkiewicz affirmed, "we were purely physical beings, that all was physical, that some force

---

227 Diary, December 19, 20, and 24, 1934, and January 27, 1935.

worked through us, not ourselves which determined our actions. She spoke of the Snake in the Garden of Eden." Adamkiewicz wondered if the belief in personal immortality was not based upon egotism. "She could not feel the reality of the transcendental – the Occult – but believed only in the physical." King countered that he felt no concern about death, that "the mind & spirit were the realities, the physical was the unreal & unenduring ... My whole talk with Madam Adam (beginning of things) -kiewicz was to state my belief in spirit, mind, matter – reality being in that order & while not denying the physical to make it the lowest order in our natures as it is in the world itself."

After re-reading the introduction to Dr. Anita Mühl's *Automatic Writing*, "which deals with sub-conscious, etc.," King concluded, "some things are automatic in our nature, e.g., the physical attraction felt in talking with Madame Adamkiewicz ... to me what I was being shewn was that so far as the physical is concerned – it is largely automatic – something hidden & buried in our beings & becomes revealed where deep answers onto deep – and leads to the 'oneness' of which Madame Adamkiewicz also spoke – the oneness of the physical world – she was speaking of the force outside like the serpent – which works through man & woman, not themselves."[228]

Five months later, King felt the serpent's outside force when "a letter from the Polish Minister's wife inviting me to dinner seemed to arouse something in my nature quite unaccountable except on some theory of magnetic attraction. It made it difficult to rest one evening, and impossible to control one's thoughts, though no words had been spoken or exchanged." He questioned his very life-long religious and spiritual constraints against engaging in sexual activity as a bachelor. "I believe that in some ways there is too much inhibition of thought as well as act and that I suffer from an unnatural kind of life. I sometimes think this pain I have is due to the conflict and nervous condition occasioned thereby, and that if my life were the normal one of a natural man, I would regain strength which has certainly been lost somewhat in the suffering the last year or two."

Yet King was once again unable to resolve the conflict between what he conceived as his lower materialist sexual drive and his higher mind and spirit. "I know no departure from the path of virtue would bring happiness; it would certainly bring remorse, and loss of power."

---

228 Diary, January 27, 1935.

At the end of 1937, he once more was "completely overcome by some influence from without, which completely possessed me within; made it impossible to rest or sleep. I am certain it was an occult influence (not mere subjective force) but some kind of mental telepathy or communication."[229]

King often saw his own life experiences reflected like a mirror in his daily reading, not only in the Bible and inspirational "little books" but also in biographies, literary works and even in newspapers and fairy tales. He finished James Matthew Barrie's marvelous ghost novella, *Farewell Miss Julie Logan*, with Joan Patteson in July 1933, a few days before he departed on a speaking tour of Western Canada and the Co-operative Commonwealth Federation met to issue its Regina Manifesto calling for the replacement of capitalism with a planned socialist economy. In the novella, a sexually repressed Minister, Adam Yestreen, snow-bound in a Scottish glen in the 1860s, encounters mysterious "Strangers," ghosts of soldiers and supporters of Bonnie Prince Charlie defeated by the English after the Jacobite rising of 1745.

In popular lore, Charles Stuart, who had attempted to regain the British throne from the Protestant House of Hanover for the Catholic House of Stuart, hid in Rev. Yestreen's glen after his defeat at the Battle of Culloden. Hunted by the British, Stuart is saved from death by the mysterious "Someone Who Was With Him" who fed him when he hid fevered in the glen. "Of course the legend has it that she was young and fair and of high degree," Rev. Yestreen records in his diary, "and that she loved much." Barrie suggests that this "wayward woman" also had a sexual relationship with Bonnie Prince Charlie but was abandoned by him when he fled to the continent. The Reverend's manse is haunted by this "Spectrum" who is also embodied in the beautiful Miss Julie Logan, grandniece of the aristocratic Old Lady of the Grand House that was loyal to Charles Stuart. Yestreen falls madly in love with Julie Logan.[230]

Much of the appeal of the mystery for the reader lies in Barrie's construction of his ghost story, which implies that Rev. Yestreen had not gone mad but that the "Strangers" and Julie Logan had been real. After King and Patteson had finished the novella, Joan "was sure Barrie was a spiritualist, that I was wrong in thinking that he was seeking

---

229   Diary, June 16, 1935, and December 5, 1937.
230   Barrie, 262.

to imply that what Adam Yestreen had seen were hallucinations, that Barrie was writing of an actual record, believing in spirits (.....)." Patteson's statement gave King "a new thought and direction to work on and I decided to read the book again." He immediately perceived a correspondence between Barrie's text and his own life – "all the characters in Barrie's book find their duplicates here."

His terrier Pat barked just like the dog "of old descent" in *Farewell Miss Julie Logan* and behaved strangely as if he had sensed a ghostly presence in his home. King "took it as meaning 'They are near' & I had thought of the dog that barked at our seances ... It is here the parallel began to make itself clear in the grand Houses, though I did not see it for a while." He had also been reading his grandfather's Bible so that "gradually there came into my mind the significance of the dream of a night or two ago – of the 2 covenants of the beast that was slain & the bible, with grandfather's writing all over it." He recalled what his aunt Jennie Lindsey told him when King was about seventeen years old, "that the Mackenzie family had in it the blood of one of 'the great Houses' of Scotland."

> Who that great personage was I have never been able to recall; she named him some Lord – or someone of very high station – there was something of a child born out of lawful wedlock ... It seemed to me as I sat there it all went back to the time of 'the fatal battle of Culloden' as grandfather spoke of it in Mackenzie's Life of [Charles] Lindsey. (There is a curious fact my hand wrote this of its own bringing in the Lindsey as if to form the connection.) He speaks of one of his ancestors following Prince Charlie abroad, fighting for him, though he was a Catholic – of all his ancestors sticking to Charles Stuart whom 'barring his religion, all Scotland deemed as their rightful sovereign' ... grandfather spoke of his 'native glen' ...
>
> It seems to me that 'the stranger,' the one who was ministering to the others, might be a spirit that visits me even now – the spirit of the one who attended the Prince – who has been in the glen, in the form of a ministering angel – that this spirit may have been the one near when Pat growled the other night – and when he barked this morning, that I have in me the blood of the prince – that the spirit is the Stranger & that she is the Julie Logan.
>
> Joan came along as I was reading. I told her of my thoughts as far as I could. She reminded me that a Julia had come & called to

me when Mrs. Wriedt was with me in Brockville. I remember it vividly. For a moment, it was as if I were in a world of spirits and this voice Julie, Julie, calling out to me. (.....)[231]

King was so struck by these apparent parallels that he put aside preparing speeches for his imminent Western tour since he felt "this is the most amazing experience of my life." He and Joan again read Barrie's novella out loud, "bearing in mind that it was paralleling facts in my own ancestry, as well as in my own personal experience." The "amazing" parallels they perceived between Prince Charlie and William Lyon Mackenzie's flight after the failed 1837 Rebellion included "the concealment in the cave, the being hunted by the British red coats, the protection of him even by his opponents, the bounty on the head, the unwillingness of any however poor to avail themselves of the bounty, etc. – the escape across the border – The parallel is complete."

But King discovered that "there is something more profound & deeper than that, and it is hidden away in Barrie's book." He recognized that Barrie had portrayed the ghostly Julie Logan as a dangerous seductress with characteristics of a vampire. She had disfigured the face of a previous minister residing in Adam's manse with her teeth. And when she helped to deliver the baby of a snow-bound resident in the glen, its mother snatched the infant from her arms because she "had a sinking that she was going to bite it." King himself felt a "spectrum bite" when he was reading before going to sleep and "felt for a moment as if the back of my hand were caught in the crack of a closing door ... I feel quite sure this was a materialization – something letting me see that I am right in believing that the spirit of Julie Logan is about, that it is the one that has been near to me all the time ... this is significant evidence & paralleling."

King also perceived that Barrie used the violin of the repressed Reverend as a symbol for his sexual desire – "a symbol of the spirit of Julie Logan. His desire to caress it – its coming towards him – his taking it to bed with him, his imaginings concerning it, this all repeated later with the spirits" – and related the parallel to his own experiences with "electric currents" sent by others that made him unable to control his sex instinct. "I thought of my own 'experiences' which I thought were related to others outside ... a spirit that was attaching itself to one & which had come perhaps down the years. I am sure an

---

231 Diary, July 16 and 18, 1933.

ancestor of mine loved some maiden in the glen at the time of Prince Charlie. That one left with the Prince for France is recorded in Mackenzie's Life – whether he was the one who left her behind & that her spirit is seeking him I cannot say, more likely she has found him in the beyond. (....)"[232]

The following day King concluded, "I was being shown that Barrie's book was a guide – taking me back by Mackenzie to his past, shewing the way to his ancestry ... also Barrie's book coming to me from Joan – Joan clearly is helping me to find myself. She is a ministering spirit & her life & mine have some link in the past as I have said to her many times." Recording in his diary still further parallels about Mackenzie's life found in Nathaniel Benson's drama *The Patriot* and his own "associating my ancestry with the Great House," King felt a sudden sexual charge. "(As I write this down I feel a singular emotional excitement which is as real as anything I have ever experienced, and which if I were to give way to it for a moment would mean the most complete union possible with some woman.) It is the blood of my ancestor & that spirit, Julie Logan, wherever she is seeking contact, or taking possession of my body ... It is clear to me that what the loved ones are seeking to get through to me is the story of my ancestry, as explaining my temptation as 'partly fate' and 'partly free-will.'" He reasoned that "If Julie Logan were left having borne a child – the basket referred to what they shared – & waited & waited, she would be the one that would lament & her spirit would haunt the glen – following down those who shared the Mackenzie blood – & so would come to me."

King composed a family genealogy tracing his ancestry to the Jacobite rising of 1745, noting that his aunt Elizabeth Mackenzie also "believed in messages, spirits." He informed Joan, "I never saw more clearly as I write now, what might account for the spirit of the wayward woman – coming to grandfather & coming to me – he speaks of the errors of the head & heart – that is what I have suffered from as well." King identified the basket with which Julie Logan brought food to Prince Charlie as a symbol of their love relationship. When his massage therapist, Dr. Ball, brought him a basket of fish, he insisted on purchasing the basket for $10 [$220 in 2023 dollars]. "Here was the last of Julie Logan ... everything had been sent to cure me of the spirit that had been following

---

232 Diary, July 16 and 17, 1933.

me, something earth bound & holding to the blood – & that seeing <u>the basket</u> ... I was able to detach & objectively view the 'influence' at work & now to understand my own nature – what was natural – attract the divine by divine fire & not the flesh by the lusts thereof." He told Joan, "she had been the ministering spirit that had helped to save my soul & reminded her of help I had been able to give her about a matter of torment, which concerned her, till it was held up objectively & discussed." They placed the basket on the hall table at Kingsmere. "There it is a symbol of the truth of [the] whole story."²³³

King and Patteson began reading Catherine Macdonald Maclean's *Dorothy Wordsworth, The Early Years* in September 1933. He noted, "Joan seemed to be guided in her selection of books" and immediately associated the poet's "Tintern Abbey" with the picture of Tintern Abbey his father had in his rooms at the University of Toronto and with two paintings sent him by Homer Watson to whom he had been introduced by his father. "This is all surpassing wonderfully. I feel that through all this beauty dear father would have me believe" – as Maclean had written of William Wordsworth – "that my life is 'being shaped and moulded by some unseen power to a definite end' ... It is all very very real & the line of division is as nothing between this world & the next – their presence & my own." He found Maclean's biography of Wordsworth "written with an understanding of the forces that influence conduct and character."²³⁴

King was struck in 1933 by "how wonderfully parallel to my life this summer – our lives at Kingsmere – my life in other regards – is the story of Dorothy & William Wordsworth ... through it all the evident Spiritualist belief – and the search for our destiny which seemed the link between Wordsworth, Coleridge & others, and is between Homer Watson & myself." He found even more profound parallels between himself and the poet when he received Hugh l'Anson Fausset's book, *The Lost Leader: A Study of Wordsworth*, in April 1934. In his chapter "The Fall," King saw a

---

233 Diary, July 17 and 18, 1933.

234 Diary, September 25 and 28, 1933, and October 8, 1933. By 1935, he considered Maclean, along with Violet Markham and Stephen Spender, "three of the best minds in Britain today." Four days before he died on July 22, 1950, he wrote the Macmillan Company of Canada regarding a contract in which he guaranteed a $4,000 [$51,000 in 2023 dollars] subsidy for two years for *Maclean* to write a *Life of William Lyon Mackenzie*. See Diary, August 22, 1935, and July 18, 1950.

parallel between himself and the poet fathering his daughter Caroline in Revolutionary France and failing to marry her mother, Annette Vallon. Wordsworth had been "false to his truer and purer being," Fausset wrote, and was thus unable to expel the poison from his blood so that "the furies of perplexity, shame and remorse were already on his track."

King wrote of his own inability to control his sex drive, "All of this might have been written of myself in bygone years – as I read it, I thought of the poison in my blood that has maimed me physically for the past half year. In Nature I pray the remedy is to come, in seeking the simple life etc. I pray too that [with] my continuous striving I may yet reach the point where 'he that overcometh, shall all things inherit.' … This writer Fausset sees deeply into spiritual experiences and by interpreting the progress of Wordsworth's spiritual life is making clear to me many truths about my own."[235]

Most significantly, Mackenzie King believed that – like Wordsworth – he had become a "Lost Leader" because of his inability to overcome his earth-bound sex instinct. "It is singular – or rather significant, that I should have a sort of recurrence of physical sensations which is almost impossible to control – & which at a time of sleep seem to pass beyond my control – just when reading this particular phase of Wordsworth's Life." "It were as though I was being taken back many years purposely to let me see the forces which had served to undermine and might have destroyed entirely my leadership. The truth is that I too have been a 'lost leader' or rather The Lost Leader. Years that might have meant very much to leadership in the party and country were sacrificed in part to compromise with what I knew to be wrong, and unwillingness to face it squarely. I have tried to do so since, and it may be that through the providence and grace of God it may not be too late, but I am sorely conscious at the present time of wherein I cannot come out and say the things I feel ought to be said, and want to say, just why I can't, I can scarcely explain to myself."

For his speech to the Women's Liberal Club, before an audience of one thousand at the Royal York on May 11, 1934, King had intended to contrast "the Spiritual & Christian note" with the materialistic one of Socialism & Communism and the note of Christian love with "the ruthlessness of dictatorship" but found himself unable to do so. "I have failed to speak out because of 'the negative self reasserting its

---

235 Diary, October 8, 1933, April 26, 1934, and May 13 and 15, 1934. Fausset, 117-18. Revelations 21:7.

claims' – the denying of Christ, preventing the assertion of His life & its example – Like Peter (In his life there is hope – he denied – but he repented – and he came to be the founder of a Church) ... I have been the Lost Leader in much that I should have led in and for the same reason that Wordsworth was."

Despite his despair, King once again demonstrated how he used his reading of the Bible and other books, his dream visions and spirit communications to cope with the 'poison in his blood" – his "past which continues, often subconsciously and unconsciously to enthrall" – so that he could become the true leader he aspired to be. He combined a basic understanding of psychology with the teachings of the Bible regarding acknowledging and confronting his failings, to forgive others, to ask those he had harmed for forgiveness, and above all to ask for the forgiveness of God, "the power of Christ – to cast out the devil – the evil influence which continues, persists – and seeks to come in whenever given a chance by association of ideas, names, etc."[236]

Ten days later, King attended a luncheon of the League of Nations Society featuring a discussion on foreign policy and peace in the world that was attended by J.S. Woodsworth, national chairman of the Co-operative Commonwealth Federation. King recorded in his diary, "I had a feeling that Woodsworth who was there had retained as Leader what I had lost (for a while), the fearlessness of speaking out, of realizing the creative & real nature of the forces at work. He spoke of the time he was in the East end of London & I was at Passmore Edwards Settlement & Hull House – those were the days of real conviction & vision. He has retained his; I have not lost mine, but like Wordsworth, [have] hesitated to speak out as I should. I believe I am emerging – that this is the moment of revival – that like Wordsworth I am finding the two things go together, one's personal life & its happenings & the part one will play in politics. I pray God I may become a real Leader of men.[237]

By the outbreak of World War II, Mackenzie King's belief in magnetic and electric forces had been firmly incorporated into his spirituality. After continuing to read Gladys Osborne Leonard's *My Life in Two Worlds* he commented, "It is a little tiresome re materialization etc., though interesting & true – coming from her. There are magnetic & electric forces possessed by some which certain connect with others

---

236 Diary, May 15, 1934.
237 Diary, May 25, 1934.

in the beyond & help to bring into being the material phenomena described. – The ether is the reality."[238]

When in 1943 Francis Mulvihill, one of his part-time labourers at Kingsmere, informed the PM that he was being treated in his abdomen with electricity and that "they were able to speak to him also," King "saw in a moment that it was a case of clear hallucination." "I said to him that that was pure imagination and that it originated in his brain...I tried to explain to him that he must dismiss the thought that there was any power of the kind that could be exercised over him, but he was very positive, refusing to admit this. I told him the sensation was real but it did not come from the source that he thought."

In 1947, King was "immensely relieved" to hear Dr. Parsons in Ottawa "say that my spine had kept in perfect shape: that he found me in good condition but that it would be wise to have a check-up...He treated my cold by applying electricity to the sinus, nostrils, etc., by letting electric current flow through his own body and bringing a point of contact with his hand. This seemed to bring quite remarkable relief."[239]

In the context of Mackenzie King's search for the origin of the "fire through the veins" he felt in his body, it is worth noting its curious parallel with the "serpentine fire" of kundalini energy. As early as 1916, he had his spine x-rayed in Ottawa and again in Baltimore where he confided to Dr. Barker that he felt sexual sensations in the perineal region behind the tip of the final segment of the vertebrae column. In 1932, he speculated about "some sensory centre that begins work on its own, as a result of an outside impulse or stimulus."

The prominent American psychic investigator Hereward Carrington presented twelve lectures delivered before the Psychological Research Society of New York in 1918 in which he explored the relationship between Yoga practices, kundalini energy, psychic centres or "chakras," and the production of psychic phenomena. He published these lectures as *Higher Psychical Development (Yoga Philosophy): An Outline of the Secret Hindu Teachings* in 1920.[240]

In a more recent collection of essays, *Kundalini Rising: Exploring the Energy of Awakening*, Stuart Sovatsky writes of kundalini yoga that "the practice can be traced back at least five thousand years to

---

238 Diary, August 15, 1939.
239 Diary, August 15, 1939, November 22, 1943, and February 6, 1947.
240 See in particular Chapter 11, "The Relation of Yoga to 'Psychics.'"

the archeological relic known as the Pashupati seal. It depicts an antler-crowned demigod, sitting cross-legged with one heel pressing his androgynous perineum and the other the root of his erect penis." Like Carrington, he also notes of the principal energy centres or "chakras" of the human body that "the primordial kundalini energy itself was seen glowing and seething at the perineum in the *muladhara* chakra, the 'root generator' center that governs the earth element."[241]

This first chakra can radiate kundalini energy upwards to the second *svadhishthana* chakra located at the root of the sexual organs. If the kundalini energy can radiate up through other principal energy centres to the highest *sahasrara* chakra located in the crown of the head, it can affect a God or cosmic consciousness. King speculated in 1932 regarding Princess Cantacuzene whether the electric and magnetic currents he was feeling were "part of a divine fire which controlled means, power and understanding." The following year he speculated with Joan Patteson whether it was possible to "attract the divine by divine fire & not the flesh by the lusts thereof."[242]

In *Kundalini Rising*, Dorothy Walters writes that for the committed aspirant, kundalini "awakens a deep sense of connection with the divine essence, the ultimate mystery of creation itself. Often, especially during the bliss states, we feel as though these visitations come from a heavenly source, almost as if the angels have descended and enfolded us in boundless love...The goal of the mystical journey is, for the religious, permanent union with the higher being, total surrender of self – annihilation into God." In his diaries, King records that his life mission was to carry out God's will on earth and references the appearances of angels in his dreams and the boundless love of his deceased mother, father, sister, and brother in their almost nightly dream visitations and in séance "conversations."[243]

Carlos S. Alvarado and Michael Nahm have noted of Hereward Carrington that he "was one of the most prolific popularisers in the history of psychical research...Carrington was clearly a vitalist, believing that human beings had a force or principle in them that defined life, independent of the workings of the body ... He argued that mediums could exteriorize a nervous energy that usually stayed

---

241 Sovatsky, 248, 250.
242 Diary, May 8, 1932, and July 18, 1933.
243 Walters, 7, 18.

in the body, to produce movement of objects and materializations ... In his view these materializations represented the condensation of this usually invisible force, what many referred to as ectoplasm."[244]

As discussed in chapter 16, King met Carrington in New York in 1933 when he took out a membership in his American Psychical Institute. King's contacts with Canada's most prominent investigator of psychic energy and ectoplasm, Winnipeg's Dr. T. Glen Hamilton, is discussed in chapter 12.

---

244 Alvarado and Nahm, 94, 95.

CHAPTER 7

Mackenzie King and the Historians

Most historians, in three *Maclean's* surveys over two decades, ranked Mackenzie King among Canada's greatest Prime Ministers for his political leadership in winning Canada's autonomy from the British Empire, keeping English and French Canada united during Canada's enormous war effort in World War II, and inaugurating the Canadian social welfare safety net by introducing old age pensions in 1927, unemployment insurance in 1940, and family allowances in 1944.[245] He ranked first in the 1997 survey, slipped to third place behind Wilfrid Laurier and John A. Macdonald in the 2011 poll, and regained the position of best Prime Minister in *Maclean's* 2016 ranking.

For J.L. Granatstein and Norman Hillmer, "Mackenzie King was Canada's greatest prime minister, party leader, and politician." Michael Bliss also judged him as "the greatest and most interesting of Canada's prime ministers." In his autobiography, *Writing History*, Bliss recalled, "the more I reflected on Mackenzie King, prime minister off and on from 1921 to 1949, whom it had become fashionable to ridicule for his strange ideas about spiritualism, his sexual anxieties, and his total lack of charisma, the more I admired his intelligence, his understanding of the country, and his effectiveness...I judged him Canada's best." Ian McKay in turn perceived King as "the country's most significant early twentieth-century liberal theorist and politician" and "so obviously one of the pivotal organic intellectuals of the twentieth-century liberal state." And in his 2011 biography, Allan Levine assessed King as "the greatest and

---

245 Hillmer and Granatstein, Granatstein and Hillmer, Hillmer and Azzi, and Azzi and Hillmer.

most peculiar prime minister Canada has ever had and likely will ever have."²⁴⁶

These laudatory appraisals contrast jarringly with commentary about King's occult practices after his death. H. Blair Neatby, one of the historians commissioned by King's executors to write his multi-volume biography, briefly summarized the whole panoply of his occult activities in the 1930s in a matter-of-fact manner. These – what Neatby called "superstitions" – included his belief in phrenology, numerology, astrology, automatic writing, fortune-tellers, horoscopes, dream interpretation and dream visions, his friendships with spiritualists, and the use of mediums and "conversations" over the "little table" to communicate with the departed in the Beyond. Neatby ascribed these activities to King's loneliness and inability to form genuine friendships. As he wrote in the third volume of the King biography, *The Prism of Unity*, published in 1976, "His ventures into the occult helped to dissipate his loneliness and also to reassure him of his significance as a person as well as a public figure ... his solution was to find reassurance in another world." Neatby had already affirmed the official position maintained by King's executors and biographers in the second volume, *The Lonely Heights*, published in 1963. "Mackenzie King's many political decisions in his long career do not need to be explained by any reference to the spirit world."²⁴⁷

Neatby's unequivocal assertion will be tested in later chapters on the influence of Rachel Bleaney on King during the 1925, 1926 and 1930 federal elections and on the impact of King's occult beliefs in his dealings with Adolf Hitler. Robert Teigrob, in *Four Days in Hitler's Germany: Mackenzie King's Mission to Avert a Second World*

---

246 Granatstein and Hillmer, 84. Bliss, *Right Honourable Men*, 123. Bliss, *Writing History*, 321. Ian McKay, 427, 403. Levine, *King*, 398. Levine entitled his conclusion "Canada's Greatest Prime Minister."

247 Neatby, *William Lyon Mackenzie King, The Prism of Unity, 1932-1939*, 70, 72, and *William Lyon Mackenzie King, The Lonely Heights, 1924-1932*, 408. Before its publication by the University of Toronto Press, *The Lonely Heights* was serialized in four parts by *Weekend Magazine*, a supplement to about forty Canadian daily newspapers. Part One, "Loneliness Was His Burden – And His Shield" was subtitled "He wanted to be liked but had little time for friends, so his mind moved slowly into the world of spiritualism." See the *Ottawa Citizen*, October 19, 1963, pp. 66, 67. See also pp. 403-412 in Neatby's chapter "The Distortions of Reality," serialized as *Weekend Magazine's* Part Four, "How The Spirit World Gave Him Reassurance: From his occult experiences he chose only views that confirmed his own ideas," *Ottawa Citizen*, November 9, 1963, 100.

War, suggested contrary to Neatby that "In crafting his approach to the troubles in Europe, King seemed to put less stock in the material evidence before him than on the false assurances of chronic fraudsters, along with cues from blankets, clouds, imaginary friends, and a host of other hallucinatory signs and wonders. These attitudes and approaches produced a mission by a Canadian prime minister that could hardly have been less illuminating or fruitful."

Roy MacLaren, in *Mackenzie King in the Age of the Dictators: Canada's Imperial and Foreign Policies*, similarly argued that "In his domestic political balancing act" between English Canada and Quebec "King was reassured by voices from Beyond counselling that, as leader of the opposition [1930-1935], he should stand clear of attempts – if there were any – to influence what the United Kingdom might do about collective security at the League of Nations and Italy's threatened invasion of Abyssinia."[248]

The military historian Charles P. Stacey, in his revisionist *A Very Double Life: The Private World of Mackenzie King*, also published in 1976 like *The Prism of Unity*, provided a much more detailed examination of the Prime Minister's spiritual and occult practices than Neatby and MacLaren and destroyed his image as an intellectual. Describing King's numerous "conversations" with the departed over the "little table" at Laurier House, Stacey wrote, "It is the extraordinary crudity of the manifestations of his spiritualism, the shattering naïveté of his judgements in these matters, that leave one with the ineradicable impression of a limited intelligence. At times, it is simply impossible to take him seriously." After extensively citing one of these "conversations" with deceased family members, friends, and the great Liberal leaders in England and Canada on King's birthday from his 1934 diary, Stacey concluded, "Once more one stands in awe before the ego that could produce such a tribute to itself out of its own viscera."

The historian also quoted from King's notes of a "conversation" over the "little table" eight days prior to the 1935 election, which returned him as Prime Minister. Among the many departed who appeared, St. John said, "Long ago I wanted to tell you that God had chosen you to shew men & nations how they should live." His late friend Lord Grey, the British Foreign Secretary during 1906-1916, added, "Long ago I saw that you would be a peace-maker ... God has chosen you for

---

248 Teigrob, 236. MacLaren, 87.

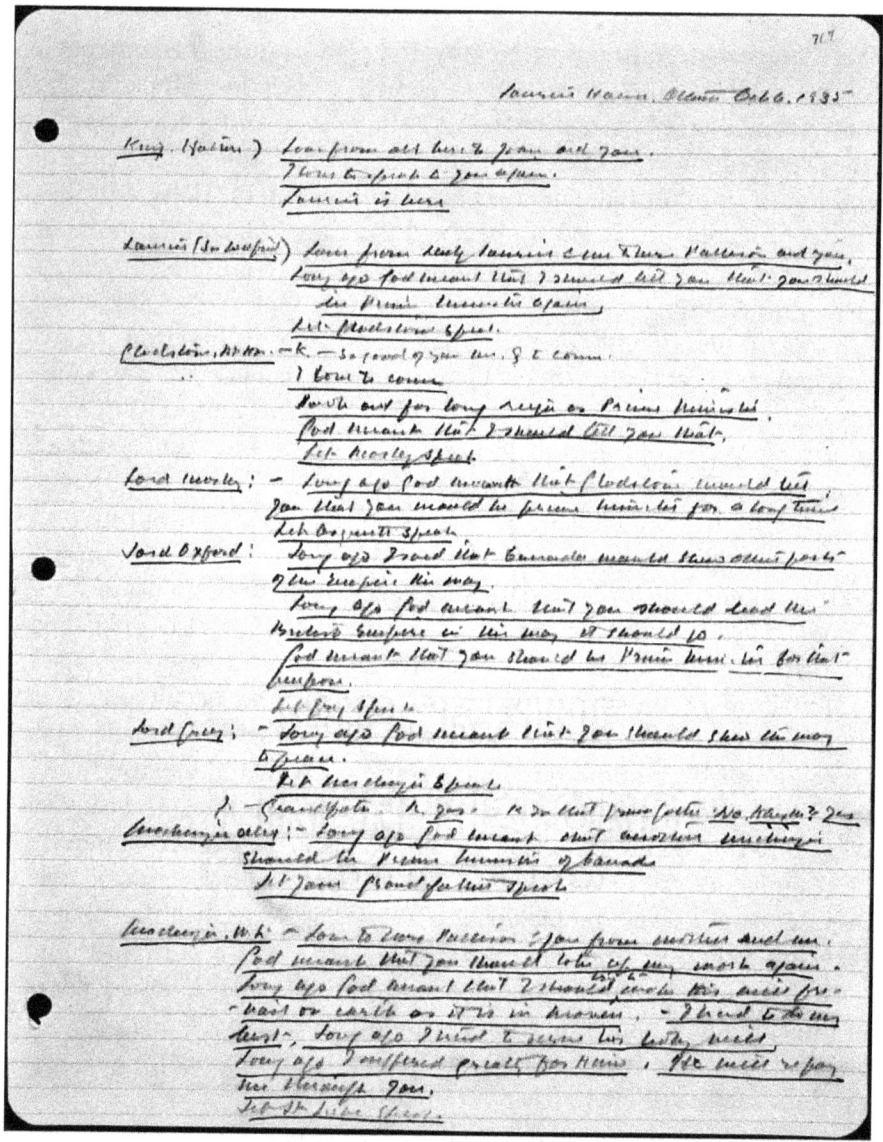

Figure 23: King's record of the "marvellous results" of his "conversation" over the "little table," October 6, 1935.

that purpose." Sir Wilfrid Laurier made several predictions about the outcome of the 1935 election, the great majority of which were proven incorrect. Stacey again suggested to his readers, "Most Canadians, if they had been confronted with the document just quoted, would have said that the Liberal leader was out of his head. Fortunately for him, however, the electorate had no knowledge of what went on behind the doors of Laurier House." On Palm Sunday in 1942, King wrote that Laurier House and the House of Commons were "both dedicated to God's work in my life."[249]

Henry Stanley Ferns – a member of King's secretarial staff from 1940 to 1943 – wrote in his memoirs *Reading from Left to Right* that "if one reads the celebrated Mackenzie King diaries for the years 1939-45 one forms the impression that Canada was governed by a superstitious lunatic." Ferns observed that "those portions of the diaries which I have read shocked me, not on account of any strange quirks that are there exhibited, but because they reveal a foolish and childish immaturity of private personality in contradiction to his great ability as a public man." Pierre Berton, after referencing passages in King's diary about his spiritualism and séances, declared on *Front Page Challenge* in 1978 that the Prime Minister was at times "a certifiable nut." He challenged the *Ottawa Journal* writer and one of King's neighbours near Laurier House, Richard Jackson, "Is it not an indictment of the Ottawa press corps, of which you were a member, that these facts did not emerge in some form during King's lifetime? … Surely in any other country, no Prime Minister could hide the fact from the press that he was that much a spiritualist." The historian and broadcaster Laurier LaPierre echoed Berton on CBC-TV *Saturday Report* in 1991: "What is dangerous about this is that he sought political advice."[250]

George Bowering suggested, "one could spend one's whole life in the National Archives, just reading that diary … There is more writing about Mackenzie King than just about any other Canadian, but no one has ever been able to explain Mackenzie King." Will Ferguson asked whether – in private – King was "a fascinating, mystical, spirit-intoxicated eccentric." He concluded, "In public, however, he was a master politician. Cunning, quiet and relentlessly bland. In many ways, he was the ultimate Canadian: bizarre yet dull, passionate yet celibate, crafty yet thick, calm yet more than a bit mad."

Charlotte Gray also "trawled through some of the endless wash of words" in King's diary while researching the life of his mother,

---

249 Stacey, *A Very Double Life*, 175-176, 183, 184. Diary, Palm Sunday, March 28, 1942. Book F, p. 87.

250 Ferns, 140, 141. Pierre Berton, *Front Page Challenge*, March 27, 1978. Laurier LaPierre, CBC-TV *Saturday Report*, November 16, 1991.

Isabel King. In a *Saturday Night* article on the Prime Minister entitled "Crazy Like a Fox," Gray queried, "How can we square the evidence of the diaries … with King's extraordinary success in government? No historian or biographer has ever managed to put together the two sides of Mackenzie King: Mr. King, the stodgy windbag, and Weird Willie, the mother-obsessed oddball."[251] As Keyserlingk observed, "King's spiritualism has been a deep source of embarrassment for most scholars, little more than a sad indication of his personal, social, or psychological weaknesses. As a result, this part of King's life has been hived-off to a private realm…the occult side of King revealed in his private papers has baffled scholars, who either have not comprehended his insights or could not forgive such quackery."[252]

A few historians speculated about the specific nature of the Prime Minister's possible mental disorders. Robert Teigrob suggested most recently that "If King were alive in our day…he might well be diagnosed with pareidolia and / or apophenia. Those with the former exhibit a marked tendency to see distinct images in random and meaningless stimuli…An apopheniac not only perceives the image detected by the pareidoliac, but deems it part of an ongoing stream of messages from the spiritual realm…Over time those demonstrating such behaviours can descend into paranoia or psychosis, but the symptoms have also been linked to increased creativity." In *Four Days in Hitler's Germany*, Teigrob proposed that it "appears logical that a person who simply cannot help but make constant connections, who is bombarded with synchronized, repetitive, portentous signals, would be drawn to spiritualism; more than that, the traits associated with apophenia in particular *require* belief in the purposeful workings of unseen forces…Perhaps, in other words, King's spirituality is not merely a peripheral and derisible curiosity, but an essential ingredient in the makeup of a political savant."[253]

Colonel Stacey, Canada's most distinguished military historian, was among those scholars who could not forgive King's occult "quackery" as revealed in what he called "that colossal compilation" and "one of the most remarkable diaries in human annals." Yet he also suggested that the Prime Minister's diary "may offer a special source of personal

---

251 Bowering, 209. Ferguson, 256, 257. Gray, "Crazy Like a Fox," 42, 44.
252 Keyserlingk, 27, 28.
253 Teigrob, 66, 67.

revelation about King that has not yet been tapped." Stacey proposed that the séance "conversations" the PM recorded "over the little table" came "straight out of King's subconscious mind...in these memoranda of seances we are coming pretty close to what I have called the quintessential King." Along with his diary, "King's meticulous records of his sessions with the little table are a revelation of his inner mind."[254]

Rachel Bleaney and Etta Wriedt had affirmed that they could establish direct contact with the spirit world. Stacey hypothesized that King now found himself able "to engage in what may be called 'do-it-yourself' spiritualism, in which he and his friend Mrs. Patteson conversed over the table with the spirits of the departed without the assistance of any third party." Stacey concluded, "It is my impression that rapping soon gave place to a more direct form of communication in which King acted, in effect, as a medium himself, receiving messages and repeating them aloud for the benefit of Mrs. Patteson." Roy MacLaren similarly determined that "In his spiritualist meanderings King was in a sense talking to himself."

The Prime Minister lends some support to this assumption that he was receiving communications in his mind as he was writing down messages from the spirit world in a reference to Andrew Lang's introduction to Alexander Mackenzie's *The Prophecies of the Brahan Seer*. "He begins to write of two experiences – and then says '<u>as I pen these words another comes to me</u>.'" King observed that this was "something I find happens so often."[255]

The Spiritualist Prime Minister explores what Stacey called King's inner mind and traces how his spiritual and religious beliefs and convictions may have influenced his political decision making. For as the eminent historian of psychoanalysis Paul Roazen suggested in 1998 in *Canada's King: An Essay in Political Psychology*, "Until we get a more rounded view of how to integrate King's spiritualism with the rest of his accomplishments, an unsatisfactory situation will remain in which King appears simply as an enigma, without any effort going into trying better to fit the pieces of this curious puzzle together."

---

254 Stacey, *Mackenzie King and the Atlantic Triangle*, 12, 13, 20. Stacey, *Canada and the Age of Conflict*, ix.

255 Stacey, *A Very Double Life*, 172. Stacey, *Mackenzie King and the Atlantic Triangle*, 12-13. MacLaren, 86. Diary, December 4, 1938. The Lang citation is from page vi of his introduction.

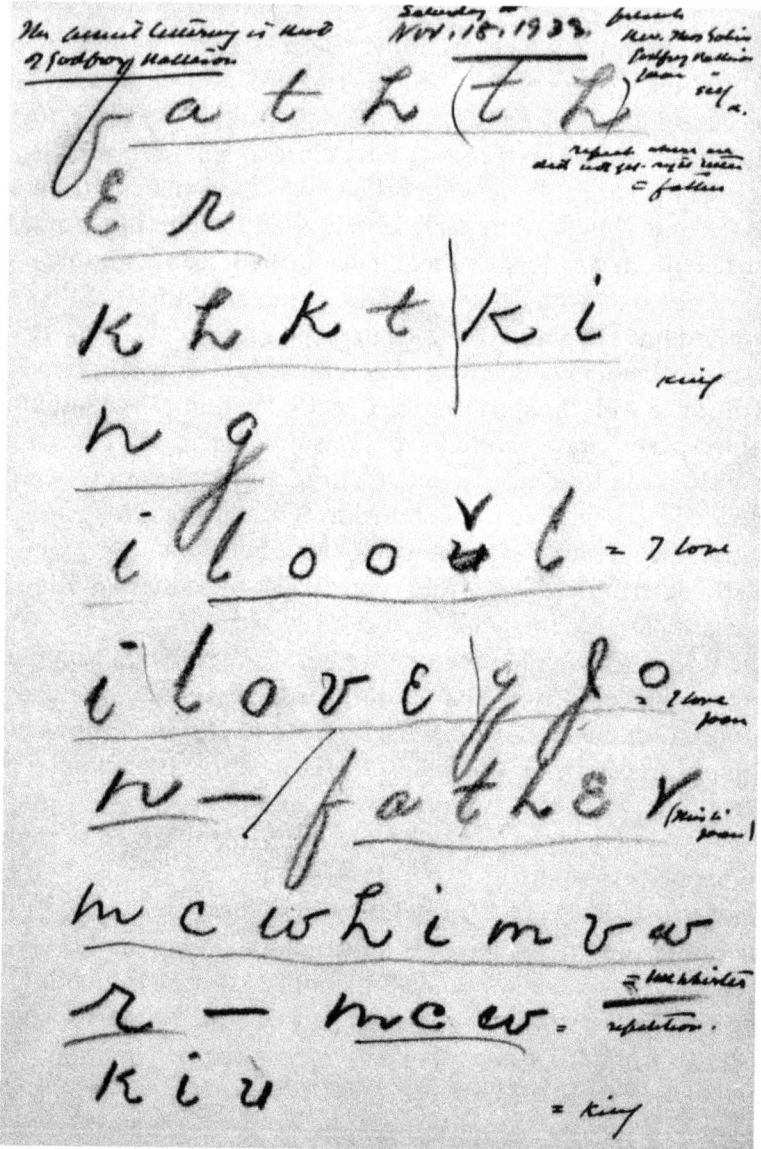

Figure 24: Record of the first table rapping effort at Laurier House, November 18, 1933. Hand lettering by Godfroy Patteson.

A decade later, Margaret Bedore asserted once more, "Despite the continuous assessments of historians, King still eludes us. There is no intellectual history of King – The Mind of Mackenzie King…There is no complete work on his religious life – The Faith of Mackenzie King. We have not appreciated how religion sustained King throughout a long career and filtrated through all his thoughts. The windows to his mind and his faith need to be opened to bring us closer to the real Mackenzie King." Roy MacLaren, in *Mackenzie King in the Age of the Dictators*, has argued more recently that "to dismiss revelations of his preoccupation with the Great Beyond as irrelevant to an understanding of the man is to overlook the insight that they provide into his complex character. Worse, such an approach ignores the truism that all democratically elected leaders should be held to account for their character, their honesty, and their effect on the nations."[256]

The Spiritualist Prime Minister attempts to achieve such a more rounded view by documenting his life-long spiritual pursuits and how Spiritualism was a fundamental element of his worldview and being. Alan Bennett entitled a similar biographical exploration *The Madness of George III*, and its subsequent film adaptation, *The Madness of King George*. Bennett postulated that King George's mental illness resulted from porphyria, an inherited disease affecting the nervous system. Its possible symptoms included hallucinations, delusions, and psychoses. Mackenzie King referred to having his teeth treated for porphyria by Dr. Snell in Toronto over a sixteen-year period. He did not have the type of porphyria triggered by exposure to sunlight, however, for he recorded in his diaries taking a "sun bath" from 1894 through to sunbathing with President Roosevelt in Warm Springs, Georgia, in 1940. (He referenced seven sun baths in 1935 alone, including lying out "quite naked" on the upper verandah of one of his cottages at Kingsmere.)[257]

Porphyria is associated with depression. King frequently highlighted his repeated periods of depression and to having inherited physical traits from his controversial grandfather and mother. Mackenzie, the tempestuous political reformer and leader of the 1837 Rebellion in Upper Canada, was accused by his detractors of being mentally unstable. According to Charlotte Gray, he "was a fearless crusader in public, but in private he could hurtle into black depressions just

---

256 Roazen, 43. See Jeremy Pearce, "Paul Roazen, 69, Scholar Who Found Flaws in Freud, Dies," *New York Times*, November 23, 2005, and Morton Schatzman, "Professor Paul Roazen," *The Independent*, November 16, 2005. Bedore, 62. MacLaren, 87.

257 Diary, November 10, 1922, November 14, 1925, November 22, 1928, February 1, 1929, December 5, 1929, November 30, 1937, September 28, 1938, and June 1, 1935.

like his daughter Barbara." His oldest daughter suffered from manic depression and was committed into New York's Asylum for the Insane in 1848 while Mackenzie lived in exile in the United States. In 1860, she burned to death in the Provincial Lunatic Asylum on Queen Street in Toronto after setting her clothes on fire.[258] Barbara had been an inmate for over a year. "Asylum records reveal that a paternal great aunt and a maternal aunt had been diagnosed insane also." Henry Stanley Ferns and Bernard Ostry, in their *The Age of Mackenzie King*, noted that after Mackenzie resigned from the Legislature of Canada "in disgust" in 1858, "he was esteemed mad." After he died in 1861 at the age of 66, Charles Lindsey recorded, "The official cause of death was given as 'softening of the brain.'"[259]

Mackenzie's youngest daughter Isabel, Mackenzie King's mother, also became seriously ill with what her father described as a "brain fever or an affliction of the brain" at the age of seven in June 1850 and, evoking her sister Barbara, later recorded a dream in which she "set my own clothes on fire twice." After Isabel married John King and had given birth to their children, "Her moods came to dominate the household as her father's had once done: the threat of her depressions was like an extra member of the family, hovering behind the curtains." In 1919, Mackenzie King recorded that he considered cancelling a trip to the United States because of a nervous strain that made him want to cry in despair. "I have had that feeling of wishing to cry all day. My nerves I fear are getting the better of me."

Two years later he wrote his physician brother Max, "Some days I have complete command of myself but there are times when I seem to lose this grip entirely, and to be overcome with depression which is next to impossible to throw off. I am beginning to discover that highly emotional nature not unlike mother's in some particulars, and that I shall have to learn to guard against all its dangers." (The following year he finished reading "the volume 'Outwitting Our Nerves' by Dr. Jackson [Josephine A. Jackson, *Outwitting Our Nerves: A Primer of Psychotherapy*. New York: The Century Co., 1921] – found it most helpful.") When he compiled a genealogy of his family in 1933, he recalled that there were also "a number of tragedies" in the Lindseys'

---

258 Gray, *Mrs. King*, 10, 5, 7, 25, 37, 174. Luno, 37-40, 59-60, 63-64.

259 Diary, June 1, 1935. Luno, 51-52, 18, 66. Ferns and Ostry, 11. Lindsey, *The Life and Times of William Lyon Mackenzie*, 13.

part of the family tree. "Mother's brother Willie ended his life with a razor ... Lyon Lindsey if I remember ended his, with his mother's picture in his hand either by drowning or shooting. Nellie Lindsey was bereft of her full reason for a time."[260]

King's historians overlooked half-a-century of references in his diaries to his periodic bouts of depression and brain pain. He had already recorded when he was twenty-four years old in 1898, "I inherit too much from mother, i.e. too much of this terrible sensitiveness" and could "see much of Mother's nature in me ... the nervous energy and desire." While working as Deputy Minister of Labour in 1904 he wrote, "This has been a day of extreme depression. I have felt since I woke as though my body were deluged with grief and as if my eyes would rain floods of tears. Do what I will I cannot throw it off, nor do I know whence it came."[261]

In 1898, King also began recording having a terrible pain in his brain. While still Leader of the Opposition in February 1921, he actively campaigned in an important by-election won by the Liberals in Peterborough, Ontario. He wrote that the victory greatly increased his political stature but also that "At times today I feared a sort of brain storm which has occurred too frequently of late ... a process of mental demoralization has been going on. It mars the hour of victory." He felt very tired and depressed two months after his defeat in the 1930 federal election. "It is a sort of brain fag more than all else. I seem to have no desire or power to write or capacity to concentrate as I should. My body is in good shape physically, but I am very wearied mentally, and the weariness centers largely in my eyes and about the brain."

In 1931, he noted how the pain in his brain had been relieved by his occult contacts with the Beyond. "I prayed as I always do before beginning to speak, prayed that dear father & mother & grandfather & the other loved ones might be very near to me – also Sir Wilfrid – I was delighted to find my mind at rest as I spoke, not that terrible pain in the brain that I have had on occasion." But when preparing for another major speech in 1935, he had at times "a pain at the back of my skull, just above the neck which was very great, and a pain over the left eye, which almost blinded me. I knew it was just

---

260 Luno, 47, Gray, *Mrs. King*, 246, 90, 360. Diary, March 9, 1919. Diary, January 13, 1922, and December 17, 1933.

261 Diary, June 22, 1898, and October 17, 1898. Cited in McIntyre and Jeffries, 22. Diary, November 28, 1904.

nervousness – fatigue – and was due to the feeling that I could not rest."²⁶²

While preparing another speech just before the twentieth anniversary of his election as Leader of the Liberal Party in August 1939, he found that "my brain seemed 'shocked'" and that he "could not drive my mind to work...It was as if I had become possessed by some evil spirit – conscious of burning up within me." The "few words on 'the table'" failed to help so that the Prime Minister "felt I wished to have nothing more to do with politics forever – Strain too great, like an extinct volcano myself, burnt out, no word or fresh thoughts." An hour before Parliament reassembled on September 7 to declare war on Germany, King suddenly became so sick to his stomach that he vomited. He recorded, "I have in the last few days experienced toward morning a good deal of pain in my stomach. I recall how mother told me to watch that side of things. She herself suffered terribly from nervousness, which has its effect in that quarter."²⁶³

The question whether the Prime Minister may have inherited genetic traits from Isabel King is also raised by J.W.L. Forster's 1905 canvas in King's Laurier House library. Not knowing the symbolism of the "famous" painting, Paul Roazen reported from family correspondence "how serious a reader Isabel King was" but noted the paradox that the portrait "showed her reading an open book in her lap, even though her letters to King displayed an inadequate command of grammer [sic]."²⁶⁴ King's handwritten diaries are also strewn with spelling mistakes and grammatical errors suggesting that he may have inherited a form of dyslexia. Though he graduated with a PhD from Harvard, he frequently transposed letters or spelled words phonetically, such as "phamplet" instead of pamphlet, "tradegy" and "tradgedies" for tragedy, "martered," "vail" and "bolders" instead of martyred, veil and boulders, "Laurier's mantel" instead of mantle, and to "prosephy" instead of "prophesy." The typists who transcribed his diaries for the King biographers inserted two thousand "[sic]" designations in what are now the online diaries to indicate that spelling or grammatical errors occurred in the original texts. Mackenzie King

---

262 Diary, February 8, 1921, September 24, 1930, June 15, 1931, and March 20, 1935. See also October 12, 1898, January 15, 1924, September 2, 1925, January 2, 1932, January 23, 1933, and June 24, 1933.

263 Diary, August 4, 1939, and September 7, 1939.

264 Roazen, 127.

himself noted in 1938, "I recognize strongly the influence of heredity, and, of course, believe firmly in the influences from Beyond."[265]

He recorded seeing the effects of madness at close hand in his relationship with Marjorie Herridge, the wife of Rev. William T. Herridge, minister of St. Andrew's in Ottawa, where he regularly attended church services. Herridge became minister at St. Andrew's, "the wealthiest Presbyterian congregation in Canada," in 1883 and was elected Moderator of the General Assembly of the Presbyterian Church in Canada in 1914. The mother of four young children and sixteen years older than the twenty-six-year-old King, Mrs. Herridge had introduced King to the poetry of Matthew Arnold in 1901 and shared his love for literature, music, painting, and theatre. According to Allan Levine, the two "instantly bonded on an emotional and possibly sexual level."[266]

The Herridges had become emotionally estranged, leading King to refer to the minister's "indifference to her, the want of any true love between them, for years past, his going his way & she hers ... The truth is she loves me, and my problem is here ... What is to be the outcome of this love, the love which binds her to me and me to her, that is the problem now. She loves me more deeply than ever before if that is possible, and can do less well without me. I have reason to love her as I had never reason to before. I tremble at moments when I think of what our lives are to each other."[267]

King's inability to enter into a love relationship with the married Marjorie undoubtedly contributed to her mental deterioration. Louise Reynolds, who examined her correspondence with King, wrote that "In late 1919, Marjorie suffered a mental breakdown and was sent to the psychiatric hospital in Guelph for treatment." In a censored diary transcription, King recorded, "I was distressed tonight to hear that Mrs. Herridge had had a complete nervous breakdown & collapse. Willie told me it was a mental breakdown. Am very very sorry. Her strain of years (.....)." C.P. Stacey noted, "It appears that her

---

265 Diary, October 17, 1899, December 11, 1914, April 4, 1933, December 16, 1934, November 30, 1935, August 23, 1949, September 4, 1926, July 3, 1938, and July 2, 1934.

266 Stacey, *A Very Double Life*, 86. Levine, *King*, 61, 66. On King's relationship with Marjorie Herridge, see Stacey, 86-105, von Baeyer, 47-51, and Reynolds, 47-69.

267 Diary, February 26, March 2, 1902, and September 21, 1902.

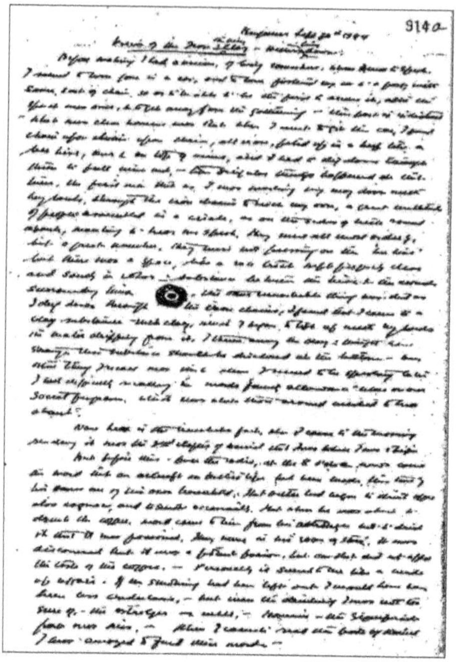

Figure 25: King's handwritten diary entry, vision of "Hitler & his doom," September 30, 1944.

mind failed a year or so before her death" in 1924. When King saw Herridge again six months before he became Prime Minister in late December 1921, he "found her greatly aged & greatly distressed over 'evil thoughts' from which she cannot free her mind. It was sad beyond words & too sad for words when I think of what a beautiful quiet nature she at one time had and how I might have helped to save all the sorrow that is now hers … It is a great warning to see a mind so overthrown."[268]

He experienced several dream visions about the Herridges while he was Leader of the Opposition in the early 1930s that he interpreted as "a soul reconciliation all round" in which a spiritual "deep love alone remained." But King also revealed an understanding of human psychology when he referred to Marjorie's love for him and to "the sub-conscious self, repressed too long" and "the Freudian repressions begetting paranoia." He felt guilt at Herridge's descent into madness. Ten years after her death, he had spirit "conversations" over the "little table" with Marjorie Herridge and George Duncan, the deceased Minister of St. Andrew's in Montreal, from which he learned not to "let the Fury of Hell accumulate – because of being 'scorned.'"

In his diary he referred to "many things Mrs. H. had said – for none of which do I blame her – though they hurt. Nature works strange havoc with our lives, and the 'scorn' of which George spoke may have worked its havoc, indeed it did, but my prayer is that is all past & I believe it is, by the words 'forget all that was unkind.' It is only the good I seek to recall … but this conversation overclouded my soul again a little." He felt guilt acknowledging that "The effort at rooting

---

268 Reynolds, 66. Diary, December 22, 1919. Stacey, *A Very Double Life*, 103. Diary, June 13, 1921.

out – root & branch – last summer was needed – but how deep the evil lies, can be seen from the quick effect of being brought by past associations into touch with it at all ... The past, with me, might well have caused my life in more than a physical sense to come under the shadow of death – in fact it did. It is from that shadow that I am seeking & praying God to be brought out of into the light."[269]

The famed diaries on which so much of our knowledge of Mackenzie King's beliefs and actions are based are not straightforward, unfiltered communications from their author. His miniscule, illegible handwritten journals from 1893 to 1935 are particularly problematic. The only person able to decipher these with a high degree of accuracy was F.A. McGregor, King's private secretary from 1909 to 1925. As Jean Dryden indicates in her analysis of the Mackenzie King Papers, McGregor "first dictated portions of the handwritten diaries deemed suitable" for R. MacGregor Dawson – the historian commissioned by the King executors to write the first "official" King biography – onto dictation belts for typing by "two trusted stenographers."[270]

But even McGregor, working with a dictaphone on the second floor of Laurier House from 1951 to 1954, periodically had to indicate "words illegible," that he could not determine certain words in the transcription process. One of the stenographers, "J.S.," in turn questioned McGregor's dictation for a 1931 diary entry, wondered whether King was confusing the poet Wordsworth with the MP James Shaver Woodsworth in 1935, suggested that a word was missing in another dictation for 1935, that the "belt [had] a blank," and corrected King's grammar in a 1937 diary. Another stenographer corrected the Prime Minister's dream description of a woman "dressed in an alluring fashion" from a "Zezubel" to a "Jezebel" type.

King's own dictation to his stenographers also resulted in errors until the end of his term as Prime Minister. When he invited Bishop Robert Jefferson to tea in the Laurier House library in 1947, the Bishop "spoke of [William] James variety of religious experiences." A year later King met with Frank Hall, a leader in the national strike by railway men, to negotiate a settlement and "he surprised me as a result of something that came in conversation, when he asked whether I was

---

269   Diary, January 17, 1932, May 27, 1932, July 20, 1933, October 8, 1933, and May 15, 1934. See also the July 1, 1934, entry regarding Herridge cited by Reynolds in full, p. 68.

270   Dryden, 55. Dummitt, 54, 136.

familiar with William James' writings. I told him I was not only familiar with the writings, but I knew them very well. I had them in the library. Mentioned a variety of religious experiences, etc." Both references are to James' influential *The Varieties of Religious Experience: A Study in Human Nature*, which King's brother Max had inscribed to him for his birthday on December 17, 1918.[271]

After his death in 1950, King's executors restricted access to his diaries and correspondence to prevent knowledge of his spiritualist beliefs and occult practices becoming part of the public record.

James Eayrs was one of three full-time assistants hired by MacGregor Dawson in 1952 to help him research and write *William Lyon Mackenzie King: A Political Biography, 1874-1923*, commissioned by the King executors. Two decades later, in "'To find the demi-god a man': King and the historians," Eayrs recalled "We were all of us participants in a kind of Manhattan Project of historiography…A national Liberal shrine, in short, was imperatively necessary." Eayrs deplored the decision to publish excerpts from King's diaries, in their "bowdlerized and truncated format," in Jack Pickersgill's four-volume *The Mackenzie King Record* as "the Pacific Scandal of Canadian letters." "What is needed is a project to publish the entire text, unabridged and unabashed."[272]

---

271   Diary, February 19, 1931, May 6, 1931, May 17, 1935, July 16, 1935, November 15, 1937, April 8, 1938, January 23, 1947, and July 13, 1948, p. 3. On James' strong influence on King, see Bedore, "King's Reading of William James" and "King's Reading on Spiritualism."

272   James Eayrs, "'To find the demi-god a man': King and the historians," *Vancouver Sun*, December 17, 1974, 6. James' stepfather was Hugh Eayrs, President of the Macmillan Company of Canada – Mackenzie King's publisher – referred to in Chapter 13.

CHAPTER 8

Fantasio, an Interview in Ectoplasm, and the Duchess of Hamilton

In 1955 Percy James Philip, the distinguished Paris and Ottawa correspondent for the *New York Times*, wrote to Norman Robertson, former Clerk of the Privy Council and the Canadian High Commissioner in London, regarding the warm public reaction to Philip's 15-minute CBC radio broadcast about Mackenzie King's spiritualism, *Fantasio*. The wide-ranging public response had convinced Philip that "a sympathetic objective book about 'The Spiritualism of Mackenzie King' is due to his memory and is eagerly awaited both in and beyond Canada."

Fantasio was the journalist's whimsical but sympathetic account of his purported conversation with King, four years after his death, on a park bench among the "ruins" of the late Prime Minister's Kingsmere estate. "It will certainly have to be done sometime," he argued on behalf of his proposed study, "and there is always the danger that, in spite of all precautions, it could be wrongly done." Philip assured Robertson, one of the King literary executors, "I shall of course accept any conditions the executors make regarding the use of, and quotations from, Mr. King's diary and papers." He would also "do my best to fit my study of this side of Mr. King's strange personality into the large scale portrait by Dr. McGregor Dawson," the first "official" historian commissioned by the King executors to write his biography.[273]

The CBC had broadcast *Fantasio* on September 24, 1954. Philip's "My Conversation with Mackenzie King's Ghost" and "I Talked with

---

273 Philip to Robertson, August 3, 1955. Executors' files, Mackenzie King Papers, Library and Archives Canada, MG 26 J 17.

Mackenzie King's Ghost" were published in *Liberty* and *Fate Magazine* in January and December 1955. To accompany Philip's piece, *Liberty* also published Frank Rasky's investigative article, "Canadian Spiritualism: Racket or Religion?" It cited Rev. T. David McQueen, the president of the Spiritualist National Union of Canada, who "conservatively estimates there are today over a half-million adherents of spiritualism in the Dominion."[274]

Mackenzie King might well have approved of Philip's proposal to his executors. He recorded attending a Canadian Club address given by the journalist following the Fall of France to the Nazis in 1940 and after the *New York Times* had transferred him from Paris to Ottawa. "It was one of the finest addresses I have ever heard in my life. A very fearless and just account of the circumstances attending the collapse of France," he noted in his diary. "Philip himself is an exceedingly fine man. It was a large gathering and he received a great ovation. The address should help in understanding by our members." Three years later, the Prime Minister phoned Philip to congratulate him for his article "The Tomorrows That Sing." "He is a son of the Manse. The article breathes Christian truth and Christian influences. It just falls short in not making perfectly clear that Christian precepts alone will save this world and make a new order."[275]

Seven decades later, *The Spiritualist Prime Minister* is the first in-depth study of the kind Philip envisioned.[276] What he was not aware of in approaching Norman Robertson in the mid-1950s was that the King trustees and executors had made a concerted effort to prevent news of King's spiritualism from becoming public knowledge. They particularly sought to avert the kind of public mockery

---

274 Rasky, 59. In their overview of the history of Spiritualism in Canada, Walter Meyer zu Erpen and Joy Lowe provided quite different statistics: "The 1901 census enumerated 616 Spiritualists. The 1911, 1921, and 1931 censuses showed a steady increase in Spiritualist numbers to 674, 1,558, and 2,263 respectively, followed in 1941 by a sharp decrease to 1,214…Finally, the 1981 census, based on twenty percent sample data, reported 1,940 Spiritualists." See Meyer zu Erpen and Joy Lowe, 77. Stan McMullin, citing these numbers, suggested "it is fair to assume many more attended, at least on a casual basis, church services, public seances, or private readings." McMullin, 21.

275 Diary, November 19, 1940. See also Diary, May 16, 1943.

276 Margaret Bedore made an excellent start with her 2008 Queen's University PhD dissertation, "The Reading of Mackenzie King," but only a third of her thesis examined his spiritualism.

the Canadian Press, Southam News and Associated Press accounts of Philip's broadcast and subsequent interviews generated.

Reginald Hardy's opening paragraph for Southam News had stated, "The Canadian Broadcasting Corporation does not intend to move its Ottawa mobile television unit to Kingsmere in the hope of getting an interview (in ectoplasm) with the shade of the late W.L. Mackenzie King." John Collins' cartoon for the September 29, 1954 *Montreal Gazette* depicted Prime Minister Louis St. Laurent on the Kingsmere bench looking up expectantly at the sky, with the caption, "Have You Anything to Say to Me?"[277]

The articles most damaging to King's reputation were published in Great Britain. The *Press and Journal* (Aberdeen), in "Mackenzie King Was a Devout Spiritualist," reported from Ottawa on Christmas Day 1951 that "Canada's most famous statesman used to slip away from Commonwealth conferences in London and Cabinet meetings in Ottawa to have private seances with his dead mother and with the late President Roosevelt." The paper asserted that "The entirely unexpected revelation that Mr. W.L. Mackenzie King was an active spiritualist has caused the greatest political sensation in Canada's history."[278]

A four-part series by John Prebble in the weekly London *Sunday Dispatch* in June 1953 was even more dismissive. With a circulation of over one million, its headlines sensationalized, "The Queer Story of Mackenzie King: Crystal-Gazing Premier Believed in Supernatural and 'Read' Tea-leaves – Believed He Made Contact with His Dead Pet Dog;" "Duchess Declared He Was 'Guided' on World Affairs: The Queer Story of Mackenzie King, Spiritualist Prime Minister;" "Roosevelt 'Message' Warned Him about Trouble in Far East;" and "Mackenzie King. Spiritualists Ask – Is He Trying to Send a Message from the Next World?"

---

277 Reginald Hardy, "Was Percy 'Pulling A Leg' or Was He Deadly Serious? Percy: 'No Comment,'" *Ottawa Citizen*, September 28, 1954. See also "On Bench at Kingsmere: Noted Newsman Says He Talked with Late Mackenzie King 3 Months Ago," *Ottawa Citizen*, September 25, 1954; "Ex-NY Times Reporter 'Talks' with Mr. King," *Ottawa Journal*, September 25, 1954; Arthur Blakely, "The Kingsmere Ruins," *Montreal Gazette*, September 28, 1954; Richard Jackson, "Believe It or Not!" *Ottawa Journal*, September 28, 1954; "Second Sight," *Montreal Gazette*, October 1, 1954; John Stevenson, *Saturday Night*, October 16, 1954; and upon Philip's death, Arthur Blakely, "Out of Thin Air," *Montreal Gazette*, November 16, 1956. For further TV and press coverage of Philip's story, see Colombo, 167-189.

278 Patrick Nicholson, "Mackenzie King Was a Devout Spiritualist," Aberdeen *Press and Journal*, December 24, 1951.

The London *Psychic News* headlined John Prebble's skepticism that King left no references in his diaries and correspondence to his interest in Spiritualism. "The executors of the late Canadian Prime Minister maintain that there is not a word about this subject in the vast legacy of such material which Mackenzie King left on his death three years ago, though he told close friends that it was his intention to publish full accounts of his psychic experiences." The paper cited Prebble's concluding *Sunday Dispatch* article, "What I have learned during the past weeks about Mackenzie King's secret life has convinced me that among the locked-up papers in Laurier House there could be found an even more fascinating story than I have been able to piece together." Fred Alexander McGregor, one of the King trustees and literary executors, wrote Norman Robertson at Canada House in London asking him to obtain copies of the June 21 *Sunday Dispatch*. "Apparently the article has referred to the efforts of Mr. King's executors to 'suppress' the story."[279]

Psychic News and *Psychic World* had begun publishing a series of items reporting the Canadian Prime Minister's involvement with British mediums and the occult within a month of King's death on July 22, 1950. The *Psychic News*' first front-page exposé headlined in bold letters, "Mackenzie King Sought Spirit Aid in State Affairs: Canadian Premier Had Proved Survival." Citing King's friend and well-known spiritualist, the Duchess of Hamilton, Fred Archer asserted that King was also a spiritualist and "always sought spirit guidance in affairs of state." According to Nina Hamilton, the Prime Minister "fully appreciated the spiritual direction of the universe and was always seeking guidance for himself in his work – though in his official capacity he couldn't allow it to be too well known."[280]

---

279 John Prebble, "The Queer Story of Mackenzie King: Crystal-Gazing Premier Believed In Supernatural and 'Read' Tea-leaves – Believed He Made Contact with His Dead Pet Dog;" "Duchess Declared He Was 'Guided' on World Affairs: The Queer Story of Mackenzie King, Spiritualist Prime Minister;" "Roosevelt 'Message' Warned Him about Trouble in Far East;" and "Mackenzie King. Spiritualists Ask – Is He Trying to Send A Message from the Next World?" *Sunday Dispatch*, June 7, 14, 21, and 28, 1953. "*Not a Word on Spiritualism in Mackenzie King's Papers* Say Canadian Premier's Executors – *Convinced a Fascinating Story Could Be Found* Declares 'Sunday Dispatch,'" *Psychic News*, July 4, 1953, 1. McGregor to Robertson, July 2, 1953.

280 Fred Archer, "Mackenzie King Sought Spirit Aid in State Affairs: Canadian Premier Had Proved Survival," *Psychic News*, August 19, 1950, 1.

Figure 26: The Duchess of Hamilton, November 29, 1926.

King had met Nina Douglas-Hamilton when he addressed the League of Nations Assembly in Geneva at the end of September 1936 following Hitler's military occupation of the Rhineland and Italy's conquest of Ethiopia and scuttled the League's principle of enforcing collective security through military intervention. The Duchess and her colleague, the Swedish-British feminist and animal rights advocate Lizzy Lind-af-Hageby, with whom she had founded the Animal Defence and Anti-Vivisection Society in London in 1906, were in Geneva at the Society's Humanitarian International Bureau in an attempt to persuade the League to accept the extension of justice to animals as part of the movement for world peace. Both were also prominent members on the Council of the London Spiritualist Alliance. Lind-af-Hageby joined its Council in 1930 and served as the Alliance's president from 1935 to 1943.

Announcing her acceptance of the LSA presidency, *Psychic Science* reported that she had undertaken four speaking tours in America and had lectured in France, Germany, Switzerland, Italy, Austria, and the Scandinavian countries. "In the course of lecture tours in recent years with the Duchess of Hamilton, she has been received by Mussolini, President Coolidge, Herr Miklas (President of Austria), the King of Norway, etc." The LSA house organ, *Light: A Journal of Psychical, Occult, and Mystical Research*, had previously called her "the greatest living authority on Strindberg, of whom she was a personal friend." Lind-af-Hageby published her *August Strindberg: The Spirit of Revolt* in London and New York in 1913. A member of a Swedish noble family, she was educated at Stockholm and at Cheltenham College and became a naturalized British subject in 1912. Following Lind-af-Hageby's death in December 1963, the LSA Secretary Mercy Phillimore's obituary recalled that her "complete conviction of individual survival of death was drawn partly from experience with the most successful mediums, but more particularly from her own personal form of mediumship, which was only used privately among her most intimate friends."[281]

In its obituary, *Psychic News* cited Hannen Swaffer who called her "the most remarkable woman in the world." The paper reported that Miss Lind "drew tremendous strength from her inspirer and spirit

---

281 "Notes by the Way," *Quarterly Transactions of the BCPS* 14:1 (April 1935), 58. "The Soul of Strindberg," *Light* 48:2457 (February 11, 1928), 61. Phillimore, "Emilie Augusta Louise Lind-af-Hageby," 456. For Lind-af-Hageby's spiritualist beliefs, see her "The Evidence for Survival," "Challenge to Modern Thought and Action: Objections to Spiritualism Answered," "Challenge of the Evidence for Survival," and "Creative Thought and the 'New World.'" Copies in the King fonds. See also "'World's Most Remarkable Woman' Passes," *Psychic News*, January 4, 1964, 1. On Lind-af-Hageby's belief that "animals be men on their upward path…the whole scale of beings is the expression in manifestation of souls in their upward path," see "The Purpose of Animal Creation as Viewed from the Spiritual Plane."

Figure 27: Lizzy Lind-af-Hageby in Psychic Science, *April 1937, seven months after meeting Mackenzie King.*

guide, Anna Kingsford," and that she was a friend of Annie Besant, the leading figure in the Theosophical movement. "She was a great friend of Mackenzie King, Prime Minister of Canada, and was responsible for introducing him to some of our best known mediums. He loved to discuss Spiritualism with her and the Duchess of Hamilton. Once, after dinner, he said, 'Let us see what we can get with the table.' This surprised Miss Lind, who regarded table communication as elementary, but Mackenzie King became more and more enthusiastic as the impromptu seance continued."[282]

---

282 "'World's Most Remarkable Woman' Passes: Spiritualist Who Was Tireless Crusader for Human Causes – She Helped Canada's Prime Minister to Attend

Lind-af-Hageby expounded her belief that Spiritualism had both a religious and scientific basis in a 1913 address to the London Spiritualist Alliance entitled "Psychic Evolution from the Points of View of the Scientist and Spiritualist." She stated that following the understanding of physical evolution presented by Charles Darwin and Alfred Russel Wallace, "that idea necessarily carried with it the theories and problems of psychical evolution. You cannot have physical evolution without its psychic side." As *Light* summarized part of her address, she believed that "psychic evolution was creating and moulding news senses and faculties and producing a new type of humanity. She believed that those who now possessed these psychic faculties were the pioneers and forerunners of the new race of the future... There would come about a new religion and a new science, and that new religion and new science would be wedded and would be one. The old feud between the religious consciousness and the scientific mind would be at an end."

Since spiritualists believed in continued existence and the continual perfecting of the human spirit, Lind-af-Hageby affirmed that spiritualists "are the true optimists, knowing that the soul is free from the ravages of time, for to realize that we are in the midst of life, perpetually evolving is to hold the secret of life in one's heart. (Applause.)" Following the outbreak of World War I, she proposed the founding of an Occultists' Peace Union and was duly elected its chair in September 1914. By contrast Usborne Moore, the LSA Vice-President, was certain that "This war will probably settle the peace of Europe for two hundred years."[283]

Lind-af-Hageby felt a oneness with nature and love for all living things, whether plant, animal, or human, and was appalled by man's cruelty and inhumanity and the preparations for another world war. As she stated six months before meeting Mackenzie King in 1936, "we know

---

Seances," *Psychic News*, no. 1648, January 4, 1964, 1.

283 Lind-af-Hageby, "Psychic Evolution from the Points of View of the Scientist and Spiritualist," *Light* 33:1716 (November 29, 1913), 571, and 33:1717 (December 6, 1913), 584, and "The Great Calamity: Its Cause and Cure." Moore, "Interview with Vice-Admiral Usborne Moore: The War, Psychic Science, and the 'Direct Voice,'" 499. See also "An Occultists Peace Union" and "Psychic Science and the War: An Occultists' Peace Union Formed," *Light* 34:1,756 and 34:1,757, September 5 and 12, 1914. Many issues of *Light* can be accessed on the website of the International Association for the Preservation of Spiritualist and Occult Periodicals http://iapsop.com/archive/materials/light/

that all material-form, all living creatures are moulded and animated by spirit – spirit that was, is and will be." She first saw the Canadian Prime Minister at a diplomatic party in Geneva. "The Duchess and I spoke to him because we had heard someone say mockingly that he believed he could communicate with his dead mother. The fact that so great a man was interested in spiritualism was enough for us, and we approached him and raised the subject. He told us how extremely important he considered it, and that he sought evidence of communication with the dead. He believed he had already made such communication with his mother and sister." "I think it was a relief for him to be able to talk so freely with us," Lind-af-Hageby informed the *Sunday Dispatch* in 1953, "he was delighted when we assured him that we would introduce him to spiritualists in Britain."[284]

In his diary, Mackenzie King in turn recorded of their meeting in Geneva that he "had a most interesting talk" with the Duchess of Hamilton, the president of the Animal Defence Society, "whose chief interest is apparently in psychic research and anti-vivisection of animals." He viewed the anti-vivisection exhibition organized by the Humanitarian International Bureau (Lind-af-Hageby was its president) on October 5, noted that its underlying belief was that "the whole animal creation is kindred to man," and sent Lady Hamilton an autographed copy of his *Industry and Humanity* he had written for the Rockefeller Foundation.[285]

Through the Duchess of Hamilton and Lind-af-Hageby, King had his first sitting with the clairaudient medium Helen Hughes at the London Spiritualist Alliance on October 23, 1936, and brought his principal secretary and stenographer, Edouard Handy, with him to record the proceedings. The medium had explained to *Light* readers how she demonstrated survival earlier in the year. "In Clairvoyance, I see a spirit form as naturally as if I were using the physical eye...But it is on my gift of Clairaudience that I mostly depend in my demonstration of survival. In Clairaudience, or clear-hearing, I hear quite

---

284 Lind-af-Hageby, "Challenge of the Evidence for Survival," 1. John Prebble, "Duchess Declared He Was 'Guided' on World Affairs," *Sunday Dispatch*, June 14, 1953, 5.

285 Diary, October 3, 1936. For the Animal Defence Society and the Humanitarian International Bureau, see Lind-af-Hageby, "Despair or Re-Dedication" and "The League of Nations and the Protection of Animals" in *Progress Today: The Humanitarian and Anti-Vivisection Review*, April-June 1936.

naturally, as though I were using the normal ear…It is in listening to the 'Voice,' that enables me to understand all other feelings that come to me, and to gather the facts by which I demonstrate survival. It is listening to the 'Voice' that enables me to give the names, facts and details, that provide the evidence."[286]

In her October séance, Hughes established contact with and heard the voice of Mackenzie King's deceased physician brother, Max. Afterwards, King "said that he knew he had been able to make contact with his brother through our sittings and they had both discussed things only they could have known about."[287] The transcribed online King diaries do not refer to this séance but he described a similar sitting with Helen Hughes at the LSA a decade later, calling their meeting "one of the most remarkable experiences of my life." "We were no sooner seated than she immediately spoke of those who were around us and named in a moment my father and mother, Max and Bella and my grand-mother Christina, calling her by name and other members of the family."

> It was an amazing experience. One after the other she described as being present. My mother putting her hand on my forehead: my brother standing by me and stroking me on the back. Through the interview, she brought special messages from each one in turn. Lent her voice to them to speak to me. There was no mistake in anything she said. Everything as natural and true as could possibly be. I kept a record for an hour…
>
> Unless one has undergone this experience, one cannot imagine what it means. My father stood in the background to let others talk to me…There was not one sentence in which all that she [Hughes] said in an hour was not wholly veridical. It was all most comforting as to the ultimate outcome though evidence of plenty of difficulties and fight in the meantime. I would not have missed this experience for anything in the world… She explained fully the relationship of my mother and myself and the psychical laws which enabled her to exert the influence and guided the power which she does on my life. There was no mistaking the absolute identity of each member of the family.[288]

---

286 Hughes, 161.

287 John Prebble, "Duchess Declared He Was 'Guided' on World Affairs," *Sunday Dispatch*, June 14, 1953, 5.

288 Diary, May 30, 1946.

The LSA was Mackenzie King's principal source of engaging sittings with mediums in England and obtaining publications by British spiritualists from 1936 to 1948. It traced its history to the founding of the British National Association of Spiritualists in 1873, re-organized as the London Spiritualist Alliance in 1884. The naturalist and prominent spiritualist Alfred Russell Wallace, co-discoverer with Darwin of the principle of natural selection and author of *Miracles and Modern Spiritualism*, was one of its early leading figures. The LSA's house organ, the weekly newspaper *Light*, had been founded in 1881. It proclaimed the Alliance's belief "in the existence and life of the spirit apart from, and independent of, the material organism, and in the reality and value of intelligent intercourse between spirits embodied and spirits discarnate." The Alliance's library contained four thousand volumes on Spiritualism and claimed to be the most comprehensive of its kind.[289]

After his personal experiences and encounters with mediums and psychic investigators, King agreed with Lind-af-Hageby that survival after death had been established scientifically and had worldwide social implications. As she stated at a public meeting about Spiritualism organized by the LSA in Caxton Hall, Westminster, in March 1936, "We hold that Survival has been proved. How? By communication from the so-called dead."

> For communications to be received and recorded, it is necessary that there should be two kinds of participants: the so-called dead and the so-called living…We hold that the evidence for Survival is of immense importance to human life, here, in this world, on this planet, and that it has clear and direct bearings on individual, social, political, national and international life…Survival has not been proved without other things being demonstrated – such as the spiritual law of cause and effect, moral obligations, results of our manner of thinking and living on the physical plane. Hence the desire of Spiritualism to present the evidence for Survival, to spread the truth.[290]

---

289 *Concerning the Origin & Aims of the London Spiritualist Alliance Ltd. and The Quest Club*, 22.
290 Lind-af-Hageby, "Challenge of the Evidence for Survival," 1.

The Duchess of Hamilton and Lind-af-Hageby organized a social gathering for King at the London Spiritualist Alliance headquarters, 16 Queensberry Place, South Kensington, on October 28, 1936. The three dozen leading spiritualists invited to meet the Canadian Prime Minister as the guest of honour included Mercy Phillimore, Stanley De Brath (the author and former editor of *Psychic Science*), the editors of *Light* and *Two Worlds*, and five of "our best mediums" with whom Phillimore scheduled sittings for King the last week of October: Rose Livingstone, Helen Hughes, Ruth Vaughan, Pamela Nash, and Naomi Bacon. Lind-af-Hageby assured King, "I shall, of course, see that the little party is entirely private & that there are NO reporters or publicity of any kind."[291]

Fourteen years later the *Psychic World* reported that at the reception King "made a speech in which he paid tribute to the great help he had received through mediumship." His diary – only transcribed in part at the direction of his executors in order to reduce King's frequent spiritualist references – records that a day after speaking with King Edward VIII in Buckingham Palace, he "Came back to the Ritz, had an hour's sleep, a bit of dinner, then to a 'party' given by Miss Lind af-Hageby, and the Duchess of Hamilton. (.....) It has been an exceptional experience coming to meet and to know so many of those who are pioneering in a new field of psychic phenomena. The character of the people interested and the years of experience they have had are the best evidence of the genuineness of the whole movement. (.....)".[292]

Sending King the list of appointments for his sittings with mediums (ranging from 1£ to 1£ six shillings [about $141 to $183 Canadian

---

291 Lind-af-Hageby to King, October 17, 1936. Phillimore attended LSA meetings from 1904 to December 1913 when she began working as the LSA librarian. Subsequently, she became Secretary of the LSA and held that position for thirty-nine years until November 30, 1952. Vice-Admiral Usborne Moore (the LSA Vice-President) invited her to her first sitting with Etta Wriedt held at the home of W.T. Stead at Wimbledon in late 1914. Hewat McKenzie, the future founder of the British College of Psychic Science in 1920, booked six sittings for Phillimore with Osborne Leonard in 1915. Mackenzie King began his sittings with Etta Wriedt in 1932 and with Leonard in 1937.

292 "Mackenzie King Paid a Great Tribute to Famous Medium," *Psychic World*, September 21, 1950, 2. Diary, October 28, 1936. The ubiquitous (.....) in the Library and Archives Canada online diaries indicate omissions in the transcriptions of King's original diaries.

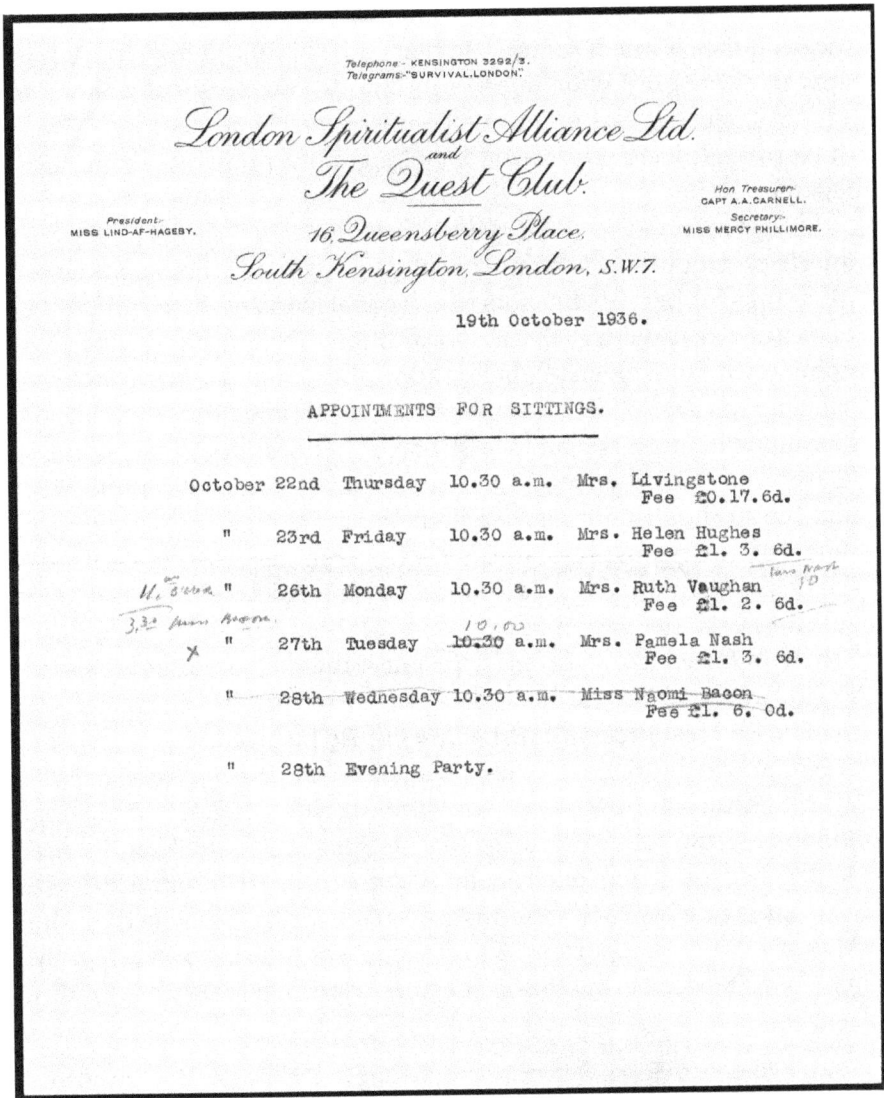

Figure 28: The London Spiritualist Alliance's Medium Appointments and Evening Party for Mackenzie King, October 1936.

in 2023 dollars]), Mercy Phillimore in turn had written the Prime Minister, "from what you told me concerning your own inner experiences, I realize what a precious thing it is for one in authority in the State to receive direct inspiration from the Unseen." King responded, "I continue to think very often of my visits to 16 Queensberry Place, and of yourself and your associates. No memory of my trip abroad means quite so much to me." He thanked Phillimore for "your kindness in expressing your interest in one or two personal matters to which I referred in one of our conversations" and sent her a copy of Norman Rogers' *Mackenzie King* biography, prepared for the 1935 federal election.[293]

In September 1950, the *Psychic World* published King's high praise for Helen Hughes, whom he consulted until 1946. "He was warm in his thanks for her psychic gifts which enabled his mother and brother to communicate with such ease. In addition to telling her that he knew nobody who had given greater comfort, he added, 'or has done more valuable war work.'" By November, Hughes claimed that King himself had made his first appearance at one of her séances in her home in Glasgow in the presence of Maurice Barbanell, editor of *Psychic News*, and the spiritualist Hannen Swaffer. "First the medium's guide mentioned that he was present. Then a few minutes later he controlled the medium and in a masculine voice expressed his pleasure at being able to speak," the weekly reported in "Mackenzie King Comes Back." "There followed a few words to the effect that he had found the spirit world, whose existence had been proved to him before, far greater than he had realised. And he had met those he loved."[294]

Not to be outdone by its spiritualist competitor, *Psychic News*, "The Spiritualist Newspaper with the World's Largest Circulation," announced the following week that its first article on King by Fred Archer had been reprinted in the October 10, 1950 *Ottawa Citizen* (under the title "WLMK: Spiritualist") and had also been cited by *Time Magazine*.[295] *Time* reported, "King's secret was indeed so well kept that his closest associates in Ottawa last week were unable either to confirm

---

293 Phillimore to King, October 19, 1936. King to Phillimore, November 20, 1936. For Phillimore's views on Spiritualism and mediums, see her "How to Sit with a Medium." Copy in the King fonds.

294 "Mackenzie King Paid a Great Tribute to Famous Medium." "Mackenzie King Comes Back," *Psychic World*, November 9, 1950. See also Pam Riva, "Searchlight on Canada's Secret Spiritualist War Leader," *Psychic News*, January 22, 1983, 4-5.

295 "Mackenzie King," *Psychic News*, November 18, 1950, 4. Fred Archer's article was also reprinted as "Mr. King Named as Spiritist" and "Mackenzie King: Spiritualist" in *Windsor Star* October 17, 1950, and *Calgary Herald*, October 20, 1950, p. 4. See also "Always on the Ground," *Victoria Times*, October 25, 1950, "Mr. King's Spiritual Beliefs," *Toronto Star*, November 9, 1950, and J.V. McAree, "New Light on Mr. King," *Globe and Mail*, November 10, 1950.

or deny that he was a practising spiritualist ... None of them could say whether in the privacy of his study, Mackenzie King actually tried to communicate with his dead mother or whether his spiritualist experiments had any effect upon his conduct of the country's affairs." The magazine suggested that the answer to this question would never be known since King, in his testament, had ordered that his diaries be destroyed. *Time* referred to *Psychic News* as "a leading publication of Britain's spiritualist cult" and noted that the son of the dowager Duchess of Hamilton, "the present Duke of Hamilton, was the owner of the estate near Glasgow where Rudolf Hess landed in 1941."[296]

Born in 1894 in Alexandria, Egypt, where his father was a prosperous German import-export merchant, Rudolf Hess "had never lost the interest in the stars awakened at his mother's side in Egypt; at his boarding school at Bad Godesberg [in Germany] he had bought and borrowed books on astronomy. By 1923 he had acquired an interest in astrology too, perhaps through Karl Haushofer, who was also a student of the occult ... he 'lived in unreality, he believed in dream-readings, prophecies and astrology.'"[297] Hess had been a student and assistant of Professor Haushofer, the former World War I Major General who had developed the field of geopolitics in Germany. Through Hess, his concept of Germany requiring greater *Lebensraum* ("living space") by means of territorial expansion into Eastern Europe and Russia found its way into Adolf Hitler's 1925-1926 political biography *Mein Kampf*, edited by Hess, and became part of Nazi ideology.

Appointed by Hitler as his Deputy in 1933, Hess had chosen his May 10 nine-hundred-mile solo flight to Scotland – in his attempt to negotiate a truce between Germany and England so that Germany would be free to attack Russia – in part based upon a propitious horoscope and reading by his astrologers Dr. Ernst Schulte-Strathaus and Dr. Ludwig Schmitt. Schulte-Strathaus had told Hess that "an unusual major conjunction would occur on 10 May 1941, with six

---

296 "Canada: 'In Quiet & Reflection,'" *Time Magazine*, October 23, 1950, 24.
297 Padfield, 21. The last sentence cites Schwerin von Krosigk. *Es geschah in Deutschland*. Tübingen: Wunderlich, 1951, 240. Howe, in *Astrology and the Third Reich* (p. 192), notes that "During the early years of the Third Reich [Hess] applied for an initial grant of 12 million Marks and an annual subvention of 2 million Marks for his projected Central Institute for Occultism. Nothing came of this grandiose plan."

planets in the sign Taurus coinciding with a full moon."[298] Hess had had a wide-ranging discussion with Karl Haushofer on August 31, 1940, about Germany extending peace feelers to Great Britain. "The Professor told Hess that he had seen him, in his dreams, on three separate occasions piloting an aeroplane, but he knew not where."[299] The Deputy *Führer* referred to their conversation in a letter to Haushofer of September 10. "Let's both keep our fingers crossed. Should success be the fate of the enterprise, the oracle given to you with regard to the month of August would yet be fulfilled." Just before his flight to Scotland, he gave a folder to his adjutant which included "'A minute on the relevant dream of the General' (Haushofer), a horoscope drawn up by Schulte-Strathaus and a prophecy given to him at Christmas 1940 by one Grete Sutter."[300]

The crucial contact between Hess and the 14th Duke of Hamilton was Haushofer's son Albrecht, whom Hess appointed as his personal advisor and as a foreign policy specialist in the German Foreign Office in 1934. He had begun visiting London two years previously and in 1936 was named by Hess as an assistant to Joachim von Ribbentrop, the new German ambassador to the United Kingdom. Secretly also a member of the German resistance, Albrecht Haushofer first met and befriended the Duchess of Hamilton's son at a special dinner party in Berlin given by Hitler for the head of the British Foreign Office in 1936 and stayed with him at his residence in Britain in 1938. In a top secret September 1940 memorandum to Hess entitled "Are There Still Possibilities of a German-English Peace?" he affirmed that the Duke of Hamilton "has access at all times to all important persons in London, even to Churchill and the King."[301]

Robert Keyserlingk, referencing King's heavily edited diary entry for October 3, 1936, and apparently confusing the Duke with his mother, the Duchess of Hamilton, asserted that "Hess' flight to England in 1941 has been attributed to the esoteric links he forged

---

298 Howe, 195. Tyson, 281, 278-280. Nesbit and van Acker, 124. Leasor, 58.

299 Padfield, 364. James Leasor, in *Rudolf Hess: The Uninvited Envoy*, cites Hess re Haushofer's premonitions that "'he was always right.' Such 'evidence' of psychic ability impressed Hess enormously" (p. 44). For a detailed account of the relationship between the Haushofers, Hess, and the Duke of Hamilton, see Douglas-Hamilton, *The Truth About Rudolf Hess*.

300 Manvell and Fraenkel, 84. Douglas-Hamilton, 123. Padfield, 363. Leasor, 221.

301 Leasor, 224.

Figure 29: Rudolf Hess and Adolf Hitler at the Nazi Party Congress in Nuremberg, September 1, 1933, in Deutschland erwacht *(1933).*

during the 1936 Berlin Olympic games with the Duke of Hamilton, a leading British spiritualist, whom Mackenzie King also visited during his trip to Britain in 1936." King recorded meeting Hess after his meeting with General Hermann Goering and before his meeting with Hitler in June 1937.[302]

The Hamiltons were the premier Scottish peers and could trace their aristocratic ancestors to the early 1600s. While the 12th Duke had squandered much of the family's fortune gambling on horses – leaving debts of £1 million on his death in 1895 – the Hamiltons still owned tens of thousands of acres containing valuable coal deposits. "At the Royal Commission on the Mines in 1919, the President of the Miners' Federation of Great Britain … claimed that the Duke of Hamilton received £240,000 per year in mining royalties while many who lived on his estates lived in abject poverty."[303]

Mackenzie King visited Ferne, the large Georgian mansion near Shaftesbury, Dorset, which served as the Hamiltons' main residence, while attending the Imperial Conference and coronation of King George VI in London in 1937. During his weekend visit, he marvelled at the 237-acre estate's beautiful grounds and gardens, its animals, and songbirds. "I have seen nothing more wholly pleasing in landscape." The Duchess "has devoted a big part of her life to seeking to preserve animal life as part of God's creation. One felt the immense companionship of the horses, the dogs, the birds, the trees, the flowers, and other green things as one walked about. Indeed, the whole place seemed a sort of earthly paradise."[304]

Lady Hamilton showed King the sanctuary where her twelve-year old daughter Mairi, who died suddenly after a freak accident, was buried. Her brother's biographer recorded that "Bizarrely, three weeks before her death, when out riding with her sister Margaret, she had a premonition that she would not live to be thirteen. She believed she was wanted elsewhere and even earmarked the spot in the garden where she was to be buried."[305] Lind-af-Hageby was also a guest and she, the Duchess and King discussed numerology and "many

---

302 Keyserlingk, 32. King's online diary entry for October 3, 1936 contains six "(…..)" omissions from the original diary. Diary, September 14, 1938, p. 6.
303 Peel, 33, 4.
304 Diary, May 15 and 16, 1937.
305 Peel, 39.

interesting experiences of those present." The eighty-six-year-old Sir Oliver Lodge, the renowned British physicist and leading proponent of psychic investigations, made a brief visit. King was "immensely impressed by his extraordinary resemblance to my father" and thanked Lodge for the inscribed books he had sent him which he had read "with great benefit" and prized deeply. He described their encounter as "a very precious and memorable hour in one's life."

He summed up his visit to Ferne – including placing a gold ring on his finger "which Mary, Queen of Scots, had been wearing and which was on her finger as she went to the scaffold to be executed" – as "psychical experiences of a very significant character." The following month he saw the Duchess again at her beautiful home, with its "peace and beauty of the garden," at 25 St. Edmund's Terrace in London where she introduced him to the medium Mrs. Gladys Osborne Leonard. King described his séance there with Leonard, "of which I have made personal notes" not found in his diary, as "the most remarkable I have had in England." In correspondence, he referred to his visit to Ferne as "the crowning event of the Coronation itself" and, citing Revelations 21:1, thanked the Duchess for helping him "glimpse not a little of 'the new heaven and a new earth.'"[306]

Lady Hamilton, in turn, had just affirmed her spiritualist beliefs in an address delivered at the Spiritualist Community Service at Grotrian Hall in London on June 13. In "Priest or Prophet?" published in *Light*, then subtitled *A Journal of Spiritualism, Psychical, Occult and Mystical Research*, she declared, "We Spiritualists know, through personal experience, that we can communicate with other spirits, whether – as St. Paul writes – in the body or out of the body." As with Mackenzie King, the Duchess' spiritualist beliefs were fortified by her strong desire to maintain contact with her mother after her death. "My Mother, who was a keen Spiritualist, described to me her experiences in this matter after she had passed on," she stated in her address. "She told me that she had discovered that she could communicate in any direction she liked by a sort of telephonic system. She was most excited when she told me she found herself, as it were, able to operate by thought-projection from such a centre." The Duchess' assertion immediately after King's death that he "always sought spirit guidance in affairs of state" derived from her conviction, "*Leadership*

---

306 Diary, May 16 and 17, 1937, and June 12, 1937. King to the Duchess of Hamilton, May 17, 1937, and June 13, 1937.

must always come from Divine Guidance, and that, I maintain, is just what we Spiritualists have."³⁰⁷

Like his deceased sister Mairi, the Duchess' oldest son Douglas Douglas-Hamilton, who became the 14th Duke of Hamilton after the death of his father in 1940, may initially have shared some of his mother's spiritualist beliefs in his youth. When elected to the House Debating Society while attending Eaton in 1919, "he made a promising debut by speaking cogently for the motion: 'That Ghosts do Exist.'"

But Mark Peel's biography of the Duke of Hamilton conveys the later strong disapproval of the Hamiltons for the Duchess' involvement with Spiritualism, the Animal Defence and Anti-Vivisection Society and Lind-af-Hageby. "A self-obsessed Swedish aristocrat of intelligence and drive, Miss Lind's success in extracting large amounts of Hamilton money to finance the animal rights movement won her few friends in the family, but Nina was devoted to her," Peel wrote. "Together they travelled the country to pronounce on the iniquities of vivisection, and the virtues of spiritualism and reincarnation, fads which she increasingly practised following the death of her daughter Mairi in 1927." Their "psychic activity in battling human diseases" rather than relying on conventional medical procedures nearly caused the death of Douglas' brother George from peritonitis and set Douglas "permanently against Miss Lind and ruptured his relationship with his mother." Both brothers threatened to take legal action over "the large amount of Hamilton money Nina ploughed into the animal rights movement."³⁰⁸

The manner of the Duchess' death – and her bequeathing the family's beloved Ferne estate to the Animal Defence and Anti-Vivisection Society for an animal sanctuary run by Lind-af-Hageby – further outraged Douglas Douglas-Hamilton and his wife Elizabeth. Lady Hamilton had developed a non-malignant throat condition that prevented her from swallowing a few weeks after receiving a papal blessing in November 1950 for her advocacy of the proper treatment of animals. She began to recover after receiving an aureomycin anti-biotic drip but refused further treatment when she discovered

---

307 Duchess of Hamilton, "Priest or Prophet?", 369, 370. Italics in original. Copy in the King fonds.

308 Peel, 21, 22, 98, 97.

aureomycin had been developed from experiments on animals. "She died slowly of starvation with Miss Lind and her followers around her yet unwilling to help her or get her the treatment she needed, a shocking state of affairs." Elizabeth, "seeing her mother-in-law lying there on her bed ... could not believe that this skeletal form was anyone she had ever known. It was a most distressing sight and one that continued to haunt her for the rest of her life."[309]

Douglas Douglas-Hamilton's avid interest in athletics, politics (he was elected to Parliament in 1930 at the age of 27), and as a pioneering aviator (he was the first to circle Mount Everest in 1933) undoubtedly also made him unsympathetic to Spiritualism. In a distinguished military career, he served as leader of the City of Glasgow 602 Squadron from 1927 to 1936 and was appointed Station Commander of RAF Turnhouse, Edinburgh, responsible for the defence of the North of England and Scotland, in 1940. Canadian Governor General Lord Tweedsmuir had already suggested Douglas-Hamilton to Mackenzie King as his successor as Governor General of Canada in December 1939. Lady Hamilton sent King a letter and sketch of the Duke in January 1941. King again discussed "Lord Hamilton who is the Duchess of Hamilton's son" as a possible Governor General with Viscount Cranborne, the Secretary of State for Dominion Affairs, in June 1945.[310]

Rudolf Hess parachuted from his Me-110 near the Duke's home in Dungavel on the night of May 10, 1941, and demanded to see the Duke. Hamilton interrogated Hess on May 11 and flew to London personally to inform Churchill and King George VI of Hess' arrival. According to Mark Peel, "When he had finished a long silence ensued before Churchill asked him with studied emphasis, 'Do you mean to tell me that the Deputy Führer of Germany is in our hands?'"[311] Three months later, Mackenzie King crossed the Atlantic in a Liberator bomber to meet with Churchill and the British War Cabinet. Churchill explained to King that "Hess had begun to get a little unbalanced and to suffer a persecution complex and finally decided that he would perhaps serve his master best if he flew across the channel and talked with the Duke of Hamilton. That the Duke was the Lord Steward of Scotland, close to

---

309 Ibid., 182.
310 Diary, December 12, 1939, January 22, 1941, March 3, 1945, and June 24 and 25, 1945.
311 Peel, 147.

the King. That there was, he believed, an anti-Churchill-Eden party in Scotland with which the King and Queen would be sympathetic and who did not desire to see the British Empire broken up. He was certain Hitler was going to win and he thought if he could persuade the Scotch [sic] of this and how generous Hitler would be in the terms of any immediate settlement, the war would be speedily ended. He would then fly back to Germany himself after having had a talk with Hamilton."[312]

Mackenzie King had also been receiving what he believed to be spirit communications about Hess' purported peace mission. Four days after his capture, a Social Credit MP presented him with a shepherd's crook cane made on the estate of the Duke of Hamilton. He recorded in his diary, "It was significant that this presentation should have been made just at the time the press is making mention of Hamilton having conferences with Hess. To me it is a symbolic link in a plan in which invisible hands are having control. It really means to attach real significance to what is transpiring between Hess and Hamilton. I think I see the situation clearly."[313]

The Prime Minister had also received a letter from "an old lady in New York," the psychic Jessie Coumbe, dated either May 11 or 12, 1941, which related to the Deputy *Führer*. "She saw an Indian Chief and others holding their hands over a man's head and, finally, the Chief pointing to the swastika, and having it shot to pieces by his slaves, who were assembled nearby ... In the course of the vision, the Indian said that Hitler would be sending some man who would land on Scotch soil – to beware of a sheep in tiger's clothes, or a tiger in sheep's clothes. Hess' flight was on the night of the 10th. No news came until the night of the 12th." Again, accompanied by his stenographer, Edouard Handy, King visited Mrs. Coumbe at her home in a Harlem slum, at 539 East 144th Street, in June 1941 and dictated seven typed pages in his diary to Handy describing their visit. "(As I dictated, H. has remarked that the Indians may have signified the help that would come from the north part of America. I agreed but added that I feel sure it means our air force.)"[314]

The following month at Kingsmere, he read to Princess Alice, the wife of the Governor General the Earl of Athlone, "extracts from Mrs.

---

312 Diary, August 22, 1941
313 Diary, May 15, 1941.
314 Diary, May 19, 1941, and June 18, 1941.

Coumbe's first letter regarding her vision of 'P.M.' and Hess' flight ... Her Excellency was immensely interested in the whole account." The Prime Minister noted that the Governor General and Princess Alice "too are believers in psychic phenomena & the spirit world." King informed Queen Mary of Coumbe's vision after attending a worship service with the King and Queen at Balmoral Castle during his stay in the United Kingdom in August. "She seemed to attach considerable importance to phenomena of the kind, but indicated the need of right interpretation ... I have been much impressed by not only how deeply religious the Queen is at heart but even more by the keen perception she has of spiritual values." During the service, the Prime Minister had himself "prayed very earnestly that my life might be made a medium through which Divine purpose might fulfil itself in some measure."[315]

In British custody, Rudolf Hess had written in a very similar occultist vein to his young son two months previously. "Take notice. There are higher, more fateful powers, which I must point out to you – let us call them higher powers – who intervene, at least when it is time for great events. I *had* to come to England to talk about an agreement and peace. Often we do not understand these hard decisions immediately; in time to come their meaning will be clearly understood."[316]

Hess' flight to Scotland and immediate failure to engage the British in peace negotiations enraged Hitler and led him to attribute the cause for his mad venture to Hess' occult beliefs. "It is high time to destroy all this nonsense of star-gazing," the *Führer* told Nazi Party leaders at a conference on May 13.[317] A Nazi radio broadcast the same day informed Germans of Hess' past medical ailments and stated that "recently he had sought relief to an increasing extent in various methods practised by mesmerists and astrologers, etc. An attempt is also being made to determine to what extent these persons are responsible for bringing about the condition of mental distraction which led him to take this step."[318]

Albrecht Haushofer and Hess' astrologers Schulte-Strathaus and Ludwig Schmitt were immediately arrested and interrogated. The

---

315 Diary, July 21, 1941, and August 31, 1941, pp. 4, 3. King also informed the painter Frank O. Salisbury of Coumbe's vision on September 3.

316 Nesbit and van Acker, 107.

317 Manvell and Fraenkel, 120.

318 Padfield, 230. Douglas-Hamilton, 222.

next month (just as King was meeting with the psychic Jessie Coumbe in New York), the Nazis' *Aktion Hess* led to the arrest of hundreds of astrologers, clairvoyants, Christian Scientists, faith healers, Anthroposophists, fortune-tellers, palmists, and other occultists. "'Public performances' were not to be allowed if they involved demonstrations of an occult, spiritualist, clairvoyant, telepathic or astrological nature. Public lectures on these themes were also forbidden...no articles on these subjects were to be published."[319] Albrecht Haushofer was again imprisoned after the attempt on Hitler's life in July 1944 and executed with other members of the resistance by the SS on April 22, 1945, a week before Hitler's suicide in his bunker in Berlin. Karl Haushofer and his wife Martha killed themselves by taking arsenic in 1946. Rudolf Hess hanged himself at the age of 93 in 1987, still in prison after forty-six years of solitary confinement in Spandau Prison.

As will be seen in Volume 2, Mackenzie King's occult beliefs – like Hess' – had also led him astray and caused him to completely misjudge Hitler when he made his own peace mission to see the *Führer* in Berlin in 1937. But he retained until his death in 1950 virtually all the occult practices and beliefs the Nazis outlawed in the *Aktion Hess*.

---

319   Howe, 193. Manvell and Fraenkel, 127-128, 131-132. Tyson, 285-286. For an exhaustive examination of the occult practices and beliefs by Hess, Heinrich Himmler, Joseph Goebbels, and other Nazi leaders and their use of astrology, divination, clairvoyance, and telepathy in conducting World War II, see Kurlander, *Hitler's Monsters: A Supernatural History of the Third Reich*.

CHAPTER 9

The Spiritualist Cover Up by the King Executors

In December 1950, *Psychic News* sought to answer *Time*'s query whether King's psychic communications had influenced state affairs with "Mackenzie King Talked with Dead Roosevelt." Desmond Stone further explored this psychic contact with the deceased American president in an even more sensational 1960 *Argosy* exposé, "How Mackenzie King Ruled Canada from Beyond the Grave." For this article, Stone interviewed members of King's family and his personal staff, colleagues in government and Parliament, and various mediums in London. The most famous of these was Geraldine Cummins whose *The Road to Immortality*, ostensibly transmitted to the author by the late F.W.H. Myers, and author of eight other books, many received through automatic writing, that King began reading in 1934. He recorded in his diary that the sections "'Communications' from Mr. Myers" in *The Road to Immortality* were "quite the most impressive work I have read. It seems to me to explain most things, to be thoroughly sound & to let one see the truth re the Hereafter. It verifies the Scriptures in a multitude of ways." To another of his psychic friends, Helen Lambert, he wrote that the book "has appealed to me as much as anything I have seen thus far."[320]

When King and Joan Patteson began reading Cummins' *The Scripts of Cleophas* about one of Christ's disciples to whom Jesus appeared after his Crucifixion and Resurrection, they found them

---

320 "Mackenzie King Talked with Dead Roosevelt," *Psychic News*, December 23, 1950, 7. Diary, March 28, 1934. King to Lambert, July 27, 1934. On King and Geraldine Cummins, see Bedore 237-239, 291-293.

Figure 30: Geraldine Cummins photographed for Psychic News, *circa 1940s.*

"most enlightening – they bring a sense of nearness to spiritual reality." As described in Chapter 5, King faced a major crisis of belief in June 1934 when it appeared that an evil lying spirit – rather than Sir Wilfrid Laurier – had given him false predictions in séances about the outcome of provincial elections in Ontario and Saskatchewan and Prime Minister Bennett's nominations of Canadians to the British

Crown for knighthoods. By contrast, Cummins' automatic writings about the conversion of Saul and Paul's public avowal of his conversion seemed to King "to be inspired writing, to be true." He stopped reading before the chapter "The Confounding of Simon the Sorcerer of Summaria" thinking "that chapter would be a good one for tomorrow – that what we would receive [in séances] meanwhile would be enlightening. I have just opened the page and the words before me were 'Ye be an evil' and adulterous generation. It was significant the reference here to evil." A year later, he inserted E.B. Gibbes' article in *Light*, "The Messenger and the Scripts," describing Cummins' writing the third volume of the Cleophas Scripts, *The Great Days of Ephesus*, in his diary.[321]

Geraldine Cummins was born in Cork, Ireland, in 1890 to a mother who participated in séances at the time of her birth. She attributed her later interest in Spiritualism and psychic research to seeing Frank Benson's company at the Cork Opera House performing Shakespeare in 1897 and enacting scenes from the plays with her brothers at home. *Richard III* "might in one sense be described as an A B C of Spiritualism. It abounds in ghosts ... the soothsayer in *Julius Caesar*, the witches and ghosts in *Macbeth*, *Richard III* and *Hamlet* were my monopoly ... It may, therefore, be truly said that I began my psychic career at the age of seven by impersonating a cricket team of ghosts." In addition to writing fiction, she also became a playwright herself, writing with Suzanne Day three plays about Irish characters and country scenes performed at the Abbey Theatre in Dublin in 1913, 1914 and 1917.[322] Her play *Till Yesterday Comes Again* was staged at the Chanticleer Theatre in London in 1938.

Cummins witnessed her first séance in Paris in June 1914 with the well-known medium Hester Dowden, with whom Mackenzie King would conduct séances two decades later. Using the Ouija board to communicate with deceased persons in the Beyond, Dowden established contact with a Frenchman who, a mere month before the sudden outbreak of World War I, predicted, "rivers of blood will flow in France." Using the Ouija board herself, Cummins conducted séances during WW I with the Irish playwright Lennox Robinson

---

321 Diary, May 26, 1934, and July 10, 1935. Gibbes, "The Messenger and the Scripts," *Light* 54:2795 (August 3, 1934), 459.

322 Cummins, *Unseen Adventures*, 16, 18, 17, 20.

(married to Dowden's daughter), the playwright and critic St. John Ervine, and the poet W.B. Yeats. She was present when Dowden established contact with the deceased Oscar Wilde through automatic writing in 1923 and was the recorder as Dowden read out the messages on the Ouija board while receiving Wilde's three-act drama *The Extraordinary Play*.

The same year, the publicity manager of the Haymarket Theatre invited Dowden and Cummins to attend a performance of *The Importance of Being Earnest* and asked for a review of the production by Oscar Wilde as seen through Dowden's eyes. Cummins was again the recorder of a scathing 1,500-word review transmitted by the playwright and received by Dowden on the Ouija board. Twenty-three years after his death, Wilde lambasted the Haymarket production. "It is delightful at any time to stand in an ecstasy of observation before what is absolutely perfect; the complete whole, as it were. Here I beheld my own child, and almost failed to recognize it. Its new gown and its new attitude were so unfamiliar."[323]

When Mackenzie King met Cummins, the medium heard voices of the dead in her unconscious mind via her "control" – an ancient Greek spirit contact named Astor who ushered in other spirits wishing to speak – and recorded these utterances through automatic writing. Edith Beatrice Gibbes, her colleague and collaborator since 1923, described her method in the introduction to *The Road to Immortality*. "She sits at a table, covers her eyes with her left hand and concentrates on 'stillness.'...Her right hand resting on a block of foolscap paper, Miss Cummins soon falls into this light trance or dream-state. When in this condition her hand begins to write. As a rule her 'control' makes a few introductory remarks and announces that another entity is waiting to speak."[324]

King described his first sitting with the medium in her sitting room at 25 Jubilee Place, Chelsea, London, just prior to meeting Prime Minister Clement Attlee at his country house Chequers, in November 1947. "I merely shook hands with Miss Cummins. She then sat behind a table. Big sheets of paper were put out in front of her. She had a pen in her hand. In a few moments, went off into a deep trance. Miss Gibbs [sic] sat beside her, indicating to her where to start writing and

---

323 Ibid., 20, 27, 32, 86-89, 116-22.
324 Cummins, *The Road to Immortality*, 20, 21.

when an end of a sheet was reached, placing a different sheet before her. She wrote in a large script on this foolscap paper." Since King could not read the writing upside down from the far side of the table where he sat facing Gibbes and Cummins, "the former suggested I take her seat and she would take mine. I was then able to read quite clearly what was being written on each line." Besides King's mother, Sir Wilfrid Laurier and President F.D. Roosevelt also spoke via the medium.

Roosevelt wanted to communicate with King regarding "my thought of retiring – of the problems of today, etc. There could be no doubting his personality for what he brought out was all related to what had been uppermost in his political fights while President; what he saw and felt concerning the present situation…Roosevelt's description of my father and mother was as accurate as anything could be. He had never known any of them in life." Before his sitting with Geraldine Cummins in the afternoon, King had already attended a séance with the trance medium Florence Jane Sharplin in the drawing room of her home at 10 Cheyne Road overlooking the Thames and hung with beautiful paintings of Ypres and other places of Europe. King had also recorded, "Roosevelt took up most of the morning."

He had communicated with the deceased American president as well in a sitting with Mrs. Sharplin in October 1945. When he dictated the record of this "really remarkable conversation" to his stenographer Edouard Handy the following July, he noted it was "so clear and connected in every way, bearing on difficult situations at the time. It leaves no doubt about one having been conversing with Roosevelt himself. The whole phenomena seems to be inexplicable, except in that way, having regard to how unknown to every one save myself, the questions were which we discussed between us, and also at that time the future unknown which has since developed exactly on lines indicated or foretold."[325] (For a transcription of these October 1945 and November 1947 séances, see Appendix A in Volume 2.)

In addition to interviewing Geraldine Cummins, Desmond Stone made photostat copies of her automatic writings and cited Roosevelt's warning to King about a forthcoming war in Korea in his *Argosy* article. "What I want to tell you is that three years from now is the critical time.

---

325 Diary, November 22, 1947, and July 24, 1946.

This is when you will be wanted for advice ... No war for about three years, as we see it here. Then you and the others may be able to prevent it, but it's going to be touch and go later ... Stalin and company have on hand a big scheme of cold war via Asia. Look out ... If they get away with their schemes, just tell your people to keep their attention on Asia. This is my warning."[326]

Stone claimed that, because of this caution from the late President, King ordered an unnamed "high official in the Canadian Government ... whose name is now a household word in Canada" – presumably Lester Pearson – to immediately travel to Washington to see President Truman. "I have been talking to Mr. Roosevelt and he tells me that we should not be on that [United Nations Korea] boundary commission. There is going to be a war in Asia; Canadian lives are going to be lost, and I want to get Canada off that commission right away. You must go at once and take this message to President Truman." According to Stone, when the "high official" duly arrived at the White House early the next morning with his top-secret message from the Prime Minister of Canada and entered the President's office, Truman stood up to meet him and asked cynically, "Well ... who has he been talking to this time?" Stone also cited Pearson, then Leader of the Opposition in the House of Commons, that King "was worried about Korea long before the war broke out because of some message he had received from FDR."[327]

When Desmond Stone interviewed the British medium Helen Hughes, she was upset that Mackenzie King kept his spiritualist activities secret and lamented, "He could have done so much to help spiritualism." Stone explained to his *Argosy* readers, "The reason was obvious to anyone with a knowledge of the workings of politics. If a word about King's spiritualistic interests ever leaked out to his enemies, the Prime Minister and his entire government could have been toppled instantly. Consider what the opposition could do with a slogan like 'Government by spooks!'" Ged Martin, referring to King's séance with Ellen Elliott and Alma Brash in Toronto in August 1942, similarly commented that "Two weeks later, Canadian troops would go into action at Dieppe. What would Canadians have thought had they learned that their wartime leader regarded death as a minor incident in the soul's voyage through the cosmos?" The PM was fully aware of the political consequences if his spiritualist beliefs

---

326 Stone, 62.
327 Ibid., 22, 65.

became public knowledge. Martin Ebon, in *They Knew the Unknown*, entitled his chapter on Mackenzie King "The Prime Minister Was Discreet." He wrote that King, "convinced that he had spoken with spirits of the dead, knew that Canadian opposition leaders would have a field day with stories that the Prime Minister was well known in London's spiritualist circles."328

Bruce Hutchison came to the same conclusion in *The Incredible Canadian*, published two years after King's death. "What would the Canadian people have thought of their leader if they had known that he consulted the dead in the midst of a war among the living?" King's perceptive biographer queried. "The breach of his secret probably would have ruined his public career. The few who knew it had long been bound in a conspiracy of silence, never to be broken until his death, and then only by his spiritualistic counselors. Some of his intimates regarded his seances as a harmless fad. Some understood that in his mind the other world had become as real as this one and more important. Therein lay his capacity to meet with composure all the larger shocks of life here and now. They mattered little when he had the promise of the life to come."329

In August 1950, Geraldine Cummins sent her and Beatrice Gibbes' condolences to Edouard Handy, King's principal secretary from 1936 to 1950, whom they had met at the Dorchester Hotel when they conducted their last séance with the Prime Minister in 1948. Handy had made all the organizational and financial arrangements with Mercy Phillimore for King's sittings with mediums while he was confined at the Dorchester with his heart condition. Cummins referred to an article in *The Times*, which published a resume of his testament and stated, "he directed that his diaries should be destroyed 'except those parts which he indicated should be available for publication or use.'" She inquired about the copies of her automatic writing sessions, which the Prime Minister had promised to return to Cummins, and affirmed, "he told us that he had every intention of publishing in his MEMOIRS, his interest in the matter about which he saw us, and of similar investigations he had made."330

---

328 Ibid., 64. Martin https://www.gedmartin.net/published-work-main-menu-11/268-w-l-mackenzie-king-canada-s-spiritualist-prime-minister. Ebon, 238.

329 Hutchison, *The Incredible Canadian*, 295.

330 Cummins to Handy, August 10, 1950. The correspondence and related materials between Cummins and the executors can be found in the King executors' files, "Correspondence with Geraldine Cummins 1950" and "1951-53."

Handy replied, "I know from what Mr. King has told me that had he been given the time and the opportunity to write his Memoirs he would have made special reference to his interest in the matter about which he saw Miss Gibbes and yourself as well as on two other similar occasions." He referred Cummins' inquiry about the return of the automatic writing transcripts to F.A. McGregor, whom King had asked shortly before his death to assist him in the writing of his memoirs. Handy expressed his surprise at reading Fred Archer's *Psychic News* article reprinted in the *Ottawa Citizen* (which "has, naturally, aroused much speculation in Canada") and asked Cummins to send the literary executors any items appearing in *Psychic News* "or, for that matter, copy of any other publication or article in which reference is made to Mr. King."[331]

Cummins sent Handy cuttings and extracts from *Time Magazine*, *Psychic News*, *Psychic World*, and *Two Worlds*, estimating the combined circulation of the spiritualist papers at about 41,000. In view of the publicity given to King's spiritualism in these publications, she thought it desirable "to put the facts in their true perspective, free from all sensationalism, by relating my own 'reminiscences' of meetings with him" in an appendix to her forthcoming autobiography, *Unseen Adventures*. Her appendix would refute the statement by the Duchess of Hamilton that King sought spirit aid in state affairs. Handy thanked the medium for sending the spiritualist clippings since "we have little or no access to such publications here in Ottawa" and requested that she send him her appendix on Mackenzie King. "It might be that I could make some suggestions that might prevent the kind of comment that both you and I would like to avoid. There is no telling what use certain of Mr. King's detractors might make of anything of the kind. Political opponents, as you know, are constantly seeking to place a wrong interpretation on many matters."[332]

---

331 Handy to Cummins, August 22, 1950, and November 2, 1950. Besides Norman Robertson and F.A. McGregor, the other literary executors were Dr. W. Kaye Lamb, the Dominion Archivist, and J.W. Pickersgill, Special Assistant to King and Prime Minister Louis St. Laurent. The other trustees of the King estate, in addition to McGregor, were D.K. MacTavish and the Royal Trust Company.

332 Cummins to Handy, November 17, 1950. Handy to Cummins, December 12, 1950.

Cummins sent Handy galley proofs of her Appendix II, entitled "Reminiscences of The Right Hon. W.L. Mackenzie King, O.M.," in December 1950. In its opening paragraph she had written, "Mr. Mackenzie King told me that, when he retired, it was his intention to write his *Memoirs*. In the last chapter he would relate his varied experiences in psychical research, describe our experiments together and declare his faith in a spiritual world."

The King executors and trustees were horrified by Cummins' appendix. "The effect," the *Globe and Mail* reported citing the London *Sunday Dispatch*, "was immediate and volcanic." It was not until after King's death that the truth was revealed, the *Globe* stated, "and this despite strong and impassioned efforts by his executors to keep it secret."[333] The executors objected to Cummins' assertions that the deceased Franklin Roosevelt had warned King about a forthcoming war in Asia, that the former President "had fallen in love" with King's mother "in that other life," (Roosevelt called her "a sweet and loveable woman – one of the best") and that Isabel King "was apparently the primary inspiration of his life."

According to the transcript of Cummins' automatic writing, Roosevelt informed King, "You will not know how we come, but when you sleep, we will put suggestions into your mind." King's executors did not want to acknowledge publicly the medium's claim that "Being a religious man and a sincere practising Christian, Mr. Mackenzie King saw no wrong in attempting to speak with the spirits of the dead." "For he was following the example of Christ who, on the mountain, spoke with the spirits of Moses and Elias, and they had been dead for many years," Cummins wrote. "Roman Catholics, who revere St. Joan of Arc, are in a better position, perhaps, than others to appreciate the rightness of Mr. Mackenzie King's view of communication ... was he morally wrong to ask what is our state, craving a diviner harmony than life supplies, or wrong to seek, as did the early Christians, communion with departed souls?"[334]

Duncan MacTavish and Leonard Brockington, first chairman of the CBC 1936-1939, a counsel in MacTavish's law firm and chairman of the Mackenzie King Scholarship established in King's will, called on

---

333 J.V. McAree, "Mr. King and Spirits," *Globe and Mail*, September 14, 1953, 6.

334 Martin, op. cit. Galley proofs, "Reminiscences of The Right Hon. W.L. Mackenzie King, O.M." in Cummins correspondence file.

Cummins and Gibbes on January 19 in their home in Chelsea where they had conducted their séance with King in 1947. Their intent was to convince the two to delete the appendix to *Unseen Adventures*. Cummins protested to Handy afterwards that the two mediums were "quite dumbfounded when, immediately on entering the drawing-room," Brockington "opened the conversation in what seemed to us a most unpleasant manner. We were quite wrongly accused by him of dishonesty and breach of confidence." Beatrice Gibbes declared, "I have never been so insulted in my own drawing-room. We were treated as though we were criminals in the dock."[335]

F.A. McGregor, who took over the correspondence with Cummins from Handy at this point, attempted to placate the medium by explaining that the King trustees and literary executors "have felt ourselves under an obligation to carry out Mr. King's wishes as we know them. Since he had kept under personal lock and key all his correspondence and notes on this subject, we considered it would be a breach of confidence on our part to disclose what he had kept so secret." L.W. Brockington "thought of your relationship to Mr. King – and I confess I share his feeling – as similar to that between solicitor and client or between priest and parishioner or between doctor and patient … His reaction is understandable … in view of his strong feeling, as a close friend of Mr. King's, that an injustice was being done and that the disclosures of the kind proposed would be seized upon by political enemies in Canada and misinterpreted."[336]

Cummins and her publisher, Rider and Company, refused to omit the offending appendix from her autobiography but agreed to alter it so as not to disclose King's identity. In a memorandum of his meetings with the two mediums and their publisher MacTavish wrote, "we achieved a document which I believe would have no internal identifying evidence which would direct the minds of readers obviously to Mr. Mackenzie King."[337] The title of the appendix was amended to

---

335 Cummins to Handy, March 1, 1951.

336 McGregor to Cummins, March 29, 1951.

337 Duncan MacTavish, "Memorandum Covering Conversations in England." He noted, "My impression of the interview was that Miss Gibbes is the dominant personality and she seemed to be much more adamant than was Miss Cummins." Christopher Dummitt commented on their relationship that "The two unmarried women had lived together for decades." Dummitt, 61.

"Reminiscences of a British Commonwealth Statesman," King's and Roosevelt's names were changed to Mr. S. and X.Y.Z., and references to Isabel King were deleted. Rider asked for "hundreds of pounds" for making these typesetting alterations in the autobiography and for the delay in publication and loss of sales resulting from concealing Mackenzie King's identity. But the publisher finally accepted the 100 pounds [£2,600 or $4,410 in 2023 Canadian dollars] in compensation offered by the executors and trustees. After Cummins asserted her copyright to her automatic writings and threatened to put the matter in the hands of the Society of Authors, McGregor returned the original scripts to the medium but asked her to destroy these upon receipt.[338]

In a revised postscript to *Unseen Adventures*, Cummins referred to Queen Victoria's many sittings with mediums and Prime Ministers Gladstone's and Balfour's open association with psychical research as well as the suppression of psychic investigations in the Soviet Union. "When will the western nations learn in their struggle for peace and freedom that psychical research and 'Spiritualism' are not things of shame to be hidden and suppressed?" she asked. "When will mankind learn that evidence and knowledge of a life after death can give the greatest happiness to individuals and could in time be the foundation of world-peace and international understanding through the foundation of a new morality?"[339]

Despite her unpleasant experience with the King executors, Cummins informed McGregor in November 1951 that Blair Fraser, the Ottawa editor of *Maclean's Magazine*, had interviewed her and Beatrice Gibbes, as well as Helen Hughes, Mercy Phillimore, and the editor of *Psychic News*, Maurice Barbanell, for his article "The Secret Life of Mackenzie King, Spiritualist" to be published by *Maclean's* in December. Although largely a summary of accounts published in London over the previous year, Fraser claimed to reveal "the best-kept secret" of King's career: "the fact that the Prime Minister of Canada had been for more than twenty-five years a convinced and practicing spiritualist." Fraser had also interviewed some of the King executors who sought "to prevent any possible misinterpretation of the facts as he knew them." As McGregor informed Cummins, "Mr. Fraser was

---

338 Cummins to McGregor, May 21, 1951. McGregor to Cummins, June 18, 1951. Gibbes to McGregor, July 9, 1951.

339 Cummins, *Unseen Adventures*, 183.

impressed by what you and Miss Phillimore told him about Mr. King's not seeking guidance on matters of public policy. We too had stressed this, and the article indicates his acceptance of this view."[340]

Fraser's revelations in *Maclean's* again generated newspaper articles across Canada that reported the Prime Minister's Spiritualism but nevertheless assured their readers that his beliefs and occult practices had not affected his actions in the political arena. "Argus" in *Le Devoir* cited these assurances by King's executors and official biographer. "Ces familiers admettent que M. King s'adonnait au spiritisme, mais ils protestent qu'il ne s'en est jamais remis aux messages ou conseils des esprits pour orienter les affaires de l'Etat canadien."[341] The general tone of this newspaper coverage followed that of the *Victoria Times* article published the previous year after reports of King's involvement with Spiritualism first emerged in London and in *Time Magazine*: "What has been said of him was true: He was a good man. Leave the rest."

Yet as Paul Roazen observed, "Fraser's story was to be the beginning of what turned into a subsequent collapse of King's political standing in Canada." Lind-af-Hageby refuted Mercy Phillimore's statement to Blair Fraser denying that King consulted mediums for advice in statecraft in the January 1952 *Psychic News*. "I can fully confirm what the Duchess [of Hamilton] has stated. The 'inner man' of Mr. Mackenzie King was animated by Spiritualism, by the knowledge of survival and communication, by knowledge of the powers of prophecy and – in the innermost part of his 'inner man' by his profound and enduring love of his mother. It is not possible that a man can go so deeply into Spiritualism as Mackenzie King did, apart from sittings with mediums and receiving messages, without this colouring his actions as a

---

340 Cummins to McGregor, November 7, 1951. Fraser, 7-8. McGregor to Cummins, November 13, 1951. Barbanell invited King for an off-the-record discussion about "your interest in psychic subjects. I understand this interest is of long standing," while the Prime Minister was in London for meetings with Churchill, the 1944 Meeting of Commonwealth Prime Ministers, and addressing Parliament. King declined, citing lack of time. "I shall hope to have this opportunity at some future occasion." Barbanell to King, May 10, 1944. King to Barbanell, May 20, 1944.

341 Argus, "Le spiritisme de Mackenzie King," *Le Devoir*, December 17, 1951. See also James McCook, "Seances at Laurier House: Spiritualist Mackenzie King Tried 'Communication' with the Dead," *Ottawa Journal*, December 10, 1951, and "M. King aurait pratiqué le spiritism durant 25 ans?," *Le Canada*, December 11, 1951.

statesman and his judgment of world events." King and Joan Patteson expressed a similar thought when the Prime Minister prepared to leave for the Paris Peace Conference in July 1946. Joan "said to me as I came away that she hoped I would fulfill my mission. That in all this, we begin with ourselves which is true. One brings to the world only what is in one's own soul."[342]

Two examples supporting Lind-af-Hageby's affirmation that Spiritualism shaped King's "inner man" occurred in 1933 during the debate in Parliament regarding government intervention to address the social and humanitarian needs arising from the Depression, and the subsequent federal election campaign in 1935. King and the Liberal Party were forced to establish a much more progressive party platform after J.S. Woodsworth of the newly founded socialist Co-operative Commonwealth Federation introduced a resolution in Parliament on February 1, 1933, calling on R.B. Bennett's Conservative Government to "immediately take measures looking to the setting up of a cooperative commonwealth." In his account of King's two-hour-long speech in Parliament on February 27, H. Blair Neatby summarized that "A Liberal government would not bring the millennium but King did imply in his peroration that liberalism was strongly influenced by the Sermon on the Mount."

While Neatby noted the strong Christian influence on King's politics, he did not acknowledge the spiritualist and occult means that conveyed what King believed to be the word of God. After attending church on Sunday, February 26, he recorded in his diary regarding his forthcoming speech, "I had meant to quote 'Let this mind which was in Christ Jesus be also in you' & will hold to it. I feel that the loved ones are urging me to strike this note...I felt a closer communion during the service & tonight than I have felt for a long time. I am truly grateful & pray that the loved ones will be with [me] to sustain & help me tomorrow & that God will guide me in all that I say." The next morning King repeated, "I believe all the loved ones are about helping & inspiring" and that his presentation of the Liberal Party platform in Parliament in the afternoon would be the real Co-operative Commonwealth, "the Kingdom of God on earth, 'Thy will be done on

---

342 "Always on the Ground," *Victoria Times*, October 25, 1950. Roazen, 2. Fred Archer, "Mackenzie King: 'I Confirm the Duchess!' – states Miss Lind-af-Hageby," *Psychic News*, no. 1025 (January 26, 1952), 1, 3. Reprinted in *Psychic Observer*, October 10, 1952, 8. Diary, July 14, 1946.

earth as it is in Heaven.' I pray God for the gift of utterance, and power to speak the words that will be helpful at this time to my country & the world."

After addressing the House of Commons, King congratulated himself for getting "an entire program on the record and to go on record myself in parliament as believing that Christianity alone could save mankind...I felt though I have been guided in what I said & that the speech will serve a great purpose...It is a speech that will have to be reckoned with & may mark a turning point in our future as a party." Neatby recorded that "King's House of Commons speech was reprinted as a pamphlet with the platform itemized in fourteen points. In future, when correspondents criticized the party for having no clear statement of its policies, King merely mailed them a copy... The pamphlet would be one of the major items of Liberal literature in the election campaign of 1935."[343]

Mackenzie King again acknowledged spiritual inspiration from the Beyond near the end of the 1935 election and just weeks before Benito Mussolini's invasion of Ethiopia on October 3. He and Joan Patteson held a séance "conversation" over the "little table" on September 8 which created "the feeling as of a divine presence surrounding us." "The presence of St. Luke and St. John seemed almost unbelievable to her and to me; one cannot just believe it; still one stops to reflect on how lives lived here would seek to influence in the hereafter the conduct of those having to do with affairs & a crisis in the world's history. To me the whole evening gave the impression of power descending, from on high – thoughts inspired from a highest source, themselves inspired from a source still higher, etc."

On the morning of his fourth radio broadcast on September 17 in the campaign that would rout Conservative Prime Minister Bennett and restore the Liberal Party to power, King came in from his garden seat at Kingsmere and "wrote out my thoughts on government vs. business – a spiritual vs. a material conception of life taking direct issue with Bennett. It was what was needed to complete the speech. I felt it was the best of all, and certainly along with what I had written last night the fulfilment of what St. Luke had said in 'the conversation.'"[344]

---

343 Neatby, *William Lyon Mackenzie King, The Prism of Unity, 1932-1939*, 35, 37, 38. Diary, February 26 and 27, 1933.

344 Diary, September 8 and 17, 1935.

In 1955, five years after King's death, Henry Stanley Ferns, a member of his secretarial staff from 1940 to 1943, published with Bernard Ostry, the first critical biography of Canada's longest-serving Prime Minister, *The Age of Mackenzie King: The Rise of the Leader*. Their biography was widely condemned by reviewers in Canada for blackening King's reputation. Ferns believed that many of these reviewers were supporters of the Liberal Party. As he related in his autobiography *Reading from Left to Right*, the authors were impeded during their research when they were denied access to King's diaries and correspondence by his executors. Bernard Ostry had to threaten to go to the media when the Public Archives refused him further access to public papers since the King Estate had appointed an "official" biographer, R. MacGregor Dawson, to research and write his life story.

Ferns wrote that at a time when the Liberals still formed the Government, "Monopoly was the policy of the literary executors of Mackenzie King because they wanted to see constructed an acceptable image *now* when the image would be of political advantage. If nothing more, they wanted 'the intellectual space' occupied at once so that alternative interpretations were impeded, delayed, or made impossible." This censorship was repeated in 1963 when another "official" biographer, H. Blair Neatby, completed his King study covering the years 1924-1932. The executors wrote to Neatby "requesting one change – the only change the literary executors ever directly asked that he make to the biography. Neatby had referenced the spiritualism binders in a footnote. [W. Kaye] Lamb asked that the reference be deleted. 'My three fellow Literary Executors are firm in their resolve that these notes are to be destroyed.'"[345]

Protests by Ferns and Ostry that King's executors were monopolizing his private papers and constructing his image for political purposes were repeated with the publication of C.P. Stacey's best-seller, *A Very Double Life*, in 1976. The editor of *Maclean's*, Peter Newman, attacked the most prominent of the King executors, John Whitney Pickersgill (1905-1997), who was not only King's and Prime Minister Louis St. Laurent's special assistant but also became clerk of the Privy Council in 1952, Secretary of State in 1953, and held Cabinet posts in the Lester Pearson Government from 1963 to 1967. As King's, St. Laurent's and Pearson's literary executor, Newman charged, Pickersgill

---

345 Ferns, *Reading from Left to Right*, 302. Dummitt, 200.

"finds himself in position to rewrite or at least re-interpret much of the Canadian history that was being made between 1919 and 1968. And he's been doing just that ... the greatest monopoly and control of historical sources this country has ever seen." When James Lorimer republished Ferns' and Ostry's *The Age of Mackenzie King*, also in 1976, the Conservatives' Dalton Camp wrote about the "'conspiracy to keep the truth about Mackenzie King from the Canadian people.' The official biographers, he wrote, 'were in on the cover-up.' Laurier House, where they worked on the official biography, 'was not so much the prime resource for King scholars ... as it was a fudge factory.'"[346]

In March 1977, three months before the King executors transferred ownership of his papers to the Public Archives of Canada, Pickersgill and Gordon Robertson, another executor and Clerk of the Privy Council (1963-1975), personally burned the separate Spiritualism binders in which the Prime Minister recorded transcriptions of sittings, automatic writing by mediums, and King's own detailed accounts of his séances from 1932 to 1950. After he became one of the King executors in 1968, Robertson examined what were probably automatic writings by mediums in what he referred to as "scribblers" – "soft-covered, ruled books all Canadian schoolchildren used from Grade 1 up."

> The "scribblers" were the right instrument for their purpose: a place for the mediums to record their communications with the spirits King had sought to contact in 'the other world'...
> No school child could get out of Grade 1 with the writing or the confusion in the scribblers. Presumably allowance has to be made for the likelihood that the writing was done by the medium in a darkened room on her lap (it seemed always to be a 'her') or on a shaking table. The incoherent scribbles were obviously what the medium thought she heard in response to questions to spirits vaguely identified with members of King's family, Sir Wilfrid Laurier, and others to whom King had been particularly close. Most of it, to any reader in broad daylight, was meaningless gibberish.
>   Two things became clear. There was nothing and could be nothing with enough coherence to constitute any 'direction' or 'comment' on policy – the kind of thing that had been imagined

---

346 Dummitt, 210, 211, 246.

by critics all-to-ready to believe that King had a streak of madness in him. The other thing was that there was nothing of any value or relevance for the public record. King would never have directed that any part be preserved. Jack and I burned the scribblers, page by page, in the Pickersgills' fireplace.[347]

Because of the immensity of the Mackenzie King Papers, totalling an estimated two million pages of documents occupying more than two hundred meters of shelf space, thousands of pages of spiritualist and occult publications, King's correspondence with mediums, psychics and fellow spiritualists, his notes, and transcriptions of séances – and even misfiled pages from his Spiritualism binders – survived the 1977 archival purge by the King executors. In December 2000, the National Archives of Canada microfilmed twelve thousand pages of these records in a Spiritualism Series of the Mackenzie King Papers, MG26, J9. These are accessible online via the Canadian Research Knowledge Network website (http://heritage.canadiana.ca/view/oocihm.lac_mikan_108986).

King also recorded his occult beliefs and practices in his regular, daily diary and in his correspondence so that we can reconstruct his encounters with the occult. The PM's Spiritualist Papers were not opened to the public until January 1, 2001. In her detailed study of the Mackenzie King Papers, Jean Dryden concluded, "by keeping the sensitive parts of the personal series closed...the Executors sought to keep the emphasis on the political side of King's career." The fact that no in-depth study of King's spiritualism has been published since more than seven decades after his death suggests that his executors were largely successful in their endeavour. Ged Martin queried, "If Mackenzie King was in reality a madman, ruling Canada at the random behest of spirits summoned from the vasty deep, was there not an obligation on those who knew to ignore confidentiality and place the issue in the public domain?" Martin affirmed that "two very basic issues must be faced. First, did Mackenzie King allow spiritualist experiences to shape political action? Secondly, was he mad? An affirmative answer to either question would have disturbing implications for his Canada – and, by extension, for that of his successors."[348]

---

347 Gordon Robertson, 55.
348 Dryden, 63, 66, 57, 68. Dummitt, 256-257. Martin, op. cit.

Walter Meyer zu Erpen and Joy Lowe lamented the dearth of archival and print sources on Spiritualism in Canada a decade before Library and Archives Canada opened the Spiritualism Series of the Mackenzie King Papers in 2001. But they confidently predicted that the King Papers "may be the single most significant source of information on Canadian Spiritualism during the first half of the twentieth century."[349] The chapters that follow more than fully bear out their prescient prediction.

---

349 Meyer zu Erpen and Lowe, 77.

CHAPTER 10

"Everybody Knew About It" – Circles of Spiritualists

In 1935, Ernest Addison Stanley Hayward, O.B.E., reported in *Light*, the organ of the London Spiritualist Alliance, that Spiritualism in Canada still manifested itself primarily in private and in secret. After spending a month in Victoria, which he considered "the most English of Canadian cities," Hayward wrote that "Victoria is a most conventional city, exceedingly orthodox in its religious beliefs, and consequently psychic subjects are, to the majority, strictly taboo. The few who happen to be interested are practically afraid to moot the question to acquaintances." He had visited two Spiritualist churches Sunday evenings and found there were less than thirty people at each, "and the atmosphere was depressing."

> Unfortunately, any mention of the word 'Spiritualism' is frowned upon almost universally throughout Canada, and, I regret to say, this state of affairs is mainly due to the poor type of Mediums, and others, who conduct services. There are, of course, some exceptions, and I know that the distances are so great and the churches so few that it is most difficult to arrange for interchange of Mediums and speakers. The consequence is that the majority of Mediums appear in public long before they are developed; and, when launched on their work so prematurely, they seldom develop further, and so eke out their powers in any way they can, by ability to read the character of the person they are addressing, by cleverly worded leading questions, or by sheer bluff and effrontery.[350]

---

350 Hayward, "Spiritualism in Canada," 712.

Mackenzie King's executors claimed to be carrying out the Prime Minister's wishes to keep his spiritualist beliefs and investigations – what came to be called his "psychic research" – secret as well. Edouard Handy affirmed the need for such secrecy in a confidential 1950 memorandum to the executors regarding King's personal and private correspondence stored at Laurier House. "In addition to personal correspondence, there are papers of very private nature [regarding psychic research] which Mr. King had also wished to consider using in his Memoirs," Handy wrote, "but instructed me to destroy were he not to be given this opportunity himself. I refer especially to private correspondence with [the London Spiritualist Alliance at] Queensberry Place, London."[351]

The King estate trustees alerted his relatives in 1951 about the forthcoming publication of Blair Fraser's "The Secret Life of Mackenzie King, Spiritualist" exposé in *Maclean's* in December. After reading Fraser's article, Margery King wrote F.A. McGregor, "I certainly feel that the whole question was handled in as dignified a way as we could hope for…While not knowing the details, I had known of Uncle Willie's interest in Spiritualism. He made no secret of it – and certainly his belief in a 'life hereafter' – was one of the corner stones of his life."[352]

The executors' primary motivation for the next several decades was really to preserve King's political reputation and that of the Liberal Party. Speaking on behalf of over a dozen mediums the Prime Minister consulted in his lifetime, Geraldine Cummins wrote McGregor, "We, also, are fully aware of Mr. King's wishes in this connection. He made no secret of them to people here or to his friends in Canada. He openly stated that he had the intention of publishing the results of his researches in his memoirs. This fact is presumably now to be suppressed by his executors." King had stated this intention to publish his psychic investigations to Dr. Glen and Lillian Hamilton when he visited the two researchers in Winnipeg in 1933. Simultaneously with the publication of Fraser's 1951 *Maclean's* exposé, Lillian Hamilton allowed the publication in the *Winnipeg Tribune* of three letters King wrote the couple after his visit. In "Mackenzie King's Secret: Newly

---

351 Edouard Handy, "Confidential Memorandum Re Personal and Private Correspondence at Laurier House," August 17, 1950. File "Archives: Disposition of Diaries and Personal Correspondence, 1950."

352 Margery [Mrs. W.L.M.] King to F.A. McGregor, January 2, 1952.

Disclosed Letters Reveal 'Spiritual' Link," Val Werier divulged, "Mrs. Hamilton reports that Mr. King said during his Winnipeg visit he intended to write a book on his spiritualist beliefs and the foundations for them. In fact he once approached a secretary with a view to engage her to do the copy work."³⁵³

When C.P. Stacey studied the diaries, he reported that after the Prime Minister and Joan Patteson held their sittings over "the little table," King "recorded these conversations in pencilled memoranda, apparently written while the séance was in progress. Usually, they are to be found attached to the original diary." These memoranda were removed before the diaries were transcribed for the historians hired by the King executors in the form they now appear online on the Library and Archives Canada website. But the executors' intention of decreasing references to King's spiritualism in his diaries was not carried out consistently. There are indexes for the years 1923-1926 with categories for astrology, Spiritualism, "psychical-horoscope etc.," and coincidences. The index for the 1937 diary lists "PSYCHICAL PHENOMENA: CONVERSATIONS, ETC., WRITTEN UP BY MR. KING PERSONALLY… (A total of 75 Conversations, etc., including records, etc., of Visions.)"³⁵⁴

In July 1946, just after studying the "transcription of sitting with Mrs. [Helen] Hughes which Handy had made," King dined with Blair Fraser on board the S.S. *Georgic* while en route to the Paris Peace Conference but apparently did not discuss his spiritualist beliefs with the journalist. What was new in Fraser's 1951 *Maclean's* article was his contention that Mackenzie King was open about his occult interests with many members of his staff, friends, and like-minded spiritualists. "To his real intimates he made no secret of these beliefs," Fraser wrote. "Some of them joined him many times in sessions with the Ouija board in Ottawa … Members of his personal staff knew it too – in some cases Mr. King didn't know they

---

353 Cummins to McGregor, May 21, 1951. Val Werier, "Mackenzie King's Secret: Newly Disclosed Letters Reveal 'Spiritual' Link," *Winnipeg Tribune*, December 14, 1951, 1. See also "Eternal Survival Said King Belief: Three Letters Written by Late Prime Minister Are Made Public," *Montreal Gazette*, December 15, 1951.

354 Stacey, *Mackenzie King and the Atlantic Triangle*, 13. Diary, January 1, 1923, 1924 and 1925, and December 31, 1937.

knew, but they all did."³⁵⁵ Mackenzie King had in fact acknowledged in 1932 that his servants knew about his séances at Laurier House when the direct-voice medium Etta Wriedt from Detroit enabled him to communicate with spirits in the Beyond. "The 'conversations' in many cases have been so loud, so clear etc.," he recorded in his diary, "that I have felt great embarrassment at the servants in other parts of the house, hearing what was said, as I am sure they have."³⁵⁶

Like Geraldine Cummins, Percy Philip, in his 1955 "My Conversation with Mackenzie King's Ghost" article for *Liberty*, observed, "There is no incompatibility between being a Christian and church goer, as Mr. King was, and being a searcher into the mystery of the hereafter." Philip commented regarding Fraser's exposé, "During his life, we had several discussions on the fascinating subject, and it came to me as a surprise when, after his death, it was 'revealed' in a magazine article that he had been a practising spiritualist. I thought everybody knew about it."³⁵⁷

Reginald Hardy, author of the 1949 biography *Mackenzie King of Canada*, cited one of the Prime Minister's employees who knew, in his Southam News article about Philip's 1954 CBC radio broadcast: "'He believed in spiritualism deeply,' my friend Bob Lay, King's chauffeur for many years, told me today."³⁵⁸ In 1960, Desmond Stone identified three further members of the Prime Minister's personal staff who were intimately familiar with his contacts with the spirit world. "One was Edouard Handy, King's loyal French-Canadian secretary. The second was Miss Lou Zavitske, confidential secretary, who kept his accounts and knew of the payments to mediums. 'But I never asked any questions,' she declares. 'It was none of my business what Mr. King did. He had one room we were forbidden to enter, and I never did. We called it the Dark Room, and that's just what it was.'" A memo from Edouard Handy, "Mr. King wishes to have the letters filed in the 'private boxes' in the dark room – most recent on top," indicates, however, that some of his secretaries did have access.

---

355 Diary, July 26, 1946. Fraser, 8.

356 Diary, June 30, 1932.

357 Percy J. Philip, original typescript "My Conversation with Mackenzie King" in executors' files, p. 3.

358 Reginald Hardy, "Was Percy 'Pulling A Leg' or Was He Deadly Serious? Percy: 'No Comment,'" *Ottawa Citizen*, September 28, 1954. King had hired Lay as his chauffeur in November 1931.

Desmond Stone named a third member of King's staff who was familiar with the windowless "Dark Room" on the third floor of Laurier House where King kept his diaries, his psychic records, the "cupboard containing my books on psychic phenomena," and where he conducted séances. Opening "the cupboard which has the psychic material," King recorded on another occasion, "involved taking a key out of the little cabinet in which I have my sacred books, grandfather's & others." Fred McGregor, his private secretary from 1909 to 1925, transcribed his handwritten diaries from 1893 to 1935 for the executors and King's biographers. Stone wrote that McGregor, now also an executor himself, "states without reservation that spiritualism played 'a much larger part in Mr. King's life than even most people today realize.'"[359] In 1919, McGregor gave to King, as a Christmas present, J. Francis Grierson's *Abraham Lincoln, The Practical Mystic*. In January 1925, he assisted the Prime Minister with preparing his Speech from the Throne while he was visiting Atlantic City. King had been so impressed by a reading by the Indian phrenologist and palmist astrologer Professor Douglas Goray that he returned with his secretary and "McGregor had his hand read along much the same lines as mine of yesterday."[360]

King's staff catered to his interest in Spiritualism until his death. In 1948, the *Halifax Herald* published "Shakespeare Contacted Through Spirit World, Drama Critic Claims." The article reported that the London drama critic Percy Allen contacted William Shakespeare, the Earl of Oxford, and Sir Francis Bacon via Hester Dowden to inquire about the authorship of Shakespeare's plays. Shakespeare admitted that the Earl of Oxford was his collaborator. "We two are Shakespeare and I have born the burden of two men's work too long. I am glad to draw the curtain aside and show you the real playwright and poet combined." One of King's secretaries annotated the press clipping "The P.M. to see" – which King did – and marked "file re Psychical Research."[361]

Mackenzie King acknowledged the assistance and loyalty of his staffers to whom he confided his spiritualist beliefs in his last will and testament. He bequeathed $10,000 each [$128,000 in 2023 dollars]

---

359   Diary, November 16, 1935, and December 22, 1935. Stone, 64.
360   Diary, December 25, 1919, and January 27 and 28, 1925.
361   "Shakespeare Contacted Through Spirit World, Drama Critic Claims," *Halifax Herald*, January 5, 1948. The article refers to Percy Allen's study *Talks with Elizabethans Revealing the Mystery of "William Shakespeare,"* published by Rider.

to McGregor and Handy, $3,000 to Lucy Zavitske to whom he also dictated his diary, and $1,500 to his chauffeur Robert Lay. The Prime Minister further recorded in 1929 that he dictated correspondence with Rachel Bleaney, the Kingston fortune-teller, to Howard Measures, another of his private secretaries in the 1920s. "I spoke with him concerning spiritual phenomena, the interpretation of dreams etc., pointing out that I felt there was little significance to be attached to what related to material things e.g. riches, marriage etc. etc. but that purely spiritual phenomena, qualities of heart & mind, purpose of life etc. might be revealed & furthered by communion with those who have gone before."[362]

And in 1931 he had a talk with Norman McLeod Rogers, his private secretary from 1927 to 1929, who then joined the faculty of Queen's University. "He was telling me of Mrs. Bleaney's reading of his hand. She had told his past remarkably well, had also told of his wife's father's death and of the present illness of his wife's mother, naming the trouble. She prophesied long life & a future for him in politics. Would have other offers than Queen's – some had already come." The following year he informed Rogers of his séances with the Detroit medium Etta Wriedt and "what the summer had meant in belief ... the existence of those who have passed beyond the veil – in etheric bodies & their power to help us, their upward progression." He concluded, "I am being guided – and that the best is yet to be."

In 1933, he "talked with Rogers of Glen Hamilton's experiments," the Winnipeg psychic researcher who had shown him the multiple cameras with which he captured photographs of ectoplasm (the spiritual substance out of which materializations are produced), and other psychic materializations. Two years later, he spoke in Parliament with MP Arthur Cardin, whom he would appoint his Minister of Public Works after the 1935 election, "of the death of his father. I spoke of his father's continued existence etc." He discussed psychic phenomena with Canon Bertal Heeney in 1936. (When the Canon, accompanied by his son Arnold Heeney – whom King would appoint his Principal Secretary in 1938 – first visited him at Kingsmere in 1933, he wrote in his diary that the visit and "the faith they shewed in me as a man was a messenger from God, to give me strength in the hour of greatest need.")[363]

---

362 Diary, January 15, 1929.

363 Diary, March 29, 1931, September 19 and 21, 1932, September 23, 1933, May

As he swept the 1935 election, "one of the earliest returns that came in & which rejoyced me beyond all else was that Rogers had won Kingston & that they were carrying [him] around the city on their shoulders." On his birthday in December 1936, the Prime Minister had another pleasant talk before the open fire in the Laurier House Library with Rogers, then Minister of Labour (1935-1939) and future Minister of National Defence (1939-1940), when – contrary to Mrs. Bleaney's prediction – he died in an air crash. King wrote that the two close colleagues had "a short talk of man's nature and of the doctrine of predestination rightly interpreted which Rogers, like myself, has much in his mind." The doctor of the ailing painter Homer Watson had noted the same year that King had confided to him that "several cabinet ministers were interested in spiritualism, and I said it wouldn't be good to talk of it. He said, 'No, it wouldn't be good for the party.'"

After the internment of Rogers' ashes in the soldiers' plot at Beechwood Cemetery, the PM met with his three brothers and "told them of the talks I had with Mrs. Wriedt, which Norman had been present at, and how impressed we had been by them." Referring to his earlier sittings with Rachel Bleaney, "I then told them the little happening at Kingston, and the flag incident of years ago. Indeed, as I talked in the room with them, it seemed to me I was getting unmistakable evidence of the fulfilment of the plan of his life by these beginnings and ends and close associations." Rogers' brother Arthur reported that King also "motioned towards a picture of his late mother on the wall in the Prime Minister's Office and announced that he had spoken to her and she had said she would be looking after Norman McLeod Rogers in the next world."

During the Dominion-Provincial Conference in 1946, there was intense conflict within King's Cabinet about making tax concessions to the provinces. King recorded in his diary, "It is interesting too that at this time when I have been contending with my own colleagues, to take a different line in the Dominion-Provincial Conference, that the line I have been trying to have them take is the one that Rogers stood out for very strongly; had he been spared, there are many things that would not have happened in this war or arising out of it which are more or less indefensible. I have not the least doubt he is in this way letting his presence and influence be made known to

---

23, 1935, July 12, 1936, and July 9, 1933.

me." And in 1947, King wrote Mrs. Rogers about "the truly amazing experience I had in London, when, through a medium, Norman asked me to let you know that he was well and happy and was constantly at the side of the boys and yourself. He referred to some particular incident which he said would assure you that it was he who was speaking."[364]

In November 1941, the Prime Minister discussed his psychic research and speaking with the departed in séances with mediums and over the "little table" with another member of his Cabinet, Ernest Lapointe, the Minister of Justice, who was in hospital dying of heart failure. "That I had made records of the talks I had had with them, and that there was no mistaking their identity or their continued existence. That I was as sure as could be that whichever of us went first, that we would keep in touch with each other. He said: I believe that." When Angus Macdonald, his Minister of National Defence for Naval Services, informed him two years later that his nephew Dr. William Lyon Mackenzie King, one of the twin sons of his brother Max, had perished in the sinking of the destroyer *Ste. Croix*, he immediately reiterated, "I felt sure Lyon's life and influence would continue to be felt in this world; that I believed strongly in survival of human personality." He confided the same thought to the grief-stricken Eleanor Roosevelt at the burial of the American President at Hyde Park two years later. "There is no such things as separation. Life goes on. He will be nearer than ever at your side."[365]

In regard to other members of King's Cabinet, Paul Roazen reported the anecdote that at one meeting "a Minister once rapped against the table with his foot 'unconsciously,' and King stopped the proceedings to find out what was going on." During the height of the Cabinet crisis over conscription in 1944 – when King finally reluctantly agreed to bring in conscription despite overwhelming opposition from Quebec – the Prime Minister showed Louis St. Laurent a letter from Odette Lapointe, the daughter of his late Quebec lieutenant, expressing her and her father's support for King. St. Laurent, who succeeded Lapointe

---

364 Diary, October 14, 1935, and December 17, 1936. Noonan, 218. Diary, June 13, 1940, pp. 5-6, and May 6, 1946. "Rogers, King and the World Beyond," *Kingston Whig-Standard Companion*, June 10, 2000, 3. King to Mrs. Norman Rogers, July 23, 1947.

365 Diary, November 19 and 20, 1941, September 27, 1943, and April 15, 1945.

as the MP for Québec East and as Justice Minister, "was deeply moved by reading it. He turned to me and said, I think you may feel this is a message direct from Beyond. Of course, I agree entirely with him, but I think it was a great relief to his heart to think that Lapointe, whom he succeeded, would be realizing completely the situation in which we are and understanding it."[366]

Already in October 1932, Mackenzie King had informed his ailing friend Senator Andrew Haydon, the former Liberal Party campaign treasurer censured by the Senate for his role in the Beauharnois bribery scandal, of his experiences with the direct-voice medium Etta Wriedt in Detroit. Visiting the dying Haydon again two weeks later, he informed Joan Patteson that he "would probably have a talk with him before long, if Mrs. Wriedt is spared." After serving as one of the pall bearers at Haydon's funeral the following month and "communing with Haydon aloud," King "felt as it were someone pressing my right shoulder. I said yes, Andrew, I know it is you; continue to press & I could feel the pressure as of a bag of air – a spiritual body, against my shoulder ... it was Haydon & mother bringing comfort and assurance to my heart & evidence of his survival."[367]

Twelve years later King felt less restraint avowing his spiritual beliefs to his political cohorts in a more public setting. After returning to Ottawa from the Meeting of Commonwealth Prime Ministers and addressing the two houses of Parliament in London, he revealed to the Liberal Party caucus on May 25, 1944, "I believed in the survival of the human personality. I felt that my parents, to whom so largely I owed whatever of good there was in me, were sharing with me the rejoicing and the home-coming." He drew the inference that "there was an eternal justice which helped to work out things in the long run, one generation reaped what another sowed, etc....the tributes paid were so from the heart, and my own feelings so intense that I more or less made a confession of my inner convictions and belief to a degree I have never done in public before." He was also open about his spiritualist beliefs while speaking for an hour at the banquet in Ottawa celebrating his 25th anniversary as Leader of the Liberal Party on August 7 the same year. "In speaking, I debated

---

366 Roazen, 144. Diary, December 1, 1944, p. 4.

367 Diary, October 4 and 19, 1932, and November 12, 1932. Neatby, *William Lyon Mackenzie King: The Lonely Heights*, 384.

a little as to how far I should go in revealing my inner beliefs and outlook on life but concluded that I owed this to the Party and did not hesitate to express quite publicly my firm belief in the survival of human personality and to make at the close a reference to the influence of childhood and home, what I owe to my parents and also to my grandfather and others."[368]

During World War II, King shared reading his tea leaves with John Nicol, his personal valet since becoming leader of the Liberal Party in 1919, and his butler MacLeod (King never gives his first name), who joined his staff on July 1, 1931. On the day of the federal election in March 1940, Nicol drew his attention to the tea leaves in the Prime Minister's cup, saying they looked like a March hare. King thought the leaves looked "like one of the sphynx [sic] on my table upstairs. Do you notice the figure standing at the top of it? A man with a plume floating over his head, the feathers of which rise above the rim of the cup. It was clearly a symbol of triumph and victory. Nicol remarked on how distinct the figures were. They were so realy [sic] that the movement of the cup through the air made the little leaf which looked like a plume wave in the air."

In January 1941, the Prime Minister felt compelled to look at the tea leaves in his cup at lunch and saw a camel "as clearly drawn as it would be possible to have it," with a figure on the camel that again looked like one of the winged sphinxes on his library table. "Without expressing any word, I showed the cup to MacLeod and asked him what he saw. He at once said: a camel and a man on wings on his back. He said it looked like something of victory." When the Prime Minister turned on the radio that evening, the first words he heard were that the Free French Camel Corps operating from Chad had begun an offensive against the Italians in southwest Libya.

> The significance of this to me is that it evidences that some mind has been seeking to communicate with me in advance, thereby giving an assurance of the presence of others who are with me helping and guiding. In other words, a testimony of the existence of the spiritual world as I believe it to be. At any rate, it all seems so directly sent that I could not but experience the comfort which it brought. Had this been the first time anything

---

368 Pickersgill and Forster. *The Mackenzie King Record. Volume 2, 1944-1945*, 13, 46.

of the kind had occurred, it might be different. Time and again, I have seen the fore-telling of an event in this way. One of the many agencies of communication. Coming at this moment was undoubtedly meant as a support to my faith on which everything else rests.[369]

In addition to members of his staff, Mackenzie King also openly spoke about Spiritualism and psychic phenomena with close friends, members of his family, government officials, VIPs, ordinary Canadians, and Canadian and non-Canadian artists. He was not an isolated religious eccentric but held occult beliefs that were much more widely held than is realized today. Four months after he became Leader of the Liberal Party on August 7, 1919, Lady Evelyn, Duchess of Devonshire, wife of the eleventh Governor General of Canada, the Duke of Devonshire, informed him that "some time ago" she and her daughter "were amusing themselves with a 'weegee' [Ouija] board, she called it." "Someone asked who is to be the next premier & the reply to use the Duchess' own words, 'the thing rammed out Mackenzie King.' She laughed quite heartily about it, said it must have been in some one's mind." The cultured art critic and future chairman of the Canadian Radio Broadcasting Commission, Hector Charlesworth, would similarly assert in his 1925 *Candid Chronicles*, "I believe in a certain nebulous form of telepathy, unconscious thought transference, which may some day be put in harness as radio has put sound waves in harness."[370]

Some of King's encounters provided warnings about the dangers of Spiritualism and spiritualists. In his first month as Prime Minister in 1922, the railroad magnate Sir Donald Mann asked for a letter of introduction to the Russian government. "He spoke of spiritualism, said he had had talks with Laurier, who had spoken of me … came in to pay respects & to speak of Russia; it was starving people; the spirit had told him to come & plead for. Laurier had said we were all one big family etc." Mann reappeared in the PM's office in 1925 and "said he had been talking with Sir Wilfrid who gave him a message for me, to go to country last week in October, not later, that I would carry the country, including provinces of Ontario & Quebec, would lose in Maritime provinces … would have a good following in West & majority of about 20." Mann asked King if he wished to ask Sir Wilfrid

---

369 Diary, March 26, 1940, and January 28, 1941.
370 Diary, December 2, 1919. Charlesworth, 91.

any questions and foresaw that he would be married shortly after the general election. The PM found his predictions "quite extraordinary" but recorded the following week that he "talked next with Sir Donald Mann who is using his spiritualism for graft purposes – if he is not wholly insane."[371]

When he showed Laurier House to Governor General Lord Julian Byng and Lady Evelyn Byng in 1923, "We talked of phrenology which Lord Byng has specially studied." Regarding his question about the methods of receiving spirit communications, Lady Byng wrote the Prime Minister on Government House stationary marked "<u>Private</u>", citing a spiritualist tract, "It is difficult to say exactly where the messages come from and how they are sent. There are so many different kinds of ways."

> The automatic writing that contains only guidance and teachings is transmitted through the head of the medium, in some cases through the brain, in others automatic. This is sent by so-called 'Guides,' Teachers, and Helpers, on our side. The personal messages come generally in another way: they are given to a guide, or Teacher, as you would give a telegram to be sent in some cases, but in a few they take on the material condition and are able to impress, or influence you themselves. Inspiration and whispers from the Beyond are much more frequent than many think: it is a kind of wireless that you are beginning to be much more able to understand now through your material scientific learning. But never forget that the spiritual part of those who are still on earth can rise and meet the spirit of those who have gone over without any intervention of writing or speech. It is a knowledge that is born in all, but very seldom understood and realized.

The following year, he discussed horoscopes with Lady Byng at a luncheon at Government House (now known as Rideau Hall) and learned that "the writer of her horoscope has said to 'beware of prestige.'" The Prime Minister had informed her that he had so often 'felt' his mother and brother since they "passed over." Lady Byng assured him, "if you can attune yourself to their key they can undoubtedly help in many ways." But she had also written King a warning that would ultimately prove prophetic. "I always feel after many years of

---

371 Diary, January 13, 1922, and May 9 and 14, 1925.

this particular sort of experience that one has to go VERY carefully, and not let oneself fall too much into the habit of trying to keep in touch. Unless all the psychic side of life – because after all it IS life, far more fully than we are apt to realise – is handled with great care it degenerates into a sort of mental dram-drinking. That is why I, personally, always walk very cautiously regarding who I talk to about it lest, in ones desire to help and encourage the honest study and understanding of these things, one should encourage the unbalanced to tamper foolishly with matter that can easily become their master – and a hard one too as I have known it in one or two cases." King did not seem to realize that Lady Byng's warning might apply to him.[372]

When he visited his life-long English friend and benefactor, the Liberal social reformer and writer Violet Markham in 1934, he "told her of some of my psychic experiences, at which she was profoundly amazed." Like Lady Byng, Markham "seemed to feel that the danger lay in 'the easy way' of having one's beliefs confirmed and in what might result through 'absence of discipline.' In this I think she is right. I explained it was but 'the fringe' – also she spoke of the dangers that had been apparent to many of the effect on one's mind & health. I told her I thought these were very real & that we had to be most careful."

Despite Markham's scepticism about the occult, King proceeded to consult a "little table." "There was a little table near, like the one at home & we tried to see what results we might get." King's mother, father, brother Max, and Markham's mother and father, communicated from the Beyond. The next day, King and Markham had another "long talk & conversation at the little table" in which the late Lord Christopher Thomson came and spoke. Thomson had been the British Air Minister responsible for the development of the hydrogen-filled R101 air dirigible built to connect Britain with India, Australia and Canada. King had seen a competing model, the privately designed R100, fly over Ottawa on August 10, 1930. Compelled by its success to show the viability of the government's still flawed R101 dirigible, Lord Thomson and his designers perished on its maiden flight to India on October 5, 1930. In their séance, Thomson "said he was very much alive & interested in long distance flying etc. He told of the destruction of the R101, of being on the bridge when it burst into flames. He woke he said in his mother's arms. Violet also

---

372 Diary, March 11, 1923, and December 23, 1924. Lady Byng to King, May 31, 1923. King to Lady Byng, June 12, 1923.

spoke with another explorer, mountain climber, about an accident of which he too gave an account. She was, I think, really impressed by these conversations and I could see did not wish to destroy the record of them."[373]

These are just a few of the numerous references to the circles of spiritualists King recorded in his diaries, correspondence, and notes on his psychic research that his executors sought to keep hidden. As he recorded in his diary after reading Wilson Harris' biography of the prominent journalist and author John Alfred Spender (*J.A. Spender*, a gift from Alice and Vincent Massey), "Eventually we all go to our own place. I have noticed this latter aspect of discovering kindred interests particularly in relation to those who are interested in psychical phenomena."

In contrast to the King executors, Reginald Hardy, in his 1949 biography *Mackenzie King of Canada*, openly discussed the Prime Minister's strong spiritual beliefs and interest in psychic research. "'I believe,' he said, on one occasion, recently, 'in the reality of a spiritual world, that this life is merely an antechamber to eternity.'" King "feels that a number of universities are now moving in the right direction in respect to psychical research," Hardy reported, "and that the day may come when man will find himself faced with incontrovertible evidence of the existence of a spiritual world, evidence so strong and irrefutable that it will provide a new and compelling sanction governing the conduct of mankind."[374]

---

373 Diary, October 6 and 7, 1934.
374 Diary, March 31, 1946. Hardy, 159, 159-160.

CHAPTER 11

King's Magical Thinking and the Canadian Origins of His Spiritualism

Blair Fraser and several of the British and Canadian newspaper accounts from the early 1950s reported that it was Lady Aberdeen who introduced the Canadian Prime Minister to the occult and to the American medium Etta Wriedt. According to the *Montreal Gazette*, he became interested in Spiritualism following the death of his mother in 1917. "The late Marchioness of Aberdeen is said to have been the first to suggest to him that he try spiritualism. He did and found it 'a great blessing.' When he was selected as Liberal Party leader at the August 1919 convention, few, if any of his supporters were aware that he was a confirmed spiritualist convinced, in his own mind, that he'd already established contact with the spirits of both of his parents."[375]

King had first met the Governor General Lord Aberdeen and Lady Aberdeen when they addressed the students at the University of Toronto in 1894 and received the couple at Laurier House when he was Prime Minister in 1925. The Aberdeens became involved in Spiritualism after the death of their son Archie in a car accident in 1909. But King did not discuss Spiritualism with the seventy-seven-year-old Lady Aberdeen until after she cabled him about the death of the former Governor General in 1934 and told him about messages received from her late husband via the automatic writing medium Hester Dowden. King in turn informed her of his "conversations"

---

375 Fraser, 9. John Prebble, "Duchess Declared He Was 'Guided' on World Affairs," *Sunday Dispatch*, June 14, 1953, 5. "Medium," *Montreal Gazette*, October 1, 1954. Fodor, 4. Ebon, 190.

with Lord Aberdeen over the "little table." "It was indeed wonderful to be able to have that talk with you last night & for you to be able to tell me about that direct message you have from Lord Aberdeen, with that extraordinary proof of identity," she wrote King in October. "It does make a wonderful difference to be able to communicate like this & I hope to be able to do it myself, without any medium later on, but I am advised it is better not to try too soon."

King recorded in his diary on October 15 that his communication with Lady Aberdeen "seemed to me to suggest that this week I might get in touch with spiritual forces, which were even now rejoicing that some evidence of their presence was here." The Marchioness then introduced King to Hester Dowden, the daughter of the late Professor Edward Dowden of Trinity College, Dublin, and other mediums in London. As C.P. Stacey commented on Blair Fraser's *Maclean's* exposé about the Prime Minister consulting with British mediums, "it is almost entirely based on interviews with King's spiritualist friends in London. Of King's do-it-yourself spiritualism with the little table Fraser knew nothing."[376]

Fraser also did not know that Mackenzie King began deliberating about the conflict between predestination and free will as early as his twenty-fifth birthday in 1899 while in London on his Harvard travelling scholarship. After reading Maurice Maeterlinck's mystical essays "On Women" and "The Tragical in Daily Life" in his *The Treasure of the Humble*, he noted in his diary, "I agree in the main with what he says in both. He lays greater stress on destiny than I think ought to be laid. We must put more on will & less on destiny." Paraphrasing *Hamlet* he added, "I believe in a Divinity that shapes our ends but I certainly believe that we rough hew them." Yet after attending a lecture the same day at Trinity College, Cambridge, on John Wesley, the founder of the Methodist Church who preached against predestination, he recorded, "I cannot but believe that He has chosen me to be

---

376 Diary, February 16, 1894, April 27, 1925, March 8, 1934, and October 12, 15, 23 and 24, 1934. Reynolds, 100. Strong-Boag, 205. Lady Aberdeen to King, October 13, 1934. Stacey, *A Very Double Life*, 188. King made time to meet with Lady Aberdeen when he arrived in Geneva for meetings of the League of Nations in September 1936. She thanked him after their nearly three-hour-long meeting, "I cannot express in words what this afternoon's talk has meant to me. I am sure that when I get to the other side & have joined your body guard there, that I shall remind you of it in the light of further knowledge." Lady Aberdeen to King, September 20, 1936.

Figure 31: Lady Ishbel Aberdeen, 1899.

one called from among men to reveal His love to men, to point them nearer to the Truth and to help this world a little to better things. Yet so unworthy do I feel, so conscious of my wasted time & careless neglect, that I hesitate on the threshold of accepting the belief...what God's plans are will become clear in time, if He has chosen me, if there is work to do, this alone is the true way of preparing myself to do it."[377]

A year later, King joined Wilfrid Laurier's Government as Deputy Minister of Labour and in 1906 strongly pressed Laurier to let him run for Parliament so that he could become the actual Minister of Labour. After meeting with Laurier, he recorded in his diary, "My feelings as a result of this interview are that I must watch matters, deliberately get to work to secure this end by legitimate means, not trust to Destiny though it may be on my side...I believe public life is to be my lot. I believe that God's purpose in my life is to help to work out His Will in the world in this way. I must seek to realize the greatness of the task, the service to be rendered such a master." F.A. McGregor, in *The Fall & Rise of Mackenzie King: 1911-1919*, emphasized the importance of his religious belief when he ran for the Leadership of the Liberal Party after Laurier's death in 1919. His private secretary from 1914 to 1925, McGregor wrote, "Mackenzie King's apparent lack of concern about the leadership...lay in his belief that the whole course of his life was, in a very special way, determined by invisible forces beyond his control or any human control. He was Calvinist enough to believe in predestination; he was realist enough to apply the doctrine to the circumstances of his own life."[378]

After taking the oath of office as Prime Minister at the end of December 1921, King struggled to consolidate his position as Leader of the Liberal Party in the face of powerful protectionist members of his cabinet who opposed his proposals to lower tariffs on imported goods to win back the hundreds of thousands of voters who had supported the Progressive Party. He was also soon worn down by intractable problems such as the transfer of natural resources to Alberta, Manitoba and Saskatchewan, the reduction of freight rates for farmers bringing their crops to markets, creating a stable government-owned transcontinental rail system, and winning greater autonomy from Great Britain in international affairs before and after the 1923 Imperial Conference in London.

In March 1924, he felt himself "completely tired out" and travelled to Atlantic City for a holiday with Andrew Haydon, the national

---

377 Diary, December 17, 1899.
378 Diary, January 2, 1906. McGregor, 330-331.

Liberal Party organizer. "I have no energy, little or no will power, can take interest in nothing and feel irritable and short-tempered...I dislike leaving parliament at the beginning in this way; on the other hand there is little use staying feeling as I do. If I do not get a rest this time, Heaven alone knows when I will."[379]

King's spiritualist belief that he was being watched and aided by his loved ones in the Beyond was a great comfort and assurance to him. The day before he was sworn in as Prime Minister in 1921, he was "sure dear Father & Mother & Bell's spiritual power & influence is a guide to me at this time. I am sure it is part of God's plan and purpose that I should be chosen for this work, though I confess I do not like the thought of a 'special providence' or predestination in any form. Yet in another sense all things are of God & all things work together for good." During the swearing-in ceremony the next day in the office of the Governor General, Lord Byng, he wrote "a little note" to his dear dead brother Max "that he might know he was in my thoughts very much at that most sacred & impressive & solemn hour."[380]

In the mid-1920s, King came to believe that astrology and its horoscopes could reveal to him what his destiny as determined by God would be. The Prime Minister departed on a five-week speaking tour of the prairie provinces and British Columbia at the beginning of October 1924. After describing his activities in Winnipeg on October 4, he recorded concluding the day by reading "a most interesting 'horoscope'" from England. He elaborated the next day that he had received his "astrological map" from M.E. Young who had contacted him after reading Macdougall King's *Nerves and Personal Power: Some Principles of Psychology as Applied to Conduct and Health*, for which King had written the introduction. The PM recalled having telephoned his brother from Winnipeg on a previous visit and travelling to Denver in January 1922 near the end of Max's long terminal illness. He remembered his conversation with his brother two months before his death from muscular atrophy, at the age of forty-three: "my conversation with him to let me know of his existence beyond the grave, to communicate with me if possible."

King perceived receiving Young's horoscope, which "impressed me very much," as a message from Max. "The amazing revelation of

---

379   Diary, March 7, 1924.
380   Diary, December 28 and 29, 1921.

my own character & possibilities in certain respects which this Astral map discloses, associated as it is with his own life & writings and the circumstances of my communication with him through space from Winnipeg, makes it all appear like a great revelation of his coming into touch and contact with me. I felt this very strongly."[381]

The PM arrived in Lethbridge and made what he felt was one of his best speeches at a crowded theatre on October 29. The following day he sent a telegram to the town mayor, W.D.L. Hardie, from Calgary. "I was born Berlin, Ontario, December seventeenth, 1874, between 9 and ten p.m. local time. Believe it to have been somewhere between nine and half past. Enjoyed seeing you again. Will be glad to have horoscope addressed Laurier House, Ottawa." Before going to sleep in Weyburn, Saskatchewan, on November 1, King read over his "horoscope as interpreted by Mr. Young in England. It is so true of what I know of myself that it is impossible not to believe in astrology as a science. My talks with Mayor Hardie of Lethbridge has awakened interest anew. It is a truly remarkable revelation & a letter from Young speaking of the last 3 years & this month is greatly remarkable."

Young's reassuring horoscope contributed to the PM feeling "a great 'Liberation' in my work. I feel I have won my place in the government of the country and that from now on further real progress will be made. I believe the Liberal Party will carry the country at the next elections. That would be the greatest victory & comfort of all. At all events I shall seek to do my utmost along right lines." Upon his return to Ottawa on November 8, King and Joan Patteson "read over my 'horoscope' by Mayor Hardie of Lethbridge, a truly remarkable document, so true in every line that one cannot but believe in a science of astrology & the influence of the stars." The next day, he and Joan and Godfroy Patteson looked at King's "Horoscope from England." A few days before his fiftieth birthday in December, the PM and his friend Peter Sims "talked in the library till lunch time, going over my 'horoscope' and talking over many matters of mutual interest and the old days."[382]

W.D.L. Hardie was unusually reputable for an astrologer. He was born in Bathgate, Scotland, in 1863, graduated from Glasgow

---

381 Diary, October 4 and 5, 1924.

382 King to Hardie, October 30, 1924. Diary, November 2, 8 and 9, 1924, and December 14, 1924.

Figure 32: William Duncan Livingstone Hardie, Mayor of Lethbridge, Alberta, 1913-1928.

University in 1883 where he studied civil and mining engineering, and worked in the United States before being hired by the Alberta Railway & Coal Company in 1889. In 1891, he became mining advisor to the Republic of Mexico and returned to Lethbridge in 1894 as superintendent of the Galt Mines where over sixteen years he became one of the pioneers of the Lethbridge coalfield. He was elected Mayor of Lethbridge in November 1912 and held that office from 1913 to 1928. His reforms included changing from the aldermanic to a commission form of local government, with Hardie serving as commissioner of finance as well, and extending municipal suffrage to women. He also served as chairman of the Hospital Board and as a member of the Public School Board.

Hardie had published a highly favourable "Character Sketch of The Hon. W.L. Mackenzie King," based on his horoscope, in the *Lethbridge*

Herald on December 22, 1921, a week before King was sworn in as Prime Minister and Secretary of State for External Affairs. He probably did not see this character sketch because he does not mention Hardie or his horoscope in his diary just before assuming the office of Prime Minister. He would have liked the Mayor's astrological reading that King "was marked at birth for positions in state or church" and that "He is possessed of a prophetic intuition and has a natural inclination to the higher aims which should rouse him to greater efforts to shake off any encumbering bad habits he may possess – he has some." The PM would have objected to his reading that King "is not a progressive, for he values the opinion of his contemporaries very highly and is seldom induced to espouse any progressive ideas which might jeopardize the respect he enjoys."[383]

Hardie looked upon astrology with the eyes of a scientist and a moralist. As he wrote the PM at the end of December 1924, "If astrology were only fully recognized, as it should be, as a science, so that it could be taught in our Colleges, and students have the expert guidance in tuition that other sciences have, it would grow into such importance, that it would in my judgment, transcend all other sciences."

When he sent his horoscope – twenty-seven typed pages in length – to King, Hardie indicated that "No part of my idea of your character has entered into the above delineation in the slightest degree. The delineations are based absolutely on the astronomical calculation which resulted in the Radix and its index." He further informed the Prime Minister that "There are three schools of astrology: (a) the fatalist; (b) the idealist; (c) the casuist. Take which you will, I am a hard shelled Presbyterian – a Calvinistic preordinationist, which must be (a)."[384]

---

383 W.D.L. Hardie, "Character Sketch of The Hon. W.L. Mackenzie King," *Lethbridge Herald*, December 22, 1921, 15. I am grateful to Belinda Crowson and the Lethbridge Historical Society for making the 1921 character sketch available to me. According to Crowson, "Hardie did not shy away from sharing his interest with people. This interest is mentioned a few times in passing in *Herald* articles." Crowson to Anton Wagner, September 6, 2022.

384 Hardie to King, December 30, 1924. W.D.L. Hardie, typed horoscope, "Hon. W.L. Mackenzie King, Laurier House, Ottawa, Canada." Hardie's horoscopes and correspondence with King can be accessed online via the Spiritualism Series of the King Papers, MG26 J9, reel H-3040, vol. 5, file 20, pp. 179-442. http://heritage.canadiana.ca/view/oocihm.lac_reel_h3040/1?r=0&s=1 King's first horoscope (pp. 352-378) was retyped by one of his secretaries when he

The Prime Minister finally found time to thank Hardie for his horoscope on December 15, 1924. "May I say that I have found your delineations amazingly accurate in many particulars and distinctly helpful, and I might add stimulating and inspiring as well... the horoscope you have given me is of quite exceptional interest ... I have become deeply interested in astrology as a science, and am really anxious to learn a little more about it and get what benefit may be possible to derive from its indications and teachings in relation to my own life."[385]

M.E. Young's and Mayor Hardie's horoscopes – with what King perceived to be their so accurate delineations of his character and past and future prospects – confirmed in his mind that astrology was indeed a science. He had hesitated to claim that he had been chosen by divine special providence or predestination to become Prime Minister but greatly welcomed the assurance that he had been predestined for greatness – if not directly by God Himself – then by His stars.

The Prime Minister was so impressed by Hardie's horoscopes that he also asked him – without offering any compensation – to prepare horoscopes for his mother, father, his brother Max and his sisters Bella and Jennie. At the end of December 1924, he was again amazed at Hardie's astrological reading of the closing years of Max's life as he knew them. "I presume that therein lies the great value to individuals of a knowledge of astrology, and the resolution of the apparent conflict between its teaching and the doctrine of free-will." Hardie responded that regarding "Free-will," "In my judgement it is an empty bubble. We will live our lives just as we were created to do without deviating a hair's breadth. This belief accounts for my Calvinistic Presbyterianism."[386]

King discovered that the hour of his birth had been 8 a.m. rather than 9 p.m. and commissioned a revised horoscope from Hardie in 1925. In the October 29 election, the Liberals and the PM and eight members of his Cabinet were defeated by Arthur Meighen's Conservatives but King

---

returned the original to Hardie for revisions. All the other horoscopes are in Hardie's handwriting.

385 King to Hardie, December 15, 1924.

386 King to Hardie, December 31, 1924. Hardie to King, January 9, 1925. King subsequently ascertained that he was born at 8 a.m., not 9 p.m., requiring Hardie and Young to prepare corrected horoscopes. For Hardie's 1925 corrected Mackenzie King horoscope, see https://heritage.canadiana.ca/view/oocihm. lac_reel_h3040/273?r=0&s=1

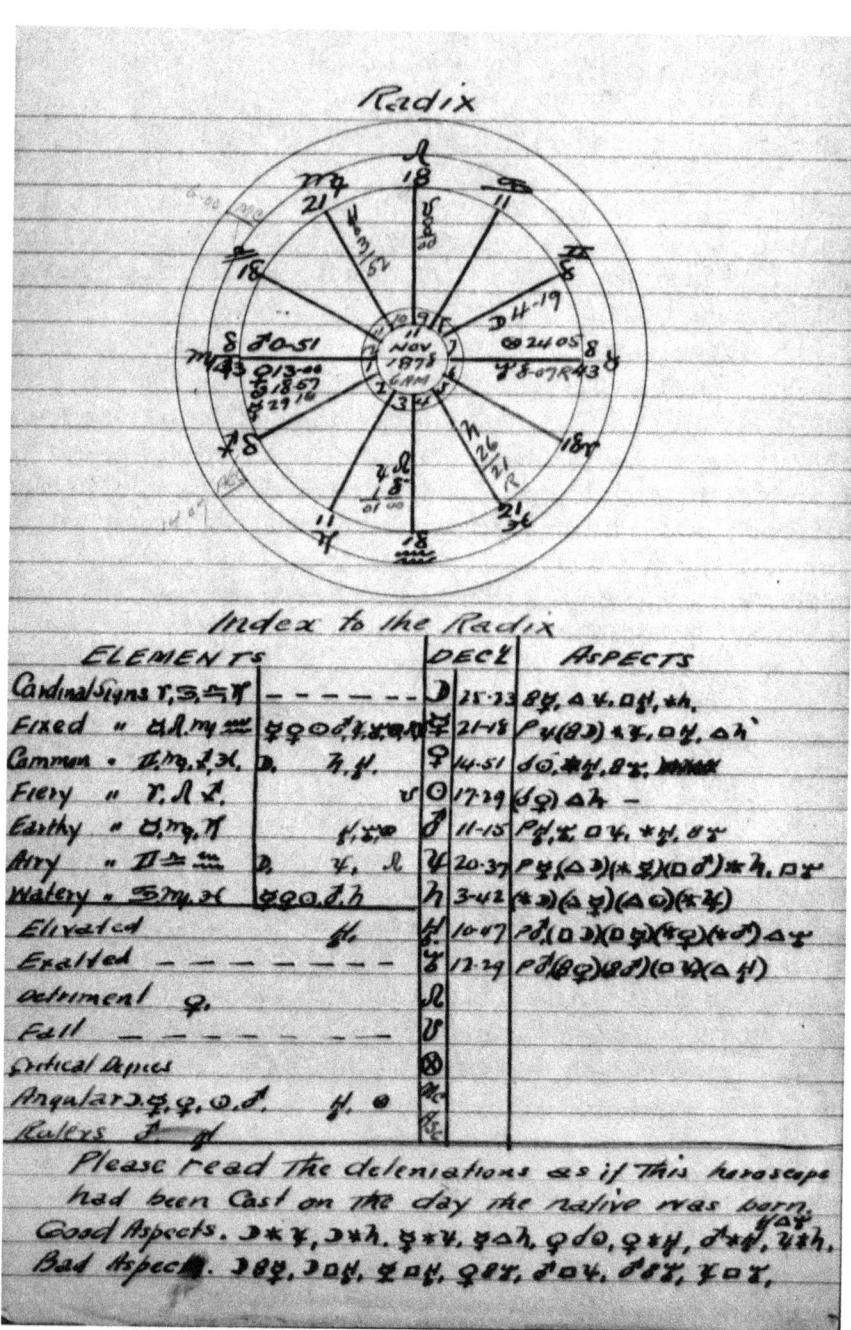

Figure 33: Mayor W.D.L. Hardie's 1924 horoscope of Macdougall King.

remained in office as Prime Minister with the support of the Progressive Party. He thanked Hardie for his horoscope at the end of December and wrote that "The New Year promises to be full of uncertainty so far as my political ventures are concerned." In view of the recent election Hardie responded, "Yes, these times are full of political uncertainty and it was just on that I was anxious to write you about. I, too, have been studying your horoscope and looking over some of the aspects in it of the future. I gave you one, which I was afraid had given you offence, because I heard no more from you. I do not believe that the fulfilment of any aspect is inevitable in all its details, but can be counteracted by proper thinking and actions." He assured King "there is no man in public life that I esteem more highly than yourself, hence my interest" and admitted that as a former railroad engineer and mining superintendent, "I did everything I could to bring about High tariff, because I believe it the only salvation for Canada. I may not be right, but that is my honest belief after many years of study and observation. That is the one thing that makes me a Conservative."

Hardie's strong views on tariffs raises the question whether these influenced his interpretation of the PM's horoscopes. He wrote King, "I am anxious that a young man (politically) like you should not make a serious mistake voluntarily, nor be drawn into one by others. There is a long future before you in the Political Arena and for a while you might accomplish more on the opposition benches than on front ones. There are two extremes in tariff and you might be a saviour by eventually leading Canada in the middle of the road to her lasting benefit." In a politically astute observation Hardie claimed, "I think astrology has pointed out your great possible error – the error of staying in office – without the majority you require for Canada's good. Now Mr. King, please do not think I have anything in my mind but your own political welfare and Canada's good."

The PM responded immediately on January 8, 1926, that Hardie's communication had given him much pleasure. "As I write the House of Commons has commenced its debate as to whether or not the present Administration is to be permitted to continue in Office. I can assure you that so far as I am concerned this question cannot be decided too soon." In his diary he added the same day, "being in office and out of parliament is not a pleasant business."[387]

---

387 King to Hardie, December 31, 1925. Hardie to King, January 8, 1926. Diary, January 8, 1926.

Two weeks after the September 14, 1926, election gave King a strong majority in Parliament, Hardie wrote the PM and informed him that he had cast horoscopes for King and Conservative Leader Arthur Meighen after Parliament was dissolved and that Meighen's showed that he would lose. He enclosed King's thirty-page handwritten horoscope which had sat uncompleted on his desk "for some time" since he had read the PM was travelling to London for the 1926 Imperial Conference in London. King studied his horoscope while crossing the ocean and while returning from England. Back in Ottawa in December, he noted in his diary that he and Joan and Godfroy Patteson spent "a very happy evening, reading over Mayor Hardie's Horoscope which is extraordinarily accurate in its delineation of character & characteristics."[388]

King had also been corresponding with the English astrologer M.E. Young in Bordon, East Hampshire, since the end of 1923 and the PM asked him to prepare his brother's horoscope. Young suggested Max's horoscope "would be the greatest help to many of us, since most truly did he 'follow his star.'" King expressed interest in having his own horoscope prepared. The astrologer observed that whereas Max's "signs were nearly all negative, your own are all positive. So that while he had wholesale patience, endurance and self-control, you have a more active courage (to be up and doing), difficulty in concentration, and considerable impulsiveness and restlessness. For solid work of his, the flashlight of intuition would get things 'out of the blue' so to speak in your own case."

The PM was "much interested in the contrast of the signs...They are quite correct so far as I am in a position to judge." Unlike Mayor Hardie, Young indicated from the outset that he was "only a student of the esoteric, and in no sense of the word a professional" and that there would be costs incurred in having astrological charts and maps made by the Modern Astrology Office, 140 Imperial Buildings, Ludgate Circus, London. It charged three shillings per chart. King forwarded a money order for 12 shillings [approximately $70 Canadian in 2023 dollars] to Young on August 1, 1924.[389] Young sent the Prime

---

388   Hardie to King, October 2, 1926. Diary, December 17, 1926. King to Hardie, December 29, 1926. Following his retirement as assistant superintendent of the Dominion Government Elevator Terminal, Hardie forwarded the PM his final horoscope in December 1936.

389   Young to King, January 13, 1924. King to Young, February 5, 1924. Young

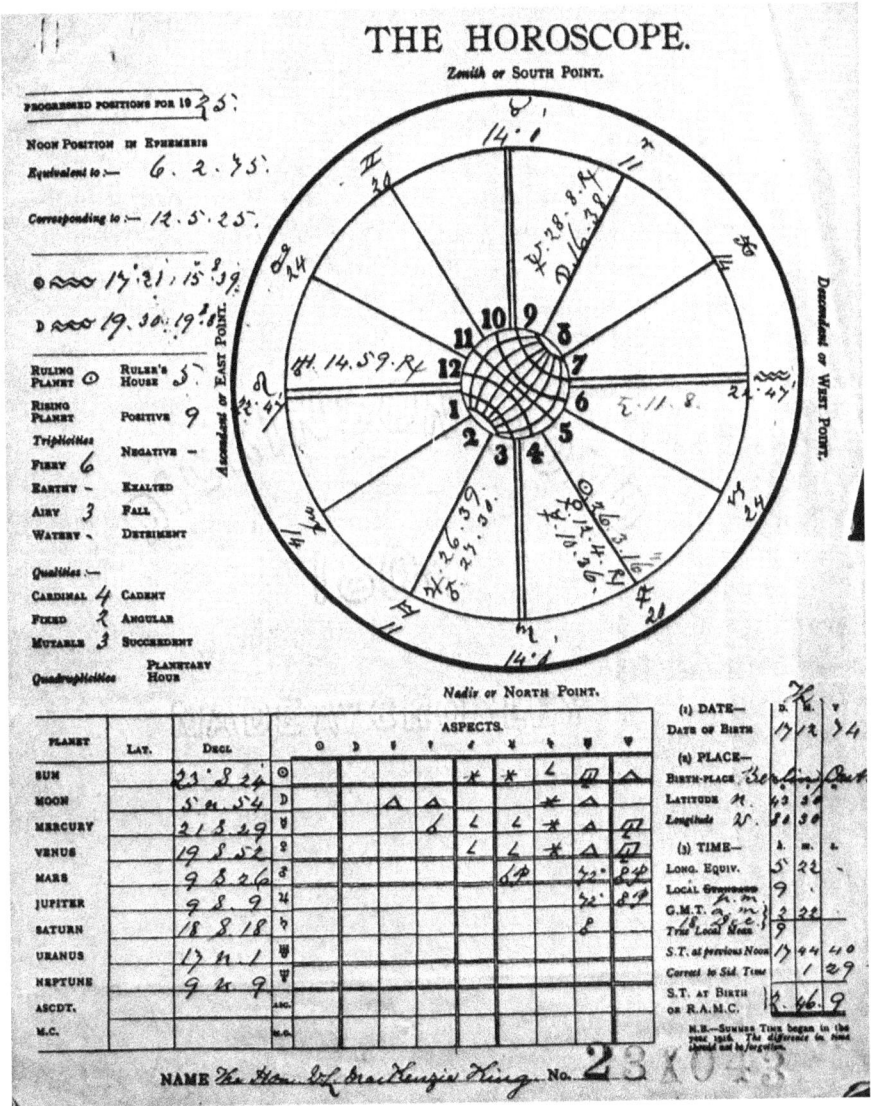

Figure 34: M.E. Young's 1925 corrected Mackenzie King horoscope.

Minister his, Max's and Isabel King's astrological charts prepared by the Modern Astrology Office and his summary of their horoscopes the day after Arthur Meighen's Conservatives defeated the Liberals in the October 29, 1925, election.

---

to King, February 22, 1924. King to Young, August 1, 1924. The monthly *Modern Astrology*, established in 1890 and edited by Alan Leo, published Leo's astrological treatise *The Art of Synthesis* in 1912.

Near the end of their correspondence, Young sent King several old magazines with astrological articles along with "some open papers" regarding the Universal Brotherhood, "the most secret of all secret organizations," so esoteric that "no definite information regarding it can be given to any outsider." He assured the Prime Minister "they are, (in the opinion of a good many) a prelude to the most extraordinary teaching. You may take it from me that there is nothing to fear but very much to gain." The following year, he urged King to submit the arcane membership obligation forms for the Brotherhood while acknowledging that these "are themselves a stumbling block to whom the series of study documents that follow the very tiresome preliminary formalities would prove invaluable. They are simply wonderful and provide a fundamental standard of logic, morals and doctrine by means of which one's own position can be ascertained & balanced." He offered to send samples of these study documents, "especially those showing the seven orders – from the cryptic to the supernatural working within the universal order. They thrill me every time I have read them. I so hope you will go on...You shall have the next papers on receipt of the obligation form."

His last letter to King in November 1926 concluded, "With regard to the open papers, I should like to say that they are a very poor and rather misleading introduction to the very real and valuable teaching that lies behind them. I hope you will be interested." The PM initially thanked Young for the magazines and "open papers which accompanied your letter. I have been particularly interested in the latter and may take the occasion to pursue the opportunity which it appears to present."[390]

Mayor Hardie and M.E. Young were genuine astrologers who viewed their calling as science, did not charge fees for their services, and had a spiritual/religious orientation which could make King believe that astrology was indeed "the voice of God speaking to the Soul." Yet horoscopes were so difficult and time consuming to cast that Young was unable to locate another knowledgeable astrologer in England who charged moderate fees. The next astrologer who offered her services to the Prime Minister, Cecilia Ruth Stevenson, born in

---

390 Young to King, October 30, 1925, July 23, 1926, and November 2, 1926. King to Young, December 31, 1925. "Instruction on the Universal Brotherhood." The "Nonobligate Obligational" open papers application form references a Guru "to whose charge I am either directly or indirectly assigned."

England in 1890 and residing at 390 Lisgar Road, Rockcliffe, Ottawa, was exactly the kind of popular psychic Young also encountered who blended horoscopes with psychology and fortune-telling in order to have a greater appeal to her clients.

Her husband, the prominent journalist John A. Stevenson, came to Canada from Scotland before World War I and settled in Winnipeg to practice law. He began his thirty-year career as a journalist with the progressive *Country Guide* and also contributed to the *Winnipeg Free Press* under the editorship of John W. Dafoe. After Mackenzie King became Leader of the Liberal Party in 1919, Stevenson wrote Dafoe in January 1920 that King was "as full of noble sentiments as a new calved cow is full of milk, but he is short on concrete plans for our regeneration." Allan Levine, in *Scrum Wars: The Prime Minister and the Media*, characterized Stevenson as "one journalist who particularly got under his skin." After King became Prime Minister, he asked Joe Atkinson, the publisher of the Liberal *Toronto Star*, to fire Stevenson from his paper. "Finally in 1923," Levine reported that after three years, "Stevenson was given notice after he had written anti-King pieces for another publication against Atkinson's direct orders." In his King biography, Levine added that Stevenson's dismissal "only embittered him further. He quickly found other work writing for American and British publications, which permitted him to continue his 'blood feud' with King." Stevenson became "one of his most bitter critics and tormentors."

To the PM's chagrin, Stevenson became the Canadian correspondent for *The Times* of London in 1927 and wrote as well for papers such as the *Manchester Guardian*, *Glasgow Herald*, *The Economist*, *Boston Transcript*, *Baltimore Sun*, *Detroit Free Press*, *New York Times*, *The Scotsman*, and several Australian and South African papers. His increased professional status enabled Stevenson to move his family to a larger home at 390 Lisgar Road in Rockcliffe, an exclusive suburb of Ottawa. The house later became the home of Russia's ambassador to Canada. A member of the Parliamentary Press Gallery, Stevenson also contributed articles to major Canadian publications such as *Maclean's*, *Saturday Night*, and the *Financial Post*. He retired from active newspaper work in December 1945 after five years as an editorial writer for the *Globe and Mail* in Toronto. In his obituary, the *Ottawa Journal* called Stevenson a journalist of the old school who "was full of strong opinions."

King periodically refers negatively to "Stevenson of the Times" in his diaries. But, in his extensive writing for Canadian newspapers, the journalist never divulged King's spiritualist beliefs and occult practices, should Cecilia Ruth Stevenson ever have confided this secret to her husband. This is all the more surprising since Stevenson's son Kerr White (he adopted the maiden of his maternal grandmother Cecilia Pretyman White) recorded that "Our father was an incorrigible gossip." Lord Tweedsmuir, Governor General from 1935 to 1940, "used to consult our father frequently and is reputed to have said about him that 'he knows everyone worth knowing in Canada and something 'bad' about each of them!'" Strangely, Prime Minister Mackenzie King did not seem to realize that Mrs. J.A. Stevenson was married to the journalist whom he so despised.[391]

The Stevensons had their two sons, Kerr in 1916, and Ian in 1918. In his recollections about his younger brother, Kerr White recounted that "after seven years, our parents' marriage was none too blissful." Mrs. Stevenson moved with the two boys to Los Angeles in 1923 because of Ian's severe bronchitis, which she thought would improve in California. She suffered from depression and "believed she was helped by a circular gadget consisting of a bundle of multiple wires covered in velvet, worn around the waist, and plugged into an electric outlet." In Los Angeles, Stevenson met Richard and Isabella Ingalese who wrote or co-wrote numerous brief occult studies in multiple editions such as *The History and Power of Mind* (1901), *From Incarnation to Re-Incarnation* (1904), *Cosmology and Evolution* (1907), *Occult Philosophy* (1920), and *Astrology and Health* (1928). "The Ingaleses wrote at least five books that our mother gave each of her children. In them they recounted the logic for their belief in reincarnation and the ubiquitous influence of karma as an explanation for the many diverse expressions of the human condition. They also spoke and wrote earnestly about a coming global 'cataclysm.'" According to Kerr White, "These dire predictions seemed to cloud our mother's viewpoint so that she acquired a cache of gold coins that we helped her bury in our

---

391 "Obituary: John A. Stevenson," *Montreal Star*, October 14, 1970, 100. Levine, *Scrum Wars*, 129. Levine, *King*, 112, 308. "John A. Stevenson," *Ottawa Journal*, October 14, 1970, 6. White, 13, 14. Stevenson refrained from acknowledging Cecilia Stevenson's extensive psychic contacts with the PM even after King's death. See his 1954 *Saturday Night* article, "Ottawa Letter: Distinguished Visitors and Apparitions."

garden behind the bungalow. When Ian was seven and I was nine, we returned to Ottawa, probably at the insistence of our father, who refused to continue the expensive trips to California. Ian's health also may have improved a little. By this time, there seems little doubt that our mother was now well fixated on the Ingaleses' view of the cosmos and on the veracity of reincarnation."[392]

Ian Stevenson credited his mother's vast library on theosophical and mystical beliefs in stimulating his own interest in supernormal phenomena and authored numerous investigations on reincarnation and survival after death. In his own recollections, he observed of one of his principal interests in medicine, psychosomatic relationships, that "My mother had believed strongly in the influence of thoughts on physical well-being, and I may owe to her my initial interest in psychosomatic medicine." He began studying history at St. Andrews University in Scotland in 1937 but, with the outbreak of World War II looming, switched to McGill University in Montreal in 1939 and graduated from its Faculty of Medicine in 1943.

After further university and medical studies and teaching in the United States, Stevenson received financial support from the medium Eileen Garrett and her Parapsychology Foundation which enabled him to travel to India and Sri Lanka in 1961 to investigate reincarnation memories in children. He was able to greatly expand this line of research as a result of further financial support from Chester Carlson, the inventor of Xerox, who endowed a chair for Stevenson at the University of Virginia where he founded the Division of Personality Studies (subsequently renamed the Division of Perceptual Studies) in 1967. He published what he considered his masterwork, the two-volume *Reincarnation and Biology*, in 1997 and was elected President of the Society for Psychical Research the following year. When he died in 2007, his *New York Times* obituary reported that Stevenson's Division at the University of Virginia investigated past lives, near-death, and out-of-body experiences, apparitions, after-death communications, and deathbed visions.[393]

---

392 White, 11, 12. Barbara McKenzie of the British College of Psychic Science describes the Ingaleses' search to find the Elixir of Life through alchemy in "The Philosopher's Stone in California," *Occult Review* 48:5 (November 1928). She notes that "*The History and Power of Mind* was amongst the first of this class of book I personally ever read."

393 Stevenson, *Some of My Journeys in Medicine*, 7. I am grateful to James

In August 1936, Prime Minister Mackenzie King invited Cecilia Ruth Stevenson and Lady Jessie Allan Foster (widow of the prominent Canadian Conservative MP, Cabinet Minister, and Senator Sir George Eulas Foster) to dinner and showed them the grounds in Kingsmere. "I discovered that to stand near the [sun] dial in the front circle & look at the Heavens gave one a feeling of a planetarium. There was very much tonight to bring home the significance of the Stars, of astrology. In the first place, Mrs. Stevenson is an astrologer, has been working on my horoscope. The conversation was mostly about astrology & the planes & spheres. (…..)" Like Mayor Hardie and M.E. Young, Stevenson connected astrology with spirituality and religion as well. She "spoke too of the higher & lower spirits, of the former as God's agents becoming interested in 'individuals – seeing their aura – or knowing they were likely to be specially helpful & working through them, concentrating on them as it were.'" Stevenson was thus reinforcing King's magical thinking that he was an agent of God and of forces in the Beyond. "Mrs. Stevenson was distinctly interesting & helpful – strong for <u>peace</u> & a constructive policy of peace…She seemed to imply that I had a special mission and might be being used in this way. She & Lady Foster both seemed to wish to infer she could help me in the fulfillment of a great purpose."[394]

In mid-April 1938, Stevenson sent the PM a fifteen-typed-page "Reading from the Horoscope for December 17, 1874 At 7:56 A.M." along with an equal sized "General Outline of Major Planetary Influences in the Near Future." Both uninspiring, humdrum readings failed to identify the imminent outbreak of World War II and King's and Canada's major role in that world conflict but nevertheless offered astrological advice. The "General Outline" proposed that if "you decide to enter some undertaking such as a practical aggressive, martial and reforming campaign, I do believe that you will get some help from the stars, through your own vigour and the law of chances." Stevenson foresaw that "The year December 1940 to December 1941

G. Matlock for the cited articles by Kerr White and Ian Stevenson. Margalit Fox, "Ian Stevenson Dies at 88; Studied Claims of Past Lives," *New York Times*, February 18, 2007.

394 Diary, August 11, 1936. Stevenson thanked King on August 21 for sending her Aldous Huxley's pamphlet *What Are You Going To Do About It?: The Case for Constructive Peace*. "I have got a 2nd copy for my son in England who has started the Pacifist Society in his school."

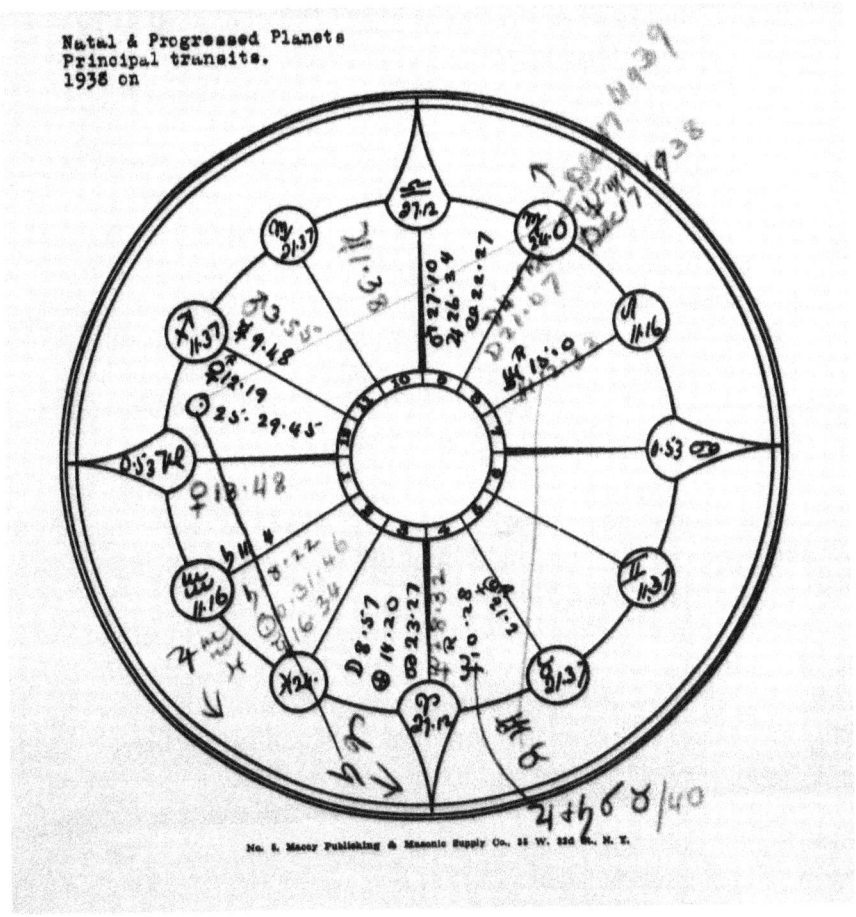

Figure 35: Cecilia Ruth Stevenson's 1938 Natal and Progressed Planets chart for Mackenzie King.

is one which is likely to bring great changes in your position. This could be either public or domestic position." She explained that "It is generally conceded by astrologers that the world is fast approaching a very momentous period in the world's history."

> It is calculated that there will probably be another terrific rise in prices culminating in 1942…there is likely to [be] another great crash & economic collapse and much discontent among the peoples of North America which will precipitate another and much worse depression than we had before. It is also calculated that the President who is elected in 1940 will die in office; let us hope naturally and not as a result of assassination by some

discontented persons. The period from 1942 to 1946 will be a very hectic one for the United States, because at that time Uranus goes into the sign Gemini, which sign has a great effect on the United States and also on Canada, I think. Every 84 years if you count back in American history you will find that there has been some kind of an upheaval on behalf of some kind of 'freedom.' This will probably result this time in some kind of civil warfare or in some severe struggle between capital and labour. It might of course also mean that foreign war could be mixed up in the vibrations, and of course at this time other parts of the world, including Europe may be upset, for England is threatened with real war from this time on for a few years by the entrance of Neptune into Libra, the house of her enemies.

Stevenson concluded her "General Outline" by advising, "Well, whether you can do more good in or out of office during these hectic years, I leave it to you to decide."[395]

She identified herself in both documents as "Personal Counsellor, Astrologer" and largely offered advice in her "Reading from The Horoscope." "I feel that I entirely understand your nature," Stevenson informed the Prime Minister. "You are really a most idealistic person, with a genuine faith and interest in those things which are real and eternal and the mystical strain in your character will make you naturally turn to that side of life, perhaps more often than the ordinary man of action and of public affairs would." One must wonder how King reacted when he read Stevenson's Freudian insights about his mother and relationship with Joan Patteson in the section "RELATIONS WITH THE OPPOSITE SEX; PARTNERSHIPS ETC." "It is quite obvious that you had an extremely close tie with your Mother, for the Moon in Aries always indicates such a close bond, sometimes a little restrictive."

> You like I do probably believe in the essential value and importance of these ties of soul with soul, mental and spiritual ties, irrespective of the physical relationship involved or not involved. If you do you would call this a good thing. If, however, one regards such things from the worldly and more materialistic viewpoint, one would be inclined to call it a Mother complex. Such a bond always makes it difficult for a man to marry but

---

395 Stevenson, "General Outline of Major Planetary Influences in the Near Future," 10, 14, 15.

that this is necessarily always a disadvantage I am not for one at all ready to agree…After seeing this horoscope, I am ready to believe that your Mother has certainly taken an interest in you since she passed into the next plane, and that no doubt many of the astral impressions which you get are from her.

No doubt the ideal so firmly fixed on your mind of your Mother may have made it difficult for you to replace her, but in any case I would say that despite all your adventures, some of them unusual if not downright mysterious, you have not found that ideal which would call forth really wholehearted concentrated devotion…No, I am inclined to think destiny was wise in not urging you to contract a legal marriage partnership.[396]

King read Stevenson's horoscope readings out loud to Joan Patteson on April 22, 1938. "The first part of it, the past & characteristics I thought good. The progression is obviously mixed up with her own thoughts & views, and I found far from comforting, or as I thought true." He and Joan then had a more satisfying sitting at the "little table." Stevenson had written him, "There is no need to send me any money for this horoscope; it is true that my husband keeps me on such a tight string that I am not in the habit of making presents to men friends!, but I trust this may be an exception since you are the Prime Minister of my adopted country." King phoned the astrologer the next day saying, "I would rather treat it as a professional matter & asked her her fee. She suggested $20.00 asking if I thought it too much. I said I would send her $25.00 [$501 in 2023 dollars] & later wrote her to England sending $5 for her library."

In his letter to Stevenson, he looked forward to her return to Kingsmere where they could look over the PM's horoscope. "I should be glad to tell you, just as honestly as I can, wherein it seems to me I have benefitted by, or fallen short of the place which the planets evidently intended I was to have at the time of my arrival in this world." Yet when he again read Stevenson's horoscope to Patteson the following year, it "seemed to me almost utter trash, as Joan and I agreed this morning. The Christian truths are the only sure guides. They are the paths which lead the right way & to the right haven at the close. Got the opposite in 'conversation' after Church tonight."[397]

---

396 Stevenson, "Reading from The Horoscope for December 17, 1874, At 7:56 A.M.," 6, 12, 13.

397 Diary, April 21 and 22, 1938. King to Stevenson, April 23, 1938. Diary,

In November 1941, like M.E. Young, Stevenson tried to interest the Prime Minister "in the teachings of true Esoteric Christianity as distinguished from Churchianity" by sending him copies of VISION, a leaflet of UNIVERSAL TRUTH. She had signed some of her previous correspondence and astrological charts as both Ruth Cecilia and Ruth P. Stevenson. In the first number of VISION she explained, "'Cecilia' in a previous incarnation was 'Philip,' companion brother of ST. FRANCIS of ASSISI. Through this link of past association she has been entrusted with the distribution of the following communication from Him, which He desires should reach all who can accept it as His MESSAGE to the suffering world today, now in the darkness before the dawn of the new AQUARIAN AGE." Two weeks after Canada declared war on Japan and Hong Kong was about to fall to the Japanese – resulting in over one thousand Canadian casualties – King responded, "You will realise, I know, how little time I am able, at the moment, to command apart from the war, for any special interests or study. Perhaps a little later on I may have a chance of talking over with you some of the profound matters in which we are mutually interested."[398]

In the early 1940s, Stevenson annotated a copy of Charles A. Ward's 1940 *Oracles of Nostradamus* and circulated the book to twenty-seven of her occult initiates through her New Era Universal Occult Truth Libraries. A copy of this edition, issued in Senneville, Quebec, was offered for sale on AbeBooks in 2022 for $5,286 USD. In her handwritten and typed annotations, Stevenson identified herself as a disciple of the 18th century Prince Rakockzy, the Comte de St. Germain. According to the AbeBooks description, "Her notes predict earthquakes, plague, famine, cataclysm, 10% of the world's population surviving, fall of the moon rock…her handwritten comments on Nostradamus successfully talk of Hitler and Mussolini, an Arab leader, World Government etc." Cecilia Ruth Stevenson died on July 24, 1968, and was buried in the Cimetière Mont-Royal in Outremont, Quebec.[399]

February 12, 1939.

398 Stevenson to King, November 4, 1941. *Vision* 1:1 (November 1941). King to Stevenson, December 23, 1941.

399 "c1940 Annotated Copy of 'Oracles of Nostradamus' with Handwritten and Typed Notes by Famed Occultist and Spiritualist and Disciple of the Enigmatic Prince Rakockzy, Comte de St. Germain," copy located through AbeBooks, 2022. For the Comte de St. Germain and his secret of prolonging life, see Isabel Cooper-Oakley. *The Comte de St. Germain: The Secret of Kings.*

Despite his lack of time for Stevenson's further astrological delineations and horoscope prognostications during World War II, astrology had become a firm part of Mackenzie King's belief system. Following the conclusion of the trilateral trade agreement between Canada, the United Kingdom and the United States, the PM recorded in his diary in March 1939 that James Samuel Taylor, the MP for Nanaimo, "said that by his reckoning in Astrology, it was just 150 years ago that the Americans and the British separated. That now they were coming together on trade matters through the agency of Canada. He had all this worked out in terms of signs of the Zodiac, and argued we had done the right thing in negotiating the Treaty." In August, he pasted Francis Drake's individual horoscope in his diary. The following year, the spiritualist Dr. John Hett recommended an astrologer friend who predicted that President Roosevelt would be elected for a third term but would be assassinated in office and that a terrible revolution would break out in the U.S. The Prime Minister responded, "I have been particularly interested in what you have written concerning astrological influences. I wonder if, some time, you could arrange for me to meet your friend." And in 1945, the Prime Minister discussed preordination with Dr. T.V. Soong, the Chinese Foreign Minister. "He said there was no doubt where date of birth was known, that a life could be worked out. His view was it was the result of careful observation and deduction that had been made over centuries by those who have come to be highly expert fortune tellers."[400]

In the 1920 and 1930s – in addition to using astrology and Rachel Bleaney's psychometric reading of handkerchiefs and neck ties to fathom his future – Mackenzie King also believed his destiny was inscribed in his hands and only required a qualified palmist for its correct interpretation. Having one's palm read was a family activity that can be traced to Isabel King's encounter with a fortune-teller as a seven-year-old in Kingston in 1850 and continued in her family in

---

Milan: G. Sulli-Rao, 1912; Virginia Milward, "The Comte de St. Germain," *Occult Review*, 15:5 (May 1912); and Arthur Edward Waite, "Comte de St. Germain as an Historical Personality," *Occult Review* 37:4 (April 1923). Waite notes that "Saint Germain is an object of particular devotion in circles of modern theosophy, and I am told that in Co-Masonic Lodges connected with this movement his portrait is saluted as that of a Master who has taken the Woman [sic] Movement in Freemasonry under his special charge."

400   Diary, March 9, 1939, and August 12, 1939. Hett to King, December 30, 1940. Diary, September 2, 1945.

Berlin, Ontario, through the 1890s. In his diary, Mackenzie King noted his first encounter with a fortune-teller after consulting the palmist Mrs. Lauretta Menden in Toronto in 1896. Following his election as Leader of the Liberal Party and while campaigning in Kamloops in 1920, a Syrian fortune-teller read his palm and foresaw his marriage. King observed, "There was nothing in the 'fortune' but common places. She was out on my being married not to one I loved first but the next one. Out on my life work being an 'easy one,' right in working by head instead of hand etc. etc. Pure fake, but some little amusement."[401]

While in Atlantic City in January 1925 working on his Speech from the Throne, the Prime Minister was much more impressed by the Indian phrenologist and palmist-astrologer Prof. Douglas Goray, who had been an inspector of post offices in India. He liked Goray's thoughtful, quiet appearance and so had a three dollar [$52 Canadian in 2023 dollars] reading. The palmist "began with astrology, "Sagittarius;" gave general horoscope, description, then got into palmistry – a long life – complete life, length depending on use I made etc. – watch stomach trouble, digestion etc.... Will always have some money. Much has come to me – some from opposite sex (Lady Laurier's gift of Laurier House). Anything attempted this year will succeed – any big change. February & Thursday good day for me (day Parliament opens)."[402]

In December 1930, ten weeks after R.B. Bennett's Conservatives defeated the Liberals, the palmist Quest Brown contacted King requesting an interview. The Montreal magazine *Passing Show* had commissioned her to write a series of articles on the hands of famous and prominent Canadians. Working out of her home at 4095 Côte-des-Neiges and the Medico-Dental Building in Montreal, 1396 Sainte Catherine Street West at Bishop St., Brown advertised herself as "Canada's accepted Palmist." When she came to Ottawa, she made appointments at the Chateau Laurier Hotel for $5 [$85 in 2023 dollars] per consultation, with another $5 for extra time, and provided "Scientific Hand Analysis for Vocational Guidance, Health Diagnosis and Life Delineation." Jane Stewart, an astrologer, was also available in Montreal for "delineation of horoscopes and major and minor aspects for one year" for $10.

Brown read Mackenzie King's hands at Laurier House on December 22, 1930, a week after his fifty-sixth birthday. The palmist detected

---

401 Diary, October 13, 1920.
402 Diary, January 27, 1925.

a new line in his lifeline. "That is when his power is coming again… The exact age is 59 [i.e. in 1933] …The beginning of the cycle of renewed power and the greatest power you have had yet … I want you to believe this scientifically, not as fortune telling…Your past success was not one-eighth of the success which is seen here." Brown also foresaw that "there is some man who will come into your life; that man, you must rely on him. He is a man who will get nearer to the heart of the people than yourself. Your strength is from the mentality." The man "will perhaps use the emotions of the people; something you have not got, and he will be absolutely necessary in your fame."

From reading his hands, Brown assessed King as "a man of great power who has not expressed himself. I would say that your life has not expressed itself…You have never expressed your heart yet. That is a thing that will come yet, I think. Your mentality has been developed at the expense of your heart." But she also forewarned him about "female influences," what surely must have made King think about his relationship with the married Joan Patteson. Studying the lines of his palms, Brown thought "there is a break that might be brought about by a female influence, between six and eight years; you could be one of the greatest men in the world, but there can be scandal over your last days."[403]

In his diary, Mackenzie King wrote enthusiastically about Quest Brown's "truly remarkable" reading, describing her as "an English woman comparatively young & really quick & intelligent." "First the line of fate on the left hand indicated a very full life – everything before me, but I had been handicapped around the age of 20 & thereafter with financial embarrassment, a parent [King's father] had died (or become unequal to the task). There had been sheltered life at home, at college and later had come the struggle to help others – a life of service it had been, thwarting to some degree the free development fate had planned."

Brown won great credibility in King's eyes by correctly identifying "the time of my greatest sorrow," the illness and death of his mother in 1917. "There had been sickness to care for – much – relief had come after great sorrow – the greatest sorrow had come about 14 years ago…The best of my life was to come around 59 & 60 [i.e. 1933-34]. I would experience a power surpassing anything up to

---

403 Brown, "Destiny, and Sir Arthur Currie," *The Passing Show*, December 1930. "Interview with Mrs. Quest Brown, December 22, 1930."

the present. 'The 59th to 60th year brings the beginning of a cycle of Fame more brilliant than experienced before...' She thought I had been very fatigued the last few years, was below par even now & for the next year would have to watch my judgment closely to making decisions; in another year or two all this would clear & I would realize a sense of power I never had before & would have fame at 60 & on greater than anything I had ever known."

Regarding the death of one of his opponents and a man who would aid him politically, King elaborated in his diary, "I had an enemy who crosses the path between now & then but he would disappear from blood pressure, clot on brain or something – that was written on my hand. I said I supposed that was present P.M. [R.B. Bennett]; she replied 'yes.' Some man would be a great help to me, he would supply the heart needed for my name and fame. I had the intellectual side very strong; he would reach the hearts of others for me & would be a great help for 4 years from now."

Brown also gained King's confidence by seeing that "my mother would mean more to me than all others – a woman born in October would be too possessive for me...She was very strong about the brilliant line on the right hand & watching the 'possessive' person as indicated on the other line running to the mound of Sagittarius...She used the word 'possessive' many times & made clear she meant some relationship to a married person...I gather she felt I would not marry & did not tell all she saw." At the close of the reading, Brown said "I was 'a boy.' 'You are a boy – with all the nature of a boy, need a wife to mother you.'"[404]

Though at first she declined to accept payment, King paid the palmist $5 and another $5 for extra time. Three days later, after reading 1 Samuel 9:9 regarding "the truth of the soothsayer – come let us go to the seer – to inquire of God," he added in his diary, "I have thought much of what Mrs. Quest Brown has told me. (I feel somehow I will hear again from her.) It seems to me in what she said about not letting any woman be 'possessive,' protecting my good name etc., she was giving me the seer's word." A week later, despondent about the Liberal electoral defeat and how to revive the Party, he had dinner with Norman Rogers, his future Minister of Labour and future Minister of National Defence. "He is really one of the very best men I know...He

---

404 Diary, December 22, 1930.

has promised to help in preparation material. He may be the man to supply 'the heart' referred to by Mrs. Quest Brown. He is truly appreciative of spiritual things and of highest values."[405]

King was even more convinced by Quest Brown's second visit in February 1931. "She is quite a remarkable woman, very sincere and with great psychic powers. I was more impressed than ever with her personality, and the real insight and power it reveals." Two months before R.B. Bennett's sister Mildred married William Herridge – the Prime Minister's senior advisor and son of the Rev. and Marjorie Herridge – Brown informed King that she had read Mildred's palm and that Mildred subsequently slammed the door in her face. Brown had seen written in her hand "two or three love affairs in her life, one that really had gone very deep" and that her forthcoming marriage was a marriage of convenience and not for love. "She spoke about an adopted child; Miss Bennett said it was her brother's."

Quest Brown assured King that Bennett himself would come to a gruesome end and that he would be returned to power. King had had an "extraordinary dream" of Bennett "lying dead on a slab." Brown foresaw that Bennett "will not last; he will have a crushing end, a crash of some kind. He may have to take precautions to protect his own life. Times are going to get much worse; in September will be riots and in the spring of next year, bloodshed & loss of life. There will be changes; there will be upheavals; conditions will be volcanic." The palmist assured King, "You will be called upon to take hold of things in ways you may not dream of. It will or may all come about suddenly – but it is coming. You have a great part to play. The country will see something in you they have never seen before. They need something, something of inspiration. You have that and will bring that. They do not begin to know you yet. It is all very clear. It is your destiny."

Quest Brown was certain King had a great future and that "it will be hard to over-estimate what may come in the way of honour & power in 3 or 4 years time." She sensed difficulties at present, "that this month & time will be a hard one, likely to pick up out of atmosphere whatever makes for irritation & stumbling, that I have to be careful in what I say & do. This due to Horoscope & position of planets, etc. She thinks by August I will come to smoother waters." King was greatly animated by Brown's assurances. "She spoke to me in a reverent way

---

405 Diary, December 25, 1930, and January 3, 1931.

of myself & her great belief in me and the part I have to take. She says she feels so sure of it all. She was full of spirit, it was clearly there & I confess to an immediate interest in all she said & to great enjoyment & sense of reality & truth in discussing these things with her."[406]

Quest Brown was a new type of medium who felt confident to speak in public and to advertise her craft and name in newspapers and on the radio. She had announced the opening of a "vocational department," the Quest Brown Studio, in the business personals of the *Montreal Star* on July 30, 1930. "Will advise you as to the work you are most suited for." The *Ottawa Citizen* for October 7, 1930, listed her 8:30 to 9:30 p.m. CFCF radio broadcast, "Laws of Palmistry by Quest Brown." The *Ottawa Journal* and *Citizen* of April 16 and May 5, 1931, announced, without referring to palmistry, that "Mrs. Quest Brown, of Montreal, is a guest at the Chateau Laurier for a few days."

Brown had addressed the Ottawa Women's Press Club on February 16, 1931, two days before her sitting with Mackenzie King at Laurier House. The *Citizen* called her "a noted palmist" and reported that she informed the journalists that "the mind and palm were directly connected, and were more in unison than other parts of the body." This "accounted for the personality being shown in the lines of the palm." But in May, Brown wrote a desperate undated letter to King from Montreal after suffering "the terrible humiliation of being searched publicly and placed in a cell with 3 disorderly women." She had been "arrested and imprisoned on the charge of fortune-telling very soon after the new chief of Police came into power." Brown was out on bail and had engaged Lucien Gendron, KC, of Gendron and Monette, 276 St. James St., "to fight for my science and livelihood. Should I lose my case it will [be] a miscarriage of justice and will be very destructive to the encouraging and constructive work that I have been doing." She wrote to King in the hope that "your power can avert a great injustice" and asked that he write Gendron, "giving him a brief impression of the sincerity and value of my work" before her case was heard in Criminal Court on May 21. There is no correspondence extant between King and Brown about her case. Lucy Zavitske, King's secretary, wrote him a memo on May 19 reporting that she had called Lucien Gendron but that he had left for lunch

---

406 Diary, February 18, 1931.

and could not be reached by telephone. "He is expected back at the office at 2 p.m., and I have left word for him to call you immediately upon his return."[407]

Quest Brown's charge of fortune-telling was first heard before Judge J.O. Lacroix in the Montreal police court on May 21. In its coverage, the *Montreal Gazette* described Brown as "a palmist with society connections and many magazine articles and radio talks to her credit." She had been "smartly attired in a brown tailor-made suit, with a fox fur and a Bangkok hat." Brown told the court she knew that the two constables who came to her office and paid $2 [$38 in 2023 dollars] for the reading were policemen because they appeared so ill at ease. The *Gazette* reported that "Miss Brown took the stand to defend palmistry as a science and to draw a sharp line of distinction between her own practice and that of the common fortune teller who frequently appears in court." She asserted that palm reading was being recognized the world over by psychologists. "It is definitely a science: the palm is a nerve centre, and changes in the mind are reflected in the lines of the hand." Lucien Gendron called Dr. George Joseph Boyce as a defence witness. Like Brown, he testified that there was an undoubted relationship between the lines of the hand and the brain and that palmistry was a science. "There was a comparison to be made between palmistry and phrenology."[408]

Judge Lacroix rendered his judgment on June 9. In contrast with magistrate Oulton's decision to convict Mercy Phillimore of fortune-telling in London in 1928, Lacroix's decision to fully acquit Brown was so one-sided that it raises the question whether he was influenced by Mackenzie King's behind the scenes intervention. The *Gazette* reported that Lacroix declared that chiromancy, the reading of palms, "has a basis in science, and is not to be confused with the vulgar art of the fortune teller...'The officers who made this case,' said the judge, 'should have known that they were not dealing with one of those common fortune tellers who have no real knowledge, have made no special study, but rely solely upon a vivid imagination and a verbal fluency that are not without a charm of their own." He characterized Brown as "a very well educated woman, who has made a special study of chiromancy. This study is

---

407 "Women's Press Club," *Ottawa Citizen*, February 17, 1931, 19. Quest Brown to King, undated letter, May 1931. Lucy Zavitske to King, May 19, 1931.

408 "Palmist Defends Craft as Science: Woman in Court on Fortune-Telling Charge Scorns Accusers," *Montreal Gazette*, May 22, 1931, 6.

Figure 36: Quest Brown at the Chateau Laurier, Ottawa, February 1939.

recognized in all civilized countries. I am informed that now in England the science known under the name of chiromancy is legalized."

Lacroix ruled that Brown had not attempted to mislead the public. "The accused has not claimed that she possessed a supernatural power or an occult science that permitted her to foretell the future." After examining previous judgements rendered under article 443, he ruled "there was no fraud on the part of the accused; there was no criminal intent and consequently there was no offence." He considered chiromancy "as a science in the infant stage in our country, based, in any case, on principles and rules that are not contrary to already existing sciences, especially medical science."[409]

Brown continued to promote palmistry and her "QUEST BROWN" branding through newspaper advertising – including several large display ads paid via corporate sponsorship from Rogers Fuels – radio broadcasts, and public presentations after her trial. Her CFCF "Quest Brown – Horoscope" and "Character Analyst" broadcasts ran from October to December 1931 and again from October to December 1932. She lectured on "The Laws of Palmistry" in the Mount Royal Hotel in February 1932 and spoke to the Business and Professional Women's Club in the Windsor Hotel in Montreal in February 1933.[410]

Mackenzie King corresponded with Brown in 1934 and 1935 but did not see her again until February 7, 1939. The day of her sitting with the PM, the *Ottawa Citizen* announced the five-day residency by the "widely known lecturer and writer" at the Chateau Laurier. The paper reported that "During her life Mrs. Brown has come in contact with leading personalities in the economic and political life of both Canada and the United States." Her sitters had included "the late Sir Arthur Currie [Commander of the Canadian Corps in WW I and principal of McGill University 1920-1933], Judge Surveyer, Dr. [Duncan] Campbell Scott [the poet and deputy superintendent of the Department of Indian Affairs 1913-1932], Hon. Charles Dunning [King's Minister of Finance 1935-1939], William Butler Yeats, the famous Irish poet who recently died; Peter Freuchen, Arctic explorer; the late Dr. Knud Rasmussen

---

409 "Court Maintains Palmistry Is Not Vulgar Chicanery," *Montreal Gazette*, June 10, 1931, 4.

410 "Bias of Scientist Bar to Palmistry," *Montreal Gazette*, February 3, 1932, 7. "More Revelation about Kreuger: Match King Mentioned in Palmistry Talk," *Montreal Gazette*, February 16, 1933, 9.

[polar explorer and anthropologist]; General Gerardo Machado, ex-president of Cuba; Faith Baldwin, novelist; Achmed Abullah, rector, and the late Ivar Kreuger, Swedish match king."[411]

Despite her denials of fortune-telling in court in 1931, Brown, in her previous sitting with King, had foretold his future and predicted Prime Minister R.B. Bennett's "crushing end," riots, bloodshed, and loss of life in the spring of 1932. King in turn had been gratified that the palmist was "full of spirit." In 1939, King was so impressed by Brown's reading that he dictated a nine-page account of his 90-minute interview with her on February 7. Brown read the PM's hands over the little square table in the Laurier House library while he took notes. From little lines at the side of the hand, she correctly identified King's porphyria infection in his teeth, hemorrhoids, a thyroid deficiency, and a valvular condition of the heart that had also been disclosed by his doctors. "The things to watch were the heart – not serious – and the teeth to be closely watched, and the little thyroid shortage." But she was wrong in predicting his very long life, "possibly to 88 or 90," and that King would die outside of Canada. "She said that the hand indicated, above all, no diminishment of power or prestige but rather increased power, increased recognition in the coming years. She showed on both the right and left hand how far the line of fate extended…She spoke about a strong sun line and said she would be completely mistaken if I did not come back to power twice more. There was every indication of that."

> Analysing the right hand from the point of view of planets, etc., she pointed first to the mount of the first finger which is: Jupiter, and said it was powerful. Indicated I would have great power. The second finger – which stood for Saturn – helped to balance the first. Saturn stood for sobriety. She found that I kept myself well in check and was balancing all tendencies. The 3rd finger – Apollo – indicated brilliancy along the line of art and writing, etc. She said had I devoted my life to literature, I might have written brilliantly or in any line of art, made great headway… She kept returning to the fact that I could have been a great writer and could do much in that direction still. Spoke of love of music, etc.… . She spoke particularly of the far side of the hand

---

[411] "Widely Known Writer Is Visiting Capital," *Ottawa Citizen*, February 7, 1939, 2.

as indicating great imaginative qualities. The 4th finger – Mercury – indicated that I was both logical and illogical – in other words, gullible. That I was very logical but might be taken in on some things. Speaking of the thumb, she used the word 'magnificent' as indicating particularly great willpower and judgment combined. She said I could be led but never could be driven.

Brown correctly foresaw that King's finances would be good to the end. When he asked her if she saw any probability of marriage in his hand, "she laughed a little and said she thought I was destined to live alone throughout my life."

Regarding world events, Brown's studies, "particularly by means of [astrological] charts," persuaded her that "conditions generally, in so many aspects, were so wholly similar to the months immediately preceding the war of 1914 that she felt convinced there would be a war this year, and she looked for it about the month of June." Yet Brown also thought "Hitler's life would end this year. That Mussolini too might not survive long. That in both countries, Italy and Germany, a critical situation would develop." What was most significant about Quest Brown's reading with the Prime Minister only months before the outbreak of World War II, was that she questioned whether he should continue in public life. King indicated that "it was a sense of duty which kept me in the other course. That I was ready to follow whatever my destiny might be. That I would shape my course as events might determine and do my utmost to serve well as I went along."

Brown felt so strongly that King should retire from public life that she wrote him the next day from the Chateau Laurier. The PM acknowledged the significance of her letter by entering it verbatim in his diary. "In spite of your apparent good health," the psychic reader of palms observed, "your vibrations were those of a weary and discouraged man. I could not do otherwise than plead with you to spare yourself as much as possible in the near future." "You can still fulfill your destinies away from the maddening crowd," Brown advised. "You have many years in front of you in which to achieve all you desire for Canada and possibly this must be achieved in the peace and silence of your own inner life…Your own spiritual freedom will enable you to help Canada far more than in any empty and soulless office…You were destined to lead Canada out of the morass of materialism that is crushing all the ideals of your great leaders in the past…You are at the turning point of your life – don't drift into a negative and empty victory – fight for your own spiritual development

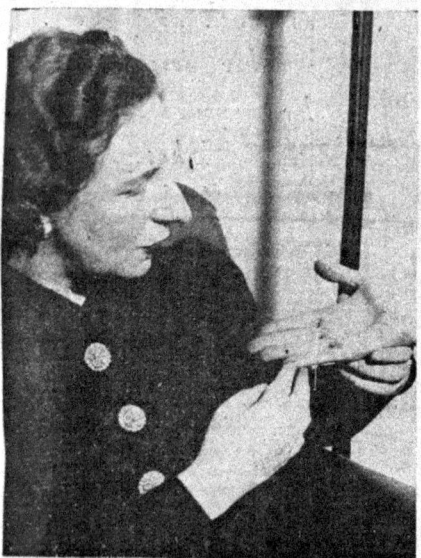

What Has Become of Hitler Astrologer?

Famous English Palmist Brings Story of Mystery After Munich

MRS. QUEST BROWN, PALMIST, WHO BRINGS REPORT ABOUT HITLER'S ASTROLOGER

Figure 37: *Quest Brown on the cover of the* Boston Globe, *November 22, 1939.*

and this may have to be worked out in solitude."

Brown strongly urged the Prime Minister, "You are a mystic and your real leadership may be in an entirely different direction. You must go into the silence and accept unreservedly the guidance that will direct you to serve Canada." In his diary, King agreed that Brown's letter forced him to consider the true purpose of his life. She "has diagnosed absolutely correctly the real conflict that I experienced and have experienced over many years... However, I feel that to go into the life of silence, congenial as it would be, would be to desert the real purpose of my life especially at times such as the present." Despite his many inadequacies, "I nevertheless can help to keep Canada on a steadier keel than possibly any other one likely to succeed at the present time, and very possibly, in the position I hold, will be able to save possibly many situations which would be full of peril to the people of this land."[412]

Quest Brown gave an illustrated lecture at the Hotel Brunswick in Boston where she had taken a suite on November 8, 1939. The *Boston Globe* featured her on its front page on November 22 under the heading "What Has Become of Hitler's Astrologer: Famous English Palmist Brings Story of Mystery After Munich." According to the paper, "The grapevine news among the astrologers is that he mysteriously vanished...According to reports which Mrs. Brown says she has received from abroad, the Fuehrer's astrologer had told Adolf the stars said thumbs down on the venture. She has not read Hitler's palm

---

412 Diary, February 7, 1939.

– although partial to astrology, he's said not to be unsympathetic to palmistry – but she has delved into Mussolini's. 'He's a man of destiny...the many lines tell that...however, the three main lines show greatly weakened resistance during the next two years."

Brown informed the *Globe* that her parents baptized her Quest after she had learned to talk because she always asked so many questions, then added Elsie May after Quest. She estimated that she had analyzed between 50,000 and 75,000 pairs of hands, including those of actors Roland Young, Mary Pickford, and Douglas Fairbanks. For her research, "hospitals and prisons throughout Europe and North America have opened their doors." She was in the United States and not England because of the outbreak of World War II. Her suite at the Hotel Brunswick was decorated, the *Boston Globe*'s Janet Jones reported, "with autographed pictures of some of the famous men and women Mrs. Brown has hand analyzed." These included "Canadian Prime Minister Mackenzie King – whose return to politics she forecast besides predicting that he'll be Prime Minister several more times to come." This news that King had been among her sitters was not republished by Canadian newspapers.[413]

In 1943, Brown was one of the "oracles" featured in a benefit party in New York "designed to attract those interested in such branches of the occult as astrology and card reading," organized by Countess M. Koutowzow-Tolstoy. In the late 1940s, she befriended Virginia Haggard, the lover of the painter Marc Chagall who had escaped from Nazi-occupied France to New York in 1941. According to the artist's biographer, Jonathan Wilson, Chagall encouraged Virginia's "burgeoning relationship with Quest Brown, an English clairvoyant and palmist. Indeed, Chagall was happy to have his own palm read and generally pleased with the results. There is an inked imprint of Chagall's hand made by Quest Brown."[414]

There was still one further pseudo-science King pursued in the late 1920s and 1930s: graphology, the belief that handwriting

---

413 Janet Jones, "What Has Become of Hitler's Astrologer: Famous English Palmist Brings Story of Mystery After Munich," *Boston Globe*, November 22, 1939, 1, 14.

414 "This Party for Those Interested in Occult," *New York Daily News*, May 22, 1943, 281. Jonathan Wilson, *Marc Chagall* (New York: Schocken, 2007), 153. Virginia Haggard describes their encounter with Quest Brown in *My Life with Chagall*. (New York: Donald I. Fine, 1986), 47-48 and 71-72. I am grateful to Allan Levine for guiding me to this Chagall reference.

revealed a person's character and could be used to diagnose physical and mental health. The Prime Minister believed it was a science because his first graphologist, Fred D. Jacob, had been the official graphologist for the Dominion government, working out of the office of the Department of the Interior. A former newspaperman, he began working as a journalist for the *Toronto World* at the beginning of the century and after a few years was sent as the paper's special correspondent to London.

Jacob analyzed "The Handwriting of Premier King" on June 28, 1927. His series of profiles also aimed to include graphological readings of King's Minister of Justice, Ernest Lapointe, his Minister of Finance, James Robb, former Prime Minister and Conservative Party Leader, Arthur Meighen, Ontario Conservative Premier Howard Ferguson, Progressive MP Agnes Macphail, the President of the Canadian National Railways, Sir Henry Thornton, and others. Jacob's inaugural article in the series, "The Handwriting of Premier King," did not appear in the *Toronto Star* until May 26, 1928. It was reprinted simultaneously as "Premier's Writing Analysed by Expert" in the *Manitoba Free Press* which identified Jacob as "the outstanding interpreter of handwriting on this continent."

The Conservative *Ottawa Journal* began publishing the series on June 2, teasing its readers with "Do You Know What Character Kinks Handwriting of Premier and Famous People of the Dominion Reveals?" It stated Jacob was "recognized on this continent and in Europe as one of the most advanced students of graphology" and entitled his reading of King "Handwriting Expert Finds Unusual Combination of Idealistic Nature and Practical Man in the Premier." The paper subtitled its article, "Broad Interests and Leadership Exemplified in His Style of Script – Declares Hon. W.L.M. King Has Power of Second Sight."

In January 1931, six months after his defeat by R.B. Bennett's Conservatives, Mackenzie King invited Fred Jacob for dinner at Laurier House to read his and Joan and Godfroy Patteson's handwriting. Not knowing King's life-long inability to restrain his sex instinct, Jacob ventured, "you have strong appetites and passions, but they are well controlled. Your temperament is like a torrent which has to be held in check. You have good control…You have strong hypnotic powers. Eyes and personality could hypnotize and could hold through personality. You have a strong healing power…You have a strong will. It is hard to budge." He returned several times to King's tremendous intuition and psychic powers which he thought "might be a trouble to you." Sitting near the portrait of Isabel King he suggested, "You could get in touch with the other side. You could get in touch with your mother. It might bother you in your politics because you would work tremendously under this influence. You could go very far in that way."[415]

What made graphology different from astrology, palmistry and numerology was that it could be used not only to assess but also to project character in a propagandistic fashion. King wanted recognized graphologists to inform Canadians about his sterling character and virtue so that his example of Christian public service could inspire other Canadians. Such publicity, of course, also had considerable political value. In 1935, six months before the federal election that would return him to power, King was asked for a sample of his handwriting by Augustus Kingsley Cuddon-Woodthorpe in Montreal for his *Penmanship and Personality*, the first Canadian book to be published on this study. He identified himself as President of the Canadian Handwriting Institute and a member of the National Vocational Guidance Association and reminded King that "I wrote a study of you a few years ago that appeared in the Press, and which delighted many of your followers, and in response to which you sent me a very kind acknowledgement." A month before the October election, Adrienne, the handwriting analyst for the *Vancouver Sun*, published her analysis of King's signature as "Liberal Chief's Writing Reveals Fine Character."[416]

The Prime Minister continued sending out samples of his handwriting over the next decade. Virginia Drew's analysis of his script for the *Globe and Mail* in 1937, "Premier King's Handwriting Shows Keen, Scholarly Mind," was as laudatory as Cuddon-Woodthorpe's. Adrienne requested a sample of his script for her column "Character Analysis," also in 1937. King sent her a handwritten response noting, "I hope you may be able to decipher it which is more than I myself find it possible to do at times." Her analysis, "Canadian Prime Minister Modest," also appeared in the *Edmonton Bulletin*, March 7, 1938. She again reproduced King's handwritten note to her in the *Vancouver Sun* in 1940

---

415 Diary, January 21, 1931. "F.D. Jacob's Delineation of the Handwriting of Mr. Mackenzie King, January 21, 1931."

416 Cuddon-Woodthorpe to King, April 16, 1935. Adrienne, "Liberal Chief's Writing Reveals Fine Character," *Vancouver Sun*, September 19, 1935.

for an appreciative analysis in her column, "What Character does your handwriting Reveal?" In 1947, Tam Deachman asked King for a sample of his handwriting for a graphological character profile of the leaders of the four major political parties in the *Canadian Business* magazine, published by the Canadian Chamber of Commerce in Montreal, entitled "Your Handwriting <u>DOES</u> reveal Your Character."[417]

---

417   Virginia Drew, "Premier King's Handwriting Shows Keen, Scholarly Mind: Thinks Carefully before He Acts," *Globe and Mail*, June 17, 1937. Adrienne to King, October 9, 1937. King to Adrienne, November 15, 1937. Adrienne, "Canadian Prime Minister Modest," *Edmonton Bulletin*, March 7, 1938, and "What Character Does Your Handwriting Reveal?" *Vancouver Sun*, February 24, 1940. Tom Deachman, "Your Handwriting DOES Reveal Your Character," *Canadian Business* 21:3 (March 1948). The *Toronto Star* noted the frequent illegibility of King's handwriting in "All Great Men Are Not Great Penmen," October 25, 1937.

CHAPTER 12

Dr. T. Glen Hamilton: Photographing Ectoplasm in Winnipeg

Mackenzie King for years relied on leading mediums and multiple forms of spirit communication, consulting the Kingston fortune-teller Rachel Bleaney from 1925 to 1933 and the Detroit direct-voice medium Etta Wriedt from 1932 to 1938, as well as working the "little table" with Joan Patteson in Ottawa from 1933 until the end of September 1949. He had such a strong belief in the continuity of personality after death, however, and such a compelling need to be in touch with his deceased loved ones, that he also simultaneously established contact with numerous additional mediums and psychic investigators in Canada, the United States and England. After his defeat in the 1930 election that relegated him to the position of Leader of the Opposition in Parliament, he asked God to "bless this Christmas to me and bring to me a helpful revelation from the dear ones in the Great Beyond. I pray that I may feel certain of the near presence of their spirits as the angels watched about the cradle at Bethlehem & as the star guided the wise men of the East 1930 years ago."[418]

In 1933 alone, King established contact with Dr. Thomas Glendenning Hamilton in Winnipeg, Helen Lambert and Marie and Hereward Carrington in New York, and with Dr. John Hett who had medical practices in Kitchener and Toronto. To an even greater extent than Rachel Bleaney, these and over a dozen additional mediums and psychic explorers discussed in this and subsequent chapters raise questions about the extent of Mackenzie King's magical thinking.

---

418 Diary, December 24, 1930.

He first heard about T. Glen Hamilton from the painter and spiritualist Homer Watson. The artist informed King during his first visit to his studio in June 1933 that there was an even greater psychic investigator than Etta Wriedt in the mid-west able to bring about the materialization of spirits whose features were clearly recognizable. "I asked if materialization were not unsatisfactory & unpleasant. He said on the contrary, it was beautiful – features all clearly recognizable etc. He said it must have been where the conception of angels came from."[419]

King's credence in Hamilton's psychic investigations was strengthened further when he visited the tuberculosis sanatorium in Ninette, Manitoba, while on his 1933 Western political speaking tour in July. After visiting the women's and men's wards, he addressed the bed-ridden patients from the lawn outside through a loudspeaker. He recalled his own brother Max's struggle with tuberculosis (his *The Battle with Tuberculosis and How to Win It* was recommended reading for the patients) and praised the loving and scientific care they were receiving from the sanatorium's medical superintendent, Dr. David A. Stewart. "It was an amazing experience – Sunday afternoon by the little lake preaching the gospel of love – that is where & how I found myself led by invisible hands, continuing on earth Max's mission here & in the great beyond. It was a glorious hour for both of us, I the instrument through him to reveal the power & nature & love of God through the life of Christ."

At their home, Mrs. Stewart spoke of Oliver Lodge's "investigation & satisfaction by Science of the existence of the survival of life & personality etc. I spoke of having met him, of our talks together, of my talks with Lord Grey etc. & of being assured in my own mind of the guidance I was receiving from beyond." The Stewarts referred to Dr. Hamilton's research and photography of psychic phenomena in Winnipeg. King asked himself, "should I not speak of what I had personally experienced. I said if they would both swear to say nothing of it I would tell them what I myself had experienced & know. It seemed to [be] ordained I should do this. So I told them of having spoken with Max, father, mother & Bell, [Bert] Harper & some 70 or 80 others [through Etta Wriedt] – by direct voice."

When they spoke of materializations, Dr. Stewart drew a photograph of Conan Doyle from his pocket, which Dr. Hamilton had taken. "Doyle had visited him, the photo was as clear as could be of a

---

419 Diary, June 18, 1933.

face, surrounded by the ectoplasm – a man with a round face – dark eyebrows etc. quite clear & distinct. He gave it to me to look at while he searched for one of an Elizabeth [Katie] King who said she was of the 17th century, was remaining in the lower plane to help her father who had been earthbound, but who was being freed. Mrs. Stewart seemed most anxious for me to see the photograph. It may relate to the John King of that period, who was in part a guide – mentioned by Dr. Sharp – to me." Mackenzie King believed what the Stewarts confided in him about Hamilton's psychic investigations because of Dr. Stewart's leading position at the Ninette tuberculosis sanatorium and because of his stature as president of the Manitoba Historical Society.

Dr. Stewart was in close touch with Hamilton and offered to write him to arrange a meeting so that he could show King "some of his strange photographs." For King this possibility of scientific proof of his belief in life after death was irresistible. "I was holding a picture of dear mother in my hand as Stewart took the one of Doyle from his pocket. I said some day I hoped to see a materialization of Mother – I should not be surprised if that may even come on the visit to Dr. Hamilton & of Max too. It is possibly to this that all is leading."

King followed up the Stewarts' introduction by writing Hamilton directly from Prince Albert on August 7, 1933. "I have been promising myself for many years past the pleasure of seeing something of the work of which you gave an account before the British Association for the Advancement of Science, and shall be pleased if you can spare me a little of your time on Sunday the 20th." After receiving an invitation to meet with the Hamiltons in Winnipeg, he again felt "this is to be the reward of all my journey, to see the photographs of the Doctor's 'materializations' – with the possibility even of seeing something which may reveal one of the dearly loved ones, mother or Max or father or Bell. Whatever comes it will be one of the really great experiences of life & will be another milestone mark in psychic research."[420]

Dr. Hamilton's interest in psychic phenomena may have been deepened by the death of one of his three-year old twin boys, Arthur, during the flu epidemic of 1918-1919. When Mackenzie King met him in August 1933, he described their encounter in his daily journal – transcribed by F.A. McGregor in the online diary – as "one of the

---

420 Stewart to King, July 25, 1933. Diary, July 23, 1933. King to Dr. Hamilton, August 7, 1933. Diary, August 13, 1933.

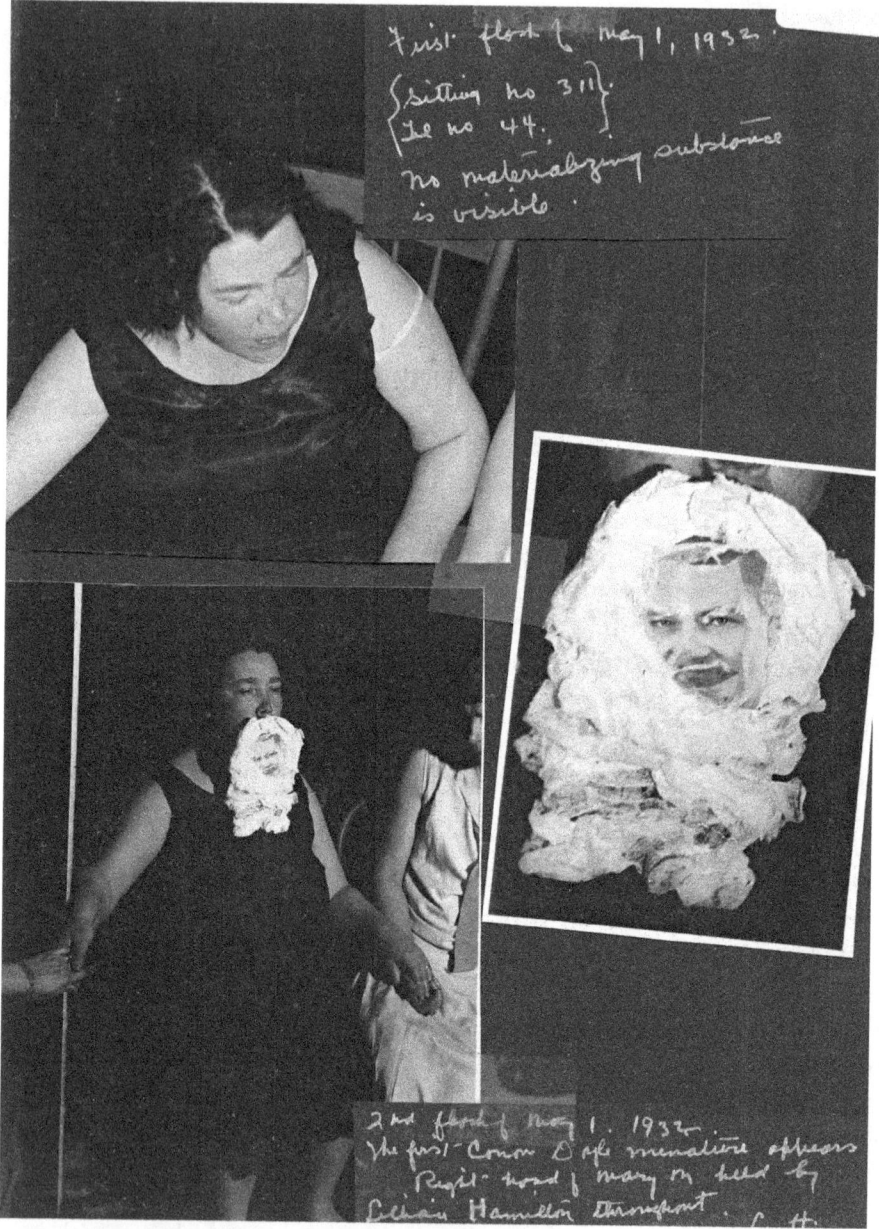

Figure 38: Medium Mary Marshall with the first Arthur Conan Doyle teleplasm, May 1, 1932. Copy also in King fonds.

really memorable days of my life. It has worked out just as I believed it would but beyond all expectations." He noted that the Dr. "practices

Figure 39: T.G. and Lillian Hamilton with their children Margaret, Glen, and James, 1932.

at large in Winnipeg & attends hospitals, is known as a 'spiritualist,' a term he does not care for but [does] not seek to combat ... Hamilton says that while the University would not allow him to lecture on his experiments, etc. in their building, that now he speaks in Churches, Universities, etc. in Winnipeg with full approval and to very large audiences."

Margaret Hamilton recalled that "Father picked up Mr. King at the Fort Garry Hotel, and brought him to our home for Sunday lunch. We had no other guests, just our family. The two men spent all afternoon sitting in our living room. Dad brought out photo after photo and King asked question after question. He appeared to be absolutely fascinated by the measures that were taken, and by the things that were revealed. He was particularly impressed by some of the trance communications from Robert Louis Stevenson." Because of the very limited time available to King on his speaking tour, "He never took part in a seance."[421]

---

421 Diary, August 20, 1933. "Interview with Margaret Hamilton Bach, November 26, 1980," 24.

Figure 40: Mary Marshall and W.B. (Barney) Cooper seated next to the teleplasm of the spirit Lucy Warnock, March 10, 1930. Copy also in King fonds.

The photographs TGH and Lillian Hamilton showed Mackenzie King were of "teleplasmic" formations, partially visible manifestations of spiritual entities. The photographs showed small images of the famous British Baptist preacher Charles Haddon Spurgeon (1834-1892); the fallen soldier Raymond Lodge; former British prime minister William Ewart Gladstone (1809-1898); and the writer and spiritualist Arthur Conan Doyle (1859-1930). Doyle was not only the author of the popular Sherlock Holmes mysteries but also of *The History of Spiritualism* and *The Coming of the Fairies*, an account of the controversial Cottingley fairies photographs, on sale at a bookstore during his visit to Winnipeg. King also mentioned in his diary "the marvellous picture of Lucy Warnock – and the marvellous picture of the ship 'the wreck of the Hesperus' and of Katie King."

Sir Arthur Conan Doyle had shown "Startling Spirit Photographs" and discussed photos of ectoplasm as part of his illustrated lecture "Proofs of Immortality," presented at the 1,800-seat Walker Theatre in Winnipeg in July 1923. Tickets ranged from 50 cents to $2 [$8.50 to $34 in 2023 dollars]. The *Winnipeg Evening Tribune* reported that the spirit and psychic photographs shown by Sir Arthur "were most remarkable and made a deep impression on the audience. He declared each and every picture he showed was genuine, and there is not the least doubt in the world that such is his belief." He had attended a séance held by Dr. Hamilton's group circle, with its first medium Elizabeth Poole, on the day of his arrival in Winnipeg on July 1 but did not mention this experience in his lecture because Hamilton did not go public with his psychic investigations until 1926.

Sir Arthur did refer to the Hamilton séance in his account of his North American tour, *Our Second American Adventure*, describing a striking case of telekinesis. When he stretched out his hand in front of the séance cabinet containing a small table, "it was like a restless dog in a kennel, springing, tossing, beating up against the supports, and finally bounding out with a velocity which caused me to get quickly out of the way. It ended by rising up in the air while our finger-tips were on it and remaining up for an appreciable period." Doyle informed his audience at the Walker Theatre, "When I consider the wonderful psychical phenomena of the one circle seen with my own eyes and the religious atmosphere of the other [a spiritualist service he had attended], I came away with the conclusion that Winnipeg stands very high among the places we have visited for its psychic possibilities. There are several Spiritualist churches and a number of local mediums of good repute."[422]

Hamilton showed King the psychic laboratory he had set up in his home at 185 Kelvin Street and introduced him to Elizabeth Poole, his first medium, during the afternoon. Doyle had referred to her in 1923 as a "small, pleasant-faced woman from the Western Highlands of Scotland" whose "psychic gifts" were "both mental and physical." In 1933, King recorded that "While at the Hamiltons, Mrs. Poole, an elderly white haired fat & dumpy little body appeared" and that she was also shown in one of the photographs Hamilton had given him. "She is a simple person, uneducated etc. but quite conscious of the fact that she is playing a very real part & making a real contribution to science."[423]

Hamilton's photographs lent great authority and credence to his other claims of contact with the Beyond such as spirit dictation and spirit descriptions of the plane of existence "behind the veil." "They began to read to me extracts from what has been received from Robert

---

422 "Conan Doyle Lectures on Spirit Phenomena: Noted British Author Convinces Audience of Sincerity in His Beliefs," *Winnipeg Evening Tribune*, July 4, 1923, 8. Homer. Rodin, 1217. Conan Doyle, *Our Second American Adventure*, 226-227, 231.

423 Homer. Diary, August 20, 1933.

Figure 41: Dr. T.G. Hamilton in front of the séance cabinet triggering a photo of Elizabeth Poole in trance, mid-1920s.

Louis Stevenson that they are taking down. The daughter has taken most of this – another story of the Donkey – another Prayer and numerous other stories etc. in style and thought & beauty equal to if not superior to anything that Stevenson has written. In their minds (and mine) there is no doubt whatever about it being Stevenson who is sending through these messages, which are to be published with his consent & I think at his request."

King rarely speculated about the continued lives of his mother, father, brother, and sister in the Beyond other than that they were instruments for carrying out God's will on earth. Dr. Hamilton provided him with a wider conception of the continued spiritual development of the departed on other planes "beyond the veil." "Hamilton told me of a wonderful vision one of the mediums had of

Stevenson – walking away as it were into the light of another region – having gone up higher ... he agrees all pass on with just what they have of character here. He spoke of one person describing the souls wandering in darkness – would create great pity – those that have lost themselves here & have not yet found the light hereafter."

King and most spiritualists believed that when they were in a séance with a medium that they were communicating with a spirit guide or control in the Beyond who put them in contact with other spirits. One of the Hamilton group's main spirit guides was Frederic W.H. Myers (1843-1901), one of the founders of the Society for Psychical Research in 1882. Hamilton "told me [he] had had numerous talks [with him] as well with David Livingstone – the explorer – with Lincoln (I think), with Carlyle – with Meyers [sic] who seems to be the one working largely with him in arranging the experiments. He read me some passages of sublime beauty from some of those beyond – Said Spurgeon had said he could not go on for a while for having preached hell fire etc. on earth when he knew there was no such thing. They all speak of getting rid of fear & substituting love. Hamilton & his wife are strong Christians & believe in all as a revelation of Christ & God. What they told me of what they are told through the mediums in trance, by their control, accords with Christian belief." Regarding Dr. Sharp, Etta Wriedt's control whose anti-Christian statements so upset King in April 1933, Hamilton agreed that Sharp's "attitude re Christ is due to a similar attitude while on earth from which he is not yet free."[424]

Eighteen months and forty séances after Mackenzie King and Joan Patteson had first met the direct-voice medium Etta Wriedt, T. Glen Hamilton once again allowed King and Patteson to feel that they, too, were taking part in psychic research that was based on solid scientific investigation, that had without question established contact with spiritual entities who in turn were working to establish contact with the physical world, and that Spiritualism was about to transform the earth. "He believes it is only a short time before heavenly voices & choruses will be broadcast on the radio. In the experiments, he says the persons tell him how they are operating to 'build up' the ectoplasm – give him directions when 'to fire' to press the button for the photographs etc. That it is clear they are just beginning to experiment as we are, and have, as they themselves

---

[424] Diary, August 20, 1933.

say, much still to learn – everything in fact … He showed me his dark [séance] room in which the experiments were made & the photographs taken, the cameras set in place – the apparatus to create magnetic music, e.g. 'Jingle Bells' – the bell which the spirits ring themselves as a signal, the equipment generally; finally he gave me a folder full of photographs – Doyle, Raymond Lodge, Spurgeon, Lucy Warnock & Katie King."[425]

For Mackenzie King, his meeting with Dr. Hamilton was another transformative experience heralding the imminent merging of the spiritual with the physical world. "The afternoon was quite the most remarkable one – save the direct voice experiences with Mrs. Wriedt – I have had in my life," he entered in his diary. "It is amazing beyond all words. It has come, as I felt on my journey it would, as a reward of the effort I have put forth, as a greater step in knowledge and guidance. I believe absolutely in all Hamilton & his wife and daughter have told me. Their children will go on, beginning with this knowledge – and in this way what is in doubt now will become accepted belief soon. The scriptures will take on new & literal & clearer meaning; the world itself will evolve to a higher plane – one can see a new significance in 'the second coming' and its nearness, but in a way a little different from that accepted by many." As he returned to Ottawa by train, King read one of Hamilton's articles and other spiritual pieces, one of which impressed him because it contained the phrase "subjective clairvoyance." "That I believe," he entered in his diary, "is a gift I am beginning to possess. Another great stage of advance has been reached, all too marvellous for words."

He thought the photograph of Katie King showed a spiritual beauty that was like Joan Patteson in appearance and showed her all the Hamilton photographs upon his return to Ottawa. He also read to her the January 1933 *Psychic Science* article reporting on the Katie King manifestations. "This was my gift to her, this new knowledge. I was about to say like your little girl 'Nancy' when I pointed out the face in the first photograph. Joan at the same moment exclaimed that is the face I saw in my vision – at the time I passed over – or nearly did – one who came to greet me & said 'You don't know me,' which I seemed to know – but did not know & which I came later to know was my little girl grown up. That is all quite strange

---

425 Idem.

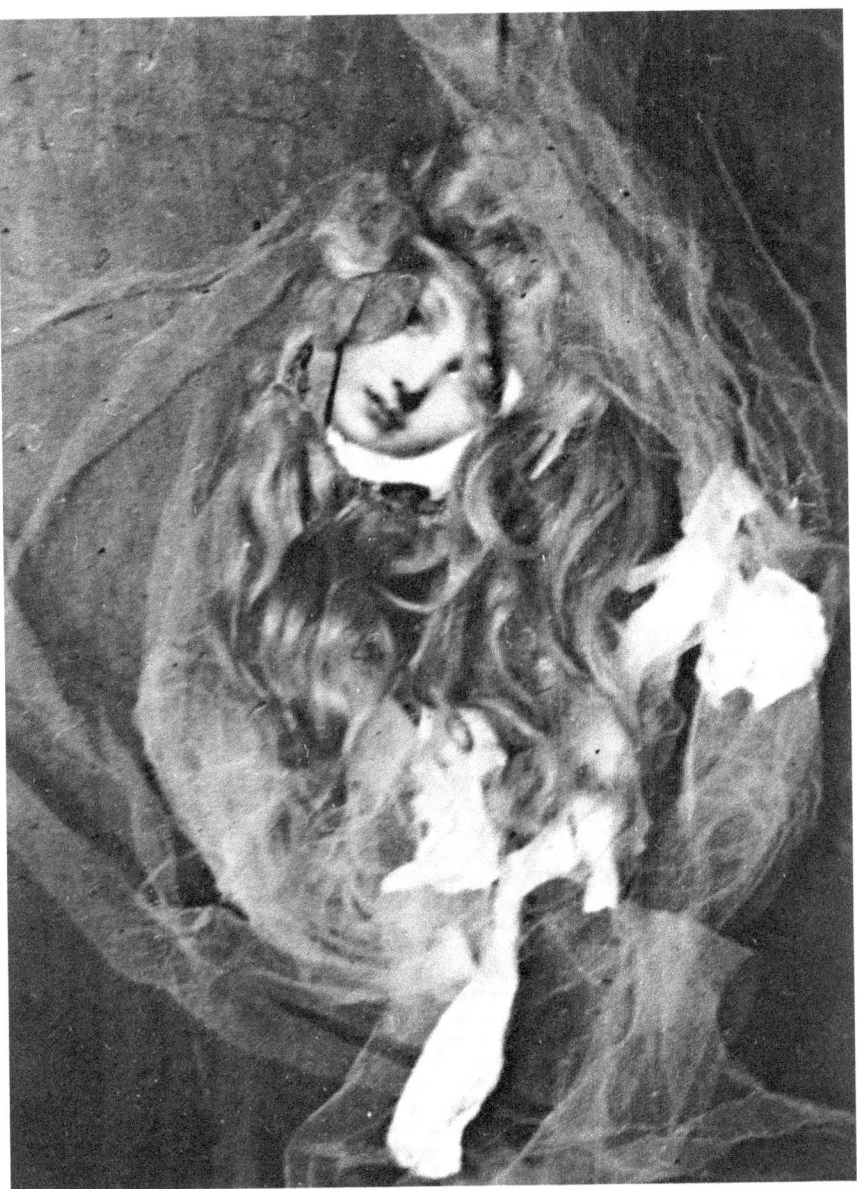

*Figure 42: Teleplasm of Katie King, November 12, 1930.
Copy also in King fonds.*

– remarkable & significant. There is more mystery, of wonder, of charm, of beauty than ever."[426]

---

426 Idem.

A week after his visit, King thanked the Hamiltons for what he called "one of the most memorable experiences of my life." "What you are achieving for science and religion and humanity; what you have received and recorded is what will be afterwards in my thoughts and remembrance. I expected very much from what I heard of your researches from others, but the results surpassed all expectations…through you a great blessing is about to be bestowed upon the world. Had I not seen the photographs you have, and heard from your lips what you read and told me, also had I not had some previous experiences of my own and some knowledge of physical science, I just could not have believed that it was possible to proceed the lengths you have."[427]

In one of the continual coincidences that King believed were not mere chance events but communications from his father, he received a loose-leaf book from Margaret Hamilton, Dr. Hamilton's daughter, in the morning mail on September 28, 1933, containing thirty-nine pages of further "communications" from Charles Spurgeon, Robert Louis Stevenson and others received by entranced mediums. "These I read aloud to Joan tonight – they are quite beautiful, reveal the nearness of the other world to us, and the growth of mind and spirit. They help to relate our lives immediately to the lives of those who have passed away and the life beyond to our present life."

On the way to his office in the Parliament Building, he read a letter from Mrs. Hamilton thanking him for his visit in August "and what it had meant to them." "I cannot tell you how much we appreciated your visit," Lillian Hamilton wrote. "Your deep and sympathetic and understanding interest in 'our subject' has indeed come to us all as a most joyous discovery. I cannot tell you how much just knowing this has given us courage to go forward at all costs, no matter how hard and difficult the way before us may at present seem to be. To share with you our 'new revelation' we will always deem a very real and lasting privilege." King in turn assured Dr. Hamilton, "I shall promise to safeguard everything you tell or send me, and I shall be more grateful for what you have time and inclination to share than words can express. I shall always look back upon that afternoon, the day I

---

427 University of Manitoba Archives and Special Collections (subsequently cited as UMASC), King to Dr. Hamilton, August 27, 1933. Published in part in Val Werier, "Mackenzie King's Secret: Newly Disclosed Letters Reveal 'Spiritual' Link," *Winnipeg Tribune*, December 14, 1951, 1.

should say, spent with you as a place of new and higher beginning in my life and life's interests. I feel I have come to a new plane of existence itself."[428]

When King reached his office, he found John David MacDonald from Winnipeg with a copy of the Sept. 29 to Oct. 5, 1932, overseas edition of the *Daily Sketch* containing articles on Hamilton's séances and psychic experiments which TGH had asked him to deliver in person. MacDonald participated in the Hamilton circle séances, at times as an auxiliary medium, from 1927 to 1936. He informed King that TGH worked until 2 am to arrange his cameras "so as to have them snap in quick succession & so that those in the beyond can touch the flash at the right moment – this by 'compressed air' arrangement from the basement."

TGH also wrote King to thank him for the gift of his brother's book, *Nerves and Personal Power*, and promised to send him "several more photographs of particular interest." "We realize more and more how great are the difficulties that confront us in this work. Nevertheless we are equally impressed with its supremely vital importance and the necessity of presenting these matters from time to time in such form as may seem practical to the public at large." King thanked Hamilton for the articles about his psychic investigations, which he had added to his "Hamilton fyle [sic]," and affirmed, "I have seen nothing which seems to me to be more interesting and in every way more worth while than the research work to which you and Mrs. Hamilton have given yourselves, not only so unselfishly and unreservedly, but with such exceptional qualifications and skill."[429]

He had believed since he was a student at university that – as he informed Dr. Stewart at the Ninette tuberculosis sanatorium – he was being guided by God and members of King's family, His ministering angels. Hamilton's psychic research appealed so strongly to King because Hamilton asserted that he was not only in communication with what he called trance personalities in the Beyond but that these spirit entities also were guiding and shaping his experiments to prove the existence of life after death. Hamilton's fusion of spirituality with Christianity also appealed to Mackenzie King.

---

428   Diary, September 29, 1933. Lillian Hamilton to King, September 25, 1933. King to Dr. Hamilton, published in Val Werier.

429   Diary, September 29, 1933. Hamilton to King, October 31, 1933. King to Hamilton, November 16, 1933.

In 1933, *Light* published seven additional articles by Hamilton about his experiments. The paper subtitled two of his pieces on the C.H. Spurgeon teleplasms "Efforts to 'Put Through' Religious Teachings from the 'Other Side'" and "Stupendous Re-statement of the Central Claims of Christianity." Hamilton described how in deep trance the medium Mary Marshall also became a direct-voice medium through whom the Baptist preacher, who died in 1892, spoke to the sitters. "His voice (or rather, the Medium's voice, under the dominations of the C.H.S. personality) took on, on these occasions, an entirely new timbre – loud and compelling, stern and denunciatory, tender and beseeching by turns." He concluded the Spurgeon articles with one of his few expressions in print of his religious worldview. "Accepting these findings as sound, and accepting also the teachings of the surviving Spurgeon as authentic," he proposed,

> have we not before us what amounts to a stupendous re-statement of the central claims of Christianity – the reality of a spiritual world; the certainty of man's survival; the reality of a living and loving Christ; the truth of His teachings and His way of life? Cautiously, indeed, must we reach out in this direction, but it would seem perhaps that we have here encountered a series of events foreshadowing that time foreseen by Myers – a time when the experimental method of research shall yet yield an extended and enduring basis of fact for many of our most cherished beliefs in the realm of religion and faith.[430]

Hamilton sent King two of the Spurgeon articles published in October. *Light* called the articles "the story of one of the most interesting and most important sustained experiments in the records of Psychical Research or Spiritualism" and referred to Hamilton's "world-wide reputation as a careful and reliable scientific investigator of psychic phenomena." At the end of the Spurgeon series, the paper commended Hamilton's "summing-up to the very earnest consideration of readers who may not yet be completely convinced of the possibility of proving Survival by experimental means."[431]

---

430 Hamilton, "Has C.H. Spurgeon Returned?: Efforts to 'Put Through' Religious Teachings From the 'Other Side,'" 679, and "The C.H. Spurgeon Case," 695.

431 Hamilton, "The C.H. Spurgeon Case," 628, and "Has C.H. Spurgeon Returned?: What the Cameras Revealed and the 'Voices' Described," 645. "Evi-

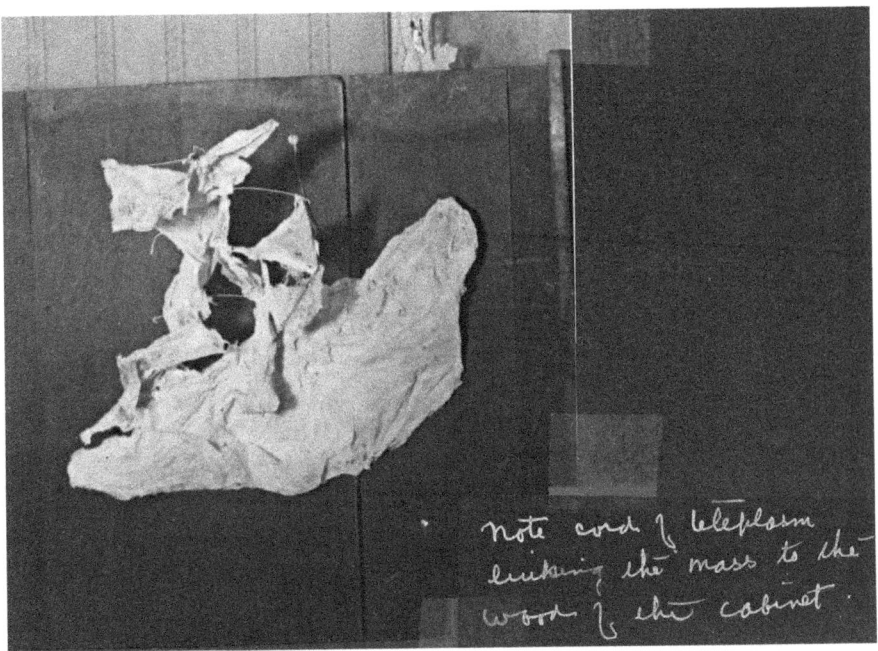

Figure 43: The ship teleplasm that floated through the air, June 4, 1930.

Unlike his rejection of Dr. Sharp's anti-Christian messages, Mackenzie King did not question Hamilton's claims about the guiding role played by spirit entities in his teleplasm experiments and thanked him for sending the articles on the Spurgeon case. "I have read them with an interest only second to what I experienced at the time you were so kind as to give me at first hand much of the information which they contain. I only wish that the readers of 'Light' might have the privilege of knowing you personally, as well as reading your marvellous researches."[432]

Impressed by Dr. Hamilton's professional reputation, personal bearing, and battery of cameras in his psychic laboratory, Mackenzie King had no doubts about his genuineness. After Hamilton's death from a heart attack on April 7, 1935, he sent condolences to Lillian Hamilton six weeks after the October 1935 election that returned him as Prime Minister. "You will not be surprised to know that I experience a very real sense of personal loss in the doctor's passing," he wrote. "I felt a very close attachment to him, and was as you know profoundly interested in his work of psychical research. I have looked

---

dence of Survival," *Light*, 53:2756 (November 3, 1933).
432 King to Hamilton, November 25, 1933.

upon him as one of the great pioneers in that field of thought and discovery. I now feel that, not only our country, but science, and even civilization itself has lost one of its great servants." To another mutual spiritualist friend in Winnipeg he added, "I feel that in his death our country, and indeed, the scientific world, has lost a truly great man, one who, in the field of psychic research, has enlarged the horizons of human knowledge. In more ways than one, I regard Dr. Hamilton's death as a national loss. How I wish I might have seen more of him and of his work. The glimpse I had of the latter will ever remain one of the really great experiences of my life."[433]

Stan McMullin noted that King's condolences to Lillian Hamilton asking her to "'let me know a little more of the circumstances of the Doctor's death. I shall be interested, too, in knowing something of your own experiences at and since that time…If it is not placing too great a strain upon you, do please send me a line or two, and tell me of the things which you know I shall wish to hear'" was King "wondering if Glen Hamilton would be able to get a message to his widow from the spirit side."

Lillian thanked King for the condolences he sent her and her family. "To have you remember us in the midst of your exceedingly busy life," she wrote the Prime Minister, "touched us all very deeply indeed, and we cannot help but feel that our Premier is also our friend." She reported that she was continuing her husband's psychic investigations, that further telekinetic phenomena and teleplasms had been received "under the same strict conditions as those imposed by Dr. Hamilton himself," and that the deceased was communicating with Lillian and her circle from the Beyond. She claimed that among the personalities TGH reported having met "over there" was King's brother, Macdougall King, and sent him a copy of the notes she had made of the sitting.

The medium at that séance stated that her husband had a message for her and that he had another man with him. "He says his name is King and that he has written a book … he met Mr. King over here through his brother." When Mrs. Hamilton did not immediately understand the reference to Max's *Nerves and Personal Power*, the medium stated that the "Dr. tells me to say 'Lillian, you have that book at home.'" She concluded by thanking the PM for "your deep interest

---

433 King to Lillian Hamilton, November 26, 1935 (UMASC). Published in part in Val Werier. King to Kathryn Ross, November 26, 1935.

in his studies ... based on a love for and insight into the deeper aspect of life and truth given only to the few."[434]

Mackenzie King And Intention And Survival

King kept a copy of Hamilton's *Intention and Survival*, his descriptions of his psychic investigations from 1920 to 1935, in his "dark room" in Laurier House where King stored his spiritualist books and records. That the Prime Minister still firmly believed in the veracity of Dr. Hamilton's research a decade after his first meeting with him is indicated when he described first reading the book in March 1943. Chapter 10 of *Intention and Survival*, he noted in his diary, explained the teleplasm phenomena as "the story of how certain entities in the Beyond had sought to construct a ship to make known their existence to Dr. Hamilton and others, and the record of how the whole story related to the trance-personality who claimed he was John King or Henry Morgan who, in the 17th century, was a buccaneer; in recognition of certain services done for King Charles II of England, he was knighted and made governor of Jamaica."

King noted that "Hamilton's book goes on to make clear that John King was a personality who had revealed itself through other mediums to different persons expert in psychical research ... Coty [Katie] King was the daughter, a name well known to students of psychical research. Hamilton refers to one aspect of the Terraplasm [sic] as the first attempt of the psychic personalities to predict a teleplasmic state representation which was finally secured in the late autumn of 1930. The chapter tells of ships' masts falling down, etc." King had seen the photo of the teleplasm representation of a sailing ship, the wreck of the Hesperus, published in *Intention and Survival*, when he first met Dr. Hamilton in 1933.

King's diary reveals how he continued to incorporate Hamilton's psychic research in his magical thinking about human survival after death. While shaving in the morning, he noticed that he had made a perfect swan with black feet with his shaving lather. Joan Patteson subsequently informed him that the film *The Black Swan*, starring

---

434   McMullin, 219. Lillian Hamilton to King, December 13, 1935. "Excerpts from Notes of Sitting held at the Home of Miss Ada Turner, October 15 [1935]." For a discussion of Lillian Hamilton's continuing psychic investigations between 1935 and 1944, see Oates.

Tyrone Power, Maureen O'Hara, and Anthony Quinn, was playing at the Capital Theatre. This made him think, "there may be a special reason why I should take in that play [sic] tonight."

He noticed that the presidential address delivered at the Manitoba Medical College in 1930, "Immortality: An Adventure in Faith," paying tribute to and sent to him by Dr. Hamilton, had been given by Dr. Rennie Swan. King had thanked Hamilton for sending him a copy of Swan's address three months after their meeting in 1933. "I was glad to see that it contained the recognition it did of your research work…It does seem to me all important that… those interested in promoting psychical research should never fail to emphasize that its results are evidencing the reality and truth of which much has hitherto been most baffling to human understanding and accepted only on faith." In addition to the Dr. Swan reference, King saw that the envelope of a letter from Jack Miner of the Miner Migratory Bird Foundation displayed "a number of Canadian wild geese flying through the air. Strong resemblance to swans … these 3 communications coming in this closely related way cause me to feel assured that what I have to record from now on is true in all respects." Patteson also "felt sure that there was something in what I had told her of Dr. T. Glen Hamilton's researches which made her feel sure that they were, in some way, connected with what was portrayed in 'The Black Swan.'"

When King read Chapter 10 of *Intention and Survival*, "Teleplasms Related to the John and Katie King Trance Personalities," it was obvious to him that "it was virtually the kind of language and scene which had been portrayed in the film 'The Black Swan' … The chapter tells of ships' masts falling down, etc. This all appeared on the film." He perceived "a parallel right in Canada itself in this year 1943 to the same false ideas and relationships portrayed in 'The Black Swan' which relates to the days of Charles II, men with knee breeches, etc. I felt my soul revolt against the kind of thing that is set forth in this life of Athlone [the Governor General, the Earl of Athlone, at Government House] as the thing toward which those highest in the State should aim." Having found the Henry Morgan connection, he phoned Joan and "told her of what I had read in the book. When I got to bed, the hands of the clock were in a straight line at 11:25. I felt wholly convinced in my own mind that the day's experience was something quite exceptional, and one of the most remarkable and convincing experiences of my whole life. That there was a real purpose behind it. That I was being shown not only the proof of survival, survival of the human personality, but also my real mission and purpose in all my work."[435]

The next day King consulted his copy of Marianne Bayley-Worthington's *My Psychic Life* which Lizzy Lind-af-Hageby had sent him in 1939 and found that a white swan represented good luck. "Some great good is coming to me arising out of apparently evil conditions." At noon, he received a telegram from Churchill that seemed to fulfill the prediction. "In the darkest days Canada, under your leadership, remained confident and true," the British Prime Minister wrote. "Now the days are brighter and when victory is won, you will be able to look back with just pride upon a record surpassed by none." King recorded in his diary, "The minute I read this message, I felt that the symbol of the swan representing good luck and the black feet of the white swan representing good coming to me out of apparently evil conditions, had been fulfilled."[436]

Mackenzie King's correspondence, diaries and reactions to *Intention and Survival* demonstrate his complete acceptance for over a decade of the spiritual truths revealed to him by T. Glen Hamilton and his psychic investigations. These truths about discarnate spirits communicating with and assisting those on earth would help to guide his "real mission and purpose in all my work." The concluding chapter to Volume 1 of *The Spiritualist Prime Minister* analyzes how Ellen Elliott, brought in psychic contact with Jesus Christ in séances with one of Lillian Hamilton's mediums, replicated this Christ Presence with King during the height of World War II. Elliott's interaction with the PM shows the very impact of occult and spiritualist beliefs on Mackenzie King that his executors had so ardently sought to obliterate from the historical record.

---

435   Diary, March 6, 1943.
436   Diary, December 5, 1939, and March 7, 1943. Secretary of State for Dominion Affairs to King, March 6, 1943.

CHAPTER 13

Mackenzie King, Ellen Elliott, and The Christ Presence

Mackenzie King first came to know Ellen Elliott in August 1941 when he signed the contract with the Macmillan Company of Canada for his collection of speeches and addresses, *Canada at Britain's Side*. He sent her text for the book, and she sent him galley proofs. Macmillan had published King's *The Message of the Carillon and Other Addresses* in 1927, a 1935 edition of *Industry and Humanity*, and was just issuing Dr. Glen Hamilton's *Intention and Survival: Psychical Research Studies and the Bearing of Intentional Actions by Trance Personalities on the Problem of Human Survival*. The PM entered in his diary, "Called on Miss Elliott at the MacMillan [sic] Company and had a most interesting talk with her. Was greatly surprised at the extent of her interest in psychical phenomena. She has been giving study to the matter for 18 years. MacMillan's, at present, are getting out a book on photography by Dr. Hamilton of Winnipeg."[437]

Ellen Charlotte Thirza Elliott was born in Eastleigh, Hampshire, in 1900 and immigrated to Canada in 1920 with her parents and twenty-three-year-old brother John, a machinist. Her father, John Elliott, aged fifty-one and born in Twickenham, Middlesex, was a house decorator. Her mother, Edith Hibbs Elliott, aged forty-six, was

---

[437] Diary, August 5, 1942. When he received copies of *The Message of the Carillon* from Macmillan in 1927, King entered in his diary, "I shall ever believe <u>The Message of the Carillon</u> was a direct inspiration from dear Mother, that her spirit was in all that therein is found expressed." Diary, December 16, 1927. Cited by Henderson, 22.

Figure 44: Ellen Elliott, 1941.

born in Dorset and worked as a dress maker. The family lived at 444 Clinton Street in Toronto, a good middle-class neighbourhood. Ellen married the thirty-five-year-old English-born Cecil Booth in Toronto on January 5, 1927. Their marriage certificate listed Booth's occupation as clerk and Ellen's as secretary. The religious denomination for both was Anglican.

Ellen began working for the Macmillan Company of Canada in 1920, became the private secretary to Hugh Eayrs, Macmillan's president, in 1925 and the secretary of the company in 1937. She signed her first letters to Lillian Hamilton in the fall of 1935 as E. Elliott Booth but subsequently corresponded as Ellen Elliott. After Eayrs' sudden heart attack in 1940, Elliot was appointed head of publishing. According to Ruth Panofsky, "among the first women to hold a senior position in Canadian publishing, she helped consolidate the growth of Macmillan from a branch-plant operation to a mature publishing house…[her] publishing expertise was fundamental to the company's survival."

Elliott worked closely with writers such as Frederick Philip Grove, W.O. Mitchell, P.K Page, and E.J. Pratt. In 1944, Macmillan published Page's first novel *The Sun and the Moon* (under the pseudonym Judith Cape) after Elliott negotiated with Eileen J. Garrett's Creative Age Press in New York to purchase one thousand copies from Macmillan for an American edition. "A consummate publisher, she guided writers through the publication process with care. Between 1940 and 1946, for example, four of her Macmillan authors won Governor General's literary awards," Panofsky noted: E.J. Pratt, *Brébeuf and His Brethren* (1940); Ringuet, *Thirty Acres* (1940); Ross Munro, *Gauntlet* to *Overlord* (1945); and Frederick Philip Grove, *In Search of Myself* (1946). "In 1944, her salary was raised to $5,000 [$86,500 in 2023 dollars], half that of president Robert Huckvale, in recognition of her valuable service to the company."[438]

Elliott told the twentieth anniversary convention of the Canadian Authors' Association in 1941 that she read hundreds of manuscripts submitted for publication to Macmillan every year. She further revealed her interest in psychic matters when she presented King with a complimentary copy of Anne Elizabeth Blochin's *That Dog of Yours* as consolation for his loss of Pat I. "When the book was being written we discovered we had a mutual interest in psychic research: her investigations have dealt with the survival of animals, while my own experiments have proved conclusively (to me, at least) the survival of human personalities. So to the astonishment of both of us a chapter called 'Have Animals Souls?' found its way into the book." She had learned of the PM's own "generous and open-minded attitude towards psychics from a very dear friend of mine in Winnipeg, the widow of the late Dr. T. Glen Hamilton whose experiments are known to you."[439]

Mackenzie King was not the only author with a strong interest in Spiritualism Ellen Elliott dealt with. When she invited Julian Cross, the wealthy businessman and mining pioneer who had financially backed the publication of *Intention and Survival*, to participate in a séance in Toronto in March 1942, she explained, "My group has three writers who live in Montreal, London, Ontario, and Aurora, respectively, so it is not very often that we can get together." Ruth Panofsky recorded that among the writers Ellen worked with, E.J. Pratt "shared Elliott's interest in spiritualism, and he and his wife Viola attended occasional seances in her home."

The poet and his wife had attended séances with the American direct-voice trumpet medium William Cartheuser in a home circle led by Jenny O'Hara Pincock in St. Catharines, Ontario, as early as 1928 and 1929. Pincock describes their participation in her *Trails of Truth* where they appear anonymously as "Dr. X, Ph.D., M.A." and "Mrs. X, B.A." She advised readers that Dr. X "deems it advisable to

---

438 Panofsky, *The Literary Legacy*, 128, 140, 141, 132.

439 Diary, August 8, 1941, and October 27, 1941. Elliott, 21. Elliott to King, October 25, 1941.

Figure 45: Ellen Elliott (left) with E.J. Pratt and Viola Pratt (centre), at an autographing party for Pratt's Dunkirk *in the Simpson's book department, Toronto, October 1941.*

remain incognito." Pratt in turn wrote the foreword to Pincock's posthumous poetry collection *Hidden Springs*, dedicated to her husband Robert Newton Pincock who died after a serious illness in 1928. The fathers of Newton Pincock and Pratt were Newfoundland clergymen. After Newton's marriage to Jenny, Pratt was frequently a guest at their home in St. Catharines. "They had worked out for themselves a philosophy of life which brought serenity in the midst of unabated illness. They spent many hours relating to me their spiritual experiences, and I could not but admire the way they bulwarked themselves against suffering by the steadfastness of their faith." In Jenny's transcendental poetry, Pratt wrote in 1950, "Newton became as real to her as in physical existence, and, when she joined him a year or so ago [1948], the journey was like going from one room to another in the same family dwelling."[440]

---

440 McMaster University Archives, Macmillan Company of Canada, Author Correspondence (subsequently cited as McMaster), Elliott to Cross, March 23, 1942. Panofsky, *The Literary Legacy*, 138. Pincock, 67. Pratt, vii. On Pincock, see

Mackenzie King had developed a similar imaginative relationship with his departed mother, father, sister, and brother. In 1930, he had a dream in which he heard his mother's voice and recorded, "It was her voice but it had a <u>celestial</u> quality about it which surpasses <u>anything</u> I have ever heard. It was most beautiful, brought a peace and a joy to my heart that was unfathomable." Pratt wrote in his foreword to Pincock's poetry, "The reader must assume a belief in psychic manifestations to overcome any sense of incredibility. With that assumption the tale becomes not just an account of a dream, but a description as natural as that of a search in daytime told by a friend in whose sincerity and truthfulness one absolutely believes…It is like hearing the voice of your friend when you are certain that he is within hail for an answer."[441]

In Pincock's and Viola's transcription of the Pratts' séance with William Cartheuser on September 11, 1928, and Viola's on November 28, 1929, hands caressed Pincock's hair and shoulders in the absolute darkness. Pratt's deceased mother patted her son and daughter-in-law on their hands and heads and tried to wrench from Pincock's hand the pencil she was using to record the séance. Her hands materialized and took a pencil from Pratt's fingers. Other communicating spirits were Newton Pincock, Pratt's father, Viola's mother, and father, and Cartheuser's spirit guide, Dr. Anderson. Newton talked to Pratt about his new book and pressed flowers in the sitters' hands. In Viola Pratt's 1929 séance, a flower was also pressed between a sitter's fingers. "Strong, cool breezes were felt by all." Newton gave Pincock an osteopathic treatment on her neck "exactly as he was accustomed to give me in life…I can swear before any court in the land *that it was my husband who touched me*." Viola conversed with her two premature babies she had lost. A luminous trumpet drifted slowly and peacefully about. Newton Pincock sang a duet and Dr. Anderson gave a beautiful prayer.[442]

Describing these sittings in his biography *E.J. Pratt: The Master Years 1927-1964*, David Pitt affirmed, "Pratt was convinced that what he heard and saw was all it purported to be. For him, moreover, it was,

---

"Jenny O'Hara Pincock: Trails of Truth" in McMullin.

441 Diary, December 9, 1930. Pratt, vii-viii. For Pincock's spiritualism and séances with William Cartheuser, see McMullin and Beth A. Robertson.

442 Pincock, 66-80, 119-130.

as Viola has said and subsequent letters of his own confirm, the final 'clench of evidence' of human immortality and of the spiritual basis of the cosmic order." Pitt noted that "So far as is known Pratt attended no more séances after the winter of 1929, apart from an occasional 'sitting' at the home of Ellen Elliott, Hugh Eayrs' long-time secretary… But for Pratt and his wife, Jenny Pincock's séances had served their purpose. The question of human immortality was for them no longer one that raised any doubts. Nearly a decade after the sittings ended, Pratt was able to write with conviction of his 'ineradicable belief' in our spiritual survival beyond the grave…there is no question, though he was generally secretive about it, that the experience remained for him one of the pivotal events in his life."

The poet refrained from branding himself as a spiritualist in public. According to his biographer, "Pratt would occasionally 'confess,' very confidentially to intimate friends, that his poetry was often composed by 'direct inspiration' from 'the spirits.'" When he met with the writer Margaret Furness MacLeod in Montreal in the 1940s, "we discussed spiritualism, the occult, ghosts, mediums, and the possibility of tapping some wave-lengths or unseen forces. He confessed that much of his best work came in a mysterious way, almost like automatic writing, but this he never discussed, as the public might take a dim view of such a belief." When Mackenzie King met "Professor Pratt of Victoria" in 1930 at a dinner given by the art critic Newton MacTavish, he described him as "a young poet – a very fine type of man. I liked him exceedingly." Five years later, he "felt impelled" to read Pratt's *The Titanic* and wrote that "The poem is exceedingly well written and I enjoyed immensely the pleasure of reading it." But there is no indication in King's diaries that the Prime Minister was aware of Pratt's participation in séances and his strong belief in Spiritualism.[443]

Ellen Elliott's beliefs in Spiritualism and psychic phenomena were greatly fortified by her contacts with the Hamiltons and their mediums. What the Hamiltons did not reveal in *Intention and Survival,* or its sequel *Is Survival a Fact?*, was the appearance of a Christ presence in Winnipeg séances in 1925 and, after TGH's death, from 1936 to the end of 1939. Lillian Hamilton assembled this historical record of "Phenomena that would appear possibly to throw light on the nature of Christ as a Person, and his possible re-manifestation among men

---

443 Pitt, 49, 50, 52. Diary, December 8, 1930, and November 17, 1935.

Figure 46: Mary Marshall's deep-trance drawing of her Jesus vision, April 9, 1933.

in some objective or tangible form" in a thirteen-page letter to her daughter Margaret dated September 25, 1939. She found the first references to Christ in the séance records of deep-trance writings obtained from Elizabeth Poole and communicated by W.T. Stead and Robert Louis Stevenson on May 19, 24 and 31, 1925. "I shall in glory see His Face. Christ shall come and call on me…Christ the Lord shall come…Wait for Him in prayer. I will then His Glory see…What of the night. Christ is coming. He is not far away. The might of the King will reign. Christ is coming."[444]

In *Is Survival a Fact?*, Margaret Hamilton cited a deep-trance script from W.T. Stead transmitted in May 1925 via Elizabeth Poole, which Margaret interpreted as foreshadowing the great death and destruction of World War II. "What of the night? Behold, it is fulfilled! Men of all nations, waking and sleeping, are in fear, and run from the carnage! Christ is coming! He is not far away! The might of the King shall reign!" In the book, she also published Mary Marshall's April 9, 1933, deep-trance drawing vision of Jesus with penitents and a December 1943 trance script message from T.G. Hamilton to Lillian that she

---

444 The September 25, 1939 "Letter to Margaret Hamilton Bach from Lillian Hamilton" is posted in its entirety on the University of Manitoba Libraries digital collections website https://digitalcollections.lib.umanitoba.ca/islandora/object/uofm%3A1409947 p. 1.

Figure 47: Isabella (Isabel) Keil Farquhar, 1937.

entitled, "A Vision of the Christ." In the spirit world, TGH transmitted to Marshall, "I had wandered off by myself and in the distance I saw a great dazzling light like the sun, only softer, and as I gazed at the light it slowly took form between me and the crowd who stood watching, and the lovely form of Jesus Christ stood in all His loveliness. He smiled and stretched out His hands in blessing. Then the scene changed and He had in His arms a snow-white lamb. He stood transfigured. Then He spoke to the large company of people who stood about, and taught them. I could hear His voice from where I stood."

In her letter to Margaret on September 25, 1939, Lillian Hamilton recorded that there were many more such visions that appeared to several additional mediums. A year after Dr. Hamilton's death in 1935, Christ manifestations reappeared with a new young medium, Isabella Farquhar, whose mediumistic faculties Lillian Hamilton discovered in February 1936. The principal spirit entities communicating with Isabella were TGH himself and Robert Louis Stevenson. The séance record described her Vision C in February: "Wakes from sleep and says she has seen a river 'with trees on either hand.' Also that she has seen the Master. He is tall with lovely hands." In March, "the Christ visions became more frequent and took on a prophetic note in some instances...Vision C. In extremely deep trance in the downstairs living room following the regular sitting. [Isabel] awakes and says she has seen the Master, that the heavens opened and she saw Him holding His arms to the world. The world needed Him."

Lillian recorded that the latter part of March and beginning of April 1936, "Isabel now and again came to me and complained that she felt as if something were bound tightly about her brow, making it sore, and that drops of water were running down her face." She "seemed to have no idea whatever as to what these sensations might portend, the phenomena of the wounds of Christ being unknown to her so far as could be discovered, and the very word 'stigmata' not in her vocabulary." On Easter Sunday, April 12, Isabel fell into an extremely deep trance in the downstairs living room. "Medium suddenly begins to cry and calls out – 'I did not know I was such a wicked girl. Oh, Jesus, what have I done? Why are you so disappointed? What can I do for You?' She sobs and falls over in her chair profoundly entranced." When Isabel awoke, three small wounds were found on her right hand and five small wounds on her right shoulder. Lillian's son, Dr. Glen Forrester Hamilton (1911-1988), pronounced the wounds to be a stigmata and signed an affidavit of his medical observations. In another séance in April at which both of Lillian's sons, James D. and Glen Hamilton, were present, Isabel became cataleptic and had another Christ vision. "Her voice whispers 'I will come back. I will not leave you alone. They nailed me to a cross. I will come back. I will walk again among men.'"[445]

During the last week of April 1936 occurred the spirit communication Lillian Hamilton published as "The Death of Kitty A.: A Case of Supernormal Cognition" in the April 1937 *Quarterly Transactions BCPS*. Two spirit personalities, Dr. Hamilton and the young Kitty Alder, one of TGH's patients who had moved to British Columbia after her marriage in 1930, manifested to Mary Marshall and Isabel Farquhar three times. The spirit of Kitty was in great distress, calling for her child. Isabel gave a loud cry, moaned and tore her hair as Kitty spoke through her. "Oh, I can't bear it! I can't bear it! Take me back! I didn't want to come here so soon!" Dr. Hamilton informed Mary Marshall that Kitty had died giving birth to a boy who was living and that he was looking after her in the spirit world. Kitty's death and the birth of her son was subsequently confirmed by her mother, Christianna Alder in Vancouver. Both Alders had participated in Hamilton séances during 1927-1929.

In her *Psychic Science* article, Lillian Hamilton reported Isabel's name as "Faith," the name she was called during séances, and described the marked stages when she entered and left the trance state: "(*a*) a brief period of onset in which the subject is excited and manifests various features of a more or less hysterical nature; (*b*) a period of muscular relaxation; (*c*) a cataleptic stage in which there is marked rigidity of the whole body musculature; (*d*) the recovery stage, which lasts anywhere from twenty to thirty minutes to occasionally an hour or more." What Lillian did not report in *Psychic Science* was that the Christ vision appeared again after Kitty's death manifestation. "The Master again appears – Isabel passes into the cataleptic state, breathing is imperceptible, body musculature intensely rigid, arms in the form of a cross. Face takes on the beauty and dignity of death. Her voice, which is now a voice of moving power, speaks softly, 'I will again walk with men.'"[446]

Lillian did inform Stanley De Brath of Isabel's Christ visions a few months after he resigned the editorship of *Psychic Science* in April

---

445 Margaret Hamilton, 98. "Letter to Margaret Hamilton Bach from Lillian Hamilton," September 25, 1939, pp. 2, 3, 4, 5.

446 Lillian Hamilton, "The Death of Kitty A.," 11, 8. "Letter to Margaret Hamilton Bach from Lillian Hamilton," September 25, 1939, p. 5.

1936, at the age of eighty-two. De Brath was convinced that he regularly received truths from the spirit world via "the Teacher brought by my unseen friend, and by many communications from her." He replied to Lillian at the end of October, "I am much interested in the charming little photograph, and in what you tell me of 'Faith' and her mediumship. You are doubtless doing the right thing in keeping her as normal as possible. It is, as you say, a new development in mediumship that she should be unaware of this connection with Christ. And you are also right in keeping careful notes of the case before printing anything about it... It may be that this little medium will show that the abiding influence of Our Lord is on the subconscious, and produces the sweet and busy disposition that you describe. I gather that the 'stigmata' are subcutaneous: they are possibly given merely as physical evidence. Her trance conversations would be worth taking down." Lillian subsequently annotated his letter, "Mr. de Brath died during the late summer of 1937 & spoke to me through 'Faith,' giving practically conclusive proof that his full memory of life had carried on."[447]

Figure 48: Stanley De Brath's portrait from Psychic Science, *October 1926.*

"Faith" was the eighteen-year-old Isabella (Isabel) Keil Farquhar whom Lillian Hamilton had hired as a companion and maid in the fall of 1934 since Dr. Hamilton was so frequently away from home because of his heavy medical practice. As a girl in Scotland, her mother Lilly Farquhar had the ability to see spirits and was very psychic. Isabel, too, saw spirits as a seven-year-old growing up on a farm in St. Vital near Winnipeg. Margaret Hamilton recorded in her *Is Survival a Fact?* that "After my father's death in 1935, my mother, in 1936 and 1937, had as a companion a young woman called Isobel Farquhar. She was an excellent psychic. Through her clairvoyance and

---

447 Stanley De Brath to Lillian Hamilton, October 31, 1936 (UMASC).

trance we received considerable evidential material, not only from my father but from other of our communicators."

Isabel moved into Margaret Hamilton's home in Dundas, Ontario, in October 1937 to help her raise her first child Frances after her marriage to James Reynolds (Jim) Bach. She continued her mediumship and Margaret kept her mother informed about their séances. It was in Margaret's home with Isabel as the medium that Ellen Elliott experienced the first unforgettable Christ manifestations that she would subsequently relate to Prime Minister Mackenzie King. She described this séance of August 18, 1939, with Isabel, Margaret and Jim Bach, and Jim's cousin Bert Bach and his wife to Lillian. In her letter, Elliott referred to the "extra rush of work at the office" six months before Hugh Eayrs' sudden death from a heart attack at the age of forty-six in 1940. She was also worrying about her elderly mother's health at home after an operation and her own worsening eyesight resulting from a muscular condition that required rest. She then reported that in an upstairs darkened room, "for almost two hours, one control was followed by another in quick succession."

Spirits who spoke through Isabel included Katie King, Charles Haddon Spurgeon, Dr. Hamilton, the Hamiltons' principal spirit control Walter, Stanley De Brath, and Grey Owl "whose short word with me I can now well understand and sympathise with." Robert Louis Stevenson "talked for quite a long time weaving the most fantastic pirate story you ever heard in your life: it was sheer delight from beginning to end." Walter was then followed by another control who called himself Castell. Castell was one of the spirit controls who gave a blessing in Winnipeg in a séance with Isabel in April 1936. Lillian Hamilton thought he appeared in England to the spiritualist George Vale Owen and that he "claims to be one of the prophets who came before Christ." Elliott reported, "Up to this time my feelings had been those of one who was interested in psychic phenomena but doesn't feel a great deal about it. I was frightfully interested with everything that had been said, and was thoroughly enjoying myself. The change of personality was astounding – even the voices were different from one another."

> However, I had seen nothing clairvoyantly excepting the face of one man which was rather dark with fine features, dark eyes, and fine dark hair which could only be described as lank. I don't know who he was, and I do not recall mentioning him at the time.

But when Castell stepped in there was an entirely different voice in the room, and the vibrations were different from anything I had ever experienced. His voice was beautifully modulated, and one sensed the presence of a serene and wise personality. When he stood up he seemed much taller than anyone else in the room. He spoke and said there was to be a manifestation, and that the medium would be carried to the floor. Margaret took her hand and the rest of us moved our chairs back slightly so that nothing could touch the medium while her body was being thus lowered. Jim, I believe, held his hand at the back of her head in case an accident should happen. From a perfectly upright standing position Isabel was lowered to the floor without any movement of her limbs. She was deeply entranced, and perfectly rigid. We all felt her and tried to raise her legs from the floor but it was an impossibility.

A voice, entirely different from Castell's voice of a few moments before, spoke, and said, rather softly, but with a timbre to it that I shall never forget, 'The cross.' The force in the room was indescribable, and I, who am not a bit religious, felt as though I should have fallen to my knees. Actually, however, I couldn't move, the voice was so strong. Whether I spoke aloud or not I do not know, but a cry was wrung from my soul, 'I am not worthy.' Then this Voice spoke again, and said, 'I am Thy Lord and Master, Jesus Christ.' I put my left hand to my eyes for fear that I should see Him. My right was holding Jim's, who was breathing as heavily [and] was in as much distress as I was.

Then the two hands were placed on mine. The force was so over-whelming I cannot describe it, and although I was really suffering my mental perception was very clear indeed, and as I write to you about this I can recall it just as clearly. The two hands were not then as rigid as they had been at the beginning of the manifestation. The Voice spoke to me: it said, 'Look!' I couldn't answer. The Voice went on, 'What do you see?' I was in agony, and could see nothing but what looked like whirling clouds in front of me, and where I knew Isabel's body to be. It was as much as I could do to force the words, 'I can't' out of my lips – and then I almost fainted because the hands left mine, and without any fumbling or hesitation whatever, pressed the tips of the fingers to my eyes. It was as though my whole being had become electrified with something wondrous and all-powerful. A decided pain was left in my eyes when the hands removed themselves.

> Then the Voice went on. 'Describe it.' To say that I actually saw anything would not be the truth and yet, so sure as God is my Maker, I did see a dark brown cross with a light behind it. And the cross was not the ordinary upright one that one usually sees in pictures. It was rough-hewn, and in the [X-] shape of the Cross of St. Andrew. It was only with great difficulty that I could force the words out of myself, and perhaps 'force' is the wrong word to use there. They were being dragged out of me and I was in agony. Then the Voice went on and said, 'The face.' Again I was compelled to say what I saw and the remarkable thing about it is that face has stayed in my memory. It was beautiful. To use the word 'saw' in this connection doesn't describe my reaction. It was as though I had been vouchsafed an inner flash of perception in which the details of that face were sensed by me.
>
> I cannot recall the actual words I used because I was speaking under great emotional stress – but of this I am sure, the words that Margaret has used in recording it to you describe the face as I have it in my memory. The sitting closed after this. It is one that I shall never forget.[448]

Margaret Hamilton had also described the August 18 séance to her mother who cited part of her account "for purposes of record" in her letter of September 25, 1939.

> Isabel's trance in the meantime was becoming more profound. Following Walter's appearance Castell took control and in the space of a few seconds the atmosphere had become almost violently 'charged' with an inrush of psychic energy. Even I could feel it in the form of wave after wave of cold shudders up my back and across my scalp. The last part of the sitting was truly amazing. Castell arose and gave a brief but beautiful prayer, partly for us all, partly for 'Faith' (Isabel) on her journey. Then he intimated that the Cross would be made visible. Isabel then slumped to the floor and became as rigidly cataleptic as I have ever seen her. We all felt her, and Bert and his wife and Miss Elliott were dumbfounded at the rigidity of her whole body. Even her hands were tightly clenched. She was like a women of iron or steel. Then as we sat quietly in the

---

[448] Elliott to Lillian Hamilton, October 16, 1939 (UMASC).

darkness waiting the Voice spoke – 'I am Thy Lord and Master, Jesus Christ.'

Both Jim and Miss Elliott were breathing heavily. I was having one chill after another although it was a warm summer night and the room was quite close. I was kneeling on the floor holding Izzie's [Isabel's] hands. I could feel a cold breeze sweeping across her body from head to foot. Then as we waited a powerful voice spoke to Miss Elliott – 'What do you see. Describe what you see.' Miss Elliott began to breathe very heavily and to say I can't, I can't. The control took my hands and placed them on hers and again commanded her to look up and describe. So she tried and it sounded as if she were being made to say it. 'I see a Cross, not the conventional cross, but like the Cross of St. Andrews. It is dark but there is light behind it.' All the while she was panting and gasping and her hands were literally dripping, and her body twitching so that I was afraid she would fall from her chair. Again the voice said, 'Describe the Face,' and again, almost with agony she said, 'I cannot, I cannot look.' And she told me afterwards that it was as if the words were being pulled from her by a will far stronger than her own. 'I cannot tell you what it is like. I don't see it, I sense it. It is a far stronger Face than any of the pictures we know, much more virile, fuller and more rounded, far more manly, not meek and resigned. The eyes are full and bright... Oh, I cannot look.'

Margaret concluded her description of the séance experience by stating that she and Elliott "could have talked for hours afterwards. We were all greatly moved by it and she, I know, will never forget it. Her powers of clairvoyance are remarkable."[449]

Two days after the séance on August 18, 1939, Elliott attended the Spiritualist Britten Memorial Church in Toronto, then under the guidance of Rev. Mae Potts. During her clairvoyant demonstration following the service, Potts pointed to Elliott and declared that she was surrounded by a most beautiful spiritual force. "'In all my years as a medium' (she has been one all her life), 'I have never come in contact with such a beautiful manifestation.' (Immediately I felt the same Power which had come to me in the séance on Friday night.) 'There are two forms standing beside you: they are so bright and so

---

[449] "Letter to Margaret Hamilton Bach from Lillian Hamilton," September 25, 1939, pp. 10-11.

Figure 49: Reverend Mae Potts inside Britten Memorial Church, Toronto, circa 1940s.

advanced that I could not describe them to you. One form is taller than the other.' (I took this to be Castell, whom I believe to be tall, and the Presence.) 'These two souls convey to you that you must have no doubts whatever as to what happened, and that you have a great work to do. The light surrounding these two forms is so beautiful and so powerful, that it is impossible for me to discern their features, but the one wears a loose-flowing robe, and he indicates to me that it is sufficient for you to know that you are within its shelter.'"

The "great work" to which Mae Potts referred was the publication of Dr. Hamilton's psychic investigations, *Intention and Survival*. "I am so sure that all these manifestations are indications of what is being planned by the forces," Elliott wrote Lillian Hamilton. "We are strangely privileged. I am rather frightened that I have been allowed to share in one experience, and it makes me humble, but on the other hand I feel I have gained immeasurably from it, and that I truly am led and guided."[450]

Lillian Hamilton's report to her daughter Margaret on September 25, 1939, was what she herself referred to as a "confession." The Christ visions had manifested not only in her own home but also in the home

---

450 Elliott to Lillian Hamilton, October 16, 1939 (UMASC).

circle of Ada Turner, a high school English teacher and long-time participant in the Hamilton séances. In the winter and spring of 1937, Mary Marshall and her sister-in-law Susan Marshall had withdrawn from the Hamilton circle. "The Presence-phenomena, of which they had seen a little, they regarded as blasphemous, and refused to attend." The new group consisted of Rev. and Mrs. T.B. MacMillan, Rev. William Robertson Wood, Mr. and Mrs. William Wither, Mr. and Mrs. Harold Shand, Lillian, Isabel, and frequently Glen and James Hamilton. Physical phenomena included the complete levitation of the two-hundred-pound Bill Wither several inches above the floor. Mrs. Jean Wither "in trance began to talk of 'Light,' a being, whom, while she was in this state, she believed to be the Master, and before whom she showed the most profound reverence."

Jack MacDonald and William Bernard (Barney) Cooper experienced the same Christ presence as Ellen Elliott. With MacDonald, "A commanding voice spoke through Isabel and commanded him to describe what he saw. Like these others, almost with agony, and with great effort, he stated that he saw before him a cloud, that the cloud parted and out looked the face of the Saviour, full, strong, beautiful, but with the eyes full of suffering. The brightness of this vision was to him well nigh overpowering. He said that it was like looking into the sun with the form of a man outlined within." A new demonstration came at the close of each sitting, "the appearance of what we came to call 'the Presence'...a Voice of great dignity and sweetness impossible to describe adequately, that spoke through Isabel, blessed us, called us His disciples, and sometimes laid His hands on us as if to give us power."[451]

The persistent occurrences of these supernormal phenomena presented Lillian Hamilton with an ethical and practical dilemma as she was working with Ellen Elliott to publish her husband's psychic investigations. "With T.G.'s great scientific work still not fully reported, and myself largely the custodian of this work, it seemed hazardous to the scientific standing of the whole output were I to reveal to any outside of our immediate and closest friends the nature of these strange communications. What was I to do about it. If it was true, then I must believe and at least record the manifestations faithfully, and some time, let them be known. If it was not true – that is if it was all the product of subconscious uprisings of some kind possibly instigated by undesirable

---

451 "Letter to Margaret Hamilton Bach from Lillian Hamilton," September 25, 1939, pp. 8, 9.

forces, and I knew, or at least believed I knew that they existed – then I must close the door on this type of phenomena for all time." Margaret Hamilton recalled in her 1980 interview that after Mary Marshall joined the séance investigations in 1928, "On two occasions Mrs. Marshall, while in the trance state, was invaded by what was obviously an evil influence...Like an insane person who has a bad epileptic seizure, she became very violent and physically almost uncontrollable. You could sense the evil. It took three men to subdue her."

Believing in the efficacy of prayer, Hamilton asked that she be given a sign, "in other words, be given cross-evidence of some kind of an experimental nature that would show from which source this unfoldment came." She received her answer in the form of a two-year old issue of the *Winnipeg Free Press* showing a picture of Christ the Good Shepherd which was used to illustrate Charles Dickens' *Life of Christ* running in the paper that appeared on the bed in the house of Ada Turner and her adopted son Harold. They had never seen this issue of the newspaper before, and no one had entered their home in their absence. In a trance, Harold Turner's control asked him to telephone Lillian. "'She will understand. It is for her.'" Lillian understood. "An apport had been produced in Harold's home as a sign that my request had been heard, and in it Christ was represented as the Good Shepherd. Following this I did not doubt, but felt at last convinced that the phenomena were indeed supernormal and that their origin was within the Good."

In her September 1939 letter, Lillian wrote Margaret, "Now Miss Elliott, also knowing nothing of the previous history of the manifestation, has had this same transcendental impact vouchsafed her, one more proof that we have in this indeed encountered phenomena lying beyond our normal comprehension...The proof seems almost as convincing as that given in several cases to Paul in his days of doubt following hard on the episode of the Manifestation on the road to Damascus. The Gates were indeed opening."

> So you see how wide is the sweep of the phenomena that have now appeared in this connection, and how excellent are the 'signs' or cross-evidence that a manifestation of great import has begun to take place. We cannot, nay, dare not too lightly set it aside. Have I the faith, have you the faith, is the experimental proof sufficient to warrant us in believing that these things shall be? Is this terrible war now beginning the beginning of the time prophesied by Stead and R.L.S. and W.O.H. fourteen years ago?

Is this Being whom these five sensitives have seen in vision-form the risen and living Christ, He who was seen apparently in like manner by John on Patmos? Was the Voice we have heard akin in any degree to the Voice he heard?

'And I, John, was in the spirit and heard behind me a great voice, and being turned I saw seven golden candlesticks, and in the midst of the seven golden candlesticks One like unto the Son of Man...His head and His hair were white like wool and His Eyes were as a flame of fire, and His feet like unto fine brass and His voice as the sound of many waters and His countenance was as the sun shineth in his strength. I am He that liveth and was dead, and behold, I am alive for evermore.'

Bereft of its beautiful imagery and language of poetry, what have we? A statement that Christ appeared to John while he was entranced, that Christ had an appearance of exceeding great brightness, and a voice, that though loud, was an exceedingly sweet one. The experiences are strangely parallel.[452]

With her own spiritualist convictions and personal friendship with Lillian and Margaret Hamilton, Ellen Elliott became part of the extended Hamilton group. In her letter to Lillian of October 16, 1939, in which she described the overwhelming August 16 séance with Isabel Farquhar and Margaret, she thanked Lillian for the "amazing record" of psychic phenomena she had sent her on September 21. "I do appreciate your faith in me, and I shall regard it as a trust from you and from the circle of friends on the other side, whom, I am aware, know far better what they are doing than I can, at the moment understand." Margaret had sent Ellen her own record of their August psychic experience and "to say that I am amazed is a mild statement. I, myself, have felt and have been told that the world is on the verge of a new spiritual awakening – but it staggers me now to know from whom the awakening will come......And to know that I have been permitted to come into contact with that person makes me feel very humble indeed."[453]

Lillian wrote Elliott in December regarding the publication of *Intention and Survival*, "You belong to my little inner circle who know

---

452 Ibid., 7, 8, 10, 8, 12-13. "Interview with Margaret Hamilton Bach, November 26, 1980," 16. W.O.H. was William Oliver Hamilton, TGH's younger brother who died of a heart attack in 1924.

453 Elliott to Lillian Hamilton, October 16, 1939 (UMASC)

of these other truths that can <u>not</u> be published. In everything we shall await the guidance of higher hands than ours. Our wills, brains, good common sense, however, have their place and on these we must build an enduring foundation for our house of truth." In April 1940 she wrote Elliott, "Added to all this is the xyz [Jesus Christ] phenomena which I do not dare believe you and I can report – at least in our lifetime. Your own experiences are wonderful and <u>exactly in line with ours</u>…in our sittings for teleplasm – the order the same as with you: first the medium saw little children seemingly in the room; next she saw 'Light'; then came the rigidity – the profound trance, and xyz's voice or the voice of xyz's representative. I love your own attitude towards xyz…Thanks so much for your most interesting letter and for sharing with me those experiences. If you see xyz again in a dream may I ask that you let me know. It was a wonderful experience."[454]

Ellen Elliott and Mackenzie King

In December 1941, Ellen Elliott sent Mackenzie King a transcript of her sitting with her trance medium Alma Brash in Toronto, which she had recorded on her portable Ediphone dictation machine. She wrote that the transcript presented the actual words spoken by Hugh Eayrs, Macmillan's late president who died in April 1940, and by "my director who prefers to be called simply the White Brother. He lived on earth many years before Christ and is a very advanced soul." She identified Alma Brash as "a frail young woman of about twenty-eight, and in a state of trance is controlled by the spirit of a Zulu child, whose name is unpronounceable, so we call her Dinah. I have been told many times through various mediums that the Dinah personality is an assumed one for a much greater personality who acts as the communicator, or spirit medium, for all of the spirit influences which come to me, in much the same way as the medium herself is the physical channel for me." The White Brother had requested that she send the record of the sitting to King. "I can assure you of their anxiety and willingness to help you bear the tremendous load you are carrying and assure you of their nearness at all times."[455]

---

454 Lillian Hamilton to Elliott, December 12, 1939, and April 13, 1940 (McMaster).
455 Elliott to King, December 17, 1941. Describing a February 24, 1942, séance

The record of the December 16, 1941, sitting Elliott forwarded to the Prime Minister – held nine days after the Japanese attack on Pearl Harbor – contained a brief personal reference and a much longer political message, which she assured him came through "entirely unsolicited on my part." The late Hugh Eayrs urged King to "throw off the shackles which are symbolic of the influence of weaker minds, and he will make the Dominion the great Dominion it really is. It will play a great part in this present struggle, and the Mother Country will have cause to be proud of it. The North American Continent will figure greatly in the building of a new order of things, the new Democratic way of life. All the spiritual and material forces of the Dominion must be gathered together: everything must be put into production, and men must work hard and fast and long. The enemy is a strong one and his own method must be used to defeat him. If your leader has the fire and the spirit to enthuse his people these things could be done and these things will be done."

Eayrs informed King via Elliott, the sitter in the séance, that the builders of Canada who went before him were working to help their country in its war emergency. "Tell him not to think for one moment that he is alone, but is surrounded continually by 'a cloud of witnesses' and in his hours of great decisions, in matters of urgent importance, they are there with him. Ask him to think of them when decisions have to be made and they will do their best to help him make the wisest possible decisions."[456]

In his diary, the PM did not comment on this political exhortation from the spirit world. But Hugh Eayrs also briefly referred to another spirit who was with him. The control Dinah gave his name as Ian but pronounced it to rhyme with lion, so Elliott wondered if this name should be Lyon. King had just received a letter from his nephew John Lay in which "he spoke of Ian, (little child) who died in infancy, being in the Beyond with others, helping to direct

---

communication with Dinah to Lillian Hamilton, Elliott reported that she had discovered that her White Brother was Abraham. Elliott to Hamilton, February 27, 1942 (UMASC). Hamilton in turn highly esteemed Alma Brash. "She is indeed a highly gifted psychic. If you ever get time to tell her story she will be acknowledged as the equal of Mrs. Osborne Leonard, if not Mrs. Piper, for subjective proof." Lillian Hamilton to Elliott, undated letter "Friday" [May 1942] (McMaster).

456 "Record of a Sitting," December 16, 1941.

our lives here. There was also a letter from Miss Elliott – a voice speaking from beyond through a medium used the expression 'Ian is here.' She was not sure whether it was Ian or Lyon. Either would be equally significant. In this Chapter [the Book of Numbers of the Hebrew Bible] a lion is a symbol of the people and its power. It is quite remarkable that that word 'Ian' should have come in both communications…Miss Elliott and others with her do not yet know of the existence of any such person. Those are all, as it were, signposts pointing to a unity of thought and direction."[457]

In February 1942, Ellen Elliott informed the PM of another séance and directions from the Beyond. "On Tuesday evening last my friend emphasized very strongly indeed the immediate need of stronger defences for the West Coast, and when I doubted my ability to get this word to you they told me that you yourself would soon give me an opportunity to do so…and your letter came on Saturday," she wrote King. "With regard to the Far Eastern situation they indicated that in the next few months it would be far graver, and that the allied forces would go through very dark days which would be relieved only by what could be called miracles…and they referred to the rain storm which blanketed the arrival of the supply ships at Singapore."[458]

The Prime Minister was sufficiently impressed by Ellen Elliott's spirit communications that when he met with her at Macmillan's in August 1942, he "arranged for a sitting at Miss Elliott's residence with a little medium she has whose name is Alma Brash, a rather frail looking little person of perhaps 30 years."[459] Elliott sent King a seven-page typed record of the séance, in which he appears as "Mr. X." Among the spirit entities who appeared were King's father, his mother ("You have often seen me in dreams"), his sister Bella, his brother Max who predicted two more years of war, William Lyon Mackenzie, Sir Frederick Banting, Lady Laurier, Florence Nightingale, William Archer ("Democracy is a

---

457 Diary, December 20, 1941.

458 Elliott to King, February 9, 1942.

459 Diary, August 5, 1942. The 1921 Census reports that Alma Brash was born about 1914. Alma and her Scottish Presbyterian parents, James and Phillippa Brash, were born in Ontario. The 1940 Canada Voters List has "Miss Alma Brash, housekeeper" living with her brother James, a city employee, and his wife at 446 Clinton Street, next to the residence of Ellen Elliott and her widowed mother at 444 Clinton. The 1953 Voters List shows "Miss Alma Brash, receptionist," suggesting she may not have married.

beautiful thing"), Anne Boleyn who brought Queen Victoria, and Grey Owl (Archibald Stansfeld Belaney), another Macmillan author with whom Elliott worked closely. Brash also clairvoyantly saw the spirit of Norman Rogers, his Minister of National Defence, who had died in a plane crash in 1940. "O dear it is terrible the sight that comes before me. He is all burnt up beyond recognition and smashed to pieces. He has been in a plane that was on fire and burnt. But he tells me to tell you he is all assembled together again and is very well and very happy and working with you and with others here."

Most significantly, the White Brother also stepped forward and declared he was interested in Mr. X, "for they have much in common."

> He welcomes him and tells him he is a leader, and as such needs great spiritual forces behind him. The leaders mentioned in the Old Testament had God behind them, and Mr. X has with him the same power of God. This is a fact, and is just as true today as it was in ancient times. Moreover, Mr. X was moved here to Toronto for this very experience by the White Brother and by the Master because they had already promised to E.E. [Ellen Elliott] that this war is now to be God's war. It is to be taken out of the hands of man, and now He is to direct Mr. X's steps in the direction He commands.
>
> The door has opened, the trumpets are blowing, and Dinah described the Presence. One cannot put into words the feeling one experiences in the presence of the Lord, but the gist of the message He conveyed is as follows: He placed a crown of thorns on Mr. X's head and told him he would suffer and be persecuted as He himself suffered and was persecuted. 'Even as I was crucified, so shall you be, but I am with you.' Dinah described Mr. X going through, now, and for some time to come, a very dark, trying, and distressing period, when he would be criticised and persecuted from all sides, but she saw him also being led by the Presence, so that finally he came out into the bright sunlight, and throwing his hands to the sky said, 'Thank God.'

Ellen Elliott was attempting to establish herself as *the* major interlocutor between Canada's Prime Minister and God.

> He [the Presence] also reminded E.E. that he had spoken to her only a week previously and had said that He had left the print of His foot in this room, and that now He was starting, indeed

this was the first step, of His new mission on earth. He said He was the Word, and handed her a torch, which was also the Word, and it was her service to carry it. She said she was willing to take it, but asked how to help, to which He replied, 'Fear not, my daughter, know and believe that I am the Word, and the opportunity for service will come to you.' He then reminded Mr. X of the impression he had received to get in touch with E.E., so that the present sitting was truly the beginning of the work, that is, taking an actual hand in the affairs of the war. Mr. X was enrolled as a member of the Christ group.[460]

In his diary, the Prime Minister noted, "Received letter from Miss Elliott with interesting account of the seance, record supplementing my own. The two together make a pretty complete story." He had written her three days after the sitting. "Naturally there is uppermost in my mind, the quite exceptional experience of Wednesday evening. Your little friend has indeed a remarkable gift. I feel she is entitled to a first place in the ranks of those of her profession." He had been running over in his mind "the many experiences and things we were told. The record is indeed quite exceptional. I shall have to wait until I see you again to talk it over but meanwhile I would like you to know that it surpassed even the expectations I had had from accounts you had given to me." The PM promised Elliott, "from now on I shall follow with a deeper interest than ever all that pertains to the researches to which, over so many years, you have devoted so much time and thought."[461]

Elliott sent King the record of another sitting on August 11, 1942, in which the White Brother relayed a message from God "that He was always with you, and now that a stronger bond was created He would use you for His work on earth. 'Only the truly great are humble, and I have chosen him for my work because of his humility.'" The White Brother attributed the PM's reluctance to increase the Canadian fighting forces "and thus in all probability send thousands of men to their death" to King's spirituality and resulting abhorrence of war. "But force must be met by equal force, even though it be abhorrent to you. 'We shall impress him with the need for action, immediate action,

---

460 Diary, August 5, 1942, p. 8, cited in "Rogers, King and The World Beyond," *Kingston Whig-Standard Companion*, June 10, 2000, 3. "Record of a Sitting with A.B. (psychic), Mr. X, and E.E.," August 5, 1942.

461 Diary, August 14, 1942. King to Elliott, August 8, 1942.

for it will forestall greater destruction of human life. Every man must fight, with his bare hands if necessary, so we urge for greater effort in the production of war material. As a servant of the Master and a member of His group, we are always with him, but we cannot make aeroplanes and guns. Tell him this, for they will be needed. He will not lose heart and courage during the dark days which are before him.'" King responded that "the record of the 11th instant is a splendid supplement" to their August 5 sitting.[462]

Ellen Elliott's exhortations on how King should conduct Canada's war effort were probably influenced by the Macmillan War Pamphlet series she organized in 1941 and 1942. The company published eight titles covering aspects of Canada's role in World War II. She wrote the PM after hearing his evening radio broadcast on selective service on August 19, 1942, the day news arrived of the disastrous Dieppe Raid with very heavy Canadian casualties. Elliott felt his summing up at the end "was one of the finest pieces of oratory I have ever listened to, and I feel it will be remembered for a long time to come." Regarding the spirit world she added, "I was talking to our friends last night, and there is no doubt that they appreciated what you said, what you plan to do, and their own now strengthened contact with you." Elliott included the record of an August 20 sitting in which the Presence applauded King for his efforts. "He is referring to the speech of last night made by the Prime Minister. It appeared to be a more decisive move on the part of Mr. King…There will be co-operation from the people. There will be criticism from some quarters, but co-operation from the masses. In the speech, the White Brother says that Mr. King was more decisive, and appeared to be more determined, and also appeared to have thrown off the shackles which had influenced him in the past…The Presence sends His 'blessing to our friend, for he is now a brother of the band.'"[463]

In December 1942, Elliott wrote the Prime Minister on the usual Macmillan Company of Canada letterhead but marked Private and Confidential. "On Tuesday evening last Alma and I had a sitting for Mr. Isaac Pitblado of Winnipeg," the former president of the Canadian Bar Association, she confided. "He received very good evidence, and

---

462 "Record of a Sitting with A.B. and E.E.," August 11, 1942. King to Elliott, August 18, 1942.

463 Panofsky, *The Literary Legacy*, 135. Elliott to King, August 21, 1942. "Record of a Sitting – E.E. & A.B. – August 20, 1942."

while a <u>certain person</u> [The Presence] was addressing him he turned to me and asked me to 'Write to William [i.e., Mackenzie King]. I am with him always. His path is my path, and my strength his strength.' For myself I am honoured to send this on to you. Your name is often mentioned, but unless I am requested to, I do not write. I shall be talking to my friends for a little while on the evening of December the 16th, and will let you know if anything comes through for you."[464]

The Prime Minister invited Elliott to lunch at Laurier House on May 7, 1943, recording "she gave me an interesting account of some experiences she had had at the Easter season. Quite remarkable as they related to the Lord's supper and the holy grail." Elliott later informed him of the very strong psychic vibrations she sensed in his dining room with its striking portraits of family members and Liberal politicians. She also found the vibrations in his library at the top of the house "so overwhelming that I could not appreciate your wonderful library as much as I know I would ordinarily. The power in that room is filled with sweetness and love and the fullest understanding, and it is not altogether your dear mother's presence there, because I am sure the Lord is there too."

She informed the PM of another séance with Alma Brash in which the White Brother imparted that he "had taken the opportunity while I was with you to make a much closer and stronger contact so that they could, through our sittings here, give you added strength, physically and spiritually." Regarding the announcement of the Prime Minister's forthcoming meeting with Churchill and Roosevelt in Quebec City in September, the White Brother assured him that "the sword of the spirit was in your hand and that the beautiful souls of the Christ band were always with you, and also your own dear friends who, I am sure, also belong to that band."

Elliott again tried to establish herself as the interlocutor between the PM, the spirit world, and Christ. The White Brother recognized King's own considerable psychic powers of perception. "If I [Elliott] would merely think of your name in our sittings they would take that thought vibration, blend it with their own higher one, and you would receive it." She asked the PM not to take the time to answer her letter and implied that it was God rather than King's mother who was the guiding entity in Laurier House. "If those minutes

---

[464] Elliott to Mackenzie King, December 10, 1942.

could be spent in the top room with your 'friend' that would be enough for me."[465]

Ellen Elliott was King's main contact at Macmillan's, overseeing the publication of his *Canada and the Fight for Freedom* in 1944 and subcontracting his titles and Ludwig's *Mackenzie King* to other publishers in the U.S. and abroad. The PM may have been susceptible to her messages regarding Christ because of his admiration for Dorothy Sayers' radio drama *The Man Born to Be King*. He had followed the broadcasts of the series on radio and contacted Sayers by telephone to obtain an autographed copy of the published scripts. He "spoke of the play she had written and my liking its representation of the manliness of the Life of Christ. Its portrayal of forces that were at work on a world scale today, similar to those which were in conflict at the time of the crucifixion of Christ."[466]

King again invited Elliott to Laurier House for tea and dinner in March 1946, fulfilling his promise to follow her psychic research with a deeper interest. The PM noted that her "truly remarkable" account, which he recorded in over five-typed pages in his diary, "really links up with a book the Macmillan Co. published dealing with Dr. Hamilton's experiences in ectoplasmic photography." Elliott informed King about a young man, George McKanday, who had served in the army and had worked with her at Macmillan's eighteen years ago. When McKanday's unit landed in Sicily in the summer of 1943, a French-Canadian friend of his by the name of Dallaire was killed at his side, splattering his clothing and face with blood. McKanday suffered from malaria and had to go into hospital. One day he phoned Elliott that his room was filling with a sort of smoke, which she declared was ectoplasm. A voice began speaking to him about photography. "It spoke of someone who had been doing photography in the war, in Italy, and who had been killed, but who was on the other side and wanted to have him work with them."

This spirit then materialized "and kept talking with the other just as though the two of them were men in a room together" and told McKanday he wanted him to make photographs without a camera by simply exposing photographic plates that had been laid on the floor of the hospital room. Elliott brought these photographs to show to the

---

465   Diary, May 7, 1943. Elliott to King, May 18, 1943.
466   Diary, May 15 and 20, 1944.

Prime Minister. Some of them revealed what he thought were Russian emblems, a cross, a hammer and a sickle, seven concentric circles, and a Russian face. "The next photograph was that of Adelard Dallaire, looking exceedingly happy. Complete picture of his head and shoulders. There could be no mistaking who he was...All had been taken without any camera, with nothing done by McKanday, except to put the plates where they were."

The Prime Minister believed Elliott because she happened to be wearing a brooch of the three graces holding hands that was almost identical to the brooch that had been worn by King's mother. Further, McKanday had also learned to communicate with the spirit that had materialized in his room using a Morse code by tapping on his knee. Igor Gouzenko, the cypher clerk in the Russian Embassy, had just revealed to King the extensive spy ring operating in Canada and the U.S. "Here again was another curious parallel to deciphering of codes, etc." The PM was therefore certain "There is no humbug or fraud about Miss Elliott."

> She is a woman of wide business experience, very alert and active. She told me all this had happened within the past two weeks. She is confident that there will be further considerable developments. No one in this wide world will make me believe that her wanting to see me, bringing these photographs and wanting to see me was a matter of chance. That she was not directed to come and to bring me what would be evidence beyond all doubt that my mother and others were working with her, or letting me see that this great Russian espionage business is something in which they are all interested and that I am being brought into contact with them. Also that they are living, preserving their personalities and helping. That there is no such thing as death as we think of it, but a continuation hereafter of life.
>
> I said to Miss Elliott that I thought the world was in the position it was in because people had lost faith in the existence of God and in the hereafter. They had constructed [a] material universe, when in reality universe is spiritual. Once they became convinced that our lives went on, we carried our personality into the world beyond, and that there was a moral order which was above all else, their conduct would change and we would have peace on earth. We would find there was no

separation between two worlds. We are moving into that new
era of psychical and spiritual knowledge.[467]

Further to Ellen Elliott's recounting of McKanday's psychic experiences to the Prime Minister, Ruth Panofsky revealed that the divorced Elliott "cohabitated with former colleague and veteran George Milton McKanday (who had worked at Macmillan from 1929 to 1931) until his estranged first wife, Doris, died in January 1955 and they were free to marry (on 1 October 1960)."[468]

McKanday was born on December 12, 1903, in Gananoque, Ontario. His father, William Hugh McKanday (1864-1943) was born in the United States and worked as a machinist in bolt works until 1930 and subsequently as a caretaker. His mother, Louise Bilnois McKanday, was born in Ontario. A 1935 voters list reports her as "married woman." George attempted to move to the U.S. in 1925 to seek work as a printer, listing his race as "Scotch." He married Doris Amy Louise Sefton in Toronto in 1928 when he was twenty-four and Doris twenty-seven. They had two daughters. Their marriage document lists his religious denomination as Presbyterian, hers as Anglican, George's occupation as manager and Doris' as proofreader.

In 1932, McKanday was elected secretary of the Gananoque Relief Association which assisted in the raising and administering of relief funds and securing work for the unemployed. He began working as a local correspondent in Gananoque for the *Kingston Whig-Standard* and was identified as its Leeds County and eastern representative in 1932 and 1933. That year, the paper devoted half a page to publish in its entirety his address on the subject of journalism to the Rockport Women's Institute. Because of his connection to the *Whig-Standard*, the paper published brief mentions of his whereabouts during World War II. In "Now In Army," the paper stated on June 3, 1940 that "George McKanday, well-known newspaperman here for the past several years, is now Gunner George McKanday, R.C.H.A., Kingston." On May 14, 1941, "Those of the Royal Canadian Artillery overseas include…George McKanday." As Ellen Elliott informed Mackenzie King, the *Whig-Standard* reported under "Personals," on October 12, 1943, that McKanday "has been in Sicily on active service since July 12" and on May 17, 1944, referred to "Gnr. [Gunner] George McKanday, RCA in Italy."

---

467 Diary, March 22, 1946.

468 Panofsky, *The Literary Legacy*, 129.

Elliott told King that McKanday had suffered from malaria and had to go to hospital. The *Whig-Standard*, in "Red Cross Gets Praise," reported on November 22, 1944, that Gunner McKanday "a Gananoque man now serving in Italy, in a letter written to a friend in Canada has expressed his appreciation of the work of the Red Cross. Gnr. McKanday has had two attacks of malaria and now has a broken ankle." The 1945 voters list for Gananoque has McKanday as "soldier Overseas."[469]

Mackenzie King invited Elliott back to Laurier House for tea in front of the fireplace in November 1946. She again brought photographs of different parts of the world and different people, including of two Canadian soldiers who were killed in Italy. "Then most interesting of all was a picture of Dr. Hamilton of Winnipeg," King recorded in a four-page typed diary entry. "His picture I could recognize myself. Mrs. Hamilton was overjoyed. She had seen it and said without question it was the picture of her husband. He of course was the one who developed pictures in his own house in Winnipeg with his own apparatus and which I saw myself and talked with him about."

King recorded that apparently Elliott's mother and sister "and she and her friend [George McKanday] all work together; also a Mr. Cross from Port Arthur or thereabouts who is helping to finance her friend, who, she says, does not expect to live very long and who at times is in a state of collapse. She says she has to guard him against drinking: also when there are times when some of the phenomena are being discussed he feels quite ill but comes out all right." The PM noted that McKanday asked the spirits how it was he was saved when the others were blown to pieces. "The voice told him that his was a case where they were demonstrating from beyond their power of healing; that, as a matter of fact, his power [body?] had been blown to pieces with the others. They had brought the body together and the spirit was restored within the body. The experience had been unknown to himself, and as it were he awakened where he had been when the disaster occurred. He told Miss Elliott that he was quite sure this was true. They both believe that."

---

469 "Gananoque Forms Relief Association," and "Gananoque Welfare Board Officers," *Kingston Whig-Standard*, June 28, 1932, 5 and September 18, 1934, 5. "Newspaper Man Turns into a Public Speaker," *Kingston Whig-Standard*, September 5, 1934, 9.

He is on a different plane of vibrations than this earth plane. He is not yet of the vibrations of the spirit world completely, but he is as it were between the two. He is perfectly conscious, is living as a man, he is actually indifferent whether he died tomorrow or the next day. In a word, he is in the truest sense a medium – a medium between the two planes of vibrations...

I could not help thinking while she was describing the story of the soldier whose life had been destroyed, but restored as evidence of the power of healing of those beyond...If, very shortly, as I believe will be the case, the world comes to be made fully aware of the human survival after death, people will see with their own eyes pictures of their loved ones beyond all mistake and get into communication with them and learn that life goes on after death and the struggle for good and evil still prevails. There will be a new sanction to conduct, a new belief in the power of good and evil and in the supremacy of God. It is all perfectly amazing.

The Prime Minister was convinced of the veracity of Ellen Elliott's account and of the genuineness of photographs showing ectoplasm emanating from McKanday's hands. Comparable to Dr. Hamilton's psychic investigations, "Ectoplasm would sometimes cover the side of a curtain or bits of furniture...The photo showed the room in which she was sitting. It is some substance that seems to come from his body and which builds up into what may become material for materialization. It returns again to the body."

King concluded that "Altogether the record is most astounding; the most astounding I have ever heard from human lips or read in any book. The whole story was told to me with perfect naturalness by Miss Elliott, as we sat with the book open on a table before us, for I could see the pictures myself. Also read the records if I had wished to do so. She has everything recorded in terms of hours, days, surroundings, questions and answers, etc." As in her previous visit he reiterated, "Miss Elliott is a highly intelligent person, Christian in her belief. Lives alone with her mother, and not the kind of a person for a moment to be duped. As a matter of fact she is keeping all these records with a view to publishing a book on the subject."[470]

---

470 Diary, November 28, 1946.

The PM invited Elliott again to Kingsmere in July 1947, just before the publication by Macmillan of another edition of *Industry and Humanity*. She had been informed by the new Macmillan management that after twenty-five years her services were no longer required. William Arthur Deacon, the literary editor of the *Globe and Mail*, called Elliott an outstanding figure in Canadian publishing and lamented that her departure from Macmillan "removes from publishing one of the very few persons who have been intimately associated with the development of Canadian literature during the past quarter century."

King thought Elliott was giving too much time to psychic studies and advised her to make them a side issue and to do executive work. During this last visit, he found her "less interesting than at other times." "She brought her books with her pictures. I did not think what they are getting at present begins to equal what they had a year ago but it is clear there are experiments coming from the other side, trying to reach this side, and gradually working out. Something might still be revealed I believe which will make co-operation between the Beyond and here quite easy in the matter of photographs, reproducing the actual faces and garments of some of those who have passed over but who are making their presence known through thought-wave, or some other way in relation to what was familiar to those they are communicating with. There is something simply amazing about what has already been achieved."[471]

Ruth Panofsky recorded that in 1949, "Elliott began a highly successful second career as entrepreneur. Together with George McKanday, she established Mailit, an advertising, printing, and mailing company, at 54 Wellington Street West in Toronto." The 1963 voters list for their 68 Glencairn Avenue address reports George as president and Elliott as secretary-treasurer. The 1965 voters list has George as president and the 1972 list as printer. Elliott died of a heart attack on March 22, 1973, shortly after she and George returned from a Caribbean cruise. McKanday died on December 21, 1977.[472]

Ellen had sent condolences to Margaret in January 1957 at the passing of Lillian Hamilton and urged Margaret to continue editing

---

471 William Arthur Deacon, "Macmillan Editor Leaves Publishing," *Globe and Mail*, June 28, 1947, 10, cited in Panofsky, *The Literary Legacy*, 146-47. Diary, May 23, 1947, and July 31, 1947.

472 Panofsky, *The Literary Legacy*, 147. "Ellen McKanday, 72, Publishing Executive," *Toronto Star*, March 26, 1973, 57.

the trance writing scripts transmitted by Robert Louis Stevenson and David Livingstone that could not be included in *Intention and Survival*. "The shock is gone now, because I know she is in good hands and when quite rested will take up a life of interest and accomplishment...I don't think you could do anything better than go ahead with the R.L.S. and L. scripts as you and she had planned. And you'll get help."

The following year she congratulated Margaret for the publication of the thirteen-part series *Is Survival a Fact?* published by the *Winnipeg Free Press* from January 18 to February 1, 1958, and reprinted by Victor Sifton, the paper's editor and publisher, as a booklet bearing the same title. The *Toronto Daily Star* published the series beginning on April 21, 1958. Psychic Press in London published *Is Survival a Fact?* in book form in 1969. Elliott wrote Margaret that the series "cannot fail to help the cause of the good work, and T.G. and Lillian, and all the gang I am sure, are feeling very satisfied...The *Star* really did you proud...your introductory article was splendid...It is wonderful and I trust the series will be picked up by other papers. It should be."

She reported that her daily work at Mailit "doesn't leave me much time for my own pursuits, and certainly not enough energy for the thing that interests me most. And George [McKanday] has been under the weather lately; sittings take so much out of him – the phenomena producing kind – that it isn't fair to expect him to sit. However, I am hoping and praying. A sitting for clairvoyance recharges all *my* batteries but it would run his down."

> When our friends are particularly anxious to carry out another experiment they get after both of us, and we don't get any mental peace until we sit for them...I do miss them. Miss actually talking to them, I mean, via someone else's mediumship rather than my own. This is sheer cowardice on my part, because I KNOW I am in touch, but they used to give me such nice little private asides through George of which he was quite unconscious, and which indicated to me that my own little excursions out to meet them were successful. One shouldn't need such assurance, but one does. Any kind of mental mediumship is so close to imagination, unless it is accompanied by clairvoyance – and sometimes when it is – that I feel the need of a check-up once in a while.[473]

---

473 Elliott to Margaret Hamilton, January 4, 1957, and April 22, 1958.

This vital role of séance mediums as communicators and connectors between life on earth and the spirit world was also suggested by Elizabeth Neres' tribute to the famous Boston medium and friend of T.G. Hamilton, the Canadian-born Mina Marguerite Crandon, known as "Margery." Hamilton had met her husband, the gynecologist Dr. Le Roi Goddard Crandon, while studying post surgery at Boston City Hospital in 1917 and attended eight séances with Margery in their home in 1925. In December 1926, he organized the Crandons' public speaking engagements in Winnipeg where they held two private séances in the Hamiltons' home. In her poem, "To Margery," published in *Light* in 1928, Neres wrote:

> You welcome Death in Life that we
> A nobler Life in Death may see;
> You give dear hours of consciousness
> That our poor wits may better guess
>   A saner scheme
>   Than we can dream
> Of order, growth and righteousness.
>
> You touch the spring that opes the door;
> We enter in. You ask no more
> Than that your light may help us scan
> The hidden Truth, the secret Plan,
>   And thereby sense
>   Intelligence
> Infused through all the world of Man.
>
> From heights of utter selflessness
> You reach to us in helpfulness;
> Through you, we glimpse what is to be;
> You prove our immortality!
>   O, Margery,
>   What words have we
> To thank you for Eternity?[474]

Canada's most famous spiritualist, Mackenzie King, first consulted the Kingston clairvoyant Rachel Bleaney when he ran for Parliament in 1919 and had his last séance over the "little table" with his spiritual

---

474 Elizabeth Neres, "To Margery," *Light* 48:2470 (May 12, 1928), 220.

partner, Joan Patteson, in 1949. Volume 2 of *The Spiritualist Prime Minister: Mackenzie King and His Mediums*, examines how prominent mediums and psychics in Canada, New York and London influenced the PM before, during and after the Second World War. The volume opens with an examination of Rachel Bleaney's crucial role in the 1925, 1926, and 1930 federal elections and proceeds to a case study of the direct-voice trumpet medium Etta Wriedt from Detroit whom W.T. Stead selected as a resident medium at his Julia's Circle in Wimbledon in 1911. Sir Arthur Conan Doyle, at the beginning of his 1922 American lecture tour, called Wriedt the "strongest medium in the world." In his legendary diaries, King vividly describes his over sixty séances with Wriedt between 1932 and 1938. Other chapters analyze his sittings with the equally famous trance mediums Eileen Garrett in New York and Gladys Osborne Leonard in London.

The volume analyzes King's appeasement of Adolf Hitler prior to and after his peace mission with the German dictator in Berlin in 1937, his views on race, his contacts with psychics during World War II, and his intimate involvement in the creation of the nuclear weapons still menacing our civilization today. After Igor Gouzenko, the cipher clerk at the Russian Embassy in Ottawa, defected in September 1945 and revealed Russian spy rings seeking atomic bomb secrets in Canada, Great Britain, and the U.S., the Prime Minister held nine séances with Hester Dowden, Florence Jane Sharplin, Gladys Osborne Leonard, Helen Hughes, and Geraldine Cummins in London. In his sittings, he sought political counsel from the deceased President F.D. Roosevelt whether he should expose the Russian spy ring or give the secret of the atom bomb to the Russians. Seven of these London séances from 1945-1947 are transcribed in Appendix A of Volume 2. In addition to an extensive bibliography, a complete chronology of major events in King's life and contacts with mediums and psychics can be found in the Chronology in this volume.

ACKNOWLEDGEMENTS

I would like to express my great appreciation to the Survival Research Institute of Canada (https://survivalresearch.ca/) for its financial support while I completed researching and writing *The Spiritualist Prime Minister*. I am particularly grateful to Walter Meyer zu Erpen, SRIC President, for generously contributing his expertise in the fields of Spiritualism and psychical research, and for biographical and genealogical examinations of the mediums included in this study. I also thank Walter for introducing me to descendants of three mediums and psychic investigators and for very substantial assistance with locating photographic images.

I extend thanks to the International Association for the Preservation of Spiritualist and Occult Periodicals, in Forest Grove, Oregon (IAPSOP). The digital resources available on the IAPSOP website (http://iapsop.com/), in particular the British, American, and European Spiritualist and psychic science journals, have proven invaluable in locating additional material, confirming the citations of known articles, and demonstrating the flow of information from one country to another.

I am grateful to Library and Archives Canada for providing ten images from its William Lyon Mackenzie King fonds and to the Canadian Research Knowledge Network for providing seven images from the nine microfilm reels of the King Spiritualism Series J9 (https://heritage.canadiana.ca/view/oocihm.lac_mikan_108986). The University of Manitoba Archives and Special Collections (UMASC) kindly provided seven images from the Hamilton Family Fonds and the Victoria University Library provided photographs of Ellen Elliott and of Ellen Elliott with E.J. Pratt.

I thank the College of Psychic Studies in London for the 1913 portrait of Lizzy Lind-af-Hageby in *Light* and the photo of Mercy Phillimore. The National Portrait Gallery in London provided the photo of the Duchess of Hamilton. Additional images were provided by Parks Canada and Laurier House in Ottawa, the J. Paul Getty Museum's Open Content Program, the Missouri Historical Society, the Survival

Research Institute of Canada, the Bedford Fine Art Gallery, Bedford, Pennsylvania, the Galt Museum & Archives | Akaisamitohkanao'pa, Ontario, and the Homer Watson House and Gallery in Kitchener, Ontario. Janice Hamilton, a granddaughter of Dr. T. Glen Hamilton and Lillian Hamilton, kindly contributed the 1932 Hamilton family photo. I am also grateful to Brian Foss for helping to locate the Homer Watson image and to Konrad Skreta for providing valuable assistance with photographs.

CHRONOLOGY

Mackenzie King's Life and His Mediums

DECEMBER 11, 1837   King's grandfather, William Lyon Mackenzie, the leader of the failed 1837 Rebellion in Upper Canada, flees to the United States.

FEBRUARY 6, 1843   Mackenzie's wife, Isabel Baxter, gives birth to their 13th child, Isabel Grace, Mackenzie King's mother, at 4 p.m. at 12 Chambers Street while the family was living in exile in New York City.

SPRING, 1850   The seven-year-old Isabel Grace visits a fortune-teller in Kingston soon after Mackenzie is pardoned and he and his family return to Canada. Her folk belief in fortune-tellers persists until the 1890s.

AUGUST 28, 1861   Death of William Lyon Mackenzie.

DECEMBER 12, 1872   Isabel Grace marries John King in Toronto at 9 a.m.

NOVEMBER 15, 1873   Birth of Mackenzie King's older sister Bella in Berlin (Kitchener), Ontario, at 2 a.m.

DECEMBER 17, 1874   Birth of William Lyon Mackenzie King at 8 a.m. in Berlin, Ontario.

AUGUST 27, 1876   Birth of King's sister Jennie in Berlin, Ontario, just after midnight.

NOVEMBER 11, 1878   Birth of King's brother Max at 6 a.m. in Berlin, Ontario.

OCTOBER 17, 1891   King begins his studies at the University of Toronto.

SEPTEMBER 6, 1893   King writes his first entry in the diary he will keep until his death in 1950.

NOVEMBER 13, 1893   King begins opening his Bible at random for messages from God directing him what to do.

JANUARY 3, 1894	King is mesmerized by the phrenologist and mesmerist Prof. William P. Seymour while a student at the University of Toronto.
SPRING OF 1895	King receives his BA in political economy from the University of Toronto.
MAY 2, 1896	The palmist Mrs. Lauretta Menden tells King's fortune in Toronto.
JUNE 12, 1896	King receives his Bachelor of Laws from the University of Toronto.
SEPTEMBER 30, 1896	King arrives in Chicago to begin graduate studies at the University of Chicago.
SPRING 1897	King receives his MA from the University of Toronto.
JUNE 1898	King receives his MA from Harvard University.
JANUARY 11, 1900	King has his head read by the phrenologist O'Dell at the London Phrenological Institute in England.
SEPTEMBER 15, 1900	King is appointed Deputy Minister of Labour in Wilfrid Laurier's Liberal Government.
SEPTEMBER 24, 1903	King buys his first property at Kingsmere, Quebec, for $400.
MARCH 3, 1906	Audience members call on King to examine the actress Eva Fay on stage to prevent possible fraud at her mind-reading performance in Ottawa.
OCTOBER 26, 1908	King is elected MP for North Waterloo, Ontario, defeating his Conservative opponent by 263 votes.
JUNE 2, 1909	King is sworn in as Minister of Labour in Wilfrid Laurier's Liberal Government.
JUNE 30, 1909	King receives his PhD from Harvard.
SEPTEMBER 21, 1911	King loses his seat as MP for North Waterloo by 315 votes as Laurier's Government is defeated by Robert Borden's Conservatives.
APRIL 15, 1912	W.T. Stead perishes in the sinking of the *Titanic*.
AUGUST 13, 1914	After meeting with John D. Rockefeller Jr. in New York, King is appointed as a labour consultant for the Rockefeller Foundation.
APRIL 4, 1915	Death of King's sister Bella in Toronto at the age of 41.
AUGUST 30, 1915	Death of King's father, John King, in Toronto at the age of 72.

JULY 1, 1916 Dr. Chevrier examines King's spine in Ottawa and subsequently diagnoses him as suffering from a severe form of neurasthenia.

OCTOBER 26- NOVEMBER 11, 1916 King is examined at the Johns Hopkins hospital and medical school in Baltimore by Dr. Lewellys Franklin Barker and the psychiatrist Dr. Adolf Meyer. Their diagnosis includes psychoneurosis and psychasthenia.

JANUARY 26, 1917 King begins faith healing through prayer to heal his dying mother.

DECEMBER 17, 1917 King is defeated by 1,078 votes running for MP in the riding of North York, Ontario. Laurier's Liberals are defeated by Robert Borden's Unionist party.

DECEMBER 18, 1917 Death of King's mother Isabel in Ottawa at midnight at the age of 74.

FEBRUARY 15, 1918 The spirit of Isabel King appears to Mackenzie King in a dream vision and declares, "I am alive."

OCTOBER 2, 1918 King invites Joan Patteson to a dinner party to celebrate the completion of his study for the Rockefeller Foundation, *Industry and Humanity: A Study in the Principles Underlying Industrial Reconstruction*.

FEBRUARY 7, 1919 The phrenologist and mesmerist William P. Seymour commits suicide in Camden, New Jersey.

FEBRUARY 17, 1919 Death of Sir Wilfrid Laurier at the age of 77.

AUGUST 7, 1919 King is elected Leader of the Liberal Party at the national Liberal Party Convention in Ottawa.

OCTOBER 17, 1919 King receives an honorary Doctor of Laws degree from Queen's University in Kingston and contacts the fortune-teller Rachel Bleaney to give him a reading.

OCTOBER 20, 1919 King is elected by acclamation as MP for the riding of Prince County in Prince Edward Island and spends his first week in Parliament as Leader of the Opposition October 27 to November 1.

NOVEMBER 5, 1919. Rachel Bleaney writes King asking him to send her a personal article such as a handkerchief so that she can give him a spiritual reading to help and guide him.

OCTOBER 13, 1920	King has his palm read by a Syrian fortune-teller in Kamloops.
NOVEMBER 1921	Rachel Bleaney tells King his fortune regarding the general election to be held on December 6, 1921.
DECEMBER 6, 1921	King is elected by 1,055 votes as MP in North York, Ontario. The Liberals win a one-seat majority over the Progressive Party and the Conservative Party.
DECEMBER 22, 1921	Mayor W.D.L. Hardie publishes King's horoscope character sketch in the *Lethbridge Herald*.
DECEMBER 29, 1921	King is sworn in as Prime Minister and Secretary of State for External Affairs.
MARCH 18, 1922	Death of King's brother Max at 9 a.m. in Denver, Colorado, at the age of 43.
JANUARY 14, 1923	King moves into Laurier House donated to him by Lady Laurier after repairs paid for by Peter Larkin.
DECEMBER 29, 1923	King first hears about Etta Wriedt from Mary Fulford, who describes one of her sittings with the medium in Brockville, Ontario.
OCTOBER 4, 1924	King receives a horoscope from Mr. M.E. Young sent from England.
NOVEMBER 8, 1924	King and Joan Patteson read his horoscope received from Mayor Hardie of Lethbridge.
DECEMBER 31, 1924	King acknowledges receipt of his brother Max's horoscope from Mayor Hardie.
JANUARY 27, 1925	King has a reading by the Indian phrenologist and palmist-astrologer Douglas Goray in Atlantic City and consults him again the next day.
MARCH 1, 1925	Rachel Bleaney gives King and Joan Patteson readings in Laurier House.
APRIL 17, 1925	Mayor Hardie sends King his corrected horoscope.
OCTOBER 20, 1925	Rachel Bleaney gives King a reading in the Chateau Belvidere Hotel in Kingston.
OCTOBER 24, 1925	King sends Bleaney a dream to interpret in which he and his family are on deck of a ship that lurches over to one side and sinks into the water.

OCTOBER 29, 1925	King loses by 494 votes to his Conservative opponent in North York. Eight members of his Cabinet are also defeated as Arthur Meighen's Conservatives win 115 seats to the Liberals 100. King remains in office as Prime Minister with the support of 22 Progressive Party MPs.
OCTOBER 30, 1925	M.E. Young sends King his, his brother's and Isabel King's horoscopes and informs the PM that he has given up all astrological work and study.
FEBRUARY 15, 1926	King is elected MP with 5,631 votes over his Independent opponent in a by-election in Prince Albert, Saskatchewan.
JUNE 28, 1926	King resigns as Prime Minister after Governor General Lord Byng refuses to grant him a dissolution of Parliament.
JUNE 29, 1926	The Conservatives' Arthur Meighen is sworn in as Prime Minister but is defeated by a vote in Parliament on July 2.
JULY 26, 1926	Rachel Bleaney gives King a reading in Laurier House.
SEPTEMBER 14, 1926	King defeats his Conservative opponent, John Diefenbaker, by 4,095 votes in Prince Albert. Liberals win 116 seats to 91 for Arthur Meighen's Conservatives. He is sworn in as prime minister on September 25.
OCTOBER 2, 1926	Mayor Hardie sends King a thirty-page handwritten horoscope which he had cast before the September election predicting the Liberals' victory.
NOVEMBER 12, 1926	King meets Sir Oliver Lodge at Lord Grey's mansion during the 1926 Imperial Conference in London.
JUNE 28, 1927	The graphologist Fred Jacob analyzes King's handwriting. His analysis is published in Canadian newspapers the following year.
AUGUST 4, 1927	Rachel Bleaney gives King and Mrs. Stanley Baldwin readings in Laurier House.
JANUARY 10, 1929	Rachel Bleaney gives King a reading in Laurier House.
JANUARY 12, 1929	King acknowledges receipt of Mayor Hardie's latest horoscope.
APRIL 8, 1929	W.D.L. Hardie sends King a revised horoscope of his brother Max.

FEBRUARY 8, 1930	Rachel Bleaney gives King a reading in Laurier House.
JULY 28, 1930	King and the Liberal Party are reduced to 90 seats as R.B. Bennett's Conservatives win 135 seats. King is re-elected in Prince Albert by 192 votes over his Conservative opponent and becomes Leader of the Opposition until 1935.
DECEMBER 22, 1930	King has a reading by the English palmist Quest Brown in Laurier House.
JANUARY 21, 1931	The graphologist Jacobs reads King's and Joan and Godfroy Patteson's handwriting in Laurier House.
FEBRUARY 18, 1931	King consults with the palmist Quest Brown in Laurier House.
APRIL 12, 1931	The Montreal numerologist W.J. Morran sends Quest Brown King's number symbology.
APRIL 16, 1931	King consults with the palmist Quest Brown in Laurier House.
AUGUST 21, 1931	Rachel Bleaney gives King a reading in Norman Rogers' home in Kingston.
FEBRUARY 21, 1932	King participates in two séances with the direct-voice medium Etta Wriedt in Fulford Place, Brockville. In his diary he records, "read over the typewritten statement of first seance Mrs. Fulford had at Fulford place with Mrs. Wreidt [sic] some 20 years ago. It was very similar to the seance of tonight, only tonight seemed to me more remarkable."
FEBRUARY 22, 1932	King participates in two séances with Etta Wriedt in Fulford Place, Brockville.
FEBRUARY 24, 1932	King participates in a séance with Etta Wriedt in Laurier House.
FEBRUARY 25, 1932	King participates in a séance with Etta Wriedt in Laurier House.
FEBRUARY 26, 1932	King participates in three séances with Etta Wriedt in Laurier House.
JUNE 26, 1932	King participates in three séances with Etta Wriedt in Kingsmere.
JUNE 27, 1932	King participates in three séances with Etta Wriedt in Kingsmere.
JUNE 28, 1932	King participates in a séance with Etta Wriedt in Kingsmere.

JUNE 29, 1932	King participates in a séance with Etta Wriedt in Kingsmere.
JUNE 30, 1932	King participates in two séances with Etta Wriedt in Kingsmere.
SEPTEMBER 8, 1932	King participates in two séances with the clairaudient medium Miss Hitchcock in Fulford Place, Brockville.
SEPTEMBER 9, 1932	King participates in a séance with Miss Hitchcock in Fulford Place, Brockville.
SEPTEMBER 26, 1932	King receives purported messages from Sir Wilfrid Laurier transmitted via automatic writing to "Miss (…..)," an unidentified medium in Ottawa.
SEPTEMBER 29, 1932	King participates in a séance with Etta Wriedt in Detroit.
SEPTEMBER 30, 1932	King participates in two séances with Etta Wriedt in Detroit.
JANUARY 6, 1933	King participates in three séances with Etta Wriedt in Detroit.
JANUARY 7, 1933	King participates in a séance with Etta Wriedt in Detroit.
JANUARY 17, 1933	Rachel Bleaney gives King a reading in Laurier House.
JANUARY 18, 1933	Rachel Bleaney gives Joan Patteson and J.W.L. Forster readings in Laurier House.
APRIL 14, 1933	King participates in a séance with Etta Wriedt in Laurier House.
APRIL 15, 1933	King participates in three séances with Etta Wriedt in Laurier House.
APRIL 16, 1933	King participates in four séances with Etta Wriedt in Laurier House.
APRIL 17, 1933	King participates in three séances with Etta Wriedt in Laurier House.
AUGUST 20, 1933	King meets the psychic investigator Dr. Thomas Glendenning Hamilton and his first medium Elizabeth Poole in Winnipeg.
OCTOBER 15, 1933	King participates in a séance with Etta Wriedt in Detroit.
OCTOBER 16, 1933	King participates in three séances with Etta Wriedt in Detroit.
OCTOBER 17, 1933	King participates in two séances with Etta Wriedt in Detroit.

OCTOBER 30?, 1933 — King meets Helen Lambert and Marie and Hereward Carrington at the American Psychical Institute in New York.

NOVEMBER 13, 1933 — The Dominion Archivist, Arthur Doughty, introduces King to table rapping. Almost daily "conversations" over the "little table" with Joan Patteson follow until the end of May 1950.

NOVEMBER 18, 1933 — Marie Carrington sends King his receipt for annual associate membership in the American Psychical Institute, under the name M.K. Venice.

DECEMBER 13, 1933 — King participates in two séances with Etta Wriedt in Laurier House.

DECEMBER 14, 1933 — King participates in four séances with Etta Wriedt in Laurier House.

MARCH 13, 1934 — Death of Rachel Bleaney in Kingston at the age of 57.

APRIL 13, 1934 — In a "conversation" over the "little table" at Homer Watson's studio in Doon, Ontario, the late Senator Lawrence Alexander Wilson predicts an election victory of 1,600 votes in the by-election of Oxford South.

MAY 24, 1934 — Death of the graphologist Fred Jacob in Ottawa at the age of 69.

AUGUST 25, 1934 — King participates in three séances with Etta Wriedt in Laurier House.

AUGUST 26, 1934 — King participates in two séances with Etta Wriedt in Laurier House.

AUGUST 27, 1934 — King participates in three séances with Etta Wriedt in Laurier House.

AUGUST 28, 1934 — King participates in three séances with Etta Wriedt in Laurier House.

OCTOBER 6 & 7, 1934 — King has a "conversation" over the "little table" with Violet Markham at her home in Kent.

OCTOBER 12, 1934 — Lady Aberdeen informs King of evidence of her deceased husband's continued existence via automatic writing. He informs her of his "conversations" with Lord Aberdeen over the "little table."

OCTOBER 15, 1934 — King visits the Society for Psychical Research and the British College of Psychic Science in London to arrange sittings with trance mediums.

OCTOBER 22, 1934	Estelle Stead arranges a sitting for King with the trance medium Ruth Vaughan in London.
OCTOBER 23, 1934	Lady Aberdeen arranges a sitting for King with the automatic writing medium Hester Dowden in London.
OCTOBER 24, 1934	King has sittings with Hester Dowden and Ruth Vaughan in London.
MAY 7, 1935	King sends a sample of his handwriting to the Montreal graphologist Augustus Kingsley Cuddon-Woodthorpe for his book *Penmanship and Personality*.
OCTOBER 14, 1935	King and the Liberal Party are returned to power in the 1935 federal election, winning 171 seats to 39 for the Conservatives and 17 for Social Credit. King is re-elected in Prince Albert by 1,553 votes. He is sworn in as prime minister on October 23.
NOVEMBER 16, 1935	King and Princess Cantacuzene (Julia Grant) have a séance sitting in Washington in which they communicate with President Ulysses S. Grant.
DECEMBER 2, 1935	King dines with Helen Lambert at her home in New York.
DECEMBER 3, 1935	King has a sitting with the clairvoyant Edwina Crunden (Miss Tweedie) in New York.
DECEMBER 4, 1935	King has a sitting with the trance medium Eileen Garrett in New York in the morning and has his fortune told from the cup at the Roma Gypsy Tea Room in the afternoon.
AUGUST 11, 1936	King dines at Kingsmere with the astrologer Ruth Cecilia Stevenson who prepares his horoscope.
AUGUST 24, 1936	King sends Etta Wriedt funds for her train transportation to Ottawa for séances at Kingsmere on August 22 and 23 that are omitted from his heavily redacted diary.
SEPTEMBER 29, 1936	King addresses the League of Nations Assembly in Geneva following Adolf Hitler's military occupation of the Rhineland and Italy's conquest of Ethiopia and scuttles the League's principle of enforcing collective security through military intervention.
OCTOBER 3, 1936	King meets the Duchess of Hamilton and Lind-af-Hageby, the President of the London Spiritualist Alliance, in Geneva.

OCTOBER 22, 1936	King has a sitting with Rose Livingstone at the London Spiritualist Alliance.
OCTOBER 23, 1936	King has a sitting with the clairaudient medium Helen Hughes at the London Spiritualist Alliance.
OCTOBER 26, 1936	King has a sitting with Ruth Vaughan at the London Spiritualist Alliance.
OCTOBER 27, 1936	King probably did not attend his scheduled 10 a.m. sitting with Pamela Nash due to his meeting with King Edward VIII at Buckingham Palace at 11:15 a.m.
OCTOBER 28, 1936	King probably cancelled his scheduled 10:30 a.m. meeting with the trance medium Naomi Bacon at the London Spiritualist Alliance.
OCTOBER 28, 1936	King purchases a crystal ball at the Partridge and Company antique shop in London and attends the evening gathering in his honour at the London Spiritualist Alliance organized by the Duchess of Hamilton, Lind-af- Hageby and Mercy Phillimore.
NOVEMBER 15, 1936	King records seeing an angel in his crystal ball at Laurier House.
DECEMBER 15, 1936	King receives his horoscope from Cecilia Ruth Stevenson.
DECEMBER 31, 1936	King acknowledges receipt of a new horoscope from W.D.L. Hardie.
MAY 9, 1937	King has a sitting with the trance medium Ruth Vaughan at the London Spiritualist Alliance.
MAY 10, 1937	King purchases a "little table" at the Partridge and Company antique shop in London and has a solo "conversation" over the "little table" at the Ritz Hotel.
MAY 12, 1937	Following the Coronation of King George VI and Queen Elizabeth, King has another solo session over the "little table" at the Ritz.
MAY 13, 1937	King receives a second crystal ball purchased at the Partridge and Company antique shop as a gift from the American millionaire Alfred H. Caspary.
MAY 15-16, 1937	King visits the Duchess of Hamilton at her country estate, Ferne, in Dorset. In addition to Lind-af-Hageby, he meets with Sir Oliver Lodge on May 16.

MAY 29, 1937 — King visits Lind-af-Hageby at her home in London.

JUNE 2, 1937 — King has a sitting with Rose Livingstone at the London Spiritualist Alliance.

JUNE 12, 1937 — King visits the Duchess of Hamilton at her home in London where he has a sitting with the trance medium Gladys Osborne Leonard.

JUNE 16, 1937 — King has a sitting with Rose Livingstone at the London Spiritualist Alliance.

JUNE 17, 1937 — King has a sitting with Pamela Nash at the London Spiritualist Alliance and shows his crystal ball to "some friends" at the [International] Institute for Psychical Research.

JUNE 29, 1937 — King meets with General Hermann Goering, Rudolf Hess, and Adolf Hitler in the Hindenburg Palace in Berlin.

NOVEMBER 15, 1937 — King sends a sample of his handwriting to Adrienne, the handwriting analyst for the *Vancouver Sun*. He begins communicating with Etta Wriedt and the Duchess of Hamilton regarding Wriedt's desire to donate her portrait and other spiritualist memorabilia to the London Spiritualist Alliance.

DECEMBER 9, 1937 — Gladys Osborne Leonard begins sending King periodic messages from the Beyond received via automatic writing and "impressions." They correspond until December 1949.

JANUARY 15, 1938 — King participates in two séances with Etta Wriedt in Laurier House.

JANUARY 16, 1938 — King participates in his last séance with Etta Wriedt in Laurier House.

JANUARY 17, 1938 — King shows the crystal ball he received from Alfred Caspary to Governor General Lord Tweedsmuir at Laurier House.

APRIL 19, 1938 — King declines Nandor Fodor's invitation to become a member of the International Institute for Psychical Research in London.

APRIL 20, 1938 — King receives a horoscope from Cecilia Ruth Stevenson.

FEBRUARY 7, 1939 — King has his hands read by the palmist Quest Brown in Laurier House.

SEPTEMBER 10, 1939 — Canada declares war on Germany.

SEPTEMBER 25, 1939	King receives a genealogical chart linking Queen Elizabeth, The Queen Mother, with the Mackenzie family from Mrs. Doughty in B.C.
OCTOBER 18, 1939	Dr. John Hett begins reporting communications to King from the spirit world in séances with Etta Wriedt before and after her death.
MARCH 26, 1940	King is re-elected in Prince Albert, defeating his National Unity (Conservative) opponent by 776 votes. The Liberals win 179 seats, National Unity 39, William D. Herridge's New Democracy 10, and J.S. Woodsworth's Co-operative Commonwealth 8.
JUNE 10, 1940	Canada declares war on Italy.
AUGUST 17, 1940	King meets with President F.D. Roosevelt and signs the Ogdensburg Agreement.
APRIL 19, 1941	King meets with Helen Lambert at her home in New York.
JUNE 18, 1941	King visits the psychic Jessie Coumbe in New York.
JULY 15, 1941	Death of King's Irish terrier Pat I at 4:20 a.m.
DECEMBER 8, 1941	Canada declares war on Japan.
DECEMBER 17, 1941	Ellen Elliott sends King the transcript of a sitting with the trance medium Alma Brash containing a message for King from the White Brother.
MARCH 3, 1942	A. Elliott Jacks in Vancouver begins sending King visions and messages from the spirit world he was instructed to forward to the Prime Minister. They correspond until July 27, 1945.
APRIL 18, 1942	King makes a second visit to Jessie Coumbe in New York.
APRIL 22, 1942	The Canadian national plebiscite on conscription frees the federal government to introduce compulsory overseas military service.
AUGUST 4, 1942	King has a sitting with the trance medium Alma Brash and Ellen Elliott in Toronto.
AUGUST 17, 1942	Death of W.D.L. Hardie in Lethbridge at the age of 80.
AUGUST 19, 1942	916 Canadians die and thousands more are injured and taken prisoner in the Dieppe Raid in France.
SEPTEMBER 13, 1942	Death of Etta Wriedt in Detroit of a stroke at the age of 81.

MAY 7, 1943	King has lunch with Ellen Elliott in Laurier House.
MAY 18, 1943	Ellen Elliott sends King a message from the White Brother received in a séance with Alma Brash.
AUGUST 17-24, 1943	King hosts the first Quebec Conference with President F.D. Roosevelt and Prime Minister Winston Churchill in Quebec City.
SEPT. 12-16, 1944	King hosts the second Quebec Conference with President Roosevelt and Prime Minister Churchill in Quebec City.
APRIL 12, 1945	President F.D. Roosevelt dies suddenly of a cerebral hemorrhage. Harry S. Truman becomes President.
APRIL 30, 1945	Adolf Hitler commits suicide in his bunker in Berlin.
MAY 8, 1945	End of World War II in Europe.
JUNE 11, 1945	King loses to his Co-operative Commonwealth opponent by 129 votes in Prince Albert. The Liberals win 118 seats, Progressive Conservatives 67, Co-operative Commonwealth 28, and Social Credit 13.
AUGUST 6, 1945	King is re-elected to Parliament in a by-election in Glengarry, Ontario, defeating an Independent opponent by 4,226 votes.
AUGUST 6, 1945	The United States drops an atomic bomb on Hiroshima.
AUGUST 9, 1945	The United States drops an atomic bomb on Nagasaki.
AUGUST 15, 1945	The Japanese surrender, ending World War II.
SEPTEMBER 5, 1945	Igor Gouzenko, the cipher clerk at the Russian Embassy in Ottawa, defects and reveals Russian spy rings seeking atomic bomb secrets in Canada, Great Britain, and the U.S.
SEPTEMBER 29, 1945	King travels to Washington to inform President Harry Truman of the Russian spy ring in Canada.
OCTOBER 7, 1945	King arrives in London and meets with Prime Minister Clement Attlee to discuss the Russian spy ring in Canada and the United Kingdom.
OCTOBER 17, 1945	King meets with Mercy Phillimore at the London Spiritualist Alliance.

OCTOBER 25, 1945	King has a sitting with the automatic writing medium Hester Dowden in London at 6 p.m. (see séance transcription in Volume 2, Appendix A).
OCTOBER 26, 1945	King has a sitting with Florence Jane Sharplin at the London Spiritualist Alliance at 9:30 a.m. (see séance transcription in Volume 2, Appendix A).
OCTOBER 27, 1945	King has a sitting with the trance medium Gladys Osborne Leonard in Tankerton, England, from 10:40 to 12:30 a.m.
OCTOBER 30, 1945	King has a sitting with the clairaudient medium Helen Hughes at the London Spiritualist Alliance at 11 a.m. (see séance transcription in Volume 2, Appendix A).
OCTOBER 31, 1945	King has a sitting with Florence Jane Sharplin in London at 9:30 a.m. (see séance transcription in Volume 2, Appendix A).
NOVEMBER 10, 1945	King and Prime Minister Attlee arrive in Washington to discuss the Russian atomic spy ring and the control over atomic energy and the atom bomb with President Truman.
FEBRUARY 13, 1946	Igor Gouzenko begins testifying before the Royal Commission on Espionage.
MARCH 4, 1946	The Royal Commission on Espionage issues its First Interim Report.
MARCH 5, 1946	Alan Nunn May is arrested in London for espionage and subsequently is sentenced to ten years' imprisonment.
MARCH 22, 1946	King has tea with Ellen Elliott in Laurier House.
MAY 19, 1946	King arrives in London to confer with Clement Attlee and participate in the June 8 Victory Day procession.
MAY 23, 1946	Mercy Phillimore shows King Etta Wriedt's watch and portrait the medium donated to the London Spiritualist Alliance.
MAY 28, 1946	King has a sitting with Florence Jane Sharplin at the London Spiritualist Alliance (see séance transcription in Volume 2, Appendix A).
MAY 29, 1946	King has a sitting with Miss Smith at the London Spiritualist Alliance.
MAY 30, 1946	King has a sitting with Helen Hughes at the London Spiritualist Alliance at 10:30 a.m.

JUNE 27, 1946	MP Fred Rose is convicted of espionage and sentenced to six years in prison.
JULY 28, 1946	King arrives in Paris for the Paris Peace Conference.
NOVEMBER 28, 1946	King has tea with Ellen Elliott in Laurier House.
JULY 31, 1947	King invites Ellen Elliott to dinner at Kingsmere.
AUGUST 11, 1947	Death of King's Irish terrier Pat II.
NOVEMBER 6, 1947	King sends a sample of his handwriting to T.W. Deachman for his graphological analysis for *Canadian Business*.
NOVEMBER 22, 1947	King has a sitting with Florence Jane Sharplin at 11 a.m. at her home in London and with the automatic writing medium Geraldine Cummins at her home in the afternoon (see séance transcriptions in Volume 2, Appendix A).
NOVEMBER 25, 1947	King sends the November 22, 1947, transcript of his séance with Geraldine Cummins to Winston Churchill who returns it to King with "a most significant little note."
AUGUST 7, 1948	King resigns as Leader of the Liberal Party. He receives Pat III as a gift.
SEPTEMBER 20, 1948	King arrives in Cherbourg, France, and takes the train to Paris to attend the Third General Assembly of the United Nations.
OCTOBER 6, 1948	King arrives in London to attend the Conference of British Prime Ministers.
OCTOBER 8, 1948	Lord Moran examines King and detects symptoms of incipient heart failure. King arranges with Mercy Phillimore for sittings with mediums in London.
OCTOBER 22, 1948	King has a sitting with the trance medium Edith Thomson at the Dorchester Hotel in London.
OCTOBER 23, 1948	King has a sitting with Geraldine Cummins and Beatrice Gibbes at the Dorchester Hotel.
OCTOBER 26, 1948	King has a sitting with Florence Jane Sharplin in the morning and a sitting with Gladys Osborne Leonard in the evening at the Dorchester Hotel.
NOVEMBER 15, 1948	King resigns as Prime Minister of Canada. Louis St. Laurent becomes Prime Minister.
APRIL 30, 1949	King relinquishes his seat in the House of Commons.

SEPTEMBER 25, 1949   King records his last diary entry having a séance on the "little table" with Joan Patteson.

DECEMBER 8, 1949   King records his last diary entry about receiving correspondence from Gladys Osborne Leonard, "on Mother & Harper (on his anniversary of passing) & in reference to importance of writing."

JULY 20, 1950   King suffers his final heart attack.

JULY 22, 1950   Death of Mackenzie King at 9:42 p.m. in Kingsmere, Quebec, at the age of 75.

AUGUST 19, 1950   *Psychic News* publishes Fred Archer's front-page exposé "Mackenzie King Sought Spirit Aid in State Affairs: Canadian Premier Had Proved Survival."

DECEMBER 15, 1951   *Maclean's Magazine* publishes Blair Fraser's "The Secret Life of Mackenzie King, Spiritualist."

APRIL 7, 1954   Death of Godfroy Patteson.

APRIL 23, 1960   Death of Joan Patteson.

APRIL 20, 1976   Macmillan in Toronto publishes C.P. Stacey's *A Very Double Life: The Private World of Mackenzie King*. Newspapers across Canada started publishing the first of five excerpts from Stacey's biography on March 6. The *Vancouver Sun* headlined its excerpt on March 8, 1976, "Sin pushed King to Brink of Insanity."

JANUARY 1, 2001   Library and Archives Canada opens the William Lyon Mackenzie King Spiritualism Series. MG 26 J 9. LAC subsequently posts the Series online at http://heritage.canadiana.ca/view/oocihm.lac_mikan_108986

2003   Library and Archives Canada digitizes *The William Lyon Mackenzie King Diaries* MG 26 J 13 and posts the diaries online at http://www.bac-lac.gc.ca/eng/discover/politics-government/prime-ministers/william-lyon-mackenzie-king/Pages/diaries-william-lyon-mackenzie-king.aspx.

BIBLIOGRAPHY

Anonymous. *Concerning the Origin & Aims of the London Spiritualist Alliance Ltd. and The Quest Club*. [London: L.S.A. Publications], 1935.

Anonymous. "Miss Lind-af-Hageby Elected President of the L.S.A.," *Light* 55:2822 (February 7, 1935).

Alvarado, Carlos S. "Frederic W.H. Myers, Psychical Research and Psychology: An Essay Review of Trevor Hamilton's *Immortal Longings: F.W.H. Myers and the Victorian Search for Life After Death*," *Journal of the Society for Psychical Research* (subsequently cited as *JSPR*) 73:896 (July 2009).

Alvarado, Carlos S., and Michael Nahm, "Psychic Phenomena and the Vital Force: Hereward Carrington on 'Vital Energy and Psychical Phenomena,'" *JSPR* 75.2, no. 903, April 2011.

American Psychiatric Association, *Diagnostic and Statistical Manual of Mental Disorders*. Fifth edition. *DSM-5*. Washington, D.C.: American Psychiatric Publishing, 2013.

Archer, Fred. "Statesmen and Spiritualism" in his *Ghost Writer*. London: W.H. Allen, 1966.

Asprem, Egil. "Science and the Occult" in Christopher Partridge, ed. *The Occult World*. London: Routledge, 2016.

Austin, Benjamin Fish. *What Converted Me to Spiritualism: One Hundred Testimonies*. Toronto: Austin Publishing, 1901. https://www.canadiana.ca/view/oocihm.78875/1?r=0&s=1

Azzi, Stephen, and Norman Hillmer, "Ranking Canada's Best and Worst Prime Ministers," *Maclean's*, October 7, 2016.

Ballstadt, Carl, Michael Peterman, and Elizabeth Hopkins. "'A Glorious Madness': Susanna Moodie and the Spiritualist Movement," *Journal of Canadian Studies* 17:4 (Winter 1982-83).

Barrie, J.M. *Farewell Miss Julie Logan: A J.M. Barrie Omnibus*. Andrew Nash, ed. Edinburgh: Canongate Classic, 2000.

Bedore, Margaret Elizabeth. "The Reading of Mackenzie King." PhD thesis, Queen's University, 2008.

Bliss, Michael. *Right Honourable Men: The Descent of Canadian Politics from Macdonald to Chrétien*. Toronto: HarperCollins, 2004.

Bliss, Michael. *Writing History: A Professor's Life*. Toronto: Dundurn, 2011.

Bogdan, Henrik, and Gordan Djurdjevic, eds. *Occultism in a Global Perspective*. London and New York: Routledge, 2014.

Bourdieu, Pierre. "Genesis and Structure of the Religious Field," *Comparative Social Research* 13 (1991).

Bourdieu, Pierre. "Legitimation and Structured Interests in Weber's Sociology of Religion" in *Max Weber, Rationality and Modernity*. Scott Lash, Sam Whimster, eds. London: Allen & Unwin, 1987.

Bourdieu, Pierre. "Some Properties of Fields" in Pierre Bourdieu. *Sociology in Question*. Richard Nice, trans. London: Sage Publications, 1993.

Bowering, George. *Egotists and Autocrats: The Prime Ministers of Canada*. Toronto: Penguin Books, 1999.

Boyko, John. *Bennett: The Rebel Who Challenged and Changed a Nation*. Fredericton: Goose Lane Editions, 2012.

Bradley, Herbert Dennis. *An Indictment of the Present Administration of the Society for Psychical Research*. London: C. Vernon, 1931. https://babel.hathitrust.org/cgi/pt?id=uc1.b4273705&view=1up&seq=7&skin=2021

Brandon, Ruth. *The Spiritualists: The Passion for the Occult in the Nineteenth and Twentieth Centuries*. London: Weidenfeld and Nicolson, 1983.

Brown, Quest. "Destiny, and Sir Arthur Currie," *The Passing Show* (Montreal), December 1930.

Bucke, Richard Maurice. *Cosmic Consciousness: A Study in the Evolution of the Human Mind*. Philadelphia: Innes, 1901 and New York: Dutton, 1969.

Campion, Nicholas. "Astrology" in Christopher Partridge, ed. *The Occult World*. London: Routledge, 2016.

Carrington, Hereward. *Higher Psychical Development (Yoga Philosophy): An Outline of the Secret Hindu Teachings*. New York: Dodd, Mead, 1920.

Charlesworth, Hector. *Candid Chronicles: Leaves from the Note Book of a Canadian Journalist*. Toronto: Macmillan, 1925.

Chéroux, Clément, et al. *The Perfect Medium: Photography and the Occult*. New Haven: Yale University Press, 2004.

Clarke, N.P. "Psychometric Experiments with Ruth Vaughan," *Quarterly Transactions of the British College of Psychic Science* (subsequently cited as *Quarterly Transactions BCPS*) 12:4 (January 1934).

Colombo, John Robert. *Mackenzie King's Ghost and Other Personal Accounts of Canadian Hauntings*. Willowdale, Ontario: Hounslow Press, 1991.

Cook, Ramsay. *The Regenerators: Social Criticism in Late Victorian English Canada*. Toronto: University of Toronto Press, 1985.

Craven, Paul. *'An Impartial Umpire': Industrial Relations and the Canadian State, 1900-1911*. Toronto: University of Toronto Press, 1980.

Cummins, Geraldine. "Experiments in Automatic Writing," *JSPR* 31:555 (May 1939).

Cummins, Geraldine. *Mind in Life and Death*. London: Aquarian Press, 1956.

Cummins, Geraldine. "My Mediumship," *Light* 56:2872 (January 23, 1936).

Cummins, Geraldine. "Problems of After-Death Messages," *Light* 51:2655 (November 27, 1931).

Cummins, Geraldine. "Problems of Automatic Writing," *Light* 55:2821 (January 31, 1935).

Cummins, Geraldine. *The Road to Immortality: Being a Description of the After-Life Purporting to be Communicated by the late F.W.H. Myers through Geraldine Cummins*. London: Ivor Nicholson & Watson, 1932.

Cummins, Geraldine. "Roosevelt's Three Prophecies to Mackenzie King," *Psychic News*, October 7, 1961.

Cummins, Geraldine. "Survival and Immortality: A Modern Revelation," *Light* 56:2886 (April 30, 1936).

Cummins, Geraldine. *Unseen Adventures: An Autobiography Covering Thirty-four Years of Work in Psychical Research*. London: Rider, 1951.

Davies, Robertson. *The Manticore* in *The Deptford Trilogy*. Bungay, Suffolk: Penguin, 1985.

Dawson, R. MacGregor. *William Lyon Mackenzie King: A Political Biography, 1874-1923*. Toronto: University of Toronto Press, 1958.

De Brath, Stanley. "Ectoplasm," *Quarterly Transactions BCPS* 14:1 (April 1935).

De Brath, Stanley. "Psychical Research and Human Survival," *Light* 40:2084 (December 18, 1920).

Denison, Flora MacDonald. *Mary Melville, The Psychic*. Toronto: Austin Publishing, 1900.

Denison, Flora MacDonald. "The Vision of Mary" in B.F. Austin, ed. *What Converted Me to Spiritualism: One Hundred Testimonies*. Toronto: Austin Publishing, 1901.

Donaghy, Greg. *Grit: The Life and Politics of Paul Martin Sr.* Vancouver: UBC Press, 2015.

Douglas-Hamilton, James. *The Truth about Rudolf Hess*. Edinburgh: Mainstream Publishing, 1993.

Dowden, Hester. "Automatic Writing: How It May Be Developed and Its Dangers Avoided," *Light* 53:2754 (October 20, 1933).

Doyle, Arthur Conan. *The History of Spiritualism*. Volume 2. London: Cassell, 1926. Reprinted London: Psychic Press, 1989, and Project Gutenberg Australia, 2014. http://gutenberg.net.au/ebooks03/0301061h.html#pic23

Doyle, Arthur Conan. "A New Revelation: Spiritualism and Religion," *Light* 36:1869 (November 4, 1916).

Doyle, Arthur Conan. "The New Revelation," *Light* 37:1922, 37:1923, 37:1924 (November 10, 17, and 24, 1917).

Doyle, Arthur Conan. *The New Revelation*. London and Toronto: Hodder & Stoughton, 1918. https://www.canadiana.ca/view/oocihm.73505/1

Doyle, Arthur Conan. *Our Second American Adventure*. London: Hodder & Stoughton, 1923.

Dryden, Jean F. "The Mackenzie King Papers: An Archival Odyssey." *Archivaria* 6 (Summer 1978).

Duchess of Hamilton. "Priest or Prophet?: The Letter Killeth but the Spirit Giveth Life," *Light* 57:2945 (June 17, 1937).

Duchess of Hamilton. "Spiritualism and the Religion of To-Morrow," *Light* 43:2020 (March 10, 1923).

Duchess of Hamilton. "What Humanity Owes to the Medium: Unjust Laws Which Should Be Removed," *Light* 55:2836 (May 9, 1935).

Dummitt, Christopher. *Unbuttoned: A History of Mackenzie King's Secret Life*. Montreal and Kingston: McGill-Queen's University Press, 2017.

Dyson, Erika White. *Spiritualism and Crime: Negotiating Prophecy and Power at the Turn of the Twentieth Century*. PhD thesis, Columbia University, 2010.

Eayrs, James. "'To find the demi-god a man': King and the historians," *Vancouver Sun*, December 17, 1974, 6.

Eayrs, James. "Will Mackenzie King Attend His 100th Anniversary?" *Toronto Star*, December 14, 1974, B6.

Ebon, Martin. *They Knew the Unknown*. New York: World Publishing, 1971.

Elliott, Ellen. *Publishing in Wartime*. Toronto: Macmillan, 1941.

English, John, and Kenneth McLaughlin. *Kitchener: An Illustrated History*. Waterloo: Wilfrid Laurier University Press, 1983.

Fausset, Hugh l'Anson. *The Lost Leader: A Study of Wordsworth*. London: Jonathan Cape, 1933.

Ferguson, Will. *Bastards & Boneheads: Canada's Glorious Leaders Past and Present*. Vancouver: Douglas & McIntyre, 1999.

Ferns, Henry S. *Reading from Left to Right: One Man's Political History*. Toronto: University of Toronto Press, 1983.

Ferns, Henry S., and Bernard Ostry. *The Age of Mackenzie King: The Rise of the Leader*. London: William Heineman and Toronto: British Book Service Canada, 1955. Reprinted, Toronto: James Lorimer, 1976.

Findlay, J. Arthur. "Mr. J. Arthur Findlay Replies: Why Spiritualism Must Become the Only World-Religion," *Light* 53:2760 (December 1, 1933).

Fodor, Nandor. "MacKenzie [sic] King's Search for Survival" in *Between Two Worlds*. West Nyack, N.Y.: Parker Publishing, 1964.

Foss, Brian. *Homer Watson: Life and Work*. Toronto: Art Canada Institute, 2018. Ebook: https://www.aci-iac.ca/art-books/homer-watson

Fraser, Blair. "The Secret Life of Mackenzie King, Spiritualist," *Maclean's Magazine* 64:24 (December 15, 1951).

Gerry, Elbridge T. *The Mumler "Spirit" Photograph Case. Argument of Elbridge T. Gerry on the Preliminary Examination of W.H. Mumler, Charged with Obtaining Money by Pretended "Spirit" Photographs*. New York: Baker, Vorhis, 1869.

Gibbes, E.B. "Alleged Communications from F.W.H. Myers," *Quarterly Transactions BCPS* 11:1 (April 1932).

Gibbes, E.B. "The Case of Elizabeth B.: Story of a Girl's Evidential Communications from the 'Other Side,'" *Light* 55:2838 (May 30, 1935).

Gibbes, E.B. *The Controls of Geraldine Cummins. Being an Attempt to Prove That They Are Entities Separate From Each Other, and From the Automatist*. London: Grosvenor Press, 1937.

Gibbes, E.B. "Notes on 'The Scripts of Cleophas,'" *Light* 48:2464 (March 31, 1928).

Gow, David. "Dr. Glen Hamilton's Research," *Light* 52:2701 (October 14, 1932).

Gow, David. "Spiritualism: Its Position and Its Prospects," *Quest* 11:2 (January 1920).

Granatstein, J.L., and Norman Hillmer. *Prime Ministers: Ranking Canada's Leaders*. Toronto: HarperCollins, 1999.

Granholm, Kennet. "Sociology and the Occult" in Christopher Partridge, ed. *The Occult World*. London and New York: Routledge, 2015.

Gray, Charlotte. "Crazy Like a Fox," *Saturday Night* 112:8 (October 1997).

Gray, Charlotte. *Mrs. King: The Life and Times of Isabel Mackenzie King*. Toronto: Viking, 1997.

Green, Henry A.V. "British Medical Association, Winnipeg," *Quarterly Transactions BCPS* 9:3 (October 1930).

Green, Nile. "The Global Occult: An Introduction," *History of Religions* 54:4 (May 2015).

Greenland, Cyril, and John Robert Colombo. *Walt Whitman's Canada*. Willowdale, Ontario: Hounslow Press, 1992.

Hamilton, Janice. "'Bring On Your Ghosts!' The Thomas Glendenning Hamilton Family Séances from 1918 to 1944, Winnipeg, Canada," *Paranormal Review* 77 (Winter 2016).

Hamilton, Lillian. "The Death of Kitty A.: A Case of Supernormal Cognition," *Quarterly Transactions BCPS* 16:1 (April 1937).

Hamilton, Lillian. "'Elizabeth M.': The Wonderful Story of Dr. Glen Hamilton's First Medium," *Light* 56:2893 (June 18, 1936).

Hamilton, Lillian. "Robert Louis Stevenson Calling!: Communications Received by the Glen Hamilton Circle in Winnipeg, Canada," *Light* 61:3147 (May 8, 1941).

Hamilton, Lillian. "Telepathy plus Spiritism in the Hamilton Researches in Winnipeg," *Light* 71:3372 (April 1951).

Hamilton, Margaret Lillian. *Is Survival a Fact?: Studies of Deep-Trance Automatic Scripts and the Bearing of Intentional Actions by Trance Personalities on the Question of Human Survival.* London: Psychic Press, 1969. https://archives.lib.umanitoba.ca/media/Hamilton_Is_Survival_A_Fact.pdf

Hamilton, Thomas Glendenning. "The C.H. Spurgeon Case: 'Stupendous Re-statement of the Central Claims of Christianity,'" *Light* 53:2756 (November 3, 1933).

Hamilton, Thomas Glendenning. "Dr. Glen Hamilton on His Experiments" [reprinted from the *Winnipeg Free Press*], *Light* 53:2741 (July 21, 1933).

Hamilton, Thomas Glendenning. "Dr. Glen Hamilton on Trance Personality" [reprinted from the *Winnipeg Free Press*], *Light* 53:2742 (July 28, 1933).

Hamilton, Thomas Glendenning. "Dr. Glen Hamilton's Psychic Studies: Human Faces in Teleplasm," *Light* 53:2751 (September 29, 1933).

Hamilton, Thomas Glendenning. "Has C.H. Spurgeon Returned?: Efforts to 'Put Through' Religious Teachings from the 'Other Side,'" *Light* 53:2755 (October 27, 1933).

Hamilton, Thomas Glendenning. "Has C.H. Spurgeon Returned?: What the Cameras Revealed and the 'Voices' Described," *Light* 53:2753 (October 13, 1933).

Hamilton, Thomas Glendenning. *Intention and Survival: Psychical Research Studies and the Bearing of Intentional Actions by Trance Personalities on the Problem of Human Survival.* Ed. J.D. Hamilton. Toronto: Macmillan, 1942. https://archives.lib.umanitoba.ca/media/Hamilton_Intention_and_Survival.pdf

Hamilton, Thomas Glendenning. *Intention and Survival: Psychical Research Studies and the Bearing of Intentional Actions by Trance Personalities on the Problem of Human Survival.* Second edition. Ed. Margaret Lillian Hamilton. London: Regency Press, 1977.

Hamilton, Thomas Glendenning. "Margery in Winnipeg: Three Seances of December 1926," *Proceedings of the American Society for Psychical Research* 21 (1933, dated 1926-1927).

Hamilton, Thomas Glendenning. "Reality of Psychic Force: Winnipeg Investigator's Clear Lead to Science," *Light* 55:2818 (January 10, 1935).

Hamilton, Thomas Glendenning. "A Summary of Ten Years of Psychical Research," *Light* 49:2513 (March 9, 1929).

Hamilton, Thomas Glendenning. "Teleplasmic Phenomena in Winnipeg," *Quarterly Transactions BCPS* 8:3 (October 1929), 8:4 (January 1930) and 9:2 (July 1930).

Hamilton, Thomas Glendenning. "The Teleplasms of Mary M. in the Winnipeg Phenomena," *JASPR* 25:1 (January 1931).

Hamilton, Trevor. *Immortal Longings: F.W.H. Myers and the Victorian Search for Life After Death*. Exeter: Academic, 2009.

Hankey, Muriel. *James Hewat McKenzie: Pioneer of Psychical Research*. London: Aquarian Press, 1963.

Hardy, H. Reginald. *Mackenzie King of Canada*. London: Oxford University Press, 1949.

Hardy, H. Reginald. "Our Fantastic Legacy from Mackenzie King," *Maclean's* July 15, 1951.

Hayward, E.A.S. "Spiritualism in Canada," *Light* 55:2861 (November 7, 1935).

Henderson, George F. *W.L. Mackenzie King: A Bibliography and Research Guide*. Toronto: University of Toronto Press, 1998.

Hillmer, Norman, and J.L. Granatstein, "Historians Rank the Best and Worst Prime Ministers," *Maclean's* 110:16 (April 21, 1997).

Hillmer, Norman, and Stephen Azzi, "Canada's Best Prime Ministers," *Maclean's* June 10, 2011.

Homer, Michael W. "Arthur Conan Doyle's Adventures in Winnipeg," *Manitoba History* 25 (Spring 1993) and http://www.mhs.mb.ca/docs/mb_history/25/doyleinwinnipeg.shtml

Howe, Ellie. *Astrology & The Third Reich*. Wellingborough, Northamptonshire: Aquarian Press, 1984.

Hughes, Helen. "How I Demonstrate Survival: Famous Clairaudient Medium Describes Her Experiences," *Light* 56:2879 (March 12, 1936).

Hutchison, Bruce. *The Incredible Canadian: A Candid Portrait of Mackenzie King: His Works, His Times, and His Nation*. Toronto: Longmans, 1952, and Don Mills, Ontario: Oxford University Press, 2011.

Hutchison, Bruce. *Mr. Prime Minister 1867-1964*. Don Mills, Ontario: Longmans Canada, 1964.

James, William. *The Varieties of Religious Experience: A Study in Human Nature*. New York: Longmans, Green, 1902.

Keshavjee, Serena, ed. *The Art of Ectoplasm*. Winnipeg: University of Manitoba Press, 2023.

Keyserlingk, Robert H. "Mackenzie King's Spiritualism and His View of Hitler in 1939," *Journal of Canadian Studies* 20:4 (Winter 1985-86), and in Donald Avery and Roger Hall, eds. *Coming of Age: Readings in Canadian History Since World War II*. Toronto: Harcourt Brace, 1996.

Kilbourn, William. *The Firebrand: William Lyon Mackenzie and the Rebellion in Upper Canada*. Toronto: Dundurn Press, 2008.

King, D. Macdougall. *The Battle with Tuberculosis and How to Win It*. Philadelphia: J.B. Lippincott, 1917.

King, D. Macdougall. *Nerves and Personal Power: Some Principles of Psychology as Applied to Conduct and Health*; with an introduction by W.L. Mackenzie King. New York: Fleming Revell, 1922.

King, William Lyon Mackenzie. *Canada and the Fight for Freedom.* Toronto: Macmillan, 1944.

King, William Lyon Mackenzie. *Industry and Humanity: A Study in the Principles Underlying Industrial Reconstruction.* Toronto: Thomas Allen, and Boston and New York: Houghton Mifflin, 1918. Toronto: Macmillan, 1935 and 1947. Toronto: University of Toronto Press, 1973.

King, William Lyon Mackenzie. "Liberalism The Principle of the Future" in *Report: First Assembly of the National Federation of Liberal Women of Canada, April 17, 18, 1928.* (Ottawa: 1928).

King, William Lyon Mackenzie. *The Secret of Heroism: A Memoir of Henry Albert Harper.* New York, Chicago, Toronto, London, and Edinburgh: Fleming H. Revell, 1906. Toronto: Ontario Pub. Co., and Toronto: Thomas Allen, 1919.

King, William Lyon Mackenzie. *The William Lyon Mackenzie King Diaries.* See http://www.bac-lac.gc.ca/eng/discover/politics-government/prime-ministers/william-lyon-mackenzie-king/Pages/diaries-william-lyon-mackenzie-king.aspx

King, William Lyon Mackenzie. William Lyon Mackenzie King Papers: *Spiritualism Series.* Library and Archives Canada. http://heritage.canadiana.ca/view/oocihm.lac_mikan_108986

Klempa, William, ed. *The Burning Bush and a Few Acres of Snow: The Presbyterian Contribution to Canadian Life and Culture.* Ottawa: Carleton University Press, 1994.

Kontou, Tatiana, and Sarah Willburn, eds. *The Ashgate Research Companion to Spiritualism and the Occult.* London: Routledge, 2012.

Kurlander, Eric. *Hitler's Monsters: A Supernatural History of the Third Reich.* New Haven: Yale University Press, 2017.

Lambert, Helen C. *A General Survey of Psychical Phenomena.* New York: Knickerbocker Press, 1928.

Lash, Scott. "Pierre Bourdieu: Cultural Economy and Social Change" in Craig Calhoun, Edward LiPuma, Moishe Postone, eds. *Bourdieu: Critical Perspectives.* Chicago: University of Chicago Press, 1993.

Leasor, James. *Rudolf Hess: The Uninvited Envoy.* London: George Allen & Unwin, 1962.

Leonard, Gladys Osborne. *My Life in Two Worlds.* London: Cassell, 1931.

Levine, Allan. *King: William Lyon Mackenzie King – A Life Guided by the Hand of Destiny.* Vancouver: Douglas & McIntyre, 2011.

Levine, Allan. *Scrum Wars: The Prime Ministers and the Media.* Toronto: Dundurn Press, 1993.

Lind-af-Hageby, Lizzy. "Challenge of the Evidence for Survival: Critics Answered and Objections Refuted," *Light* 56:2880 (March 19, 1936).

Lind-af-Hageby, Lizzy. "Creative Thought and the 'New World,'" *Light* 61:3152 and 61:3153 (June 12 and 19, 1941).

Lind-af-Hageby, Lizzy. "Despair or Re-Dedication," *Progress Today: The Humanitarian and Anti-Vivisection Review*, April-June 1936.

Lind-af-Hageby, Lizzy. "The Evidence for Survival: Its Challenge to Modern Thought and Action" and "Challenge to Modern Thought and Action: Objections to Spiritualism Answered," *Light* 55:2864 (November 28, 1935) and 55:2865 (December 5, 1935).

Lind-af-Hageby, Lizzy. "The Great Calamity: Its Cause and Cure," *Light* 34:1,757 (September 12, 1914).

Lind-af-Hageby, Lizzy. "An Occultists' Peace Union," *Light* 34:1,756 (September 5, 1914).

Lind-af-Hageby, Lizzy. "Place of Spiritualism in Modern Thought: Meeting Place of Science and Religion," *Light* 55:2822 (February 7, 1935).

Lind-af-Hageby, Lizzy. "Psychic Evolution from the Points of View of the Scientist and Spiritualist," *Light* 33:1716 (November 29, 1913) and 33:1717 (December 6, 1913).

Lind-af-Hageby, Lizzy. "The Purpose of Animal Creation as Viewed from the Spiritual Plane," *Light* 28:1408 (January 4, 1908).

Lind-af-Hageby, Lizzy. "Questions for the Bishop of London: Reply to His Attack on Spiritualism," *Light* 55:2844, (July 11, 1935).

Lind-af-Hageby, Lizzy. "The Rapid Growth of Spiritualism: Should Societies Amalgamate?," *Light* 55:2842 (June 27, 1935).

Lind-af-Hageby, Lizzy. "Reconciling Science and Religion," *Light* 56:2872 (January 23, 1936).

Lind-af-Hageby, Lizzy. "Spiritualism and the Crisis: Prayer, Thought and Action Needed to Remove the Causes of War," *Light* 58:3012 (October 6, 1938).

Lind-af-Hageby, Lizzy. "World Regeneration and Spiritualism," *Light* 43:2212 (June 2, 1923).

Lindsey, Charles. *The Life and Times of William Lyon Mackenzie*. Toronto: Randall, 1862.

Lindsey, Charles. *William Lyon Mackenzie*. Toronto: Morang, 1908.

Lodge, Oliver. "On the Asserted Difficulty of the Spiritualistic Hypothesis from a Scientific Point of View," *Proceedings of the Society for Psychical Research* 38, part 111 (1928-1929).

Lodge, Oliver. *Raymond, or, Life and Death*. London: Methuen, 1916.

Lodge, Oliver. *The Reality of a Spiritual World*. London: Ernest Benn, 1931.

Ludwig, Emil. *Mackenzie King: A Portrait Sketch*. Toronto: Macmillan, 1944.

Luno, Nancy. *A Genteel Exterior: The Domestic Life of William Lyon Mackenzie and his Family*. Toronto: Toronto Historical Board, 1990.

MacDonald, Malcolm J. "King: The View from London" in John English and J.O. Stubbs, eds. *Mackenzie King: Widening the Debate*. Toronto: Macmillan, 1977.

MacLaren, Roy. *Mackenzie King in the Age of the Dictators: Canada's Imperial and Foreign Policies*. Montreal and Kingston: McGill-Queen's University Press, 2019.

McCabe, Joseph. *Is Spiritualism Based on Fraud?: The Evidence Given by Sir A.C. Doyle and Others Drastically Examined*. London: Watts, 1920.

McGregor, F.A. *The Fall & Rise of Mackenzie King: 1911-1919*. Toronto: Macmillan, 1962.

McIntyre, Lynn, and Joel J. Jeffries. "The King of Clubs: A Psychobiography of William Lyon Mackenzie King 1893-1900." Undated and unpublished typescript. Heather Robertson fonds, University of Manitoba Archives and Special Collections, MSS 77, Box 1, Folder 2.

McKay, Ian. "Canada as a Long Liberal Revolution: On Writing the History of Actually Existing Canadian Liberalisms, 1840s-1940s," in *Liberalism and Hegemony: Debating the Canadian Liberal Revolution*, eds. Jean-François Constant and Michel Ducharme. Toronto: University of Toronto Press, 2009.

McKenzie, Barbara. "Can Spiritualism Replace Christianity," *Light* 54:2797 (August 17, 1934).

McKenzie, Barbara. "A Knight Errant of Psychic Science: James Hewat McKenzie," *Quarterly Transactions BCPS* 8:3 (October 1929).

McKenzie, J. Hewat. *Spirit Intercourse: Its Theory and Practice*. New York: Mitchell Kennerley, 1917.

McMullin, Stan. *Anatomy of a Seance: A History of Spirit Communication in Central Canada*. Montreal and Kingston: McGill-Queen's University Press, 2004.

Manseau, Peter. *The Apparitionists: A Tale of Phantoms, Fraud, Photography, and the Man Who Captured Lincoln's Ghost*. Boston: Houghton Mifflin Harcourt, 2017.

Manvell, Roger, and Heinrich Fraenkel. *Hess: A Biography*. London: MacGibbon & Kee, 1971.

Martin, Ged. "Mackenzie King, The Medium and the Messages," *British Journal of Canadian Studies* 4:1 (1989), and "W.L. Mackenzie King: Canada's Spiritualist Prime Minister," https://www.gedmartin.net/published-work-mainmenu-11/268-w-l-mackenzie-king-canada-s-spiritualist-prime-minister

Massicotte, Claudie. *Talking Nonsense: Spiritual Mediums and Female Subjectivity in Victorian and Edwardian Canada*. PhD thesis, University of Western Ontario, 2013. https://ir.lib.uwo.ca/cgi/viewcontent.cgi?article=2885&context=etd

Massicotte, Claudie. *Trance Speakers: Femininity and Authorship in Spiritual Séances, 1850-1930*. Montreal and Kingston, McGill-Queen's University Press, 2017.

Meyer zu Erpen, Walter J. "Canadian Psychical Research Experiments with Table Tilting and Ectoplasm Phenomena in the Séance Room," in Christopher M. Moreman, ed. *The Spiritualist Movement: Volume 2, The Belief, Practice, and Evidence for Life after Death*. Santa Barbara, CA: Praeger, 2013.

Meyer zu Erpen, Walter J. "Do Tables Fly? The Hamilton Family's Experiments with 'Psychic Force,' 1921-1927," *Paranormal Review* 77 (Winter 2016).

Meyer zu Erpen, Walter J. "Fact of Fraud? Evidence for the Authenticity of the Mary Marshall Teleplasms," *Paranormal Review* 77 (Winter 2016).

Meyer zu Erpen, Walter J., and Joy Lowe. "The Canadian Spiritualist Movement and Sources for its Study," *Archivaria* 30 (Summer 1990) with corrigenda in *Archivaria* 32 (Summer 1991).

Meyer zu Erpen, Walter J., and Shelley Sweeney. "What Does It All Mean? Physical Phenomena as Evidence of Life after Death," *Paranormal Review* 77 (Winter 2016).

Moore, William Usborne. *Glimpses of the Next State (The Education of an Agnostic)*. London: Watts, 1911.

Moore, William Usborne. "Interview with Vice-Admiral Usborne Moore: The War, Psychic Science, and the 'Direct Voice,'" *Light* 34:1,762 (October 17, 1914.)

Moore, William Usborne. *The Voices*. London: Watts, 1913.

Myers, Frederic William Henry. *Human Personality and Its Survival of Bodily Death*. London: Longmans, Green, 1903.

Myers, Frederic William Henry. "The Psychical Research Society and Its Work," *Borderland* 2:10 (October 1895), 347.

Neatby, H. Blair. *William Lyon Mackenzie King: The Lonely Heights, 1924-1932*. Toronto: University of Toronto Press, 1963.

Neatby, H. Blair. *William Lyon Mackenzie King, The Prism of Unity, 1932-1939*. Toronto: University of Toronto Press, 1976.

Nesbit, Roy Conyers, and Georges van Acker. *The Flight of Rudolf Hess: Myths and Reality*. Thrupp, Stroud, Gloucestershire: Sutton, 1999.

Nicol, J. Fraser. "The Fox Sisters and the Development of Spiritualism," *JSPR* 34:648 (September 1948).

Nicolson, Murray W. *Woodside and the Victorian Family of John King*. Ottawa: Parks Canada, 1984.

Noonan, Gerald. *Refining the Real Canada: Homer Watson's Spiritual Landscape*. Waterloo, Ontario: Mir Editions Canada, 1997.

Oates, Katie. *Women, Spirit Photography & Psychical Research: Negotiating Gender Conventions and Loss*. PhD thesis, University of Western Ontario, 2022. https://ir.lib.uwo.ca/etd/8405/

O'Dell, Stackpool E., and Geelossapuss E. O'Dell. *Phrenology: Essays and Studies*. London: London Phrenological Institution, 1899.

Oppenheim, Janet. *The Other World: Spiritualism and Psychical Research in England, 1850-1914.* London: Cambridge University Press, 1985.

Owen, Alex. *The Place of Enchantment: British Occultism and the Culture of the Modern.* Chicago: University of Chicago Press, 2004.

Padfield, Peter. *Hess: The Führer's Disciple.* London: Cassell, 2001.

Panofsky, Ruth. "Head of the Publishing Side of the Business: Ellen Elliott of the Macmillan Company of Canada," *Papers of the Bibliographical Society of Canada* 44:2 (Fall 2006).

Panofsky, Ruth. *The Literary Legacy of the Macmillan Company of Canada: Making Books and Mapping Culture.* Toronto: University of Toronto Press, 2012.

Peel, Mark. *The Patriotic Duke: The Life of the 14th Duke of Hamilton.* London: Thistle Publishing, 2013.

Philip, Percy James. "I Talked with Mackenzie King's Ghost," *Fate Magazine*, December 1955, and in John Robert Colombo. *Mackenzie King's Ghost and Other Personal Accounts of Canadian Hauntings.* Willowdale, Ontario: Hounslow Press, 1991.

Philip, Percy James. "My Conversation with Mackenzie King's Ghost," *Liberty*, January 1955.

Phillimore, Mercy. *A Brief History of the London Spiritualist Society.* London: London Spiritualist Society, 1944.

Phillimore, Mercy. "Direct Voice: Some Difficulties and a Warning," *Light* November 26, 1942, and *Psypioneer Journal* 11:4/5 (April/May 2015).

Phillimore, Mercy. "Emilie Augusta Louise Lind-af-Hageby," *Light* 84:3456 (1964).

Phillimore, Mercy. "How I Became Interested in the Paranormal," *Light* 3448 (Spring 1962) and *Psypioneer Journal* 10:2 (February 2014).

Phillimore, Mercy. "How to Sit with a Medium," *Light* 57:2929 (February 25, 1937).

Phillimore, Mercy. "The Relation of the Inquirer to the Professional Medium," *Light* 40:2048 (April 10, 1920).

Phillimore, Mercy. *Spiritualism: A Statement for the Inquirer.* London: L.S.A. Publications, 1941.

Pickersgill, J.W. *The Mackenzie King Record, Volume 1, 1939-1944.* Toronto: University of Toronto Press, 1960.

Pickersgill, J.W., and D.F. Forster. *The Mackenzie King Record, Volume 2, 1944-1945.* Toronto: University of Toronto Press, 1968.

Pickersgill, J.W., and D.F. Forster. *The Mackenzie King Record, Volume 3, 1945-1946.* Toronto: University of Toronto Press, 1969.

Pickersgill, J.W., and D.F. Forster. *The Mackenzie King Record, Volume 4, 1947-1948.* Toronto: University of Toronto Press, 1970.

Pincock, Jenny O'Hara. *Trails of Truth.* Los Angeles: Austin Publishing, 1930.

Pitt, David G. *E.J. Pratt: The Master Years, 1927-1964*. Toronto: University of Toronto Press, 1987.

Pringle, Gertrude. "Your Character and Vocation: How Frederick D. Jacob, Amazingly Expert Graphologist, is Helping Thousands to Solve Life's Most Difficult Problems," *Canadian Magazine*, December 1927.

Rasky, Frank. "Canadian Spiritualism: Racket or Religion?" *Liberty*, January 1955.

Reynolds, Louise. *Mackenzie King: Friends and Lovers*. Victoria: Trafford Publishing, 2005.

Roazen, Paul. *Canada's King: An Essay in Political Psychology*. Oakville, Ontario: Mosaic Press, 1998.

Robertson, Beth A. *Science of the Seance: Transnational Networks and Gendered Bodies in the Study of Psychic Phenomena, 1918-40*. Vancouver: UBC Press, 2016.

Robertson, Gordon. *Memoirs of a Very Civil Servant: Mackenzie King to Pierre Trudeau*. Toronto: University of Toronto Press, 2000.

Robertson, Heather. *More Than a Rose: Prime Ministers, Wives and Other Women*. Toronto: Seal Books, 1991.

Robertson, Heather. *Willie: A Romance*. Toronto: James Lorimer, 1983.

Rodin, Alvin E., Audrey M. Kerr, and Jack D. Key. "Kindred souls: The meeting of Drs. Arthur Conan Doyle and Thomas Hamilton," *Canadian Medical Association Journal* 135:10 (November 15, 1986). https://www.ncbi.nlm.nih.gov/pmc/articles/PMC1491806/pdf/cmaj00130-0170.pdf

Rogers, Norman McLeod. *Mackenzie King*. Toronto: George N. Morang, 1935.

Saunders, R.H. "The Chief Apostle of Spiritualism," *International Psychic Gazette* 18:203 (August 1930).

Serban, George. *The Tyranny of Magical Thinking: The Child's World of Belief and Adult Neurosis*. New York: Dutton, 1982.

Seymour, William. *Key to Phrenology*. Philadelphia: Prof. W. Seymour & Son, 1890.

Seymour, William. *Seymour's Key to Phrenology and Mathematical Scale for Reading Character*. Revised edition. Philadelphia: n.p., 1893.

Shortt, S.E.D. "Physicians and Psychics: The Anglo-American Medical Response to Spiritualism, 1870-1890," *Journal of the History of Medicine and Allied Science* 29 (July 1984).

Sidgwick, Eleanor Mildred. "On Spirit Photographs; A Reply to Mr. A.R. Wallace," *PSPR* 7, supplement 2 (1891).

Sidgwick, Eleanor Mildred. "Review: *Raymond, or, Life and Death*," *PSPR* 7, supplement (1918).

Sovatsky, Stuart. "On Being Moved: Kundalini and the Complete Maturation of the Spiritual Body" in Gurmukh Kaur Khalsa, Ken Wilber, Swami Radha, Gopi Krishna, and John White, eds. *Kundalini Rising: Exploring the Energy of Awakening*. Boulder, Colorado: Sounds True, 2009.

Spalding, K.J. "First Sitting with Mrs. Dowden," "Second Sitting with Mrs. Dowden," and "Third Sitting with Mrs. Dowden," *Quarterly Transactions BCPS* 13:1 (April 1934).

Stacey, C.P. *Canada and the Age of Conflict: A History of Canadian External Policies, Volume 2: 1921-1948. The Mackenzie King Era*. Toronto: University of Toronto Press, 1981.

Stacey, C.P. "Divine Mission: Mackenzie King and Hitler," *Canadian Historical Review* 61:4 (December 1980).

Stacey, C.P. *Mackenzie King and the Atlantic Triangle*. Toronto: Macmillan, 1976.

Stacey, C.P. *A True and Faithful Account: Based on the Diaries of William Lyon Mackenzie King*. CBC-TV Take 30, November 30, 1976. https://www.cbc.ca/archives/c-p-stacey-explores-mackenzie-king-s-fascinating-diaries-1.3592447

Stacey, C.P. *A Very Double Life: The Private World of Mackenzie King*. Toronto: Macmillan, 1976, and Halifax: Formac Publishing (Goodread Biographies), 1985.

Stead, Estelle W. *My Father: Personal & Spiritual Reminiscences*. London: William Heinemann, 1913.

Stead, William T. "Julia's Bureau: An Attempt to Bridge the Grave," *The Review of Reviews* 39 (May 1909). https://attackingthedevil.co.uk/reviews/bureau.php

Stevenson, Ian. *Reincarnation and Biology*. Westport, Connecticut: Praeger, 1997.

Stevenson, Ian. *Some of My Journeys in Medicine*. Lafayette: University of Southwestern Louisiana, 1990.

Stevenson, John. "Ottawa Letter: Distinguished Visitors and Apparitions," *Saturday Night* 70:2 (October 16, 1954).

Stone, Desmond. "How Mackenzie King Ruled Canada from Beyond the Grave: Here, for the first time, is the incredible secret that Canada's great Prime Minister William Lyon Mackenzie King took to his death – the story of a leader who ran his government on advice from beyond the grave!" *Argosy*, September 1960.

Strong-Boag, Veronica. *Liberal Hearts and Coronets: The Lives and Times of Ishbel Marjoribanks Gordon and John Campbell Gordon, The Aberdeens*. Toronto: University of Toronto Press, 2015.

Swaffer, Hannen. "Hannen Swaffer on Future of Spiritualism," *Light* 53:2755 (October 27, 1933).

Swan, R. Rennie. *Immortality: An Adventure in Faith*. Winnipeg: Winnipeg Medical Society, 1930.

Swartz, David. *Culture & Power: The Sociology of Pierre Bourdieu*. Chicago, University of Chicago Press, 1997.

Sylvain, Robert. "Quand les tables dansaient et parlaient: Les débuts du spiritisme au dix-neuvième siècle," *Proceedings and Transactions of The Royal Society of Canada*, 4th series, vol. 1 (June 1963).

Teigrob, Robert. *Four Days in Hitler's Germany: Mackenzie King's Mission to Avert a Second World War*. Toronto: University of Toronto Press, 2019.

Tyson, Joseph Howard. *The Surreal Reich*. Bloomington: iUniverse, 2010.

von Baeyer, Edwinna. *Garden of Dreams: Kingsmere and Mackenzie King*. Toronto: Dundurn, 1990.

Wagner, Anton. "The Habitus of Mackenzie King: Canadian Artists, Cultural Capital and the Struggle for Power." PhD thesis, York University, 2014.

Walters, Dorothy. "Kundalini and the Mystic Path" in Gurmukh Kaur Khalsa, Ken Wilber, Swami Radha, Gopi Krishna, and John White, eds. *Kundalini Rising: Exploring the Energy of Awakening*. Boulder, Colorado: Sounds True, 2009.

Watson, Alfred Durrant. *Birth Through Death: The Ethics of the Twentieth Plane; A Revelation Received Through the Psychic Consciousness of Louis Benjamin*. Toronto: McClelland and Stewart, 1920.

Watson, Alfred Durrant. *The Twentieth Plane: A Psychic Revelation*. Toronto: McClelland and Stewart, 1918, and Philadelphia: George Jacobs, 1919.

Watson, Alfred Durrant, and Margaret Lawrence. *Mediums and Mystics: A Study in Spiritual Laws and Psychic Forces*. Toronto: Ryerson, 1923.

Whitaker, Reginald. "Mackenzie King and the Dominion of the Dead," *Canadian Forum*, 45 (February 1976).

White, Kerr. "Ian Stevenson: Recollections," *Journal of Scientific Exploration* 22:1 (2008).

Wiley, Barry H. *The Indescribable Phenomenon: The Life and Mysteries of Anna Eva Fay*. Seattle: Hermetic Press, 2005.

Wingett, Matt. *Conan Doyle and The Mysterious World of Light, 1887-1920*. Portsmouth, England: Life Is Amazing, 2016.

Yeatman, Ruby. "Mercy Phillimore," *Light* 95:3 (Autumn 1975), and *Psypioneer Journal* 12:6 (Nov.-Dec. 2016).

Yeats, W.B. "Ghosts and Dreams," *Light* 34:1738 (May 2, 1914) and 34:1739 (May 9, 1914).

LIST OF ILLUSTRATIONS AND PHOTO CREDITS

CRKN   Canadian Research and Knowledge Network
LAC   Library and Archives Canada
UMASC   University of Manitoba Archives and Special Collections

FIGURE 01   Sir Arthur Conan Doyle's portrait in his 1923 *Our American Adventure*. Courtesy of the Survival Research Institute of Canada.

FIGURE 02   J.W.L. Forster's 1902 portrait of Mackenzie King. LAC PA-151422.

FIGURE 03   Mackenzie King in his Laurier House study in Ottawa in 1932. LAC C-009063.

FIGURE 04   A phrenological chart from William Seymour's *Key to Phrenology* (1890).

FIGURE 05   Barbara McKenzie's portrait in *Psychic Science*, January 1926.

FIGURE 06   Louise (Lizzy) Lind-af-Hageby's portrait in *Light*, November 1913. Courtesy of the College of Psychic Studies collection, London.

FIGURE 07   Mercy Phillimore at the London Spiritualist Alliance in 1926. Courtesy of the College of Psychic Studies collection, London.

FIGURE 08: William H. Mumler's 1872 photograph of Bronson Murray with the spirit of Ella Bonner. Image courtesy of the J. Paul Getty Museum's Open Content Program.

FIGURE 09   Etta Wriedt at Mackenzie King's Kingsmere estate, August 28, 1934. LAC PA-178407.

FIGURE 10 AND COVER   Prime Minister Mackenzie King in his Laurier House study, circa 1945. LAC C-075053.

FIGURE 11   Thomas M. Easterly's 1852 daguerreotype of Kate and Margaret Fox, Spirit Mediums from Rochester, New York. Courtesy of Missouri Historical Society, St. Louis. N17196.

FIGURE 12   Dr. Richard Maurice Bucke's frontispiece portrait published in *Cosmic Consciousness* (1901).

FIGURE 13 Giuseppe Guastalla's 1922 marble bust of Isabel King. LAC C-046512.

FIGURE 14 Mackenzie and Isabel King at Kingsmere, circa 1915. LAC C-046560.

FIGURE 15 King's shrine to his mother in his library at Laurier House. Courtesy of Parks Canada.

FIGURE 16 George Goodwin Kilburne's 1896 "The Trysting Place." Courtesy of the Bedford Fine Art Gallery, Bedford, Pennsylvania.

FIGURE 17 King with Etta Wriedt, Joan Patteson, Pat I, and Derry at Kingsmere, August 28, 1934. LAC C-079191.

FIGURE 18 Record of King's and Joan Patteson's table rapping on his birthday, 202 Elgin St., Ottawa, December 17, 1933. CRKN reel H-3042, image 1319.

FIGURE 19 Joan Patteson at Kingsmere Lake, mid-1920s. LAC C-014174.

FIGURE 20 Homer Watson surrounded by spirits, 1930. Courtesy of Homer Watson House and Gallery, Kitchener, Ontario.

FIGURE 21 After *Meet the Navy*, Ottawa, September 15, 1943. LAC C-068677.

FIGURE 22 Princess Cantacuzene from the frontispiece of her *Revolutionary Days* (1919).

FIGURE 23 King's record of the "marvellous results" of his "conversation" over the "little table," October 6, 1935. LAC C-083734.

FIGURE 24 Record of the first table rapping effort at Laurier House, November 18, 1933. CRKN reel 3042, image 1286.

FIGURE 25 King's handwritten diary entry, vision of "Hitler & his doom," September 30, 1944.

FIGURE 26 The Duchess of Hamilton, November 29, 1926. Courtesy of the National Portrait Gallery, London, x36598.

FIGURE 27 Lizzy Lind-af-Hageby in *Psychic Science*, April 1937, seven months after meeting Mackenzie King.

FIGURE 28 The London Spiritualist Alliance's Medium Appointments and Evening Party for Mackenzie King, October 1936. CRKN reel H-3035, image 610.

FIGURE 29 Rudolf Hess and Adolf Hitler at Nazi Party Congress in Nuremberg, September 1, 1933, in *Deutschland erwacht* (1933).

List of Illustrations and Photo Credits / 385

FIGURE 30 Geraldine Cummins photographed for *Psychic News*, circa 1940s. Courtesy of Psychic News, Coggeshall, Essex.

FIGURE 31 Lady Ishbel Aberdeen, 1899. Courtesy of Wikipedia Creative Commons.

FIGURE 32 William Duncan Livingstone Hardie, Mayor of Lethbridge, Alberta, 1913-1928. Courtesy of the Galt Museum & Archives | Akaisamitohkanao'pa, Ontario, photo 198610788012.

FIGURE 33 Mayor W.D.L. Hardie's 1924 horoscope of Macdougall King. CRKN reel H-3040, image 201.

FIGURE 34 M.E. Young's 1925 corrected Mackenzie King horoscope. CRKN reel H-3039, image 926.

FIGURE 35 Cecilia Ruth Stevenson's 1938 Natal and Progressed Planets chart for Mackenzie King. CRKN reel H-3039, image 1068.

FIGURE 36 Quest Brown at the Chateau Laurier, Ottawa, February 1939. CRKN reel H-3042, image 1126.

FIGURE 37 Quest Brown on the cover of the *Boston Globe*, November 22, 1939.

FIGURE 38 Medium Mary Marshall with the first Arthur Conan Doyle teleplasm, May 1, 1932. UMASC, PC 12, Box 8, Folder 6, Item 1, http://hdl.handle.net/10719/1411482

FIGURE 39 T.G. and Lillian Hamilton with their children Margaret, Glen, and James, 1932. Courtesy of Janice Hamilton.

FIGURE 40 Mary Marshall and W.B. (Barney) Cooper seated next to the teleplasm of the spirit Lucy Warnock, March 10, 1930. UMASC, H.A.V. Green Fonds, MSS 439, Box 1, Folder 2, Item 1.17

FIGURE 41 Dr. T.G. Hamilton in front of the séance cabinet triggering a photo of Elizabeth Poole in trance, mid-1920s. UMASC, PC 12, Box 9, Folder 2, Item 28, http://hdl.handle.net/10719/1411304

FIGURE 42 Teleplasm of Katie King, November 12, 1930. UMASC, PC 12, Box 10, Folder 2, Item 32, http://hdl.handle.net/10719/1410729

FIGURE 43 The ship teleplasm that floated through the air, June 4, 1930. UMASC, PC 12, Box 8, Folder 4, Item 20, http://hdl.handle.net/10719/1412183

FIGURE 44 Ellen Elliott in 1941. Courtesy of Victoria University Library, Toronto.

FIGURE 45 Ellen Elliott (left) with E.J. Pratt and Viola Pratt (centre), at an autographing party for Pratt's *Dunkirk* in the Simpson's book department, Toronto, October 1941. Courtesy of Victoria University Library, Toronto.

FIGURE 46 Mary Marshall's deep-trance drawing of her Jesus vision, April 9, 1933. UMASC, PC 12, Box 8, Folder 6, Item 7, http://hdl.handle.net/10719/1408915

FIGURE 47 Isabella (Isabel) Keil Farquhar, 1937. UMASC, PC 12, Box 10, Folder 13, Item 6, http://hdl.handle.net/10719/1524063

FIGURE 48 Stanley De Brath's portrait from *Psychic Science*, October 1926.

FIGURE 49 Reverend Mae Potts inside Britten Memorial Church, Toronto, circa 1940s. Courtesy of the Survival Research Institute of Canada.

FIGURE 50 Anton Wagner editing *In Exile*, Film House, Toronto, 1971. Courtesy of Anton Wagner Productions.

ABOUT THE AUTHOR

Figure 50: Anton Wagner editing In Exile, *Film House, Toronto, 1971.*

Anton Wagner was a founding executive member of the Association for Canadian Theatre Research and has edited ten books on Canadian theatre and drama. He was the Director of Research and Managing Editor of *The World Encyclopedia of Contemporary Theatre*, published by Routledge. He holds doctorates in drama (University of Toronto) and theatre (York University).

Born in Wels, Austria, in 1949, Reinhold Anton Wagner moved with his parents to the United States in 1960. Anton moved to Canada during the Vietnam War in 1969 and edited his first documentary, *In Exile: American Draft Resisters and Deserters in Canada*, completed with the assistance of the Canadian and U.S. Council of Churches. He served as Secretary of the Canadian Centre of the International Theatre Institute and edited *Contemporary Canadian Theatre: New World Visions* for the 21st World Congress of the ITI held in Montreal and Toronto. He served on the executive of the Canadian Theatre Critics Association and edited *Establishing Our Boundaries: English Canadian Theatre Criticism* for the University of Toronto Press. Anton was a member of the Hiroshima Nagasaki Day Coalition steering committee in Toronto for more than a decade, and produced and directed *Our Hiroshima* on Canada, Mackenzie King, and the atom bomb for Canadian and international television.

Anton has produced and directed ten documentaries on arts and culture, including *The Photographer: An Artist's Journey*. His video interviews with members of the queer community in Canada are in the Wagner/Cabrera fonds at the ArQuives in Toronto. In his documentary film work, Anton has explored the interplay between political, religious, and spiritual beliefs in *At the Crossroads: Faith in Cuba*. Anton's two-volume revisionist biography of Mackenzie King, *The Spiritualist Prime Minister*, is his first publication by White Crow Books. He has dedicated the biography to his mother, Dr. Maria Wagner, and to his brother, Dr. Burkhard Eric Wagner.

www.ingramcontent.com/pod-product-compliance
Lightning Source LLC
Chambersburg PA
CBHW021140160426
43194CB00007B/637